DONNINGTON CASTLE.

# THE
## FIRST AND SECOND
# BATTLES OF NEWBURY

AND THE

## SIEGE OF DONNINGTON CASTLE

DURING THE CIVIL WAR,

A.D. 1643-6.

BY

## WALTER MONEY, F.S.A.,

SECOND EDITION.

# The Naval & Military Press Ltd

Published by the
# The Naval & Military Press
*in association with the Royal Armouries*

Unit 10 Ridgewood Industrial Park,
Uckfield, East Sussex, TN22 5QE
Tel: +44 (0) 1825 749494
Fax: +44 (0) 1825 765701

For a full listing of all N&MP titles, visit:
www.naval-military-press.com

MILITARY HISTORY AT YOUR FINGERTIPS

Online genealogy research:
www.military-genealogy.com

*In reprinting in facsimile from the original, any imperfections are inevitably reproduced and the quality may fall short of modern type and cartographic standards.*

TO

# THE EARL OF CARNARVON,

D.C.L., F.R.S.

PRESIDENT OF THE ROYAL SOCIETY OF ANTIQUARIES, ETC., ETC., ETC.

## This Volume is Dedicated,

AS A TRIBUTE OF SINCERE RESPECT FOR HIS ENCOURAGEMENT OF
HISTORICAL AND ANTIQUARIAN STUDY.

# PREFACE.

THE FIRST EDITION of this Book, published in 1881, having met with a favourable reception, and being now out of print, I have been induced to bring out a Second Edition. In doing so, an endeavour has been made to render the eventful story of the two Battles of Newbury, and the Siege of Donnington Castle, more worthy of public acceptance by a considerable enlargement of the general subject, and by the insertion of additional plans illustrative of some of the more interesting local incidents which are described in this work.

The Civil Wars of the Seventeenth Century will always have a peculiar attraction for all classes of Englishmen, and local associations connected with this important epoch in our national history are deeply interesting to those who reside in the particular locality where many of the more prominent events relating to that stirring period occurred. Especially is this the case in places which have been the Battle-fields of the contending armies, and where our gallant forefathers, both Cavalier and Roundhead, acquired distinction and fame which will live in the pages of history to the end of time.

It has been remarked that no periods of history are so intricate, or so difficult to relate with clearness, as those of Civil War; and in attempting to construct, out of a mass of conflicting evidence, an intelligible narrative of the important historical incidents of the great struggle with which the town of Newbury and its surroundings must ever be associated, I feel conscious of many deficiencies, and that I have good reasons to appeal to the kind indulgence of my readers for the inadequate performance of a task which has so long and pleasantly occupied my leisure hours. But if I have succeeded in removing some of the obscurity and confusion which has hitherto existed respecting these civil dissensions, and rendered them not only intelligible, but interesting, my labours will be fully rewarded.

In concluding my undertaking, I desire to express my acknowledgements to all those persons who were good enough to give their support to the work on its first publication; and to other friends who have encouraged me in these researches. Lastly, but none the less gratefully, I have to express my thanks to Professor T. Rupert Jones, F.R.S., late of the Staff College, Sandhurst; Major C. Cooper King, R.M.A., Professor of Tactics, Administration, &c., Royal Military College, Sandhurst; and to Professor Montagu Burrows, Chichele Professor of Modern History in the University of Oxford; who have afforded me most kind and ready assistance.

WALTER MONEY, F.S.A.

*Newbury, April,* 1884.

# ERRATA ET CORRIGENDA.

Page   5, 16th line from top, *for* he directly ascribed *read* be directly ascribed.

—   52, 24th line from top, *for* or *read* of.

—   61, Colonel Fielding. The name of this Royalist occurs in the list of the wounded at the first battle of Newbury. It has since been ascertained that this officer was Colonel Edward Fielding of Newnham-Paddox, co. Warwick. He died of his wounds at Oxford, shortly after the battle, and was buried in St. Mary's Church in that City. The inscription on his monument is given by Hearne in the Appendix to the Liber Niger Scaccarii, vol. ii, p. 582.

— 102, Bernard Brocas, 12th line from bottom, *for* 800 *read* 500.

— 103, 2nd line from top, *omit* Robert *to the end of the sentence.*
7th line from top, *omit* the said.
16th line from top, *omit* killed at Worcester; *and after* in *insert* a branch of.

— 113, Protestations. These returns were made pursuant to an Order of the House of Commons of the 30th July, 1641, and are dated for the most part February, or March, 1641-2.

— 115, Little Shefford, *for* John Prime, rector, *read* John Prince, rector.

— 253, 28th line from top substitute u *for* n in subsequently.

       29th line from top substitute c *for* e in actions.

— 270, The John Chamberlayne who sold Donnington Castle to Mr. John Packer belonged to the family of Chamberlayne, of Sherborne or Shirbourne Castle, co. Oxon. He was son of Bryan Chamberlayne of Newbury, a person of some note in his time; and was Mayor of Newbury in 1601. Add. MS., 4961, fo. 38; C. 18, Coll. Arm. fo. 114.

# TABLE OF CONTENTS.

|  | PAGE |
|---|---|
| Dedication | iii |
| Preface | v |
| Errata et Corrigenda | vii |
| Table of Contents | viii |
| List of Plans and Illustrations | xii |
| THE FIRST BATTLE OF NEWBURY, SEPTEMBER 20TH, 1643 | 1 |

APPENDIX.

I. A list of those Regiments of Trained Bands and Auxiliaries of the City of London which were engaged at the First Battle of Newbury .. .. .. .. 77

II. The Attack on Essex's Rear the day after the First Battle of Newbury .. .. .. .. 80

III. The presence of Queen Henrietta Maria at the Battle (disproved) .. .. .. .. 82

IV. A case of Witch-murder at Newbury .. 84

V. The discovery of the Coffin and Remains of the Vault of Robert Devereux, third Earl of Essex, in the Chapel of St. John the Baptist in Westminster Abbey, June 1879 .. 86

VI. Biographical Notices of Officers and others mentioned in connection with the First Battle of Newbury—

§ 1. Royalist Officers.

| | PAGE | | PAGE |
|---|---|---|---|
| Patrick Ruthven, Earl of Forth | 88 | Sir Thomas Aston | 101 |
| Prince Rupert | 89 | Sir Anthony Mansel | 101 |
| Sir John Byron | 89 | Sir Edward Stradling | 101 |
| Lord Wilmot | 89 | Sir Michael Wodehouse | 101 |
| Earl of Carnarvon | 89 | Sir Jacob Astley | 101 |
| Earl of Sunderland | 91 | Sir John Frechville | 101 |
| Lord Falkland | 92 | Sir John Hurry | 101 |
| Earl of Lindsey | 95 | Bernard Brocas (see also List | |
| Earl of Northampton | 95 | of *Corrigenda*) .. vii. | 102 |
| Earl of Nottingham | 96 | Col. St. John | 103 |
| Earl of Cleveland | 96 | Col. Edward Villiers | 103 |
| Earl of Holland | 96 | Col. Will. Legge | 103 |
| Earl of Bedford | 97 | Col. Richard | 103 |
| Earl of Clare | 97 | Col. Daniel O'Neill | 104 |
| Earl of Crawford | 97 | Col. Morgan | 104 |
| John, Lord Belasyse | 97 | Col. Thomas Eure | 104 |
| George, Lord Digby | 98 | Col. Richard Platt | 104 |
| Lord Jermyn | 98 | Col. Charles Gerard | 104 |
| Lord Percy | 98 | Col. Thomas Rawdon | 105 |
| Lord Chandos | 98 | Col. Pinchbeck | 105 |
| Lord Molineux | 99 | Col. Edward Fielding vii. and | 61 |
| Hon. Henry Bertie | 99 | Capt. Thomas Bagehot | 105 |
| Sir Charles Lucas | 99 | Capt. Basil Woodd | 105 |
| Sir George Lisle | 100 | Capt. Clifton | 106 |
| Sir Edward Waldegrave | 100 | Capt. Newman | 106 |
| Sir Lewis Kirke | 100 | George Porter | 106 |
| Sir William Vavasour | 101 | Capt. Gwynne | 106 |

# TABLE OF CONTENTS.

### § 2. Parliamentarian Officers and others.

| | PAGE | | PAGE |
|---|---|---|---|
| Earl of Essex | 106 | Col. Edward Massey, (or Massie) | 109 |
| Lord Robartes or Roberts | 107 | Col. Sheffield | 110 |
| Lord Grey of Groby | 107 | Col. John Meldrum | 110 |
| Sir John Meyrick | 107 | Col. Norton | 110 |
| Sir Philip Stapleton | 107 | Col. Dalbier | 110 |
| Sir William Constable | 107 | Capt. Hunt | 111 |
| Sir William Brooke | 107 | Capt. Francis St.-Barbe | 111 |
| Sir William Balfour | 108 | Capt. Hammond | 111 |
| Sir Samuel Luke | 108 | Capt. Charles Fleetwood | 111 |
| Major-General Skippon | 108 | Capt. Charles Pym | 111 |
| Major-General Deane | 109 | William Twisse, D.D. | 111 |
| Lieut.-General Middleton | 109 | Robert Codrington | 112 |
| Col. Arthur Goodwin | 109 | | |

VII. Extracts from the Certificates of Returns of those Persons, who, pursuant to the Order of the House of Commons, made the Protestation in the County of Berks, 30th July, 1641—

| | PAGE | | PAGE |
|---|---|---|---|
| Brimpton Parish | 113 | Inkpen | 114 |
| Chaddleworth | 113 | Kintbury | 114 |
| Chieveley | 113 | Leckhamstead | 114 |
| Compton | 113 | Midgham | 114 |
| Enborne | 113 | Newbury | 114 |
| Frilsham | 114 | Peasemore | 115 |
| Greenham (a Tything of Thatcham) | 114 | Shaw-cum-Donnington | 115 |
| | | Little Shefford | 115 |
| Hamstead Marshall | 114 | Great Shefford | 115 |
| Hamstead Norris | 114 | Speen | 115 |
| West Ilsley | 114 | Wasing | 115 |
| East Ilsley | 114 | Welford | 115 |
| | | Winterborne Danvers | 115 |

VIII. List of the Sequestrators of the Estates of "Delinquents, Papists, Spyes, and Intelligencers," for the County of Berks, appointed under Ordinance of the Lords and Commons, April 1, 1643—

| | PAGE | | PAGE |
|---|---|---|---|
| Sir Francis Pile | 116 | Roger Knight | 117 |
| Sir Francis Knollys, junior | 116 | Henry Powle | 117 |
| Peregrine Hoby | 116 | Thomas Fettiplace | 117 |
| Henry Marten | 116 | Tanfield Vachell | 117 |

IX.—The Commissioners for raising Money and Forces within the County of Berks, and for Maintenance of Garrisons within the said County for use of Parliament, appointed June 27, 1644—

| | PAGE | | PAGE |
|---|---|---|---|
| William Lenthall | 118 | Daniel Blagrave | 120 |
| Sir Robert Pye | 118 | Richard Browne | 120 |
| Sir Benjamin Rudyerd | 118 | John Packer | 121 |
| Edmund Dunch | 119 | Robert Packer | 121 |
| | | Cornelius Holland | 121 |

X. Ship Money .. .. .. .. 121
XI. State of Public Feeling in the County in 1643 .. 123
XII. Agreement between Charles I. and the County of Berks respecting a Contribution to be levied for the support of the King's Army .. .. .. 125

# TABLE OF CONTENTS.

|  | PAGE |
|---|---|
| THE SECOND BATTLE AT NEWBURY, OCTOBER 27TH, 1644 | 128 |

APPENDIX.

| I. The King's March to Newbury | 213 |
|---|---|
| II. The King's Stay at Newbury | 215 |
| III. Red Heath and Red Hill | 217 |
| IV. Descriptive Accounts of the Second Battle of Newbury | 219 |
| V. Newbury Church as a Prison and Hospital | 224 |
| VI. Boxford | 224 |
| VII. Bucklebury | 225 |
| VIII. License of War | 226 |
| IX. Capture of Lady Forth, Countess of Brentford | 231 |
| X. Captain Knight's Relation of the Siege of Donnington Castle | 234 |
| XI. Major Ryves' Letter relating to the Siege of Donnington Castle | 241 |
| XII. Dismantling of Donnington Castle | 243 |
| XIII. Depositions of Witnesses at the Trial of King Charles 1., as to the presence of the King at the Two Battles of Newbury | 245 |
| XIV. Letter from the Earl of Manchester to the House of Lords, giving an opinion on the conduct of Oliver Cromwell | 246 |
| XV. Biographical Notices of some of the Officers and others mentioned in connection with the Second Battle of Newbury | |

§ 1. Royalist Officers.

| | PAGE | | |
|---|---|---|---|
| Prince Maurice | 248 | Sir Thomas Hooper | 253 |
| Duke of Richmond | 248 | Sir Richard Page | 253 |
| Lord Bernard Stuart | 249 | Sir Richard Lane | 253 |
| Earl of Newport | 249 | Sir Thomas Basset, or Bassett | 253 |
| Earl of Berkshire | 249 | Sir Humphrey Benett | 253 |
| Earl Rivers | 249 | Sir John Granville | 253 |
| Lord Capel | 249 | Sir Joseph Wagstaffe | 253 |
| Lord Hopton | 250 | Sir Charles Lloyd | 254 |
| Lord Colepeper | 250 | Sir Edward Walker | 254 |
| Lord Goring | 251 | Col. William Ashburnham | 254 |
| Sir John Boys | 251 | Col. Leke | 254 |
| Sir Bernard Astley | 252 | Col. Anthony Thelwall | 254 |
| Sir John Cansfield | 252 | Col. Giles Strangways | 254 |
| Sir William Brouncker | 253 | Col. Hoghton | 254 |
| Sir William St. Leger | 253 | Captain Catelyn | 255 |
| Sir John Owen | 253 | Robert Stradling | 255 |
| | | Captain Symonds | 255 |

§ 2. Parliamentarian Officers.

| | PAGE | | |
|---|---|---|---|
| Earl of Manchester | 256 | Col. Richard Norton | 257 |
| Sir William Waller | 256 | Lieut.-Col. White | 258 |
| Sir Arthur Hesilrige | 256 | Col. Sir Richard Ingoldsby | 258 |
| Major-General Crawford | 257 | Col. John Birch | 258 |
| Lieut.-General Middleton | 257 | Captain Mason | 258 |
| Lieut.-General Ludlow | 257 | Capt. Richard Wolfall | 259 |
| | | Capt. Thomas Whittingham | 259 |

| XVI. Historical Notices of the Manor and Castle of Donnington | 259 |
|---|---|
| XVII. Description of Donnington Castle | 272 |
| INDEX | 278 |

# LIST OF THE PLANS AND ILLUSTRATIONS.

1 VIEW OF DONNINGTON CASTLE (FRONTISPIECE) Opposite Title-page.
2 PORTRAIT OF THE EARL OF ESSEX             Opposite Page  36
3 PLATE OF ARMS AND ARMOUR    ..     ..       ,,          64
4 PLAN OF THE FIRST BATTLE OF NEWBURY ..     ,,          76
5 PLAN OF THE DEFENCES OF DONNINGTON CASTLE  ,,         134
6 VIEW OF SHAW HOUSE      ..     ..         ,,         152
7 PLAN OF THE KING'S ARMY BEFORE NEWBURY    ,,         186
8 PORTRAIT OF SIR JOHN BOYS  ..     ..      ,,         208
9 PLAN OF THE SECOND BATTLE OF NEWBURY      ,,         212
10 PLAN OF THE LAST SKIRMISH AT DONNINGTON CASTLE ,,   242

# THE FIRST BATTLE OF NEWBURY.

## CHAPTER I.

### INTRODUCTORY.

IN order to understand the political situation of the precise period of English History under review, a brief description, first, of the events which preceded the actual outbreak of hostilities and, then, of the previous operations of the hostile armies which eventually met at Newbury, may be acceptable. At the same time the means will be provided of rightly estimating the value and effect of the engagements fought at that place, on the fortunes of the two Parties.

The causes which led to the Great Civil War between the King and Parliament, in which the Battles round Newbury occupied a prominent position, were probably not of sudden occurrence, nor entirely due to the errors of the Stuart Dynasty. There had been a great increase in the extent and power of public feeling since Elizabeth's reign. The independence and political importance of the Middle Class had increased with extended trade and with its natural consequence, accumulation of wealth. A reasonable desire to obtain and to secure the full freedom of the subject had been surely and steadily growing the opposition to feudal government had followed as a matter of course. This desire was moreover strongly tinged with religious sentiment. "It was," to use the words of M. Guizot, an eminent writer on this subject, "the fortune of England in the seventeenth century to be governed by the spirit of religious faith as well as by the spirit of political liberty, and to enter upon the two revolutions at the same time. All the great passions of human nature were thus brought into duly controlled activity; and the hopes and aspirations of eternity remained to men even when they beheld the failure of all their earthly ambitions and hopes.

"The English Reformers, especially those whose object was

B

merely political, did not think a revolution necessary. The laws, the traditions, the precedents, the whole past annals of their country, were dear and sacred in their eyes; and they found in them a foundation for their pretensions, as well as the sanction of their ideas. It was in the name of the Great Charter, and of the innumerable statutes which had been passed during four centuries in confirmation of it, that they demanded their liberties. For four centuries not a generation of Englishmen had passed away without uttering the name and beholding the assemblage of Parliament. The great barons and the people, the country gentlemen and the city burgesses, met together in 1640, not to contend for new acquisitions, but to regain their common inheritance; they came to repossess themselves of their ancient and positive rights, and not to pursue the infinite but unknown combinations and experiences of the human mind."

But with the advent of the House of Stuart had come a retrogressive spirit on the part of Sovereign and Noble; or, at least what a large section of the English people considered to be so. James the First had many strong and extravagant convictions as to the divine origin and extent of the regal power. In his reign, however, these convictions merely strengthened; but when his son ascended the throne, and it was felt, with how much regret on the part of many who opposed him it is unnecessary to say, that he, a firmer man, was not merely more assured than his father of the importance of his kingly trust, but more purposed to fulfil it, the breach between King and People slowly but surely increased, until there was no resource but division and civil war. The struggle between the popular and monarchical principles of the constitution now assumed a definite form, soon to be decided by the terrible arbitrament of the sword. Clarendon assigns the true cause of Charles's haughty refusal of all concessions to the influence of the Queen, Henrietta Maria, to whom must undoubtedly be imputed many of the misfortunes which attended the life of the luckless King. This fascinating and beautiful woman, says the same historian, had obtained, by degrees, a plenitude of power over her husband, which, almost absolute, did much to precipitate the inevitable conflict. His history affords abundant proof of this. Unhappily too, the King with exalted notions of his prerogative, had taken it into his head that the nation might be governed without Parliaments; or at least that they were only the instruments of the Sovereign to furnish him with supplies. He had dissolved *three* in the first four years of his reign; and even signified his intention of calling no more. Twelve years passed without one parliament being summoned, during which the King was perplexed with the war of the Palatinate, in which his sister was concerned, and which the puritanic party, as well as others, had continually urged as necessary for the maintenance of the Protestant cause in Europe. To furnish the means for this and other foreign expeditions, he levied taxes on his subjects at pleasure, and exposed a policy that was inimical to the best interests of the established government. "All the foreign expeditions of Charles the First," observes the elder Disraeli, "were alike disastrous; the vast genius of Richelieu, at its meridian, had paled our ineffectual star! The dreadful surrender of Rochelle had sent back our army and navy baffled and disgraced; and Buckingham had timely perished, to be saved from having one more reproach, one more political crime, attached to his name. Such failures did not improve the temper of the times; but the most brilliant victory would not have changed the fate of the King, nor allayed the fiery spirits in the Commons, who, as Charles said, 'not satisfied in hearing complainers, had erected themselves into inquisitors after complaints.'" Numerous objections had been raised to arbitrary and illegal impositions; but the tax which of all others appeared most grievous to the subject, and raised the greatest clamour, was that which Noy, the Attorney-General, invented or revived under the name of Ship-money. A feeble and distracted Government at home had lessened the respect in which England had been formerly held by foreign nations. Her ancient prestige on the seas was slighted by her neighbours, and her national glory diminished. To restore somewhat the naval supremacy of England, the sea-ports were required to equip vessels for the King's service; and the demand was soon afterwards extended to the whole kingdom, the inland towns compounding for their assessments in money. The amount of the whole tax was very moderate, scarcely exceeding £200,000; it was levied on the people with perfect equality, and the funds were honestly and successfully applied to the purposes for which they were raised. One of the most memorable and important processes in judicial history, is that by which the legality of this impost was tried in the case of Hampden. The assessment upon his extensive landed property was twenty shillings, and on so small a point turned the issue of a great constitutional question, namely the power of the Crown to tax the people without the the consent of Parliament. It was against this innovation that Hampden resolved to make a decisive stand. Judgment was given for the Crown; but as the judges were believed to be corrupted, and as the elaborate arguments of Hampden's counsel had convinced the nation that substantial right, if not the technical construction of statutes, favoured his cause, "the judgment," says Clarendon, "proved of more advantage to the gentleman condemned than to the King's service."

In the first fifteen years of the reign of Charles the First under the mistaken advice, first of Buckingham, and then of Strafford, continual breaches were made in the constitution, and the principles and rights of Parliament invaded. But the Ecclesiastical grievances, for which Laud is chiefly responsible, had a still more powerful effect. The harsh and cruel sentences by which the Star-Chamber, the High Commission, and the other Ecclesiastical Courts endeavoured to enforce religious uniformity were especially obnoxious, most of those who were not submissive enough to the King being looked upon as Puritans, and frequently oppressed as such. So by a calamitous policy, men well affected to the Church of England, but enemies to arbitrary power, were driven in spite of themselves to side with the Puritans, in order to strengthen their party, and enable them to oppose the designs of the Court. The Parliament which opposed and levied war against the King consisted almost entirely of persons who were members of the Church of England. They were men attached to the constitution, as well in Church as in State, and enemies only to the abuse of power in both. The subversion therefore of the Civil and Ecclesiastical Constitution, which afterwards happened, was certainly not owing to any settled design at the first, but to accidents and circumstances which could not possibly have been foreseen by those concerned in it.

Charles the First's last and greatest Parliament, which has been described as "the most extraordinary and eventful Parliament in English History," met on the 3rd of November 1640.

On the 10th May following, the King, harassed out of his senses, committed the extraordinary imprudence of giving his consent to a Bill that Parliament should be elected once every three years, and that no future Parliament should be *dissolved or adjourned except by its own consent*. By this Bill some of the most valued prerogatives of the Crown were annihilated; but Charles, finding that nothing less would satisfy his parliament and people, had at last given his assent to this measure, which not only precipitated the war, but prepared the way for all that followed. It has been noticed that on the very day on which he took this, for him, fatal and impolitic step, in the agony of irresolution and much to his discredit, he was induced to give the royal assent to the Bill of Attainder, consigning to the scaffold his firmest friend, Thomas Wentworth, Earl of Strafford; an act upon which the King looked back with deep regret during the remainder of his life. In his last sad moments, it is said, the memory of this unfortunate circumstance recurred to him with sorrow and remorse.

On the 4th January, 1641-2, although hostilities had not yet actually commenced, began what has been termed "the first act in the great drama of the Civil War." On that day the King determined to seize in person the five Members of the House of Commons, Pym, Hampden, Hollis, Haslerig, and Strode;—a breach of the privileges of the House to which all the ensuing disorders and civil wars may in a great measure be directly ascribed. The King, soon after this ill-advised step, retired from Whitehall to Hampton Court, and returned no more until he was brought there a prisoner shortly before his death.

All prospects of reconciliation were now closed. The demands of Parliament amounted to a total abolition of monarchical authority; and war on any terms was considered by the King and his advisers preferable to an ignominious peace on such conditions.

Charles accordingly determined to support his authority by force. "His towns," he said, "were taken from him, his ships, his arms, his money; but there still remained to him a good cause, and the hearts of his loyal subjects, which, with God's blessing, he doubted not, would recover all the rest." It was resolved that the Queen should go over to Holland, for the ostensible purpose of conducting the Princess Mary, a child of ten, to her affianced husband the Prince of Orange. The Parliament was not deceived, however, respecting the real object of this journey, which was to solicit aid from foreign powers, and to purchase arms and ammunition with money to be raised on the valuable crown jewels the Queen took out with her, including the diamond ornaments and pearl necklace that had been part of her marriage trousseau. The Parliament passed the "ordinance for the militia," commanding it to be obeyed as the fundamental law of the kingdom; and pronouncing the King's appointment of lieutenants over the respective Counties to be illegal and void. This momentous vote completed the separation of the royalist and parliamentarian parties in the legislature. Charles, meantime, arrived at York, where he found himself again in possession of power.

## THE FIRST BATTLE OF NEWBURY.

On the 23rd April, 1642, the King, accompanied by a large gathering of royalist gentlemen, rode over from York, and demanded admittance into Hull, at that time the arsenal of the north. He was refused by Sir John Hotham, the governor, who, though he had accepted a commission from the Parliament, was not thought to be much disaffected to the King's interest. Charles immediately proclaimed Hotham as a traitor, and complained to the Parliament of his conduct. But the latter avowed and justified the action. The breach between the King and the Parliament daily grew wider, and preparations for war now proceeded rapidly. The Commons fixed on the Earl of Essex as the general for their army. Several members of the Parliament received commands; St.-John, Hampden, Hollis, were named colonels of regiments of foot; Cromwell, Haslerig, Fiennes, of regiments of horse. Great excitement prevailed in London; everybody went about decorated with orange ribands, the colour of Essex's House; the shops were closed, and civil business was almost at a standstill. Some trifling skirmishes had already occurred in the North; and at Portsmouth the war had actually commenced.

The King now judged that the time was come when he could no longer delay an appeal to his loyal subjects to support his authority, and therefore published a proclamation, requiring all those who could bear arms to meet him at Nottingham by the twenty-third of August, on which day he intended to set up his royal standard. Munitions of war had been sent from Holland by the Queen, and landed with difficulty on the Yorkshire coast. The King with his shadow of an army, consisting of about three hundred foot, and a few troops of horse, rode towards Nottingham on the day appointed, "very melancholy," as his own historian relates. The weather was wild and rough, and the royal cavalcade could scarcely make way against it. Lord Clarendon, who was present, thus describes the scene:—"The Standard was erected, about six of the clock in the evening of a very stormy and tempestuous day. The King himself, with a small train, rode to the top of the Castle Hill; Verney, the knight-marshall, who was Standard Bearer, carrying the Standard, which was then erected in that place, with little other ceremony than the sound of Drums and Trumpets: melancholy men observed many ill presages about that time. There was but one regiment of foot yet brought thither; so that the train-bands, which the sheriff had drawn together, were all the strength the King had for his person and the guard of his Standard. There appeared no conflux of men in obedience to the proclamation; the arms and ammunition were not yet come from York, and a general sadness covered the whole town. The Standard was blown down the same night by a very strong and unruly wind, and could not be fixed again for a day or two, until the tempest was allayed. This was the melancholy state of the King's affairs when the Standard was set up." The royal army having been increased by reinforcements, and contributions having come in, the King with his little train of artillery, brought up from York, marched across Derbyshire towards the Welsh borders, designing to fix his head-quarters at Shrewsbury. His nephews, Rupert and Maurice, sons of his sister Elizabeth, came over from Germany to fight for him, and by the middle of October, he mustered at Shrewsbury an army of about 12,000 men. Finding himself at the head of an army little inferior to that raised by the Parliament, the King considered he ought to seek means to put a termination to hostilities, either by trying his strength with his opponents, or, by forced marches to appear in London before Essex could put himself in his way, or overtake him. On the 22nd October, the two armies, however, were within six miles of one another, without receiving notice of each other's march. And although celerity was so great an object with the King, Essex had considerably outstripped him in his progress. The King now judging it extremely hazardous to carry out his intention of marching upon London with his opponents so closely on his heels, resolved to try the issue of the sword. The next day, Sunday, the 23rd of October, was fought the first important conflict of the Great Civil War, that of Kineton Heath or Edgehill, on the borders of Warwickshire. Ere evening closed, Charles's general (the Earl of Lindsey), Sir Edward Verney, the Royal Standard-bearer, and about five thousand men belonging to the two rival forces, were lying dead on the field of this indecisive battle.

After the struggle at Edgehill, the King, failing in an attempted march upon London, had retired to Oxford, which became from thenceforward his head-quarters; and, through the winter of 1642-3 and the early summer of 1643, the war continued, skirmishes and sieges taking place in various parts of England, so that there was scarcely a county free from internecine strife. The following summary may be useful.

During the month of December two or three warmly contested actions took place in the North; and in the South Sir William Waller, commander for the Parliament, blew up Farnham Castle, and made the garrison prisoners of war. Shortly after, he took Winchester, and then Chichester, after an eight days' siege. In the Western Counties, the royalists attacked the town of Marlborough, which had been fortified by the Parliament, who had placed there a numerous garrison. The town being carried by storm was plundered, and many of the defenders slain and taken prisoners.

In January 1642-3 Sir Ralph Hopton engaged the Parliamentary forces at Liskeard, and afterwards took Saltash, whereby the Royalists became absolute masters of all Cornwall. On the 2nd of February, Prince Rupert took Cirencester by storm and made twelve hundred prisoners. On the 22nd, the Queen set foot again in England, having been absent almost exactly a year. She had raised in a few months no less than two millions sterling, an enormous sum for that period, and it was chiefly owing to her exertions that Charles was enabled to bring an army into the field. In March Lord Brooke attacked some of the King's troops intrenched in the Close of Lichfield Cathedral, and was there killed. On the 19th of the same month a battle was fought at Hopton-Heath near Stafford, in which, though the Earl of Northampton, who commanded for the King, was slain, the result was considered unfavourable to the Parliament. About the same time, Waller surprised a detachment under Lord Herbert, son of the Marquis of Worcester, who was besieging Gloucester, and took about a thousand prisoners. In April, Reading surrendered to the Earl of Essex after a siege of ten days. The following month, Hopton defeated the Parliamentary levies under the Earl of Stamford at Stratton, in Cornwall. Hampden fell at Chalgrove in June. Waller suffered a reverse on Lansdown Heath, and at Roundway Down, Devizes, in July; and a little later on the city of Bristol, insufficiently defended, surrendered to Prince Rupert. Thus the balance had turned in favour of Charles. Extreme danger now threatened the Parliament. There was no force between Oxford and London to oppose the King's approach except Essex's diminished army, whose thinned ranks had not yet been refilled. The Parliament, says May, its own historian, "was then in a low ebb; and before the end of that July, they had no forces at all to keep the field, their main armies being quite ruined. Thus seemed the Parliament to be quite sunk beyond any hope of recovery, and was so believed by many men. The King was possessed of all the western counties from the farthest part of Cornwall, and from thence northward as far as the borders of Scotland. His armies were full and flourishing, free to march wherever they pleased, and numerous enough to be divided for several exploits."

## INTRODUCTORY.

After the surrender of Bristol to the Royalists, the King had again joined the camp; and, having sent Prince Maurice with a detachment into Devonshire, he deliberated how to employ his remaining forces in an enterprise of moment. Some of his followers proposed that he should march direct to London, where everything was in confusion, though this undertaking, by reason of the great strength of the London Militia or Trained Bands, was thought to be attended with great difficulties; but Gloucester, lying within 20 miles of Bristol, presented a possibly easier conquest. This was the only remaining garrison possessed by the Parliament in the west of the kingdom; and, by interrupting the communications of the royal armies between the south-west and north-east, prevented these from acting in concert. Hence the King at last assented to the plan of besieging this important town. The questionable policy of this measure is thus noticed by one of Charles's most faithful adherents, Sir Philip Warwick; —"One (or the like) councill in both quarters, north and west, soon blasted the prosperity in each place; for the King pitcht upon that fatall resolution, recommended to him, it is said, by the Lord Culpeper (who wanted no loyalty), of besieging Glocester, who thought it a good policy not to leave a strong towne behind him. But the counsell proved fatall; for had the King at that time resolv'd in himself to have struck at the proud head of London and had had authority enough at that time to have required the Earl of Newcastle to have joyned with him, (both armies being never in so good a state, and the countries, which they commanded, so free and secure), humanely speaking, he had rais'd such confusion among the two Houses and the Londoners, that they had either sent him his owne terms, or if they had fought him, most probably he had bin victorious. For the countries about London were well-affected to the King's cause; and many in London passionately wished for his approach. But the King fixes on Gloucester, and the Earle of Newcastle as fatally about the same time setts down before Hull." *

After all, it is by no means certain that this proposed march to London would have been so effectual and so little opposed as it is here taken for granted it would have been.

The King's army, under his immediate command, occupied the heights above the City of Gloucester, on the 10th August, which was defended by a garrison of only fifteen hundred men, besides the inhabitants; and the Governor (Massey) was peremptorily summoned to surrender, under the promise of a

---

* Sir Ph. Warwick's 'Memoires,' pp. 260—2.

general amnesty, two hours being allowed for an answer. Before the expiration of that time, two deputies from the city, Sergeant-Major * Pudsey and a citizen, presented themselves at the camp. They were pale, thin men, dressed in black, and closely shaven: "We bring to his Majesty," said they, "an answer from the godly city of Gloucester;" and on being introduced to Charles, they read a letter, which ran thus: "We, the inhabitants, magistrates, officers, and soldiers within the garrison of Gloucester unto his Majesty's gracious message return this humble answer, That we do keep this city, according to our oath and allegiance, to and for the use of his Majesty signified by both houses of Parliament; and are resolved by God's help, to keep this city accordingly."

Clarendon states, that on hearing this brief reply, delivered in a firm, clear tone, and perceiving the strange appearance of the messengers, who stood motionless before the King awaiting his answer, a movement at once of surprise, derision, and anger was about to manifest itself on the part of the courtiers; but Charles, as grave as his enemies, repressed it with a gesture, and dismissed the deputies with these words: "If you expect help, you are deceived; Waller is extinct, and Essex cannot come." The deputation had no sooner entered the city, than the inhabitants set fire to the suburbs, and left themselves nothing to defend but what was within the walls, on the principle that "a city without skirts left nothing for the enemy to sit upon." For twenty-six days, from August 10th to September 5th, the citizens, by their indefatigable exertions, frustrated all the efforts of the besiegers. Except a hundred and fifty men kept in reserve, the whole garrison were constantly on foot. In all their labours, in all their dangers, the people took part with the soldiers, the women with their husbands, the children with their mothers. Massey even made frequent sallies, and only three men took advantage of them to desert. Tired of so long a delay, attended by neither glory nor rest, the royal army in a spirit of revenge licentiously devastated the country round, the officers frequently employing their men to carry off from his house some rich farmer or peaceable freeholder of the other side, who only regained his liberty on payment of ransom. †

The news of the siege of Gloucester caused the greatest consternation in London; and the Parliament, seeing the

---

* "Sergeant-Major" formerly signified the officer now styled Major, and the "Sergeant-Major General" was what is now called Major-General.

† Clarendon's 'Hist. of the Rebellion,' vol. ii, p. 341.

absolute necessity of relieving the town as the only means of supporting their cause, now exerted to the utmost their power and authority. Trading was for a time suspended, in order that none should decline military service upon whom the lot should fall. The relief of Gloucester was urged in every pulpit. A force of 8000 horse and 4000 foot was expeditiously put into a condition of marching against the King; and a committee, comprising some of the warmest partisans of war, went to the Earl of Essex on the 4th August to inform him of the measures that had been taken to recruit and make full provision for his army, and to enquire what else he needed. In a word, they entrusted the destiny of the country to his hands, with assurance of the complete confidence reposed in him by Parliament. The Earl, in a letter to the Speaker, assured the House he would never desert the cause " as long as I have any blood in my veins, until this kingdom may be made happy by a blessed peace (which is all honest men's prayers) or to have an end by the sword."\*

Essex mustered his forces at Hounslow on the 24th of August; and, after a solemn review in the presence of nearly all the Members of both Houses, marched by way of Colnbrook, Beaconsfield, and Aylesbury to the assistance of Gloucester. On the first of September he arrived at Brackley Heath, the general rendezvous, where he was joined by a reinforcement of horse and a train of artillery, which brought his force up to about 14,000 men. He then proceeded by way of Bicester, Chipping Norton, and Stow-on-the-Wold; here he was attacked by a detached corps of cavalry under Prince Rupert, who vainly endeavoured to stop him; but the Earl advanced, without suffering himself to be turned from his road, driving the enemy before him. He was already within a few miles of the Royalist Camp, already the King's horse had fallen back on the advanced posts of his infantry, when, in the hope of delaying the Earl, if only for a day, Charles sent him a messenger with proposals of peace. " The Parliament," answered Essex, " gave me no commission to treat, but to relieve Gloucester; I will do it, or leave my body beneath its walls!" The soldiers were equally determined. " No propositions: no propositions!" shouted they when they heard of the arrival of a trumpeter from the King. So Essex continued his march, and on the 5th September he appeared on Prestbury Hills within view of the city. Here the thunder of his cannon announced to the belea-

---

\* Carte's MS. Letters; Bibl. Bodl.

guered citizens that their deliverance had come; and soon the sight of the King's quarters in flames informed them that the siege was raised.

The important services performed by Massey and the garrison at Gloucester called forth the thanks of Parliament, who granted £1,000 to the governor, and proportionate largess to the officers and soldiers; and, in order to preserve the memory of the transaction, the 5th of September was ordered by the Mayor and Corporation to be observed as an annual holiday, and was so kept until the Restoration. The south gate of the city, which had been battered down during the siege, was rebuilt the same year, with these mottoes inscribed round the arch : on one side "A CITY ASSAULTED BY MAN, BUT SAVED BY GOD ; " and on the other side, next the city, "EVER REMEMBER THE VTH SEPT. 1643—GIVE GOD THE GLORY." At the Restoration these inscriptions were effaced, and the royal arms substituted. The walls and fortifications of the city were destroyed by order of King Charles II. ; although the citizens sent early congratulations on his safe return, "lauded his singular patience in his long and disconsolate exile, implored pardon, and cheerfully yielded up the fee-farm rents due to the crown, which they had been forced to purchase by the threatening violence of the times." Massey eventually left the Parliament's service, being set aside by the Independents upon the passing of the Self-denying Ordinance, and joined Prince Charles in Holland, under whose standard he fought at Worcester; but, being taken prisoner, he was committed to the Tower. He managed however to escape, and, after the death of Cromwell, he undertook to seize Gloucester, but was taken in the attempt. A second time he slipped from his captors; and, on the restoration of the secluded Members in 1660, he appeared in Parliament, and represented Gloucester the two following years, in the last of which he was knighted.

Such an easy success as that gained by Essex in this expedition may be attributed to supineness on the part of his adversary; but it is probable that, as Clarendon says, the Royalists could not believe he was coming, and "laid their account " in the nearly thirty miles of champaign country that he would have to traverse, after the King's soldiers had eaten it bare; and where, if he attempted the expedition, the royal horse would perpetually infest his march and probably destroy his army. *

By a fortunate coincidence of circumstances, the day that

---

* Clarendon's 'Hist. of the Rebellion,' vol. ii, p. 343.

the Parliamentary troops entered Gloucester had been set apart for a public fast, but on their arrival it was turned into a day of rejoicing. Provisions of all kinds were conveyed to the city, the Governor and his soldiers were loaded with praise, the citizens congratulated on their courage, and the Earl was received everywhere with demonstrations of gratitude.

It was generally conceded that the march of Essex to Gloucester was one of the most able exploits in the whole course of the war; for his troops were untrained and ill-disciplined, and for the greater part of the way he was in the enemy's country. From Brackley to Prestbury, Wilmot and four other royalist commanders were hanging on his rear; and in the encounter at Stow, Prince Rupert with 4,000 horse made a desperate attempt to cut off his advanced guard, but in vain. It would appear, from the following remarks by Lord Orrery that there was more of a fight here than the historians have mentioned: he says "When Essex marched to relieve Gloucester, Prince Rupert advanced with his cavalry to meet the relieving army on the Downs, which doubtless he had defended, had not some brigades of Essex's infantry done wonders on that day."\*

At Gloucester the Lord-General left his heavy ordnance with forty barrels of powder and the greater part of his baggage, the better to expedite his march over an unusually hilly country. Having strengthened and victualled the garrison, which had been driven to great extremities, his mission was accomplished; but, fearing an engagement with the enemy on account of their superiority in cavalry, he determined to manœuvre his way back to London without risking a battle. Moreover the London trained-bands and auxiliaries, supposing their work already done, earnestly desired to direct their footsteps homewards.

Leaving Gloucester, Essex, with the object of dividing the King's forces, made a demonstration, as though he intended to proceed northward to Worcester; but, changing his route on a sudden, he marched to Tewkesbury, where, having thrown a bridge over the Severn and dispatched a body of troops to Upton as a feint, he quartered till Friday, 15th September. Succeeding by this skilful manœuvre in drawing the King's attention towards Worcester, Essex with the remainder of his army took advantage of a dark night, and moved for Cirencester. His vanguard, arriving in the town about 1 a.m. on Saturday morning, surprised two newly raised regiments of Royal horse, intended for service in Kent, and

\* Orrery's 'Art of War,' p. 180.

commanded by Sir Nicholas Crispe and Col. Spencer, both of whom were then absent. In the fight which ensued, the Parliamentarians took 300 prisoners, 400 horses, with six stands of colours; and, what was of more consequence, obtained possession of a large store of provisions; thus enabling the Earl to refresh his exhausted forces, and perhaps mainly contributing to his success at Newbury. This skirmish is referred to in Corbet's "Relation of the Siege of Gloucester" in the following terms: "The forlorn hope entered Cirencester, whilst the rest surrounded it, killed the centinell sleeping, march'd up to the market-house without opposition (the enemy supposing them Prince Maurice, his forces that night expected) till they entered the houses and surprised them in bed, took 400 men and thirty cart-loads of bread and cheese and other provisions, a great relief in a wasted country, and the only support of the soldiers against the battle of Newbury."

The royalist troopers taken prisoners at Cirencester were secured in the fine old parish church, which, fortunately, escaped injury during the siege in the previous year, the inhabitants having carefully protected it by suspending woolpacks around the exterior. After a few hours' rest, Essex was again on the march, his means being augmented on the way by the addition of some 1,000 sheep and 60 head of cattle, which had been taken from Royalist adherents *en route*. These were afterwards lost during the action on Aldbourne Chase, " every man's care then being to secure himself." On Saturday a halt was made at Cricklade, and on Sunday at Swindon, where the Earl of Essex attended service at the parish church, and the same night, with the van of the army quartered at Chiseldon, the artillery and trained-bands remaining at Swindon. Very early next morning, September 18th, the army broke up from Swindon and Chisledon, and got upon the Down, called Aldbourne Chase, near Shipley Bottom, and the march was resumed towards Hungerford. In a contemporary letter from Lord George Digby, Essex is said to have had 2,000 horse and 5,000 foot when he marched from Tewkesbury; but he had left some of his troops at Gloucester and others at Upton, and had lost a number of his men in several skirmishes; and this will account to some extent for the diminution of the force with which he had left London. There were also numerous stragglers on the march; and many of the Parliamentary soldiers, who remained behind drinking and who neglected to march with the colours, were slain by the Royalists on entering the towns and villages, or were taken prisoners. Essex's numerical strength, however, afterwards at Newbury, was evidently beyond Lord Digby's computation; for when the Earl marched from Brackley he had an army of about 14,000 men, and no regular engagement had taken place to account for a diminution to the extent of *one-half* of his available force.

CHAPTER II.

## THE ACTION ON ALDBOURNE CHASE.

To the royal cause the raising of the siege of Gloucester was a fatal blow. The future of the Royalist party was gloomy enough at this time, and Charles felt it fully. Since retiring from before the city, the defeated King had halted in the neighbourhood of Winchcombe and at Sudeley Castle, about eight miles from Gloucester, awaiting the motions of the enemy. Finally the Royal army retired towards Painswick, and occupied the position known as "Sponebed Hill." Here it is related that the King being seated on a stone near the Camp, with his two elder sons (the Prince of Wales and the Duke of York), one of them asked him when they should return home,—" Alas ! my son," mournfully replied the unfortunate monarch, "I have no home to go to."

It is mentioned in Warburton's 'Memoirs and Correspondence of Prince Rupert,' that the latter had sent notice of the movements of Essex to his Majesty; but he, believing himself better informed, allowed the enemy twenty-four hours advantage before he followed him. But there appears to be some discrepancy between the statements here made and those of Lord Byron * in a letter to Lord Clarendon † wherein he says :—" that had Prince Rupert been pleased to credit my intelligence, the advantage which Essex gained might have been prevented; which neglect obliged the army to go so hasty and painful a march, that before he reached Newbury there was about 2,000 horse and as many foot lost by the way." This is corroborated by Capt. John Gwynne, who says, ‡ " And when we drew off from Gloucester it proved to be most miserible tempestuous rainy weather so that few or none could take little or no rest on the hills where they were,

---

* For memoirs of persons of note, see APPENDIX.
† Lord Byron's account of the Battles of Newbury, in a letter to Lord Clarendon, in MS. Clar. State Papers, in Bodleian Lib., No. 1738.
‡ Gwynne's ' Milit. Memoirs,' pp. 36—37.

the winds next morning soon dryed up our through-wet clothes we lay pickled in all night (as a convenient washing for us at our coming from the trenches), and we made such haste in pursuit of Essex's army that there was an account of 1,500 foot quite tired and spent, not possible to come up to their colours before we engaged the enemy; and a night or two before we lost two regiments of horse, of Kentish men, and new raised regiments, which were surprised and taken prisoners in their quarters, and what was worse in most men's opinion, we were like to drop down every step we made with want of sleepe, yet notwithstanding we marcht on till we overtook the enemy's army at Newberry Towns-end."

As soon, however, as the King felt assured as to Essex's march and route, he dispatched Prince Rupert with a strong body of horse * to overtake him before he should get so far in advance as to form a junction with Waller's army, which was daily expected to leave London. The Prince accordingly, mustering his cavalry on Broadway Down, gave immediate pursuit, and by the time that Essex reached Swindon, Rupert arrived at Faringdon, having taken a route through Fairford and Lechlade, with the main part of his troops, and only dispatched a single regiment of horse under Colonel Hurry, on the same track that the Earl of Essex was taking. So that at this moment Rupert, by astonishing rapidity, was almost as near to Hungerford as the Parliamentary army was, while a body of 1,000 cavalry was advancing on their rear.

The force at the disposal of the King at this time may be estimated at 10,000 men. According to Rapin, † he commanded when before Gloucester about "8,000 horse and foot;" but this may probably be read as 8,000 of each arm, since, from the facts that such a considerable deduction has to be made for stragglers, and that a garrison of 3,000 infantry and 500 cavalry was left in Reading after the Newbury battle, and in addition a force was placed in Donnington Castle, it certainly seems that the army of the Royalists was far more numerous than the historian would lead us to believe. Rudge, in his 'History of Gloucester,' indeed, computes the King's forces as 30,000 strong, which is doubtless an exaggeration; and Lord Byron states that the army before Gloucester was the greatest the King had during the war; so that the estimate of 10,000 men for the Royalist force that fought afterwards at Newbury is fairly accurate. Clarendon also

---

* Warburton's 'Prince Rupert,' vol. ii, 291.
† Rapin's 'Hist. Eng.', vol. ii, p. 478.

THE ACTION ON ALDBOURNE CHASE. 17

bears this out in his statement that the King's army contained "above 8,000 horse" when his Majesty left Gloucester.*

Prince Rupert's detachment, therefore, may well have numbered 3,000 sabres, exclusive of the regiment sent under Hurry to harass the rear of the Parliamentary forces; and their order of march was such as to offer every advantage to such a dashing cavalier as the nephew of King Charles. Upon the Monday morning, September 18th, Rupert sent on Colonel Hurry, who had followed in Essex's track by way of Cricklade, to reconnoitre, and soon learnt that the Parliamentary troops were passing over Aldbourne Chase, on their way to Newbury. Essex's column of infantry was moving with wide intervals "between their divisions;" and his cavalry were nearly a mile in the rear. Thus, though in actual presence of the enemy, they did little to ascertain where that enemy was. The opportunity was a good one for a bold and intelligent adversary; for a force of all arms indifferently accustomed to combined action, would, as all history tells us, be subject to grave disadvantage if attacked under these circumstances. Lord Byron, after describing the position of the Parliamentary army on Aldbourne Chase as of "great advantage for our horse," says, "we were so placed that we had it in our power both to charge their horse in flank and at the same time to have sent another party to engage their artillery, yet that fair occasion was omitted, and the enemy allowed to join all their forces together, and then we very courageously charged them." It is a most noticeable fact that the Parliamentary army was singularly unaccustomed, at this time, to the movement of mixed bodies. To keep so great a distance between the different fractions, was, from every point of view, likely to lead to disaster, inasmuch as each might be taken individually, and thus the value of the united force be entirely destroyed.

This engagement took place on the open down between Chisledon and Aldbourne, near Dudmore Lodge, about two miles to the north-west of the latter village, and in this locality a cannon ball and other relics of the skirmish have been found. The encounter is graphically referred to in two contemporary tracts, which give both the Royalist and Parliamentarian version of the affair. In Robert Codrington's "Life and Death of the Earl of Essex," the author, after an account of the siege of Gloucester, relates that "From hence [Cirencester] his Excellency marched into Wiltshire, and, being advanced towards Auburn Hills, he had a sight of his

---

* Clarendon, 'Life,' vol. i, p. 164.

Majesty's horse, which appeared in several great bodies, and were so marshalled to charge our army of foot, being then on their march in several divisions; which caused our foot to unite themselves into one gross, our horse perpetually skirmishing with them, to keep them off the foot. In the meantime, the dragoons on both sides gave fire in full bodies on one another, on the side of the Hill, that the woods above, and the vallies below, did echo with the thunder of the charge. There were about fourscore slain upon the place, and more than as many more were sorely wounded. Our horse also made great impression upon the Queen's regiment of horse, and charged them again and again, and cut in pieces many of her life-guard. In this service, the Marquis of Viville was taken prisoner : it seems he would not be known who he was ; but endeavouring to rescue himself from a Lieutenant that took him Prisoner, and thereupon, having his head almost cloven asunder with a pole ax, he acknowledged himself, in the last words he spoke, which were, *Vous voyez un grand Marquis mourant;* that is, *You see a great Marquis dying.* His dead body was carried to Hungerford by the Lord General's command. It had not been long there, but the King did send a Trumpet to his Excellency, conceiving that the Marquis had been wounded only, and taken Prisoner, and desired that his Chirurgeons and Doctors might have free Access unto him for his Recovery. His Excellency certified the Trumpet that he was dead, and returned his Body to the King, to receive those funeral rites as his Majesty would give it. Some say, that his body was ransomed for three hundred Pieces of Gold." This latter statement is borne out by Whitelock in his Memoirs, who further narrates that the money was divided by Essex among his soldiers : and that this statement, as to the disposal of the body of the Marquis is probable, may be inferred from the fact that the registers of the Parish Church of Hungerford, though containing records of the burial of soldiers, make no reference to any who are of higher rank or greater note. *

Monsieur de Larrey observes in reference to the Marquis : —" The French, who never fail of illustrating the actions of their countrymen, extol the prowess of Chartre, Persans, and

---

* The Aldbourne Registers are blank during the period of the Civil War, and they do not recommence until 1646. In the Hungerford Registers, however, are the following entries : 1643, Sept. 18, buried four soldiers : Sept. 25, buried another soldier ; Oct. 4, Henry Chorbley a soldier. It would seem from the dates that these were some of the victims of the skirmish above described. Had De Vieuville been interred there, doubtless it would have been mentioned.

THE ACTION ON ALDBOURNE CHASE. 19

Beaveau, [and Vieuville*] four of their heroes who were in this engagement near Hungerford. These came over with the Count de Harcourt, whom the young King Lewis the 14th, or rather the Queen Regent, sent into England, in quality of Ambassador Extraordinary, to negociate a reconciliation between the King and the Parliament; these four lords suffering themselves to be carried away with the fire natural to their nation, and forgetting the occasion of their journey, came and offer'd their services to the King, and were actually in the battle. It cost the Marquis of Vieuville his life, for he was killed by Col. Kilson, whom he had wounded and was pursuing with too much obstinacy; and the bravery of these four adventurers was the occasion of the Ambassador's negociation proving abortive. For the Parliament, resenting his partiality, would not hearken to his proposals. This was what they signified to him by the Earls of Stamford and Salisbury, who were deputed by the two Houses. The Ambassador excus'd it as an imprudent action, which he said could not be imputed to him; and for which the other had been sufficiently punish'd by the death of one of their companions: but these excuses were rejected. Even he himself was accus'd as coming rather as a spy than an Ambassador, and with a design rather to foment the troubles than to appease them." †

As might be expected, the Royalist's account is somewhat more lengthy, and he evidently views the affair of Aldbourne Chase as a minor victory, though the success was so partial as scarcely to make it worth claiming. Still the preliminary movements of the Royalists were not unskilfully taken, for while Col. Hurry with 1,000 troopers was dispatched to harass the rear, the remainder of the cavalry under Rupert himself moved off to

---

*This name is omitted in the text, but referred to in a marginal note. See Clarendon's Hist. v. ii, p. 346.

† 'History of the Reign of King Charles I.', Lond. 1716, vol ii., pp. 165—6. An excellent portrait of the Marquis de Vieuville by Vandyke, was formerly in the collection of the Duke of Buckingham, at Stowe, and is thus described in the 'Tour by a German Prince,' vol. iii., p. 277. "The dress is odd, but picturesque—a white 'just eau corps à la Henri quatre,' with a black mantle thrown over it; full, short, black breeches falling over the knee, with silver points; pale violet stockings, with gold clocks, and white shoes with gold roses. On the mantle is embroidered the star of the Holy Ghost, five times as large as it is now worn, the blue ribbon 'en sautoir,' but hanging very low, and the cross worn in the present fashion on the side; it is narrower and smaller than now, and hangs by the broad ribbon almost under the arm." This portrait was sold at the Stowe sale, in 1848, for £220 10s. 0d. The purchaser was Mr. Emanuel, of Bond Street, London.

intercept and assail the head of the hostile column. Here let the Royalist writer, "a noble person from the South," tell the story in his own words. "It was our good lucke to cross his army just as our party had overtaken it upon the open Downe, two miles on the *north-west* side of *Auburne*. The Rebells descrying us drew up in Battalia, leaving onely a body of some 200 Horse upon a Hill, somewhat distant from the Grosse of their Army, which we found means so to steale upon with Hurryes party, as to charge and route them, and taking two Cornetts, and killing forty or fifty Men, without any losse on our part, we beat them into their Foot, and Cannon; upon which occasion we discovered such evident symptomes of feare and distraction in their whole Army, as that the Prince was well nigh tempted from his temper, and was once resolved to have charged with three thousand Horse alone; their whole Army consisting of two thousand Horse, and five thousand Foot at least, and store of Cannon. But newes arriving at the instant, That our Foot, was beyond expectation, advanced within six or seven miles Miles of us, it imposed upon his Highnesse prudence this caution, not to adventure upon halfe our strength, that rest, which the next day he might be sure to fight for with double power: Upon which consideration he made a stand, resolving that night, onely to attend them and hinder their March. We had not stood long, when we discovered that the enemy prepared for a retreat, and by degrees drew away their Baggage first, then their Foot, leaving their Horse at a good distance from them. The Prince his designe hereupon, was, to have charged them, when halfe their forces should have been drawne off the field into those Lanes whereunto their Baggage was already advanced, But their Motions being so very slow, and the Night drawing on; upon second thoughts, his Highnesse judged it the best course, to try if by a small party he could ingage their Horse, which was then grown to be a good distance from their Foot. This party he committed to the care of Hurrey, with two Regiments onely neer at hand to second him, keeping the Body of his Horse at such a distance, as might incourage the enemy to venture on that sever'd part, which they did with a little too much incouragement, for to say the truth, the Regiment that should have seconded Hurrey, not doing their part so well as they ought, forced his party almost to make somewhat a disorderly retreat, and the Prince to send hasty succours to them; which the Queenes Regiment (commanded by my Lord Jermine) was ordered to doe, which his Lordship performed with much gallantry, being received very steadily by a strong body of the enemies' Horse, and with a composednesse in the Officer that commanded them, very remarkable, for his Lordship advancing before his Regiment, with the Marquesse of *Viville* on one hand, and the Lord *Digby* on the other, the enemies volley of Carbines (given them smartly at lesse than ten yards) being past, the Commander (somewhat forwarder than the rest) was plainly seen to prye into their Countenances, and removing his levell from one to another to discharge his Pistoll, as it were by election at the Lord Digbyes head, but without any more hurt (saving onely the burning of his face) then he himselfe received by my Lord *Jerman's* sword, who (upon the Lord *Digbyes* Pistoll missing fire) ran him with it into the back: but he was as much beholding there to his Arms, as the Lord Digby to his head-piece. Immediately upon this shock, the Queene's Regiment was so charged in the reare by a fresh body of theirs, that the greatest part of it shifting for themselves, the Lord *Jermine* accompanied with the French Marquesse, and the Officers onely of his regiment thought it as safe a way, as well as the most honourable, to venture forward through their whole Army, rather than to charge back through those that invironed him, and so with admirable successe (the unhappy losse of that gallant *Marquesse* excepted) he brought himselfe, foure Coullers, and all his Officers off safe, having made their way round through the grosse of the Enemies foot. The Lord *Digby* (being stunn'd and for the present blinded with his shot,) was fortunately received out of the middle of a Regiment of the Enemies by a brave Charge, which Prince *Rupert* in Person made upon them with His one Troope, where in His Highnesse Horse was shot in the Head under Him; but yet by God's blessing brought him off. And so the Enemies' Horse being beaten quite up to their Foot and Cannon, the night comming upon us, gave a Period to that action." \*

After this the Royalists proceeded towards Newbury, and the Parliamentarians to Hungerford, where crossing the Kennet they also prepared for a further advance towards the former town, though by the opposite bank of the stream. It is evident that Essex had originally designed to proceed to Reading by the London Road on the left bank of the river, but the sudden irruption of Rupert's cavalry led him of necessity to change his plan. If the skirmish was not completely successful, it at any rate forced the Parliamentarians off their direct road and compelled them to place an obstacle

---

\* 'A Copy of a Letter written to his Excellence the Marquesse of Newcastle by a noble person from the South' &c., &c., 1643, p. 5, *et seq.*

between themselves and their pursuers. Throughout it must be borne in mind that Essex's chief desire was to reach London. To fight his way there was apparently not his intention, if it could be avoided. But the cavalry action delayed him by driving him off the London Road, and enabled the King's infantry to reach Newbury; and thus the royal army appeared in menacing force on the flank of the line of march of the Parliamentarians, obliging the Earl to form front to his flank and attempt to defeat the King before he continued his own advance towards the Capital. Probably he hoped to pass the Kennet at Newbury; but having failed there, he chose the next available passage, that of Padworth, after the battle on the 20th September had been decided in his favour. The skirmish, however, though well conceived and, as we have seen, partially successful, was but feebly executed. The opportunity afforded by the lengthy division of the Earl's column of march on open ground, for a demoralizing blow at the Army of the Parliament was almost lost through the want of order and method of the attack.

"The Armies" writes Byron again, "were then drawne so near together that it was impossible the enemy could avoid fighting with us if we pleased; and hereupon a fourth error may be observed, for notwithstanding the necessity there was of fighting (at least if they persisted in their marching to London and we in ours of preventing them) yet no orders were given out for the manner of our fighting and how the army should be embattled as usually is done on the like occasions." Skill must be combined with courage to reap the full fruits of victory; and these only partially rested with the troopers of the King, for the army of the Parliament made good its march to Hungerford though it left behind it according to the 'Mercurius Aulicus' "17 carts heavily laden with ammunition and victual, three whereof were bullet, the rest wheat and other provisions, leaving there also the 1,000 sheep (previously mentioned) tyed by the legs, 200 whereof were at once restored to their owners, the rest left till those who had a just right to them should come and claim them." * Both sides suffered considerable loss in this encounter. Of the officers of the Parliament, Capt. Middleton and Capt. Hacket are recorded as being slain, and Capt. Roper of Lord Fielding's regiment severely wounded. Whitelock estimates the killed on both sides at about 80; and the 'True Informer' of September 23rd, 1643, says "Of persons of note slain on the King's side in the skirmish was the Marquis of Vieuville, his

---

* 'Mercurius Aulicus,' Friday, October 6th, 1643.

son, and Sir John Throgmorton," but this appears to be one of the frequent exaggerations of party pamphleteers. Two of the Throckmortons, Colonels Ambrose and Thomas, were in the service of King Charles, but it is not recorded in any other account of the skirmish that either of them fell here, or that the Marquis de Vieuville had a son killed in the action. Some traces of the fight were found in May, 1815, when the workmen, in widening the turnpike road from Swindon to Hungerford, exhumed sixty skeletons on removing a bank at Preston at the spot where the parishes of Aldbourne and Ramsbury join, a few yards from the turning leading to the latter place. The skeletons were those of young men, and lay scattered about two feet below the surface. The bones were placed in carts and conveyed to the churchyards of Aldbourne and Ramsbury where they were re-interred. If, as in all probability, these remains were those of the soldiers killed in the skirmish on the Chase, it is a singular coincidence that the boundary-line of two parishes should have been chosen, as at Newbury, for the place of burial for the slain. It is probable that as this "running fight" extended over both parishes, the parochial authorities undertook jointly to gather up and inter the dead, the union point of their respective parishes being selected as significant of the mutual character of their obligation, and also as an enduring landmark. A considerable portion of this bank, which has the appearance of having been artificially raised, still remains at the side of the road, and can be identified by a row of fir trees growing at the top. In Lovers' Coppice, about 1,500 yards west from where the bodies were found, a number of silver coins of Elizabeth, James I., and Charles I. (280) were discovered in the year 1867, the greater portion of which came into the possession of the late Major Seymour, of Crowood, on whose property the wood is situate, who had them converted into a tankard. A tradition exists, that during "The Troubles" many of the inhabitants of Ramsbury, fearful of being plundered and of losing their lives, took shelter in this wood; these coins may have been buried at this time by one of the refugees, and by some accident never again recovered.

CHAPTER III.

## MARCH OF THE ARMIES TO NEWBURY.

The King, with the foot and artillery, continued to advance steadily, and on Sunday morning, Sept. 17th, wrote to he Prince Rupert, by John Ashburnham, as follows:—

"May it please your Highness, His Majesty hath commanded me to let your Highness know that he has altered his resolution of quartering this night at Burford, and now intends to quarter at Alvesscott at the Lady Ashcome's house where he will be better furnished with provisions for his army, and being the straighter way, will save three or four miles march. It is within 5 miles of Farringdon, whither his Majesty desires you would advertise him this night of your proceedings. With my humble service presented, I kiss your Highness's hand, and am, Sir, your most humble Servant, JOHN ASHBURNHAM. Northleach, 12 of the clock, Sept. 17th, 1643." *

The same evening another letter, written by Lord George Digby, was sent by the King:—

"May it please your Highness, The King hath received your Highness's letter written from Stamford, at five of the clock this evening, and commands me thereupon to let your Highness know, that since it appears by your intelligence that my Lord of Essex is not so far out of reach as was feared, he is desirous to make all haste towards him; his Majesty's army being all, except stragglers, well up hither to Alvesscott; his Majesty's desire therefore is that if your intelligence of the Rebells not being further advanced than Cricklade continue true, your Highness will be pleased to send speedily your opinion which way and to what place it will be fit for the King to march with his army tomorrow. As we looke uppon the map here, supposing that Essex points for Reading, we conceive Wantage will be the aptest place, but in this His Majesty conceives he is to be governed wholly by directions from your Highness according to your discoveries of their motions, or the impressions you shall make upon

---

* Warburton's 'Prince Rupert,' vol. ii, 289.

them, and therefore, he desires your Highness to send him speedy advertisements, of what you shall conceive best. Your Highness's most humble servant, GEORGE DIGBY. Alvesscott, at 8 at night, this Sunday. I am commanded to add, that you should consider to allow the foot here as much rest as can well be without losing the opportunity. Sept. 17th, 1643. Digby."*

At one o'clock in the morning of the following day, Charles dispatched another missive to Rupert, in reply to a letter from the Prince, this time written by the Duke of Richmond:

"Your Highness. I have let the King see what you writt, who approves of all in it, and will accordingly perform his part, only desires to have certain knowledge when Essex moved, or shall move from Cricklade, that if His Majesty's armie can arrive time enough (which he will the presently he receives the answer), he will take up his quarters at or about Wantage, so as to reach Newbury as you propose, but if that cannot be, he is loth to wearie the foot after so great a march as they have had, which you know infers that many are behind. Last night my Lord Digby writt to your Highness by the King's order upon the receipt of yours from Stamford, to which I can add what is only known since, that besides Vavasour and some other forces, Woodhouse will, I feel confident, come to-day with the Prince of Wales's regiment, say 700. * * * The motion of our armie depends much on [what] the advertisement from you will give [us] information. RICHMOND and LENNOX, September 18, at 1 morning." †

After a brief halt at Faringdon, where the King dined, the troops were soon again on the move; and that evening they reached Wantage, his Majesty sleeping at the house of Sir Geo. Wilmot at Charlton. Thither Rupert sent an express messenger to the King urging him to advance with all speed in the direction of Newbury, as Essex was now fairly on his way to that place, the possession of the town being the object chiefly aimed at by the enemy. The Prince meanwhile marched with his horse from Aldbourne to Lamborne, where he refreshed his wearied troopers, and then eagerly pressed onwards to anticipate the Earl of Essex and check his progress. He was just in time, not a minute too soon; for arriving at Newbury early on Tuesday morning, the 19th September, he found the Lord General's advanced guard already in the town, engaged in preparing quarters for the

---

* Warburton's 'Prince Rupert,' vol. ii, p. 290.
† The above extract is taken from one of the many original letters discovered at Pyt House, Wilts.

on-coming troops of the Parliament.* With scarcely a moment's halt, the leading squadron of the King's troops, headed by the untiring Rupert, confronted the startled Parliament men, who were ignorant of the nearness of the royal cavalry, but who, perceiving that resistance with so small a force was useless, made a precipitate flight, leaving several of their quarter-masters in the hands of the enemy. Troop after troop now poured into the town, which the Prince secured, and left Essex to the scanty resources of its immediate vicinity.

The march of the Royal Army from Gloucester had been thus conducted:—

|  |  | NIGHTS. | MILES. |
|---|---|---|---|
| "Sept. 14. | To Evisham | 2 | 4 |
| ,, 16. | To Snowshill | 1 | 6 |
| ,, 17. | To Norlich [Northleach] dinner, Alscot, supper.. | 1 | 12 |
| ,, 18. | To Faringdon dinner, to Wantage Sir George Wilmot's, [Charlton] supper and bed | 1 | 10 |
| ,, 19. | Dinner in the field Newbury, to supper and bed Mr. Cox's, and on Wednesday, the 20th, the great battle was struck there | 4 | 10 |
| ,, 23. | To Oxford during pleasure | 0 | 20 " |

*Iter Carolinum.*

NOTE.—The actual distance from Wantage to Newbury and from the latter town to Oxford somewhat exceeds that above stated.

A few hours later, the brilliant troop of Life Guards, composed of the noblest and wealthiest cavaliers who had no separate command, with casque and plume and glittering cuirass, came moving on in stately and martial style. They heralded the approach of the ill-starred but gallant King, who, conspicuous in his steel armour, and on whose breast glittered the Star and George, rode at the head of his infantry; and for the first time during the war entered the good old town of Newbury, a place so soon to be associated with events of the deepest significance in connection with the great national revolution.

Lord Clarendon computes the amount of income possessed by this single troop as at least equal to that of all the Lords and Commons [in London] who made and maintained that war. Sir Philip Warwick, who tells us he himself " rode therein," computes this income at £100,000 per annum, equal,

---

* 'Mercurius Aulicus,' September 19, 1643.

perhaps, to three times that sum according to our present standard.

In the "Memoirs of a Cavalier, or, a Military Journal of the Wars in Germany, and the Wars of England from the year 1632 to the year 1648," ascribed to De Foe, the hero of the narrative, said to have been Col. Andrew Newport, in referring to this troop remarks :—" As for me, I rode a volunteer in the royal troop of guards, which may very well deserve that title, being composed of young gentlemen, sons of the nobility and prime gentlemen of the nation, and I think not a person of so mean a birth or fortune as myself. We reckoned in this troop thirty-two lords, or who came afterward to be such, thirty-eight younger sons of the nobility, five French noblemen, and the rest gentlemen of very good families and estates. And that I may give the due to their personal valour, many of this troop lived to have regiments and troops under their command, in the service of the King; many of them lost their lives for him, and most of them their estates: nor did they behave unworthy of themselves in their first shewing their faces to the enemy, as shall be mentioned in its place." From a memorandum made by Capt. Symonds, the author of the Diary of the Royal Marches, concerning the King's army in 1644, we learn that the First, or King's regiment of Life Guards, and the Second, or Queen's regiment, wore red coats, Lord Percy's regiment white, Lord Hopton's and Col. Charles Gerard's regiments blue, Col. Pinchbeck's gray, Col. Aspley's red, and Col. Talbot's yellow coats.

The town of Newbury was the pivot, so to speak, around which much of the fighting, during the Civil War, in the southern part of England for a long period centred; and it is to the share it took in this most eventful and important period in our country's annals that its political and historical prominence are mainly due. The history of Newbury carries us back to the time when the masters of the ancient world— the Romans, were in possession of our island. Frequent traces of their occupation have been found in the town, and the station called "Spinæ" mentioned in the Roman itineraries can be reasonably reconciled with the adjacent parish of Speen. We may even be justified in supposing that Newbury from its situation on the river Kennet, and the presence of so many Celtic hill-forts and strongholds in its neighbourhood, was a place of settlement chosen by the early colonists of this part of ancient Britain. But whatever may have been the origin of the town of Newbury, it was undoubtedly known by its present name at least some ten years before the taking of the Domesday Survey.* The Saxon town of Newberie, which was probably within the area of the Domesday manor of Ulvri-tone, *i.e.* the town of Ulfrid or Ulfric, fell to the share of one of the Conqueror's followers named Ernulf de Hesding, who founded a Church in Newbury, which he gave with a hide of land and a priest's house, to the Abbot and Convent of Préaux in Normandy. In subsequent times, the Manor, when held by the Crown, was frequently assigned, as a jointure, to the queens of England. Thus on the marriage of Henry VIII. with Lady Jane Seymour it passed to the queen as part of her dower, and was granted in a like manner to Queen Anne, of Denmark, mother of Charles I. The latter made over the Manor to the Corporation of Newbury,† in consideration of £50 and an annual payment of £20 4s. 2¼d., in answer to the following petition for its purchase, apparently presented to the House of Commons: ‡

"Rt. Honble. That the Mair, Aldermen, and Burgesses might take the Manor and liberties thereof in fee farme. Your honble. House hath bin informed that the said suite is only the desire of some few within the town, and not general, and yet that your honble. House hath bin obliged to admit the said Corporation to compound for the same, make bold to testifie your honble. House that we specially desire the said Corporation to be possessed thereof before any other. Wee having good experience of their great love and regard for the welfare of the Town and of helping to safe [save] the poor inhabitants thereof in all taxes and payments within the town that they possibly can, and in keeping the town in good order, for which your honble favour shewed to them in their behalf, wee and all our posteritie with many more shall be each bound to pray to God for your honbles. long life and prosperous estate.

William Howes, Mair.

| Gabriell Coxe, the elder. | Thomas Chokke. | Richard Money. |
| William Twisse (Rector). | William Grove. | Timothie Avery. |
| Thomas Dolman. | Robert Daunce. | William Wilmot. |
| &c. | &c. | &c. |

---

* See 'Ordericus Vitalis,' Bohn's Ed., vol. ii, p. 264.

† The lands which comprise a portion of the Manor of Newberry, Co. Cork, Ireland, are said to have been granted by the Crown to Capt. Newman, an ancestor of its present possessor, for his eminent services in the battle of the 20th September, the name of 'Newberry' being bestowed on the property in commemoration of the circumstance.

‡ Copied from a contemporary duplicate of the original in the Corporation archives.

Like many other places engaged in the staple manufacture of England—woollen cloth, the town of Newbury was well affected to the Parliament. The reasons are not far to seek. Besides being influenced by religion and a sense of independence, the inhabitants of manufacturing towns had especially suffered from the monopolies and extortions which had raised the price of necessaries and shackled the enterprise of trade. Again, the Protestant Nonconformists were a numerous and influential body; and in the same ranks, says Macaulay,[*] were to be found most of those members of the Established Church, who still adhered to the Calvinistic opinions, which, forty years before, had been generally held by the prelates and clergy. Such a man was Dr. Twisse, the Puritan Rector of Newbury, whose teaching must have exercised a decided influence in forming the opinions of the town and neighbourhood. Newbury had also, from its position on the great western road, its proximity to Oxford (the King's head-quarters), and the royal garrisons at Donnington, Basing, Faringdon, and Wallingford, suffered perhaps to a greater extent than any other town in the kingdom from the disastrous effects of this unhappy war. Its inhabitants were therefore induced by the strongest motives to espouse the cause of Parliament.

The following letters, written by members of each party, will enable the reader to form an impartial view of the proclivities of the people of Newbury at this juncture:—

Lord Grandison to Prince Rupert.

Marlboro' 8 Dec. [1642].

May itt please your High$^{es}$ I know not how well to give credite to it, but there is two gentlemen nowe come from Newberie frighted from thence the lastt nightt by intelligence they had of some of the enemies forces were to come into Newberie *invited thether by the townsmen*, who have only reported the plague to bee there to keepe the King's troopes oute, how slight soever this may be, sure I AM THAT DIS-AFFECTED TOWNE CAN NOTT BEE TO MUCH PUNISHED BY YOUR HIGH$^{s.}$ for att my coming from Basingstoke they stopped all our baggage and had detained itt butt thatt they hered wee were strong enough to reveng itt. The Sherife of this Countie intends to be heer this day to order some things for his Maj$^{ties.}$ service, these same are the reasons thatt keept mee a day in this burnt and plundered quarter.   \*   \*   \*

From your High$^{es}$ most humble faithful servant,

GRANDISON.

---

[*] 'Hist. of England,' vol. i, p. 106.

This letter, from the Pyt House Collection, appears to have been written immediately after the capture and plunder of Marlborough by the Royalists ("the most notoriously disaffected town of all the country," says Clarendon). This was the first garrison taken on either side; when a great part of the town was burnt. Lord Grandison died from the effects of wounds received at the siege of Bristol the following year.

Two days previously the Earl of Essex wrote to the Parliamentary Colonels Goodwin and Hurry :—

Sirs,—Since I receiv'd your letter I have had information that Marlborough has been 2 days assaulted by the King's forces [Essex here gives instructions to the two Colonels to march with all speed to its relief]. * * * *You have Newberry, a very honest towne*, to march to in ye way, where you may encourage forces to follow you, *and it is a very good place to assist you upon all occasions*. Your assured friend,

Windsor, Dec. 6, 1642, 8 o'clock at night.      ESSEX.
Endorsed for Col. Goodwin, Col. Hurry, or either of them.*

Col. Goodwin, on his return to Newbury from Marlborough, gave the following account of his proceedings in a letter without superscription, but probably addressed to Philip, Lord Wharton, his son-in-law, with whom he was in frequent correspondence at this time :—

My Lord,—We have had many painful journies since I saw you, but none like that of Thursday, when we missed meeting the King's forces, and only because we could not get out our dragoons till noon. We went then on to Wantage, where were 3 regiments, 1 of horse, 1 of foot, 1 of dragoons, and my Lord Digby with certain ladies, they had intelligence before we came up, which was in dark night, and hasted away, we caught about 50 prisoners, my Lord Jermyn's lady and 3 or 4 other women, Sir Robt. Lee and his broth<sup>r.</sup> and there were some thirty slaine, some ammunition was left, which because we could not bring away was spoyled. I can write no more to night, the rather because I must be up by 5 in the morning to visit Andover, where my Lord Grandison is, they say, with 3,000 horse and dragoons, but I hope not so many. I think I shall run away and be with you shortly for we are all most abominable plunderers, as bad as Prince Robert [Rupert], and shall be as much hated, as when complaints come, I am ashamed to look an honest man in the face, truly, it is as bad to me as a bullet. It is now nearing

---

* Tanner MSS., Bibl. Bodl. v. 62/2.

morning, excuse me to all my friends: the Lord be with you all. Yours ever to command.    A. G., Newbury.
Sunday morninge, Dec. [12th]. P.S.—Our letters to my Lord Genl. surely are intercepted.*

In a letter written by Col. Dalbier † from Newbury, and presented to the House of Lords by the Committee of Oxon, Bucks, and Berks, requesting the payment of the forces under his command then lying in the town, it was ordered by their Lordships, "That some course be speedily and effectually taken for the maintenance of these forces, lest they disband and be lost, and that town [Newbury] *which hath on all occasions manifested so much affection for the Parliament*, come again within the power of the enemy."‡

From all this it will be seen that though the town was frequently in the Royalists' hands, and the neighbouring Castle of Donnington maintained a royal garrison during the whole of the years 1643 to 1646, the general sympathy of the people was rather with Roundhead than with Cavalier.

To the Royalist cause it was a place of great military value. Situated as it is on one of the most ancient and important passages of the Kennet, it is a place of considerable strategical importance. If occupied by an enemy, it menaced the main roads leading from the west by Reading to London; and for the Royal Army, based as it was on Oxford, its possession enabled them to intercept any movement that might be attempted in the Kennet Valley, while their own line of retreat was completely covered. In addition to this, Donnington Castle, an ancient fortress the strength of which had been enormously increased by the construction of fieldworks of good trace and profile, further protected a retrograde movement if it became necessary, and acted, so to speak, as an advanced fort on this side of the Thames. The castle was at the time held by a staunch Royalist, Sir John Boys, and was situated about one mile north of Newbury, near the Oxford road, which it completely commanded. South of the town, the ground rises gradually to a narrow plateau occupying the area between the Kennet and the En or Wash Rivulet, the western extremity of which towards Hungerford was known as Enborne Heath, and the eastern, in the immediate neighbourhood of Newbury, as Wash Common, over

---

* Carte's MSS., Letters, Bibl. Bodl. v. 103. For particulars of this service at Marlborough and Wantage, see Waylen's 'History of Marlborough,' pp. 166—9.

† Sometimes written D'Albier, Dalbiere, or Dulbier.

‡ 'Journal of the House of Lords,' 8 Jan. 1645.

which the road from Oxford to Andover and Salisbury passed. It was on this latter portion of the high land that the First Battle of Newbury was fought. So that while the Army of Essex, which had crossed the Kennet at Hungerford, was moving on the outer arc, as it were, to gain the passages of the stream lower down and so reach Reading, that of the King, after the cavalry skirmish just described on Aldbourne Chase, was marching by the shorter chord, and had occupied the town as well as the fields to the South of it before their adversaries had reached the Wash. The option of giving or refusing battle therefore rested with the King, and as he encamped his troops on the night of 19th September in the fields below the heights his choice had evidently been made.

Meanwhile the Parliamentary General, after the engagement on Aldbourne Chase, marched to the eastward under discouraging circumstances. "We were much distressed," says one of his men, "for want of sleep as also for other sustenance. It was a night of much rain and we were wet to the skin."

In passing through the principal street of Aldbourne on his way to Hungerford, two of his ammunition wagons broke down, but to prevent their falling into the hands of the enemy, matches were put to them and they were left to explode. This proved some hindrance to the pursuers, and the Earl managed to reach Chilton without further interference. Here some of his army lodged that night in the fields. Others were at Hungerford. Essex himself quartered at Chilton House.* The army of the Parliament suffered greatly from want of food and from exposure of the weather, and for three days could get no supplies for man or horse beyond the scanty stock they carried with them. The enemy's force followed them so closely, and the royalist horse were so far above them in

---

* Chilton House, at this time, appears to have been the property of Mr. John Packer, proprietor of Donnington Castle. His second son, John, a Fellow of the Royal College of Physicians of London, described himself in his Will, dated 22 June, 1703, as of Chilton-Foliott, Wilts. It was at Dr. Packer's house at Chilton that the Marquis of Halifax, the Earl of Nottingham, and Lord Godolphin, the Commissioners appointed by James II. to treat with the Prince of Orange, slept on the night of Friday, 7th December 1688. Chilton Lodge another seat in this village was the property of the eminent Cromwellian statesman Sir Bulstrode Whitelock, and here the "Memorials" and other works were chiefly written. He died at Chilton, in 1675, and was buried at Fawley, near Henley-on-Thames, but there is no memorial of him in the church. His widow, Lady Whitelock, died at Chilton, in 1684.

MARCH OF THE ARMIES TO NEWBURY. 33

number, that they could not with any safety send out parties to forage, as their opponents did.

By six o'clock on Tuesday morning, 19th September, Essex and his troops again met at Hungerford,* where what little sustenance could be obtained was portioned out to the men. The order to march was soon given, and the columns of the Parliament, with the brave Earl leading the van, advanced on their desperate enterprise.

The route taken by the Lord-General, who appears even at this time to have been ignorant of the King's intentions, and not to have anticipated his rapid movements, was through Kintbury and Hamstead to Enborne, by the road parallel with and south of the Kennet; but on approaching Newbury, where he had designed to quarter, he found to his surprise that his advanced guard had been dislodged and driven out, and that the King occupied the town and its approaches. Thereupon he drew his army into a favourable position in the fields screened by the woods at Enborne, and here encamped; his men, notwithstanding all the perils and trials of a long and toilsome march, being "full of courage and in no way disheartened at their hard service." Essex himself, it is said, sought shelter in a poor thatched cottage, which is still pointed out as the head-quarters of the Parliament's General.†

The "True Informer" contains the following piece of news dated Thursday, Sept. 21st, 1643. "Parliament was informed by several Clothiers, who came from Wiltshire, to this effect— That the Towne of Newbury having intelligence of his Excellency the Parliament's Lieutenant-General his advancing that way, had provided great store of provisions and other necessaries both for horse and man, for the entertainment of

---

* Hungerford Park, with all manorial rights within its limits, had been granted by the Crown in 1595 to the Trustees of Essex's unfortunate father, who was beheaded in 1601. There was no house in Hungerford Park when granted to the Earl of Essex, and it is not improbable that he was the builder of the ancient mansion pulled down by a later owner, Mr. Dalbiac, at the east end of which were the arms of Queen Elizabeth: a large and lofty room over the servants' hall was called Queen Elizabeth's room. Lysons' 'Magna Britannia,' vol. i. p. 296.

† Bigg's Cottage, where local tradition records that Essex slept, the night before the battle, is a time-worn old tenement, apparently of an age anterior to these events, situate at the foot of Bigg's Hill (hereafter referred to) on the borders of what was formerly Enborne Heath or Down, and in about the centre of Essex's position. The occupier of the cottage states that, in clearing out a well near the spot a few years since, some coins of the Caroline period and a diamond ring were found. A pike-head turned up by the plough near Enborne Schools was presented to the Newbury Museum by the late Dr. Palmer.

his army, of which the King's forces having notice, contrary to their purposes wheeled about that way, and got into the Towne unexpectedly before the Parliament's army." Tradition supports this statement, and it is said that many of the inhabitants of Newbury had been sitting up all the preceding night engaged in cooking provisions for the refreshment of the Parliamentary troops after their long march and privations. These preparations were, however, equally acceptable to the wearied troops of the King.

Essex found himself in a position of considerable difficulty and danger. It was essential, for his plans, that he should convey his army as far as possible intact to London, and his object would have been gained by avoiding a general action altogether. But speed was also essential, and with ill-disciplined troops, the inferior equipment, cumbrous artillery, baggage, and supply-trains of those times, the shortest road was more than ever the quickest. Divergence from the most direct route was not only difficult and slow of execution, both from the want of accurate maps or information and the lack of experience in directing the movements of large bodies of men, but also from the inferior nature of all the roads save those that formed the great arteries of communication. But there was yet another reason. The land was not so well drained in those days as in ours. Low lands were more liable to periodical inundations, and were therefore more generally impassable to men and horses, let alone wheeled vehicles; and naturally dry heath or high land, such as characterises the ridge of hills between the Kennet and the En Brook, afforded as a rule more ready and more certain facilities for marching. Hence it was that, even at the risk of a battle, the line of advance was directed in front of Newbury by Crockham, Greenham, and Crookham Heaths on London.

The presence of the Royalist Army at Newbury, the possession therefore of all the points of passage of the river in this neighbourhood, and the occupation of the London road, all compelled Essex to execute that most difficult of all manœuvres, a flank march in the presence of the enemy.

Military criticism on the Earl's difficulties seems almost unnecessary. It is evident that to pass by the hostile force without offering battle exposed him to three dangers; an attack on his left flank as he passed, an assault on his rear after he *had* passed, and the possible capture of his baggage which would move by the best road and in rear of his columns. The first danger would lead to his defeat in detail, for the left wing would have had to stand the attack of the whole of the King's army perhaps before the right wing could come to its assistance, thus breaking through the elementary principle of never offering your divided fractions to the blows of a vastly superior force. The second might have been still more disastrous, as the forces not arrayed in battle order and marching along several roads might have been both crushed and routed. The last danger was all important, for without supplies of ammunition, let alone food, large bodies of troops must either spread for forage and food, and become disorganised and scattered, or remain concentrated and starve. There was, and is, but one way of effecting this strategic manœuvre, namely to place a sufficient obstacle between the advancing force and the enemy, such as a river, which either cannot be crossed, or the passages of which are in the hands of strong detachments of the force. But these conditions were not available, for Newbury was then the Royal head-quarters, so that the Parliamentary Army could not hope to pass rapidly by, while flanking detachments resisted the enemy's attempt to debouch on the exposed flank. He was prevented from marching by the roads south of the En, probably, both because of the wide detour, which would have given the Royalists time to concentrate larger forces, and, moving more rapidly by the better roads in the Kennet Valley, again to present themselves before him under perhaps even more disadvantageous circumstances, and also by the inferior character of the roads. So it was that the Earl of Essex drawing up his forces between the Kennet and Bigg's Hill, resolved to cut his way through the army of the King, should it attempt to bar his path to London.

From contemporary accounts it appears that Essex's camping ground extended from the irregularly enclosed fields on the left, which protected him against a surprise by the Newbury and Kintbury Road, to Crockham Heath on the left. A natural ravine of some depth sheltered him in front, whilst his left flank had the protection of the woods at Hamstead, and of the Kennet river, and his right rested on the little river En. Here, with the rain falling in torrents, no fire! no food! the weary but resolute soldiers of the Parliament remained under arms all night, "impatient of the sloth of darkness, and wishing for the morning's light to exercise their valour." Essex's dispositions were well made. An attack by the Royalists along the Kintbury-Enborne-Newbury road might have captured his baggage, and, if pushed successfully, have "turned" his left flank, cutting him off from the best road of retreat (that by Kintbury and Hungerford), and possibly driving his army back in disorder on the En Brook. To cross this by bad roads and few bridges would have led to the abandonment of his artillery and baggage, to his being driven south and thus far off his road to London, and would have increased the demoralization and disorder of his troops. Hence it is that his reserve guarded this important road and took post at Enborne, while close to it lay the strong left wing of the main army. By occupying so extended a front as that from Enborne to the En he obtained other advantages. His flanks, resting closely on the stream and on the wooded headland of Hamstead Park, were not liable to be turned,—that is, the enemy could not get round them and attack his flank or rear without his knowledge. Lastly, with the large force at his command, it was well to utilize as many roads as possible, as at all times movement is easier by beaten tracks than across country; and, so long as his forces were not too widely disseminated, he displayed a sound appreciation of the military situation in covering the three lines of advance by the roads, Bigg's Hill—Trundle Hill, Crockham—Wash Common, by Skinner's Green, and Enborne—Newbury, which led him out on to the open land where he meant to give battle to the King. It seems exceedingly probable that, though the artillery (marching by the best road as all wheeled vehicles naturally would) may have halted at the "Slings" near Enborne, it was eventually brought up to Crockham Heath, both because its advance thence could be directed by any of the roads to the front (then partly in the occupation of the cavalier outposts) which might eventually seem best, and also because, being centrally situated, it would be safer: artillery, always cumbrous, was terribly so then; guns were easily captured, and difficult to move away. There, however, they were not only in safety, but as in all times good artillery positions are on high land because the extended view thence enables the gunner to obtain the greatest possible advantage from the range the weapon has, the slow-moving guns of the Parliamentary army were at any rate somewhat nearer their work, nearer their probable point of application, than down in the low-lying road that led from Enborne to Newbury.

THE EARL OF ESSEX.

## CHAPTER IV.

## PREPARATIONS FOR BATTLE.

All his arrangements being completed, Essex determined to direct his attack against that position of the Royalist line on the Wash which barred the upper way to London, rather than attempt a passage through the town. In the stillness of the early dawn the Parliamentary General, favoured by the cover which sheltered his camping ground, got his men under arms; and, riding from regiment to regiment, he told his soldiers that the enemy had all the advantages, "the Hill, the Town, Hedges, Lane, and River"; but with calm determination they unanimously cried out, "Let us fall upon them! We will, by God's assistance, beat them from them all!"\* and every man prepared himself promptly for the momentous struggle.

"And you that know the gain at Newberry!
Seeing the General, how undauntedly
He then encouraged you for England's right!
When Royal forces fled, he stood the fight!" †

The disposition of the army was effected with great military skill. The right, under Major General Skippon was on the rising ground by "Biggs Hill" ‡ and Hill Farm, extending along the Enborne Valley towards the Wash, the centre on the plateau, and the left in a more northerly direction towards Hamstead (Crockham Heath). The baggage or train was placed in or near what is now the front of Hamstead Park, opposite the Rectory, Enborne, described in the Parish Map as "The Slings," § under the shelter of the Hamstead Woods; and here also was their reserve both of horse and foot.

---

\* Vicar's 'Parliamentary Chronicle.'

† 'A Funerall Monument to the most renowned Earl of Essex,' printed in London, 1646.

‡ *Biggs Hill*. The Hill referred to by Lord Clarendon and other writers on the Civil Wars as the spot where Essex drew up his army in order of battle. This Hill of considerable length and elevation, is near Hill Farm (in the occupation of Mr. George Heath) on the line of march of Essex from Kintbury *viâ* Hamstead village and Enborne Street. Biggs Hill comprises the portions of land denoted as "The Common" and "Hill Ground" in the Tithe Map. Enborne Heath, Down, or Common, was enclosed about 70 years ago.

§ Ludlow, in his 'Memoires,' refers to "Slings" as a species of Artillery used by the Parliamentarians.

It has been said "there is no sound that ever rent the air so terrible as the deep silence of suspense before the battle-word is given; it is the moment when the soul sinks under the awe of something that thrills deeper than any fear"; and during that dread pause at Newbury many a fervent prayer was doubtless offered up to the God of Battles by the true hearts that abounded in both armies. They were prayerful men in those days, though superstitious and believers in witchcraft, as will be seen by the story of the death of the witch at Newbury, given in the Appendix. No action was commenced without previous prayer for success; no success was achieved without solemn thanksgiving, and each regiment had its own chaplain. The religious *petitions* of the Parliamentarians were frequently drawn out to a great length, while those of the Cavaliers were brief and to the purpose. Such was old Sir Jacob Astley's at the battle of Edgehill, who dismounting from his horse, and taking a pike in his hand, offered up the following prayer at the head of his troops; "O Lord, Thou knowest how busy I must be this day; if I forget Thee, do not Thou forget me.—March on, boys!" Dr. Jeremy Taylor, the learned author of "Holy Living and Dying," is reported to have been present at the first engagement at Newbury, and to have been busy in consoling the wounded after the battle. He attended the King in the capacity of chaplain, and is said to have 'laid the foundation' of several works in defence of Episcopacy during his service with the army.

No sooner had the mists of an autumn morning cleared away, and disclosed the Royalists in battle array on the Wash, than Essex, anticipating their tactics, began to move forward to meet the enemy. The left division of the army under his own personal command, marched from Crockham Heath to Skinner's Green, and took possession of a neglected position of considerable military importance, a rounded hill or spur in front of the lane leading from the Wash to the Enborne road, from whence a battery could "command all the plain before Newbury." *

The King was not unprepared for active operations, and early the same morning, September 20th, the royal standard was moved forward, and floated proudly on the Wash. Charles stationed his left wing and centre upon the brow of the hill sloping towards Newbury, his right wing resting on the

---

* Lord Digby, in a letter written from Newbury the day after the battle, describes this elevation as "a round hill from whence a battery could command all the plain before Newbury"; this is literally the case. In the Tithe Map it is marked "Hilly Ground."

## PREPARATIONS FOR BATTLE.

low ground in front of the town, where it was protected by hedges lined by Dragoons.* The heavy guns were planted on a roughly raised battery, remains of which still exist,† extending from near the "Gun" public-house obliquely across the plateau, whence they could play upon any attacking column advancing up the hill, and open an enfilading fire on any flank movement of Essex, should he show himself on the brow of the opposite eminence. Whitelock corroborates this view. He states that the King had on his right hand the advantage of the river, and on the left a hill about half-a-mile from the town, *where he had planted his ordnance*. Oldmixon adds, " by reason of this disposition the Parliamentarians had no passage to them, but what was exposed to the fire of the enemy's cannon." And that this position is the true one is proved further both by the remains still existing and by the "Mercurius Aulicus," which, in relating the King's preparations the night before the battle, informs us that "The London pamphlets gape wide upon Aulicus for saying the King at Newbury was forced to fight for a place to fight on, still alledging that His Majesty on the Tuesday night *had his cannon planted on the hill*. To which I answer once for all, that their dead bodies left behind on the place the next day manifest the contrary." As in all controversies, there are two sides to the question whether the King occupied the Common with his guns the night before the battle or not; and in the statements of either side there is a basis of truth. For though the Parliamentary writers may assert, and truthfully enough, that the King had to fight from the early morning of the 20th, in order to complete the deployment of his troops for battle, it is not the less likely that the level ground of the plateau was, at least partially, occupied the evening before. The fact that the bulk of the King's army had encamped, late on the afternoon of the 19th, after a wearisome march, on the fields south of Newbury, shows that at any rate, the front of battle taken up the next day from the En to the Kennet was not assumed until the very morning of the great fight. Yet it is probable that the entrenchment for the guns was chosen and

---

* "So called from 'Dragon,' as they fought in air or on the ground, mounted or on foot. Except in cases of surprise, however, they seldom fired on horseback, and never charged; they were, in fact, infantry with horses, to enable them to make more rapid movements: they were thrown forward to feel the way, skirmishing from behind ditches as they advanced, or covering a retreat in the same fashion: one man held ten horses in the rear, while his comrades, their riders, fought. Their long carbines were called 'dragons' from the cock being made in that shape."—Orrery's 'Art of War.'

† See Plan of the Battle.

prepared the evening before the battle, though possibly it was only partially armed.

The scene on Wash Common this September morning has thus been described in the picturesque language of Lord Carnarvon:—"There, on that ground, the features of which to this day reflect the local incidents of the battle, the two armies were drawn up in hostile array. Could we recall that scene, how different, probably, the features in either host! On the Parliamentarian side you would have seen the Roundheads mustering in heavy masses on the brow of that heathy hill, with their steeple-crowned hats and basket-hilted swords, whilst from their dull-featured, but resolute ranks there ascended the hum of some psalm, invoking God, as of old, to strike for His chosen people, and to smite the enemy; or there passed from mouth to mouth the watchword, as at Marston Moor, 'God with us'; or in the skilful disposition of their array you might have distinguished the different colours and insignia of each leader and his followers. Here Lord Saye-and-Sele's men in blue; there Lord Brooke's in purple; here some of Hampden's men in green; and there, perhaps, Colonel Meyrick's regiment in grey; here, Sir Arthur Haslerigg's cuirassiers, who went by the name of 'The Lobsters'; and there, the London bands—who turned the fortune of that day, and who, as an old writer says, showed that they could use a sword in the field as well as a mete-yard in the shop—in their well-known red uniform; whilst in the centre of the host, under the guidance of the saturnine Essex, you might have seen his followers with their orange colours, and have heard the homely cry, with which they went to battle—'Hey for old Robin!' But if you had cast your eye to the other side of the valley, you would have witnessed a different scene. There you would have seen the cavaliers and gentlemen, with their troops of tenants, retainers, and servants, gathering fast around their standards, in all the pride of strength and birth, and high spirit, their red scarfs flaunting in the cool breeze of an autumn morning; their spurs jingling, their plumes waving, their long hair (so much abominated by the Puritan divines) floating on their shoulders; in one word, with all that exquisite grace of dress and manner which even yet breathes from the canvas of the great painter of the day. They, too, had their watchword, as at Marston Moor, 'God and the King': they, too, stood ranged in their different battalia and other different leaders. Here Newcastle's 'Lambs,' as they were called, glistened in their white dresses; there Lord Northampton's men, in green; here, perhaps, rode Lunsford, as he is described in the ballad, in

## PREPARATIONS FOR BATTLE.

his blue rocket, surrounded by his fire-eating horse; while on the edge of the hill, under a black banner, edged with yellow, and bearing the arms of the Palatine, might have been seen Prince Rupert's impetuous cavalry, clothed in their black uniform—black, a fitting colour for that thunder-storm of war which broke with resistless fury on the ranks of the enemy." *

Obviously the relative situations of the two armies were greatly different. The King possessed immense advantages if they had been properly turned to account. His army was strongly posted between the enemy and London, well supplied with a great store of provisions and other necessaries both for horse and man, which, as previously mentioned, the town and people of Newbury, on intelligence that Essex was advancing towards them, had provided for his troops. The King's line of retreat was safe, and he had the town of Newbury to protect him, if he found it necessary to fall back; while the enemy was in want and shelterless, and must either fight or starve. Though sensible of the strength of the position, even the impetuous Rupert advised passive resistance instead of taking the offensive; and the King himself, while conscious of his superiority, resolved to engage only on such terms as should ensure success.

Essex's hopes, on the other hand, when he found himself out-stripped in the race, were chiefly based on the supposition that the King's troops were tired and unable to come to an actual engagement, and strengthened by a confidence that Waller (his old rival), who had been desired by the Parliament to march to the relief of his army, would be with him that night. But at this time, Waller was quietly lying at Windsor, with 2,000 horse and as many foot, quite unconcerned as to what might befall the Earl at Newbury, as the Earl had been on his behalf at Roundway Down; otherwise, had he moved against the King at Newbury when the Earl was on the south side of the Kennet, the Royalists might have been in great danger of an utter defeat.

The anxiety of the Royalists to gain the passages of the Kennet on the road to London is equally evident. Referring again to Lord Byron:—he says, "the day following, both armies march't as if it had been for a wager, which should come to Newbury first, and it was our fortune to prevent them of that quarter, and likewise of Donnington Castle."

---

* 'Hampshire: Its early and later History'; two Lectures delivered at the Basingstoke Mechanics' Institution, by the Earl of Carnarvon, 1857.

On arriving at Newbury,* the King, finding Essex encamped so close at hand, had no alternative but to prevent his further advance, and without loss of time took up a position extending from the town to Wash Common, where a portion of the horse was already posted; his front was strengthened by several hasty entrenchments, portions of which still remain, and every preparation was made for decisive battle.

Wash Common, before its enclosure and the construction of modern roads, comprised a large area of land now under cultivation on both sides of the Andover Road from Newbury, thus giving at the time of the battle a much more extended field of operations than is now presented by the existing *terrain*.

There is no doubt that the rapid movements of the Parliamentary troops led the Royalists to disregard the very common precaution of a study of the ground. They in all probability pushed beyond the town towards Wash Common by the main road leading south out of Newbury; but the value of the rounded spurs near Skinner's Lane, which commanded the whole of the low-lying ground between the Town and the Wash, had escaped their notice either through negligence or fatigue after their hasty march. Byron's account fully bears out this view, he states, "Here another error was committed, and that a most gross and absurd one, in not viewing the ground, though we had day enough to have done it, and not possessing ourselves of those hills above the town by which the enemy was necessarily to march the next day to Reading."

The Royal forces were commanded by King Charles in person; Lord Forth,† subsequently created Earl of Brentford, being the General immediately under the King. The Cavalry was led by Prince Rupert and Sir John Byron, Lord Wilmot acting as Lieutenant-General. The Foot was "ordered" by Sir Nicholas Byron (uncle to Sir John, afterwards Lord Byron). Amongst the more distinguished cavalier officers holding commands at Newbury were the following—*Earls:* Carnarvon, Lindsey, Northampton, Nottingham, Cleveland, Holland, Clare, and Bedford;—*Lords:* Bellasyse, Digby, Jermyn, Percy,

---

* The King during his stay in Newbury quartered at the house of the Mayor, Mr. Gabriel Coxe. Afterwards when Charles II. who had been present with his father in the last engagement, visited the town in 1663, and went over the battle-fields, Mr. Coxe presented a petition to his Majesty for payment of the expenses incurred in entertaining and providing for the Royal suite; but he does not appear to have obtained any redress.

† This and many of the following names are referred to in the Biographical Appendix.

PREPARATIONS FOR BATTLE. 43

Somerset (second son of Henry, first Marquis of Worcester), Andover, Chandos, and Molyneux;—also the Hon. Henry Bertie, Sir Charles Lucas, Sir George Lisle, Sir Edward Waldegrave, Sir Lewis Kirke, Sir Henry Slingsby, Sir William Vavasour, Sir Thomas Aston, Sir Anthony Mansel, Sir Michael Wodehouse, Sir Jacob Astley, Sir John Frechville, Sir John Hurry, and Major-General Daniel (commanding Prince of Wales' regiment);—*Colonels*: Spencer, St. John, Edward Villiers, Will. Legge, Daniel O'Neill, Morgan, Eure, D'Arcy, Poole, Platt, Wheatly, Murray, Charles Gerard, Edward Gerard, Richard or Richaut and Constable;— *Captains*: Bagehot (who took the command of the Earl of Carnarvon's troop when its gallant leader fell), Basil Woodd, Panton, Sheldon, Scott (of Sir Arthur Aston's regiment), Singleton, Clifton, and Newman.

The following are mentioned as serving in the royal ranks as Volunteers:—Henry Spencer (first Earl of Sunderland), James Hay (second Earl of Carlisle), Henry Mordaunt (Earl of Peterborough), Lucius Cary (Viscount Falkland, whose duties as the King's Secretary gave him no position in the field), the Hon. Edward Sackville (son of Edward, fourth Earl of Dorset), severely wounded in the battle,* Sir John Russell (son of Francis, fourth Earl of Bedford), Hon. Henry Howard (son of the Earl of Berkshire and brother to Lord Andover), Colonel Richard Fielding,† Colonel Stroud, George Porter, and Bernard Brocas, with some of his brothers.

On the side of the Parliament, the Earl of Essex was Lord General of the army; and amongst the more conspicuous leaders were Lord Robarts or Roberts, Lord Grey of Groby, Sir John Meyrick, who "ordered" the artillery, Sir Philip Stapleton, Sir James Ramsay, Sir William Constable, Sir William Balfour, Sir William Boteler, Sir Samuel Luke, Sir William Brooke, Sir Richard Bulstrode, Sir William Springer,‡

---

* In April, 1646, being with a party of the King's forces at Chawley, near Abingdon, he was taken prisoner by those of the Parliament, and slain by a Parliamentary soldier.

† Previously Governor of Reading, which he was thought to have surrendered too easily; he was tried by court-martial and sentenced to be shot; but, being afterwards pardoned, he fought valiantly for the King.

‡ Printed "Springer" in the 'Relation of the Battle' printed for the House of Commons shortly after the Fight, but no doubt a mistake for Sir William Springett, who was knighted at Hampton Court 10th February, 1641-2, called "of Langley, Kent." He was son of Herbert Springett, of. Ringmer, Sussex, Esq.; and the Pedigree ('Berry's Sussex,' 33,) says that Sir William died in 1643. If not killed at Newbury, he probably died of wounds received in that action; but it is not improbable that he died a natural death.

Major-General Skippon, Major-General Deane, and Lieut.-General Middleton; and Colonels Sheffield, John Meldrum, Mainwaring, Berkeley or Barclay, Arthur Goodwin, Norton, Dalbier, Holmsted, Tyrill, Thompson, Greaves, Langham, Draper, Brackley, Harvey, Holbourne, Tucker, White, and Fortescue.

CHAPTER V.

## THE BATTLE.

Owing to the close proximity of the two combatants several skirmishes had ensued during the night between advanced parties of each army. In one sharp encounter between a party of Royalist horse under Hurry and a detached body of the enemy, Lord Percy was cut in the hand and Lord Jermyn had a narrow escape, his head-piece being battered about his ears and his eye injured. These attacks on the outposts continued until the long night wore gradually away, and the first faint glimmering of light disclosed to the Royalists that the Parliamentarians were in possession of the little hill above Cope Hall. \* Sir John Byron with a portion of the right wing of horse and foot was at once despatched to assault and engage this threatening point, the circumstances of which he thus narrates:—" The next day my brigade of horse was to have the van, and about 5 in the morning I had orders to march towards a little hill full of enclosures, which the enemy (through the negligence before mentioned) had possessed himself of and had brought up two small field pieces and was bringing up more, whereby they would both have secured their march on Reading (the highway was lying hard by) and withal so annoyed our army which was drawn up in the bottom, where the King himself was, that it would have been impossible for us to have kept the ground. The hill, as I mentioned, was full of enclosures and extremely difficult for horse service, so that my orders were, only with my own and Sir Thos. Aston's regiment to draw behind the commanded foot led by Lord Wentworth and Col. George Lisle, and to be ready to second them, in case the enemy's horse should advance towards them : the rest of my brigade was by Prince

---

\* In an old terrier of the lands held by the town of Newbury, in the time of Queen Elizabeth, "Copped Hall" is mentioned as having been given for a yearly obit by Robert Long.

## THE BATTLE.

Rupert commanded to the Heath, where most of the other horse and foot were drawn."

This advance of the King's right wing, which was nearest the enemy and under his fire, was a movement absolutely necessary to cover the deployment of the remainder of the army to the left over the Wash and towards the En. The transference of Rupert's cavalry to the Wash fully coincided with and supported this movement, for they could get there and block the road before the left wing and centre (of foot) could gain the heights. Meanwhile the cavalry of the right wing, unable to operate directly over the enclosed intricate land below the position occupied by the Parliamentarians, was compelled to support the movement by inclining away to the left flank till the open ground of Wash Common was reached and a charge could be delivered. They could find no charging ground before this, owing to the hedge-rows and escarpments which lay opposite the right flank; and even when the right was so assisted by this advance of "horse" on their left, the first attempt to force the hedgerows proved absolutely fruitless.

Simultaneously with the advance of Essex's left to Cope Hall, a corresponding movement was made by the veteran Skippon, who pushed forward the right on Enborne Heath, to co-operate with his Chief. The efforts of both divisions were principally directed against the King's position on the Wash, where the storm of battle was especially maintained throughout the day; and from straggling shots the battle widened until nearly 20,000 men were engaged in deadly conflict.

Charles, as previously mentioned, had determined to stand on the defensive and await the attack of Essex, but the uncontrollable ardour and impetuosity which urged on some of the young cavalier commanders frustrated his intentions and confused his whole order of battle. Scarcely had part of the Parliamentary right wing shown on Enborne Heath, when a party of the royal cavalry bore down upon them.

"Then 'spur and sword' was the battle word, and we
    made their helmets ring,
Shouting like madmen all the while 'For God and for the
    King!'
And, though they snuffled psalms, to give the rebel dogs
    their due,
Where the roaring shot poured thick and hot they were
    stalwart men and true."
                            *Song—" The Old Cavalier."*

Soon the battle became general, and obliged the Royalists to support these advanced troops, leaving their artillery behind them unavailable on the Common: "many of the officers flinging off their doublets in bravado and leading on their men in their shirts, as if armour was a useless encumbrance in dealing with the base-born London apprentices whom they came rather to triumph over than to fight."

The left wing of the Parliamentary army, led by Essex, and with Lord Roberts' brigade of horse in front, now moves against the Royalist force on the Wash. Stimulated by the example of their chief, and charging gallantly up the slopes below the heath, in face of a biting fire of musquetry and grape, they sweep onward up the heights. They are gaining ground!

But at this crisis Sir John Byron, at whose side a few minutes before had ridden the noble-hearted Falkland, now "stretched coldly in the sleep of death" under a hawthorn hedge, advances at the head of the right wing of the royal cavalry, and, under the fire of two guns at musket distance and a deadly shower of bullets, charges them in front and flank with a determination that even the soldiers of the Parliament with all their spirited enthusiasm are unable to withstand. Staggered by the fierce onslaught, for a moment they recoil, but it is only to rally instantly and renew the fight with "undiminished resolution."

Two regiments of the London trained-bands are now brought forward in support of the Parliamentary cavalry, and cheerfully approach to share the contest; the remainder of that force meanwhile being hotly engaged on Enborne Heath, with their brave old leader Skippon, under the protection of his formidable cavalry commanded by Middleton. Essex steadily leads his young citizen-soldiers fresh and ready for the struggle "up the hill," who, confident in themselves, and satisfied with the strength of their cause nobly acquitted themselves throughout this well-fought action. The royalists have now received a reinforcement, and Prince Rupert with his daring followers ride to the very points of the pikes. The firmness and intrinsic worth of the London brigade was now to be tested, and not in vain; for the foaming squadrons of steel-clad cuirassiers came rushing forward, but these dashing troops failed again and again to penetrate those serried lines, which "stood undaunted and conquerors against all, and like a grove of pines in a day of wind and tempest, they only moved their legs, heads, or arms but kept their footing sure." The action here was long and bloody, and told fearfully on the Parliamentary ranks. Charge succeeds charge! cheer for cheer is given! Fearless amidst the storm of battle boldly urging on his men,

## THE BATTLE.

is seen the gallant King,* and the Royal colours for a time are borne triumphant. But the tide of battle turns, Essex's reserve of foot is near, the cavalry rally on their supports, the defiant banner of the Earl is borne aloft,† and waving his hat, with cries of " Forward! brave hearts!" he quickly re-forms his disordered troops and again confronts the foe. A furious *melée* ensues. The plumed helmet and the steel cap get mixed together, the combatants close and fight hand-to-hand, but at length the Parliamentary cavalry are hurled back, their scattered infantry are no longer able to support themselves, but fighting heroically to the last are driven " to the lane's end where they first came in." The royalists follow, but in their victorious excitement pursue too far, and before those who enter the lane can disengage themselves, they are well nigh cut to pieces by the Puritan troopers, who at length have made a stand. And well they did their duty. The carnage was terrible; and a tradition is preserved in the village of Enborne to this day, that the narrow lane leading to Skinner's Green was so choked with the slain that a passage had to be cleared before the troops and guns could again be moved forward.

For hours the fight was maintained with unflinching and uniform gallantry on both sides. Again and again the Roundhead squadrons charged up the hill—and as regularly were they met sword to sword, repulsed and beaten back. It was a succession of determined attacks and obstinate resistance, both parties fighting with indomitable ardour, but as yet no decisive advantage was gained by either side. The conflict was now at its height, and the artillery fire of the Royalists

---

* It would seem that the King took an active part in this battle. Sergt. Foster in his ' True Relation ' says, "I am creditably informed by those who were this day in the King's army, that the King himself brought up a regiment of foot, and another of horse into the field, and gave fire to two pieces of ordnance, riding up and down all that day in a soldier's grey coat." In the 'Mercurius Aulicus' (the Royalist journal) of September 21, 1643, it is related that "the Rebels espying from the Hill, that many stood bareheaded in a part of the field, supposed the King to be there, and made great shott at the place," and characteristically adds " The Lord covered the head of His Anointed."

† The Cornet or flag of the Earl of Essex was—" orange, on it a label, like the King's, [that is ' With God and my Right'] of silver, with this motto in roman letters, sable, VIRTVTIS COMES INVIDIA; the lining of the motto or back, of gold ; fringed with gold and silver, tasselled gold." (Prestwick's ' Respublica,' p. 24.) It is related that Essex was advised to leave off his *white hat,* because it rendered him so conspicuous an object to the enemy. "No !" replied the Earl, " It is not the hat, but the heart ! the hat is not capable of either fear or honour ! "

was committing fearful havoc in the ranks of the trained-bands, still not an inch of ground was lost. "The enemies cannon," says Sergeant Foster, one of the City brigade, "did play most against the Red Regiment of Trained-Bands, and it was somewhat dreadful when men's bowells and brains flew in our faces. But blessed be God, that gave us courage." It was a trying moment for the London Volunteers, their situation was most critical. Had the gallant City 'prentices given way nothing could have saved them from being destroyed, but they showed the same bold front they had presented at the commencement of the action, "and were, in truth, the preservation of the army of the Parliament that day." An eye witness thus describes the charge of the King's cavalry on the Blue regiment of trained-bands:—"Two regiments of the King's horse with a fierce charge, saluted the Blew regiment of the London Trained-bands, who gallantly discharged upon them, and did beat them backe, but they being no whit daunted at it, wheeled about, and on a suddaine charged them againe. Our musketeers did againe discharge, and that with so much violence and successe, that they sent them now, not wheeling but reeling from them, and yet for all that, they made a third assault, and coming in full squadrons, they did the utmost of their endeavour to breake through our ranks, but a cloud of bullets came at once so thick from our muskets, and made such a havocke amongst them, both of men and horse, that in a feare, full of confused speed, they did flye before us, and did no more adventure upon so warme a service."‡ This momentary success was however dearly purchased; the Royalists were not so easily disconcerted. Rupert, who had seen the effect produced by the encounter of the Parliamentary cavalry, came boldly on with "Byron's Blacks" and Colepepper's brigade to the relief of their comrades. Nothing could surpass the reckless daring of the Royal horse. The Roundhead column could not stand the shock of that wild charge. They now lost ground, but were quickly re-formed into solid squares with their front rank kneeling, and steadily awaited the attack. Not till the Royalist's steel was glittering in their faces, did the rear ranks pour in a well-directed volley on Rupert's brilliant cavalry. The charge was repulsed—the Royalist ranks disorganised—and men and horses were rolling on the heath in death. But this repulse did not daunt the valiant troopers, and they still fought on in some confusion, though without

---

‡ 'Life and Death of the Illustrious Robert, Earl of Essex, 1646;' by Robert Codrington, M.A., p. 33.

any decided advantage. Their leader's efforts were at this time chiefly directed against his adversary's right wing, which was being rapidly pushed forward towards the King's position on the Wash. But it was unavailing; and Essex profiting by the advantage gained on this flank, towards Enborne, obtained a footing on the plateau of the Wash, and was on equal terms with his opponents.

It is hardly necessary to point out that the temporary repulse of Essex's left in Skinner's Lane was somewhat due to the series of brilliant charges which were made over the level ground of the Common, excellent for such a purpose. The Parliamentary centre touched the left wing at the point where the lane debouches on the flat; and naturally when the enemy, driven back into this close ground, had rallied on his supports, the hand-to-hand *melée* must have resulted in disorder to the horse and have choked the narrow road with bodies. In fact the check sustained by the Parliamentary left led to the consequent speedy withdrawal of the centre, hastened too by the influence of Rupert's charges, and the battle on this side probably remained more or less stationary without marked advantage on either side until, the advance of Essex's right wing brought greater numerical superiority on his side upon the level ground of the plateau.

The following letter extracted from the Rupert correspondence * more especially refers to the engagement near Cope Hall, and supports the view here taken. This document having no signature, and being apparently a transcript, it is difficult to identify the author, but it seems to have been written by a leading officer of horse in the King's right wing, explanatory of his own part in the action:—" The King's army being drawne up on a Heath neere Newbury, the enemy were discovered approaching ye town, Prince Rupert was pleased to command mee and Major Smith with a party through the town to face the enemy, afterwards His Highness commanded mee to advance with ye party to ye hill upon our left hand, from thence we sent out parties all night, which gave His Highness satisfactory intelligence, and when it was day, His Highness went with his own troope, a party of mosqueteers and my horse to take possession of a Hill [the hill in front of Skinner's Green Lane above Cope Hall], I drew ye party into a close † that contained a considerable part

---

* Add. MS.S. 18980—2, Brit. Mus.

† A meadow in the position indicated by the writer of the above letter is known as "Jacob's Mead." Some time since, two cannon balls (6lb. and 3lb.) were found in removing a bank in this field, and are both in the author's possession.

of the hill, then we discovered the enemy and there began the service. But before relief could come to the mosqueteers, they retreated, and I drew ye horse into the next close though not without losse both with great and small shot where wee stood, untill in which time my horse received a shott in his neere shoulder. But ye foot crying out for ye horse, I returned into ye first mentioned close and was very slowly followed by reason of the straitness of the passage, but when I thought I had men enough to doe ye service, I went to ye furthest part of ye said close wheere were neere about 1,000 of ye enemies foot drawne up in order and one piece of artillery, and as I was charging my horse was shott againe into ye breast and faltered with mee, for that, I being out of hopes to do other service than to lose myself, I gave orders to ye party in these very words in Major Smith's hearing,—' Fall on, my Masters! for I must goe change my horse.' And in my coming I met with my Lord Byron. My distresse at that time compelled mee to desire him to lend mee a horse. I likewise desired ye same favour of Sir Lewis Kirke, but presently meeting with Sergeant-Major Daniel, major to ye Prince of Wales his regiment, hee lent mee a horse. That horse I changed for one of Capt. Sheldon's of His Highness Prince Maurice his regiment, which I conceived to be much better. When I was thus supplied I was going back to my charge, which I thought Major Smith would have had a care of in my absence, as I conceived in duty he ought, I being for that present disabled, but in my way back contrary to my expectation I found Captain Scot of Sir Arthur Aston's regiment and Capt. Panton of Lord Carnarvon's regiment,* and some other officers of ye party with neere about 40 men, I desired that wee might goe up ye Hill again, Capt. Panton answered mee that my Lord Lieut.-General [Earl of Brentford] commanded them to stay in that same place, whereupon I sent one to him to know his further commands. In the meantime came Sir Lewis Kirke to mee with commands from ye King to goe looke to ye passe by the river side which the enemy were then endeavouring to gaine [the road, now called Guyer's Lane, leading to the Kennet, where the river appears to have been fordable], but when I came to ye place I found Sir William Vavasour there with his brigade, which I conceived sufficiently secured that place. Whereupon I sent Capt. Scot to ye King to desire His Majesty that I might goe to some place where I might doe him better service, which His Majesty did not grant."

---

* This officer became a Major-General in the King's service, and fell mortally wounded at Cropredy Bridge, 29th June, 1644.

This view of the result of the fight about Cope Hall is fully borne out by a study of the various narratives of the battle and by an inspection of the ground. The Parliamentary left gaining the rounded hill by Skinner's Green Lane, before referred to, pushed their infantry forward beyond it, to still further check the attack of the Royalist right moving over the enclosed ground towards the guns. A small round-contoured hill just in front of the latter was gained by the rush above described; and this advance, reaching as it did the hedgerows of Dark Lane,* would have been pushed further but for the action of the cavalry of the right wing, which, diverted from a direct advance by the character of the ground, now came upon the scene. In fact the Royalist right wing seems to have been roughly handled up to this time.

Byron, who gives his own account, without considering what the other fractions were doing, and naturally lays considerable stress on his share or part in the action of the right wing to which he was attached, writes : " The commanded foot not being able to make good the place, my uncle Byron, who commanded the first tertia, instantly came up with part of the regiment of guards and Sir Michael Woodhouse's and my Lord Gerard's regiments of foot, commanded by his Lieut.-Col. Ned Villiers, but the service grew so hot, that in a very short time, of twelve ensigns that marched up with my Lord Gerard's regiment, eleven were brought off the field

---

\* Byron's advance appears to have been over the ground between the boundary-line of the parishes of Newbury and Enborne (defined by a bank and hedge, and at the point shown on Plan passable for cavalry) and the old road called "Dark Lane" which formerly ran from near Enborne Farm obliquely over the fields below the Wash to the Enborne Road, which it entered by Enborne-gate Farm, another road (Guyer's Lane) leading from this point to the Kennet. There was also a lane entering from the Skinner's Green Road below "Cope Hall" and joining the Wash Road. Most of these roads have been stopped, and it is now difficult to trace them. In removing the bank of "Dark Lane" a few years ago, a 15-lb. cannon-ball was found imbedded in the soil. The correctness of the tradition that Falkland fell on the spot until recently indicated by a poplar tree in front of the farm-house known as "Falkland Farm" is extremely doubtful: he certainly fell as the royal cavalry were advancing towards the body of the Parliamentarians, who were endeavouring to gain the Heath, but at this early period of the fight Essex had not secured a footing on the Wash. Clarendon relates that "the enemy had lined the hedges on both sides with musqueteers from whence he [Falkland] was shot with a musquet in the lower part of the belly, and in the instant falling from his horse, his body was not found till next morning." The hedges on both sides of "Dark Lane" would perfectly accord in position with Byron's narrative and with Clarendon's description.

hurt, and Ned Villiers shot through the shoulder. Upon this a confusion was heard among the foot, calling, horse! horse! whereupon I advanced with those two regiments I had, and commanded them to halt while I went to view the ground, and to see what way there was to that place where the enemy's foot was drawn up, which I found to be enclosed with a high quick hedge and no passage into it, but by a narrow gap through which but one horse at a time could go and that not without difficulty. My Lord of Falkland did me the honour to ride in my troop this day, and I would needs go along with him, the enemy had beat our foot out of the close, and was drawne up near the hedge; I went to view, and as I was giving orders for making the gapp wide enough, my horse was shott in the throat with a musket bullet and his bit broken in his mouth so that I was forced to call for another horse, in the meanwhile my Lord Falkland (more gallantly than advisedly) spurred his horse through the gapp, where both he and his horse were immediately killed. The passage being then made somewhat wide, and I not having another horse, drew in my own troop first, giving orders for the rest to follow and charged the enemy, who entertained us with a great salvo of musket shott, and discharged their two drakes upon us laden with case shott, which killed some and hurt many or my men, so that we were forced to wheel off and could not meet them at that charge. I rallied my men together again, but not so soon but that the enemy had got away their field-pieces for fear of the worst, seeing us resolved not to give over, so I charged them a second time, Sir Thomas Aston being then come up with his regiment, we then beat them to the end of the close, where they faced us again, having the advantage of a hedge at their backs, and poured in another volley of shott upon us, when Sir Thomas Aston's horse was killed under him, and withal kept us off so with their pikes we could not break them, but were forced to wheel off again, they in the meantime retreating into another little close and making haste to recover a lane which was very near unto it [Skinner's Green Lane], finding then they could keep the ground, which before they could do, I rallied the horse again, and charged them a third time, and then utterly routed them, and had not left a man of them unkilled, but that the hedges were so high the horse could not pursue them, and besides, a great body of their own foot advanced toward the lane to relieve them. Our foot then drew upon the ground from whence we had beaten the enemy and kept it, and drew the horse back to the former station; for this service I lost near upon a hundred horse and men out of my regiment,

THE BATTLE. 53

whereof out of my own troop twenty-six. The enemy drew up fresh supplies to regain the ground again, but to my uncle's good conduct (who that day did extraordinary service) was entirely beaten off."

This road was a short distance in the rear of that Falkland Farm which is situated on the Wash,\* and a tradition that the body on its recovery the next morning was first carried to the farm-house is no doubt founded upon fact. This farmhouse and Yew-tree Cottage are said to have been the only buildings on the Wash at the time of the battle, and the former is still especially associated with several incidents of the fight in local traditions. The lanes at this period, as we have above noticed, had high banks and hedges on either side, and formed a series of stout defences as well as serious obstacles to the movement of troops, being in many places equal to well constructed entrenchments. In 'Heath's Chronicle,' it is stated that "the left wing of the Parliament and the right wing of the King could not be engaged only in small parties by reason of the hedges." That this was the case is quite clear. The steep embankment forming the western boundary of the parish of Newbury would alone be an insurmountable barrier to the free action of large bodies either of horse or foot. The horse, however, on the King's left found a free passage down Skinner's Green Lane, by which Essex had intended to advance his right, and here it was that the close and sanguinary contest which has been already described took place.

Lord Clarendon gives the following account of the death of Lord Falkland, who, as has been seen, met his death while charging with the right wing of Byron's horse, in his advance upon the hill in front of Skinner's Green Lane, above Cope Hall. "In this battle of Newbury, the Chancellor of the Exchequer lost the joy and comfort of his life; which he lamented so passionately, that he could not for many days compose himself to any thoughts of business. His dear friend the Lord Falkland, hurried by his fate, in the morning of the battle, as he was naturally inquisitive after danger, put him-

---

\* There is however another building bearing the name of "Falkland Farm," situated on the south of the En near Wash Mill; but it is exceedingly unlikely that it has any established associations connected with Lord Falkland. The name may have been given it, and probably was, for purely fanciful reasons. The fighting however, as will be seen by the map, extended to this locality, and several human skeletons were taken out of the bed of the En bourne or stream when the milldam was constructed many years since. A foot-way over the stream near the Farm is known as "Battle-bridge."

self into the head of Sir John Byron's regiment, which he believed, was like to be in the hottest service, and was then appointed to charge a body of foot, and in that charge was shot with a musket bullet, so that he fell dead from his horse. The same day that the news came to Oxford of his death, which was the next day after he was killed, the Chancellor received a letter from him, written at the time when the army rose from Gloucestor: but the messenger had been employed in other service, so that he came not to Oxford till that day; the letter was an answer to one the Chancellor had then sent to him, in which he had told him, how much he suffered in his reputation with all discreet men, by engaging himself unnecessarily in all places of danger: and that it was not the office of a privy counseller and secretary of State to visit the trenches, as he usually did; and conjured him, out of the conscience of his duty to the King, and to free his friends from those continual uneasy apprehensions, not to engage his person to those dangers, which were not incumbent to him. His answer was, that the trenches were now at an end, there could be no more danger there. That his case was different from other men's, that he was so much taken notice of for an impatient desire of peace, that it was necessary he should likewise make it appear, that it was not out of fear of the utmost hazard of war: he said some melancholy things of the time; and concluded, that in few days, they should come to a battle, the issue whereof he hoped would put an end to the misery of the kingdom." *

The Royalist accounts of this part of the action are equally detailed, and the 'Mercurius Aulicus' thus describes it.† "Many of their living have cause to remember how the little enclosed Hill commanding the town of Newbury, and the plaine, where His Majesty in person was drawne up (being the first place attempted by our foot by daybreak), was then prepossessed by a great body of their foot, till in their advance to it, ours beate them off into the hedgerows, under which shelter they much annoyed both our foot and horse, the right valiant L.-Col. Villiers and ten of his ensigns being hurt upon the ground ͵the rebels first stood on, yet though they lost the hill, they kept the hedges all the forenoon, till a fresh supply of neare 200 musqueteers advancing up a lane to surprise our pykes and colours by that gallant resolute charge made by Sir Thos. Aston with his own troope (through a double quickset hedge), those poachers were dislodged, their fresh supply

---

* 'Life of Edward, Earl of Clarendon,' vol. i, pp. 164-5.
† October 14th, 1643.

routed, and fled before him in such haste, that though his horse was shot in the entrance to the lane and drew him by the leg amongst them, they had not the civility to help him up, but let him walk away on foot leaving their pykes and colours to shift for themselves, and never after regained the place. But Prince Rupert himselfe drew down a fresh relief of foot and made good the lane against them, and about three of the clock two small pieces of ours being then drawn up to that hill, *which was the place of most concernment,* and was never quit by us till the King drew off all his foot in a body to Newbury field, nor ever after mann'd by them. This is the naked truth, which for three weeks together they have so loudly rail'd at, but shall never heare more of it, if now they are unsatisfied."

While these conflicts are going forward on the hill, the battle rages with fury on Enborne Heath, where Essex's right wing, heedless of the gallant charges of the royal cavalry, are making a strenuous effort to surmount the broken ground that the approach to the Wash everywhere presented. Excited nearly to frenzy by reports that their comrades are being worsted on the left and may be cut off from their support, they charge with an ardour which passionate zeal for their cause alone could give. The general officers Skippon, Stapleton, and Meyrick expose themselves as fearlessly as the common soldiers, and the very domestics, workmen, and campfollowers rush to the field, and, animating each other to the highest pitch of fanatical excitement, fight as bravely as the bravest officers.

Almost paralyzed by the prowess of the men, of whom till then "they had too cheap an estimation," the Royalists are straining every nerve to keep at bay the foe they cannot overcome. Meteor-like, Rupert flashes from one point of the position to another, and is always to be seen in the thickest of the fight; but nothing can keep back his fierce assailants. On they come through gorse and brushwood, in face of a heavy cannonads from the Royalist guns on the heath,— through a storm of musketry bullets flying amidst the darkened air—and in a few minutes they breast the western slope of the Wash.

"Now comes the brunt, the crisis of the day!"

Old Skippon who had coolly watched the progress of the advance, calls on his men to "charge!" an enthusiastic cheer answers the order! and with an impetuosity not to be resisted, Stapleton's mailed curassiers cleave their way through the royal squadrons, and gallantly clear the ridge, the remainder of the troops pour up the ascent, the head of the royalist column is overwhelmed, and the battle virtually won! The Royalists' left flank being completely turned by this brilliant charge, the successful co-operation of the centre and finally of the left, as the Royalists are pushed back towards the town, completes the victory, and the soldiers of the Parliament are at length left masters of the hard-fought field, which, in the early morning, they had so defiantly promised their general to win.

A final effort was made by "the enemy," says Lord Digby, "on a passe by the river" (apparently Guyer's Lane); but Sir William Vavasour with the King's life-guard defeated it with heavy loss. The struggle was however practically at an end, though the ground was still stubbornly contested. It was no headlong flight down the northern slopes of the Wash to Newbury, but a dogged sullen retreat, in which the pursuer dared not press his unquestioned advantage by endeavouring to force the King beyond the line of the Kennet.

The losses had been heavy and important on both sides. On Enborne Heath, fell the brave young Lord Carnarvon, who, "emulating the noblest actions recorded in the annals of war," was struck down as he was returning from a successful attack. Also the gallant Sunderland, "a lord of great fortune, tender years, and an early judgement," who, putting himself in the King's troop as a volunteer, fell pierced by "a cannon bullet" while he was gathering up his bridle reins for the first charge. But equal courage, so Lord Byron asserts, was not shown by all of those engaged: he says, "What was done upon the Heath (where the main body of our horse and foot fought) I will not relate, because I was not an eye-witness of it, only this is generally confest, that had not our foot play'd the poultroons extremely that day, we in all probability had set a period to the war, our horse having behaved themselves with as much gallantry as could be, however, the advantage was extremely on our side, and had been more apparent had it not been lost by another very great error then committed, which was, that when we had beaten the enemy wholly from the ground we fought upon, so that not one of them appeared, and had possest ourselves of it, and drawne off a piece of their cannon, and might have done so by all the rest, had not our foot play'd the jades, and that intelligence was brought us of the great fright they were in, many of them stealing from their arms in the darkness of the night, we then upon a foolish and knavish suggestion of want of powder quitted all our advantages, and about 12 o'clock at night drew off all our men as if we had been the beaten party,

## THE BATTLE.

leaving to the enemy the field which from 6 o'clock in the morning till that time we had fought for and gained with the expense of so much good blood. My Lord of Carnarvon (than whom no man acted a more honourable part in this war) and many other valiant men being slaine that day."

It is unnecessary to give a detailed recital of all the various turns of fortune experienced by the two armies throughout the latter part of the action; but the following extract from Robert Codrington's narrative, quoted by Mr. Forster in his 'Life of Cromwell,' which appears, though somewhat tinctured by the feelings of a partisan, to be very superior in clearness to other statements, may be introduced at this point. It enables us to define one or two of the localities.

"After six hours long fight, with the assistance of his horse Essex gained those advantages which the enemy possessed in the morning, which were 'the Hill, the Hedges, and the River.' In the meantime, a party of the enemies' horse did wheel about, in a great body, and about three quarters of a mile below the Hill fell upon the rear of our army, where our carriages were placed,* to relieve which his Excellency sent a selected party from the hill to assist their friends who were deeply engaged in the fight; these forces marching down the hill, did meet a regiment of horse of the enemy's, who in their hats did wear branches of furze and broom, which our army did that day wear for distinction sake to be known by one another from their adversaries, and they cried out to our men, "Friends! Friends!" but being discovered to be enemies, our men gave fire upon them, and having some horse to second the execution, they did force them further from them. Our men being now marched to the bottom of the hill † they increased the courage of their friends, and after a sharp conflict, they forced the King's horse to fly with remarkable loss, having left the ground strewed with the carcasses of their horses and riders. In the meantime His Excellency having planted his ordnance on the top of the hill, did thunder against the enemy where he found their number to be thickest, and the King's ordnance being yet on the same hill, did play with a like fury against the forces of His Excel-

---

* Shown on the plan.

† The fields on either side of the Enborne Road. A skeleton of a young man, presumably one who fell in the battle, was found in excavating for the abutments of the Railway Bridge in the Enborne Road, in 1881.

I

lency :—the cannon on each side did dispute with one another, as, if the battle was but new begun."*

Night came on, but still the fight was continued by isolated parties, though it was now more immediately confined to the valley between Newbury and Enborne, which is about half-a-mile in length. "The glimmer of the matches † and the flashing of the fire-arms served to show each other where the other lay;" and the contest raged in a desultory way till midnight or thereabouts, when the King's troops finally retired, and by day-break had quitted the ground of the previous day's actions. The chief part of the horse crossed the river into the fields on the Speen side, and quartered in detachments in the neighbouring villages; while the foot were drawn into the town.

Essex, at the close of this well-fought day, established himself upon the ground abandoned by the Royalists, and his troops bivouacked on the field of battle in a very cheerless state, being absolutely without food. It is said that the night was very damp and chilly, and not a drop of anything to drink was to be had, though the wounded were dreadfully tormented with thirst; and a Parliamentary journal relates that one officer offered ten shillings for a quart of water! The infantry rested on their pikes, and the cavalry stretched themselves beside their horses, anticipating a bloodier and fiercer day on the morrow. Like Prince Rupert, the Parliamentary General was in the saddle all night, and as he rode over the heath while the moon shed an uncertain light on the wide scene of carnage, he "could not," says the 'Parliamentary Scout,' "understand his own happiness in the victory, and could hardly entertain it with a private joy." But the feelings of the man triumphed over those of the general,

---

\* By *The Hill* the plateau of the Wash was meant, by *The Hedges* those more especially crossing the fields between the Wash and the Kennet, and by *The River* the Kennet, now called the Old River, the canal being a modern work. It is evident Essex did not cross the river, for Vicars says, "during the whole day our soldiers could not get a drop of water to drink; and Sergeant Foster in his 'Marching of the Trained Bands,' adds, we were in great distress of water or any accommodation to refresh our poor soldiers, our men walking up and down to seek for it." In one respect at least the country is little changed since then, for the furze still grows plentifully on many parts of the field, and the "bonny, bonny broom" yet blossoms on "Broom Hill."

† The *Matchlock* had a long coil of twisted tow steeped in saltpetre attached to it; this was only lighted in time of action, a cock bringing it down to the touch-hole of the piece when it was to be discharged.

## THE BATTLE.

and the pious veteran is stated to have prayed fervently that peace might once more shine upon the land.

Glancing critically at the conduct of the action, there is little doubt but that it was more or less of a running fight extending over, at the very close of the day, even the southern suburbs of Newbury. This is supported by the authority of Oldmixon and Whitelock, and also in 'The True Relation' of a Parliamentary trooper. Bullets, spurs, portions of swords, &c., of the period, have been found in excavating for buildings in the upper or south-west side of the town, and the traces of the fight are widespread. "It was a kind of hedge fight," says a Cavalier, who was present, "for neither army was drawn out into the field; if it had, it would never have held from six in the morning till ten at night. But they fought for advantages; sometimes one side had the better, sometimes the other. They fought twice through the town, in at one end and out at the other; and in the hedges and lanes with great fury. The King lost the most men, his foot having suffered for want of succour from the horse, which, on two several occasions could not come at them. But the Parliament's foot suffered also, and two regiments were entirely cut in pieces, but the King kept the field. Essex, the Parliament general, had the pillage of the dead, but left us to bury them; for while we stood all day to arms, having given them a fair field to fight us in, their camp rabble stript the dead bodies, and they, not daring to venture a second engagement with us, marched away towards London." *

This statement can scarcely be deemed, however, an impartial one. Whether through an error in judgment or through party bias, it certainly does not express a true view of the actual circumstances, as this and the following extract both show:—

"At Newbury 1st fight, when we beat the enemy upon all disadvantage from the town's end to the top of the hill by the Heath, a wing of Essex, his horse moving gently towards us made us leave our execution of the enemy and retreat into the next field, where were several gaps to get to it, but not direct in any way, yet with the colours in my hand I jumpt over hedge and ditch, or I had died by a multitude of hands: we kept this field till midnight, and until intelligence came that Essex was marching away with a great part of his army, and that he had buried a great many of his great guns, by two o'clock in the afternoon; near unto this field, upon the Heath, lay a whole file of men six deep with their heads all

---

* 'Memoirs of a Cavalier,' pp. 250-1.

struck off by one cannon shot of ours [!]: we pursued Essex in his retreat, took Reading without opposition, made it a garrison, and Sir Jacob Astley governor."* This endeavour to blind themselves to the real facts of the case is not singular in the correspondence of parties at that time.

The casualties of the two armies in this hard contested battle, it would be difficult to estimate with anything like exactness. In Heath's 'Chronicle' it is stated that the loss on both sides together was between 5,000 and 6,000, and that the greatest loss, if there were any difference, was on the side of the Parliament. This engagement is represented by several writers as having been more obstinately contested than that at Edgehill, where 5,000 were slain; the estimate therefore in the 'Chronicle' is probably not exaggerated. M. de Larrey, the French historian, states that "8,000 men were killed on the spot, and nothing but the night could separate these furious Englishmen, who seem'd delighted to shed the blood of each other.,' Clarendon does not give the number of the slain, but mentions—"there were above 20 officers of the field and persons of honour and publick name slain upon the place, and more of the same quality hurt." Oldmixon (a violent opponent of the Stuarts) relates that 2,000 Royalists were slain from the time of Essex's removal from Hungerford to the end of Newbury fight, and that the Parliamentary loss was only 500! A Parliamentary trooper describes the action as having been "long and terrible." He writes:—"Some talke of thousands slaine on the King's side. I viewed the field and cannot guess about 500, but the townsmen informed me that they had carried 60 cart-loads of dead and wounded men into the towne before I came to view the place, and such crying there was for the Surgeons as never was the like heard." Sergeant Foster in his relation of the actions of the Trained-bands in the battle, says:—The next day I viewed the dead bodies, there being about 100 stript naked in that field where our two regiments stood in Battalia. This night the enemy conveyed away about 30 cart loads of maimed and dead men, and I think they might have carried away 20 cart loads more of their dead men the next morning." Both these writers endeavour to put the losses of the Royalists at their worst, and are not equally anxious to proclaim the loss sustained by their own party.

On the Royalists' side the following names of officers killed are recorded:—The Earl of Carnarvon, the Earl of Sunderland, Lord Falkland, the Hon. Henry Bertie, and Sir Anthony

---

* Gwynne's 'Memoirs,' ch. x, pp. 46, 47.

Mansel. *Colonels*—Joseph Constable, Poole, **Murray,** Richard Platt, Pinchbeck, Wheatley, Eure, Slingsby, Thomas Morgan, and Stroud. *Captains*—Robert Molineux (of the Wood, Lancashire), Wm. Symcocks (Captain in Lord Percy's troop), Francis Bartis, Thos. Singleton (of Stanyng, Lancashire), Francis Clifton (of Westby in the same county), Sheldon, of Broadway Court, Worcester, who served in Prince Maurice's regiment of horse, and Bernard Brocas. *Lieutenants*—Henry Butler, George Collingwood, and Wm. Culcheth. Algernon Simes, of the Little Park, Windsor, Esq., according to an inscription on the Beaver monument in Wokingham Church, was killed in this action. He served with Sir Richard Harrison, of Hurst, who jointly with Richard Beaver, Esq., of Binfield, his brother-in-law, raised three troops of horse for the King, and maintained them at their own cost, Sir Richard Harrison supporting two troops and Richard Beaver one. The estates of Algernon Simes and his friend Richard Beaver were sequestrated by the Parliament, and their families ruined in consequence. Algernon Simes married Louisa, daughter of Sir William Kippax, Bart., of Becket, near Faringdon. It is reported in the Parliamentary Journal, entitled 'Certain Information, from severall parts of the Kingdome' from the 25th of September to the 2nd of October, 1643, that a Bishop was amongst the number of those who fell at Newbury. The paragraph runs as follows:—"It hath been related that a Cavalier Bishop was also slaine in the said Battell, whose name is *Lesley*, he had been heretofore a Preacher under S. Pauls, in London, and when he died was Bishop of Kafore [*sic*] in Ireland." In the 'Mercurius Britanicus' for the week ending the 3rd of October, 1643, a "Lt. Colonell Lisly" is announced as being one of those killed on the King's side. Probably the name of this person may have been confounded with John Lesley, successively Bishop of the Orkneys and of Raphoe, the "Kafore" of the 'Certain Information,' but this Prelate died in 1671. There is no Bishop named in Cotton's 'Irish Fasti' who can be identified as the "Cavalier Bishop" of the Parliamentary pamphlet. Among the wounded were the Earl of Carlisle, the Earl of Peterborough, Lord Andover, Lord Chandos, the Hon. Edward Sackville, Sir Charles Lucas, Sir John Russell, Sir Edward Waldegrave. *Colonels*—George Lisle, Fielding, Thos. Dalton,*

---

* Col. Dalton, of Thurnham, Lancashire. An enthusiastic and gallant royalist, who raised a troop of horse for the King's service. He was severely wounded in this battle, and, dying at Andover the 2nd November following, was buried in the Church of St. Mary in that town, as the parish register records.

Gerard, Ivers, D'Arcy, Villiers, Howard, Spencer. *Captains*—Panton (fell 29th June, 1644, at Banbury), Thurston Andrews (died of his wounds at Oxford), Mr. Progers (groom of the bed-chamber to the Prince of Wales), and George Porter, a gentleman volunteer.* The Royalist prisoners taken at Newbury and Cirencester, according to the 'Mercurius Britanicus,' numbered 500, including a colonel, a major of horse, and some other officers, who were confined in Windsor Castle. Among these was Lieut. Daniel Kingsmill, of Sydmonton.†

On the Parliamentary side, the name of no officer of note is given as having fallen in this battle. *Colonels*—Davies, Bamfield, Tucker, Mainwaring (of the London Brigade), Greaves, and White. *Captains*—Hunt, Ware, ‡ Talbot, St. Barbe, and Massey are mentioned as being amongst the slain; and Captains Bolton, Mosse, Stoning, Juxon, and Willet died of their wounds a short time after the battle. The name of "Mr. John Salloway, one of the gentlemen of my Lord General's Lifeguard, who died of a wound he received at the Battle of Newbury," occurs in an Order of the House of Lords, under date of January 29th, 1643-4. This John "Salloway" was John Salwey, fifth son of Humphrey Salwey, of Stanford, co. Hereford, by Anne, second daughter of Sir Edward Littleton, Kt., of Pillaton Hall, co. Stafford. His father, Humphrey Salwey, was a member of the Long Parliament.

The following entries in the register of All Hallows the Less, Thames Street, London, record the burial of two of the Trained-bands who died of wounds received at Newbury :—

> 1643 Sep. 28, Robert Maddock, Clothworker, one of whose leggs was shot off at the battaile near Newbury.
> ,, Oct. 11, Henry Delves, Citizen and Dyer of London, who was wounded with a great shot in both his leggs at the same battaile.

Colonel Dalbier, Commissary-General Copley, § Captains

---

\* See 'Illustrations to Grammont's Memoirs,' p. 381.

† See MS. Letter, No. 127, Addl. MSS., Mus. Brit., No. 18980.

‡ On the 20th November, 1651, it was ordered that the petition of Lady Anne Crosby, widow of Capt. Peter Ware, "killed at the service at Newbury, be referred to the Committee of the Army, to be taken into consideration."—'Journals of the House of Commons.'

§ The 'Mercurius Britannicus' (30 Nov. to 7 Dec., 1643) says :— "Commissary Copley, who lost as much bloud as would write a chronicle of that battle, is now well and abroad, and refreshed, to recruit his veines again with his enemies' bloud."

## THE BATTLE.

Hammond, Fleetwood, and Pym, and Cornet D'Oyley, are reported as having been wounded.

The loss in officers and men was very heavy; and the 'Weekly Account' of September 28th, 1643, bears vivid testimony to this fact. In it the writer says, "It was a lamentable spectacle the next morning to behold what heaps of bodies and diversities of slaughter in one field this tragedy had compiled, and that the consanguineous foes, whom the sun could never hope to see reconciled, should on his return, with cold arms be observed to embrace one another, and to mingle themselves in each other's blood, by the incestuous cruelty and union of death."

Again, Sir Henry Anderson in a letter to Hollis, dated September 25th, 1643, says :—" The sight of so many brought to Oxford, some dead, some wounded, since the battle, would make any true English heart bleed."

Of all those who fell on this memorable day no one was so missed as Falkland, none so frequently referred to at these and later times. Ward,* writing in 1757, a hundred years after the great fight, fully endorses the opinion as to the single heartedness of one of the earliest victims to the Civil War. He says:—

> "Maintaining still his secretary's post,
> Till he at once his life and office lost,
> Resigning both at Newb'ry, in the field
> Of battle, by a fatal bullet kill'd,
> As boldly charging with undaunted force,
> In the front rank of noble Byron's horse.
> Falling among the valiant and the just,
> Who dy'd that day an honour to their Trust."

Both parties seem to have displayed great solicitude for the decent interment of the dead left upon the field. Previous to his advance from Newbury, Essex issued the following order to the Rector (the Rev. Mr. Elke) and Churchwardens of the parish of Enborne :—" These are to will and require, and straightly command you forthwith in sight hereof, to bury all the dead bodies lying in and about Enborne and Newbury Wash, as you or any of you will answer the contrary at his peril. Dated one and twentieth September, 1643. ESSEX."

The King also issued the following warrant to the Mayor of Newbury (Mr. Gabriel Coxe) :—" Our will and command is that you forthwith send into the town and villages adjacent and bring thence all the sick and hurt soldiers of the Earl of Essex's army; and, altho' they be rebels and deserve the

---

* 'England's Reformation,' vol. ii, p. 327.

punishment of traytors, yet out of our tender consideration upon them, being our subjects, our will and pleasure is that you carefully provide for their recovery as well as for those of our own army; and then send them on to Oxford. The one and twentieth day of September, 1643. RUPERT."

The dead bodies were principally buried in several tumuli on the Wash, some of which have become nearly obliterated. The largest mound, known in Borough perambulations as "Bumper's Hill," is situate midway between the parishes of Newbury and Enborne, the boundary line passing over its apex. In a plantation near the large barrow is a circular embankment with an outer ditch, at first sight presenting the appearance of an ancient earthwork; but it was no doubt prepared as an additional burial place for the slain, some of whom were probably buried round its margin. In the year 1855 when Wash Common was enclosed, the levelling of these receptacles of the dead was commenced for the purpose of making a road; but the desecration was stayed by the then owner of the land. The workmen, however, found indications of the bodies having been thrown in a heap and the earth cast over them, the floor of the mound being the natural surface. Human bones, soldiers' buttons, buckles, and portions of accoutrements, bullets, and cannon balls were mixed with the soil which was removed. In addition to the bodies buried on the Wash, it is said, a number were thrown down a deep well, and others cast into ditches and pits. It is evident from the Churchwardens' accounts for the parish of Newbury that many of those who were killed or mortally wounded were buried in the churchyard of St. Nicholas, as will appear from the following extracts:—

|  | £ | s. | d. |
|---|---|---|---|
| Paid for burying dead Soldiers in the Churchyard and Wash | 3 | 0 | 1 |
| Paid for Shrouds | 0 | 6 | 4 |
| Burying Soldiers in the Church | 3 | 4 | 4 |

Many cannon balls, chain and case shot, swords, pike-heads, stirrup-irons, bridle-bits, an amulet of large beads, and other relics have been found on Enborne Heath and in the fields near the Wash. Several other articles from the battle-field, including a musqueteer's cap or helmet, two leathern costrels or wine bottles (one silver-mounted), swords, buckles, spurs, &c., are to be seen in the Museum at Newbury. The 'Parliamentary Scout' also notices that "there were divers fine and rich crucifixes found about the dead, whom we pillaged, so that his Holiness has lost some blood as well as the Parliament," and adds "That of those slaine in the fight of his

Majesty's party there were more brave personal men than could be picked out of all my Lord's army, that is for stature."*
A very remarkable seal has been recently found on Wash Common, near the spot where the Falkland Memorial stands. The seal is of brass, circular, and measures one inch and eight-tenths in diameter. It bears the device of a skeleton, with a surgeon's knife in the dexter hand, and an hour-glass on the sinister side. The legend with which it is inscribed is as follows :—THE SOSCIETY AND LOYALTY OF CHYRVRGEONS HALL LONDON. The 'Mercurius Aulicus' under date of Thursday, September 21st, the day succeeding the engagement, mentions that the Parliamentarians left behind them on the battle-field "very many Chirurgions Chests full of Medicaments." The seal above described was probably that used by a Guild or fraternity of Surgeons attached to the City forces.

Several human skeletons have been discovered from time to time in the fields below the Wash. Cannon and musquet balls have also been met with in Newbury; and probably the upper part of the town suffered considerably from stray shot.†  The tower of the Church is also said to have sustained damage from the artillery.

CHAPTER VI.

ESSEX MARCHES TO LONDON, AND TRIUMPHANTLY ENTERS THE CITY.
PARTY EXCUSES. ANECDOTES OF THE BATTLE.
THE RESULTS AND CONDUCT OF THE ACTION.

The morning after the battle, Essex drew up the remnant of his shattered forces on the Wash, and announced his willingness to renew the fight, "if the enemy had any stomach for the field," by the firing of artillery. The challenge not being accepted, Essex, finding his way to London by Green-

---

* September 22nd to 29th, 1643.

† With the many petitions presented to the Parliament for redress, after the war, and preserved at the Public Record Office, is one from a farmer of the name of Daniel, who states he has a lease of a farm at Enborne at £60 per annum, and that in the first fight at Newbury the mounds and fences were utterly destroyed, the ground laid waste, and the farmer's house and out-buildings battered with shot—the damage being estimated at £100, or nearly £300 according to the present value of money.

ham open before him, proceeded on his march towards Reading without opposition.

From this it is evident how complete his victory was. Had there been any power of renewing the engagement, doubtless the Royalists would gladly have availed themselves of another attack on Essex's diminished battalions. But beaten back after an action which had lasted from dawn to dusk, their demoralization and fatigue must have been extreme. So the Parliamentary call to battle passed unheeded. The spirit of the King's army crushed by recent defeat had "little stomach" to try again the fortunes of another day. The army of Essex prepared to fight again, if necessary, to obtain the right of passage past the town of Newbury, but no longer had any such need. Re-forming his column of march from battle array, the Earl resumed his movement eastward with no further fear of immediate interruption.

The route taken by the Parliamentary troops was by Monkey Lane,\* Greenham Common, Brimpton, and Aldermaston. No sooner had Essex and his men entered the narrow lane between the latter village and Padworth,† than Prince Rupert, who, with a column of cavalry and 800 musqueteers had unperceived taken up a position in his line of march, fell suddenly on the rear-guard under Sir Philip Stapleton, throwing it into considerable disorder. The horse galloped through the foot, crying, panic struck, "Away! away! every man for his life! you are all dead men." But the foot soon rallied, and, spreading themselves along the hedges on either side, poured in such telling volleys on Rupert's wearied cavalry, that after a desperate struggle, in which great courage was shown by both parties, the Royalists, having no force to support them, were compelled to abandon the attack, and fall back, losing (it is said) in this short and murderous affair something like 300 men.‡ After this, the final rencontre,

---

\* *Monkey Lane.* An ingenious origin has been assigned to this name —that it was a favourite walk of the Monks at the neighbouring priory at Sandleford, and hence was called "Monks' Lane," which has been corrupted into the present unmeaning appellation. A Monks' or Abbot's Walk or Lane is frequently found in the vicinity of monastic establishments.

† See notes on this encounter in the Appendix.

‡ The 'Mercurius Aulicus' states that the party sent in pursuit of Essex was under the Earl of Northampton and Lord Wilmot, the Prince being the prime leader, and computes his loss at 100. Oldmixon, following an earlier writer, gives Hurry the credit of leading the horse under Rupert, and estimates the King's loss at 80 men, and that of the Parliament at 8. The foot were under Sir George Lisle.

Essex crossed the Kennet at Padworth,* and pushed on to Theale, where he arrived about ten o'clock and quartered for the night.

After a solemn thanksgiving had been performed in the presence of the Royal army for the safety of the King's person, " which had been so fearlessly exposed both on the long march from Gloucester, and on the day of battle," the King's immediate care was bestowed on the wounded, who were lying in frightful numbers all around; every neighbouring cottage, and the old farm house at Enborne,† being crowded with those who had been able to crawl to a place of shelter. Nor was his care limited to mere enquiry, for the 'Parliamentary Scout' ‡ of the time states, that "It is reported that His Majesty desired to see the wounded, which, some say, having viewed, he went sadly away." The more severely injured were left upon the battle-field the whole night. The bodies of the King's chief officers, many of whom there was reason to suppose had fallen, were first sought for, and, when discovered, it was seen that they had been spoiled and stripped by Essex's camp followers. Charles, whose silence evinced his deep sorrow, ordered an escort of their own regiments to attend the remains of their gallant leaders to the town, where they were respectfully deposited in the Town Hall (at that time standing in the centre of the Market-place §), and covered with the ensigns of their loyalty, till the necessary preparations could be made for honourable interment.‖

On Friday morning, September 22nd, Essex marched from Theale to Reading, where he was met by a committee of the Lords and Commons, who complimented him on his signal service to their cause, and desired to learn the wants of his army. Here he remained two days, and then moved on by way of Maidenhead to Windsor. The Royalist prisoners

---

\* *Padworth.* Near this place an iron casket, of the time of Charles I., with an iron chain attached to it, was found some few years since. It is supposed to have been used as a military money chest. The relic is in the possession of W. G. Mount, Esq., President of the Newbury District Field Club.

† Near Enborne Lodge, and in the occupation of Mr. Wm. Heath. It is still known as "The Hospital," and is an old-fashioned gabled building, apparently little changed since the time of the battle.

‡ September 22 to 29, 1643.

§ This building was erected in 1611, enlarged in 1684, the south front "beautified" the latter end of the reign of George II., and the entire structure taken down in 1828.

‖ See Appendix.

taken in the battle were left in the Castle, and so cruelly treated, it was said, by the Governor, that three men dropped down dead in the streets on their release.

Essex made a triumphal entry into London on Thursday, the 28th. The Lord Mayor (Pennington) and the Aldermen, in scarlet robes, received him and his troops at Temple Bar, and they entered the city amidst the enthusiastic acclamations of the people. The next day Essex was waited upon by the Speaker and the members of both Houses of Parliament, who congratulated him on his safety and success, and tendered the thanks of the kingdom for his incomparable conduct and courage; which acknowledgment they had ordered to be inscribed in their Journals as a monument of his valour and record of their gratitude.

The Earl used the occasion for presenting several colours captured from the enemy. On one of these, taken at Cirencester, was a representation of the Parliament-house with two traitors' heads upon it, with the motto " *Sicut extra sic intus* " (as without, so within), which being supposed to belong to Colonel Spencer's regiment, that officer and his family were ordered to be exiled from the kingdom; but it appears after all not to have been the Colonel's ensign. A second colour bore the Harp and Crown Royal, with the motto, " *Lyrica Monarchica.*" Another had the figure of a melancholy virgin in whose face were depicted all the characters of distress and sorrow, with the figure of a cross, pulled down by violent hands, lying despised at her feet, with the inscription " *Meliora spero.*" A fourth represented an angel bearing a flaming sword and treading on a dragon, with the motto " *Quis ut Deus.*" A fifth bore the French motto " *Courage pour la Cause.*" Lastly, in the Hall of the Chapel Royal, Whitehall, is a silk flag bearing the motto " *Constanter et fideliter,*" to which the following account is appended : " This flag was taken by Bernard Brocas, of Beaurepaire, from Cromwell's army,* at the battle of Newbury, August 20th

---

* The Parliamentary army is here spoken of as "Cromwell's Army," but at this time the future Protector held only a subordinate command, and was not engaged in this battle. The estate of the Brocas family at Beaurepaire, near Sherborne St. John, has now passed into other hands, and the house has been modernized. The Vyne is an interesting old mansion, and was originally built by the first Lord Sandys in the early part of the 16th century, but was greatly altered by Inigo Jones and his son-in-law Webb. In the private chapel, which Horace Walpole described "as the most heavenly chapel in the world," is an altar tomb, with an effigy of Chaloner Chute, Speaker of the House of Commons in Richard Cromwell's Parliament.

## ESSEX TRIUMPHANTLY ENTERS THE CITY.

[September 20th], 1643. He was taunted by the Royalist party with indifference to their cause, on account of his love for a daughter of Lord Sandys, who held the adjoining property [The Vyne], and was in Cromwell's army, and stung by the imputation of cowardice, swore in the next engagement to take a standard or die in the attempt. This flag was found in his hand after the battle, and the standard-bearer dead by his side."

The flags taken by the Parliamentary troops at Newbury were exhibited to public view, the people thronging round these trophies, while the trained-bands and auxiliaries, who had shared in the expedition, related all the details. Everywhere, in domestic conversations, in sermons, and in groups formed in the streets, the name of Essex was loudly shouted or silently blessed. It was ordered by the House of Commons that a public thanksgiving " be given in all churches for the great success it pleased God to give the army under the command of the Earl of Essex," and it was also agreed that an order for a collection should be made " on the next publick Fast-day," for the relief of the soldiers wounded in the Parliament's service. The Royalist journal 'Mercurius Aulicus' of October 1st, relates that on this occasion, Master Evans, of St. Clement Danes, preaching before his Excellence, said, " O, beloved, can you forget the Souldiers? I say the Souldiers who have spent their bloud for Christ, as Christ did for them, even their owne precious bloud in Gods cause at Newbury."

Lord Grey of Groby, Sir Philip Stapleton, Sir John Meyrick, Sir Samuel Luke, and Captain Charles Pym, members of the House of Commons, were rewarded with the thanks of Parliament for their distinguished services at Newbury.

In referring to this engagement, Fuller, the eminent historian and divine, author of 'The Worthies of England,' who strenuously adhered to the Royal cause, quaintly remarks:—
" Both armies may be said to *beat* and be *beaten*, neither winning the *Day*, but both the *Twi-light*. Hence it is said that both sides were so sadly filled with their *supper* over night, neither next morning had any stomach to *breakfast*, but keeping their stations, were rather contented to *face* than willing to *fight* one another. * * * * Many here lost their lives, as if Newbury were so named by a sad Prolepsis, fore-signifying that that Town should afford a *new burying* place to many slain in two bloody battles." *

---

* 'Worthies,' Lond., 1662, pp. 111—112.

## THE FIRST BATTLE OF NEWBURY.

That the battle was looked upon as grave and serious by both sides is very evident. The loyal historian, Sir Richard Baker, considers, for example, that "this was a harder bout then that of Edgehill; so that neither party having any stomach to renew the fight, they marched away one from the other, both the King and Essex having first sent their warrants to Newbury and Enborne for the Burial of the Dead Bodies. Essex his aym was to relieve Gloucester, which he accordingly effected, though not without some damage: for Colonel Hurrey with a good party of horse fell upon the rear of his army, commanded by Sir Philip Stapleton, whom in a narrow lane they charged so furiously, that they forced them to a run directly forward through their own foot, till at length getting into the field they faced about, and forced the King's party back again: many colours of the King's cornets were carried up to London, and much reputation was gained by this expedition to General Essex and the London Trained Bands; not that there had been wanting the height of gallantry and resolution (however Fortune fail'd) on the King's side."\*

Naturally, excuses were made by the Royalists for their defeat. Lord George Digby asserted that they were short of powder, being disappointed of a supply of 100 barrels from Oxford. They spent, as it was, four-score barrels during the action, or "a score more than had turned the fight at Edgehill." To this "foolish and knavish suggestion of want of powder" Lord Byron attributes the withdrawal of the Royalist army from the advantages "they had gained with the expense of so much good blood." Certain it is, that though the conflict was most obstinate, the King's infantry do not appear to have acted well in this battle; and the cavalry, which was by far the most effective branch of the service, bore the brunt of the actual fighting. Nor were the Parliamentarians without their complaints and excuses. Sergeant Foster, of the Trained-bands, a staunch Roundhead, in narrating the opening phases of the fight, says:—"They began their battery against us with their great guns halfe an houre before we could get any of our guns up to them, as our gunners dealt very ill with us, delaying to come up to us. Our noble Col. Tucker fired one piece of ordnance against the enemy, and aiming to fire the second time was shot in the head with a cannon bullet."

---

\* 'Chronicle of the Kings of England,' by Sir Richard Baker, knight, 4th edition, London, 1664, p. 570.

Many interesting anecdotes have been left of this battle, and though, like all such traditions, they may possibly not be strictly true, they were probably based on facts, and to that extent are therefore worth preserving.

For example, it is said, on the authority of the descendant of a man who resided at Enborne on a small farm which had been in the possession of his family for many generations,* that a party of Parliamentarians were regaling themselves in "Lushy Gully," on the south side of Enborne Lodge, thinking that they were out of danger, when, to their great consternation, a cannon ball passed through the party, without doing any more injury than carrying away a roasted pig which they were eating.

Old books relating to the War have many anecdotes; Whitelock in his 'Memorials,' instances two which are noteworthy. He says, "A passage or two I shall here remember of extraordinary mettle and boldness of spirit. One is of Sir Philip Stapleton (though he would not acknowledge it), that he being with other Parliament Commanders in the head of a body of horse facing another body of the King's horse, before whom stood their commanders, and the chief of them was Prince Rupert. The Parliament Officer desiring to cope singly with the Prince, he rode from before his company up to the body of horse, before whom the Prince with divers other Commanders were, and had his pistol in his hand ready cockt and fitted. Coming up to them alone, he looked one and another of them in the face, and when he came to Prince Rupert, whom he knew, he fired his pistol in the Prince's face, but his armour defended him from any hurt, and having done this, he turned his horse about, and came gently off again without any hurt, though many pistols were fired at him.

"Another passage was of Sir Philip Stapleton's groom, a Yorkshire man, and stout, if not too rash. By this story, he was attending on his master in a charge, where the groom's mare was killed under him, but he came off on foot back again to his own company. To some of whom he complained

---

* The late Mr. John Matthews, of Enborne, one of whose ancestors, it is said, was an officer of the Trained-bands and fought in this battle. A sword, rapier, and pair of pistol-holsters, elaborately worked, reported to have formed part of his equipment on that memorable occasion, were in the possession of his descendant above-named till his death, which occurred a few years since, when these interesting relics passed into the hands of A. B. Heath, Esq., of Burley Lodge, East Woodhay, now of Faccombe Manor, in whose possession they still remain in excellent preservation.

that he had forgotten to take off his saddle and bridle from his mare, and to bring them away with him; and said that they were a new saddle and bridle, and that the cavaliers should not get so much by him, but he would go again and fetch them: his master and friends persuaded him not to adventure in so rash an act, the mare lying dead close to the enemy who would mall him, if he came so near them, and his master promised to give him another new saddle and bridle. But all this would not persuade the groom to leave his saddle and bridle to the cavaliers, but he went again to fetch them, and stayed to pull off the saddle and bridle, whilst hundreds of bullets flew about his ears, and brought them back with him, and had no hurt at all." *

This battle was important in two ways. Politically it disheartened the Royalist party. From a military point of view it gave courage to the Parliamentarians, for it showed that the apprentices of London and the Roundhead horsemen were as dauntless as any of those who wore the Royalist badge, and could even meet the charge of Prince Rupert's cavaliers with coolness and steadfast valour. Essex did not aim at gaining the town of Newbury. His object was to push past the place and pursue his journey unmolested to London. This he accomplished, although he left the town in the King's hands. The Parliamentary organ 'Mercurius Britannicus' † boldly ventured to advance that "the towne of Newbery is a just witness who won the field"; but this is fully counteracted by the opinion held by the Royalist journal 'Mercurius Aulicus' ‡ the following week, that "It is your Moderator's § own towne, and is a very indifferent judge."

---

* Whitelock's 'Memorials,' p. 71.

† Friday, September 29th, 1643. The 'Mercurius Britannicus' was conducted by Marchmont Needham, who, educated at the Poor School at Burford, was one of the Choristers at All Souls College, Oxford, and B.A., 1637. During the Civil War he distinguished himself by his political pamphlets, first against the King, and afterwards against the Parliament, so that at the Restoration it was with difficulty that he obtained his pardon.

‡ The 'Mercurius Aulicus' was written by John Birkenhead, born of poor parents in Cheshire, a Fellow of All Souls College, Oxford. He suffered much in His Majesty's cause, being frequently in prison, and deprived of all preferments. Soon after the Restoration he was made LL.D. Elected a Burgess for Wilton, knighted by His Majesty, and made Master of the Faculties, one of the Masters of Requests, Fellow of the Royal Society, he died in 1679 without having, as it seems, made such returns as he might to those who befriended him in his necessities. See Walker's 'Sufferings of the Clergy,' pt. ii, p. 98.

§ Dr Twisse, Prolocutor of the Assembly of Divines.

RESULTS AND CONDUCT OF THE ACTION. 73

Lord Clarendon, the Royalist historian, in commenting on this action, observes :—" Though the King's army had all the trophies of victory, in, and after this battle, as is before related (it kept the Field, and had the spoil of it ; It took some pieces of the enemies' cannon, who march'd off in the night, and were pursued with some considerable loss beyond Reading, where a garrison was again placed for his majesty, under the command of Sir Jacob Ashley, Major-General of the army, an excellent officer ; so that the Parliament was in so much a worse state than they were in the Spring, as the loss of Bristol, and most of the West amounted to ; for by this time Exeter was likewise reduced by Prince Maurice), yet notwithstanding all this, the Earl of Essex, as is said before, was receiv'd at London with all imaginable Gratulation and Triumph ; he had done all that was expected from him, with many circumstances of great, soldierly, and notable courage, and the heart and spirit of the Parliament was visibly much exalted, and their impatience for Peace quite abated.

" On the contrary, upon the King's return to Oxford, there appear'd nothing but dejection of mind, discontent, and secret mutiny in the army, anger and jealousy among the officers, every one accusing another of want of courage and conduct in the actions of the Field ; and they who were not of the army, blaming them all for their several failings and gross oversights. The siege of Gloucester was not believ'd to have been well conducted, and that it might have been taken in half the time they were before it, if it had been skilfully gone about. The not engaging the Earl of Essex in all the march over so open a country, was thought unexcusable, and was imputed to the want of courage in Wilmot ; whom Prince Rupert did in no degree favour: nor was the Prince himself without some reproaches, for suffering the Earl of Essex, after all the horse was joyn'd, to march down a long steep hill into the Vale of Gloucester, without any disturbance ; and that the whole army, when it was found necessary to quit the siege, had not been brought to fight in that Vale, and at some distance from the town, when the King's men were fresh, and the other side tired with so long a march.

" But then all men renewed their execrations against those who advised sitting down before Gloucester ; the Officers, who had been present, and consenting to all the counsels, disclaiming as much as any, the whole design ; and all conspired to lay the whole reproach upon the Master of the Rolls [Lord Colepeper], who spoke most in those debates, and was not at all gracious to the soldiers ; and this clamour against

K

that engagement was so popular and universal, that no man took upon himself to speak in defence of it; though, besides the reasons which have been formerly alleged for it, what happen'd in this last action, in the relief of Gloucester, might well seem to justify it; for since it appear'd, that the City was so much united to the Parliament, that it supply'd their army with such a body of their Train'd-bands (without which it could never have march'd) with what success could His Majesty have approach'd London, after the taking of Bristol with his harassed army? and would not the whole body of the Train'd-bands have defended that, when so considerable a part of them could be perswaded to undertake a march of two hundred miles? for less they did not march, from the time they went out, to that in which they return'd. But no reason could ever convert those who looked upon that undertaking at Gloucester, as the ruin of the King's affairs." *

There is little to criticise in the conduct of the action on the Parliamentary side; certain it is that, despite the unquestionable valour of their opponents, they were able to carry out their object, that of marching on London. This point must be clearly kept in view. The destruction of the King's army, and the pursuit that should always follow a victory in order to reap the full results of the success, were not necessary here. Essex wanted the right of way and he obtained it. Though the King's army still held Newbury, it had been definitely forced back into the town. The pursuit effected by Rupert was practically barren of results, and cannot be taken as a proof that the King could claim to have won the hard-fought field. If a few enthusiastic troopers could, as they did, follow the plume of the dashing cavalier, the rest of the army could not; and the barren occupation of the battle-field, which can be the only grounds on which the Royalists could base their claim, was solely possible because Essex did not want it. The advance of the weak force by Guyer's Lane on the passage of the Kennet may be looked at as a mere petty reconnaissance on that side, and could exercise no influence on the fortune of the day. To get hold of the river line and Newbury was not Essex's object, and no importance should be attached to this affair. The value of the reserves and their usefulness in checking the counter attack of the Royalist cavalry on the then exposed left flank of the left wing, resting as it was almost "en l'air," in the field, so to speak, is clearly noticeable, and on this side the fight was ably and well conducted;

---

* Clarendon's 'History' II. pp. 360-361.

RESULTS AND CONDUCT OF THE ACTION. 75

but it is difficult to see why the attack of the right wing was not more vigorously pressed.

A more determined advance by Trundle Hill † would have taken in flank and soon in reverse the line of Royalist guns, already fully engaged with the musketeers and artillery of the left wing from Skinner's Green. Moreover an advance in echelon from the right, that is gradually advancing that wing further than the other, without destroying connection and communication between them, would not merely have brought his force across the flank of the Royalist army, but have prevented altogether an advance of the King's right on the Kintbury road, which was always possible and might have been dangerous. The probable explanation is that the open nature of the ground rendered the advance on this flank difficult against troops that could display such bravery and tenacity as the cavaliers of the King.

Turning to the Royal forces there is less to comment upon, the more so as the details of their dispositions are somewhat wanting. Their left wing seems to have been well posted, and to have effectually checked the advance of Essex's right; but it is a question whether the massing of all their artillery from the commencement so far back on the Wash was advisable. Evidently their chief wish was to block the way simply; and the King appeared desirous of offering a passive resistance, so that the artillery position as selected, resting as it did with both flanks on the slope, north and south of the narrow neck of the Wash, across which the entrenchment stretched and the main road ran, seems well chosen at first glance to fulfil the object, especially bearing in mind the short range of the field artillery of the period. But the left was liable to be taken in enfilade from Trundle Hill, and the right could be threatened from the cover of the hedge-rows of Dark Lane which approached to within musket shot of the King's guns.

Further, the Royalist account states that they were much annoyed by the fire of the Parliamentary guns on the Round Hill, and it was owing to their position that the counter attack along the valley towards Newbury was mainly checked. It has been already pointed out that this side was for Essex that which was most vital to him.

---

† Trundle Hill. *Trundle* was a kind of shot used at this period. Within the area of the battle-field the names of " Coward's Mead," "King's Mead," " War-end," "Steel Hill," " Ball Hill," and many other names occur which probably originated from some incident connected with the fight.

It would have been wiser therefore for the Royalists to have prevented the occupation of the round spur above Cope Hall; and this need not have been done, as suggested by them, by the actual occupation of the ridge, but by holding with their foot the hedge-rows of Dark Lane, and placing their right wing artillery, or a portion of them, on the spur to the right rear of the lane, whence they could both cover the low valley towards the Kennet, and at the same time bring so powerful a fire on the "round hill" as to preclude the possibillity of the guns of the attack coming into action. In fact, two batteries, one on the spur east of Dark Lane, the other at about the same position as the entrenchment actually occupied, with the left flank well "refused" or thrown back so as to meet the fire from Trundle Hill, would have made the occupation of the "round hill" impracticable. The right wing battery thus echelloned would have been protected from cavalry attack by the hedge-rows, and could have fired over the heads of the musketeers there, on the opposing artillery when endeavouring to unlimber. Though not definitely stated, the piercing the Royal centre by Falkland Farm, which seems to have been Essex's main attack, must have been coupled by an advance of his right from Trundle Hill, and the greatest credit is due to the King's commander in having been able, as he did, to withdraw under these circumstances all his forces into Newbury, without having, as is often the case, the two wings separated and driven in diverging directions from the field.

Although the charge of the Royalist cavalry under Falkland against the hedge-rows of Dark Lane was a daring and gallant action, it was but a useless waste of life. In all probability it would have been difficult even for a good horse and rider in the hunting field; how much more so with the weight of armour and the intense excitement of the charge.

The same gallant spirit animated the breasts of those who rode to death up the Balaklava Valley against the Russian guns; but the French Marshal's remark that "c'est magnifique, mais ce n'est pas la guerre," is as true of the gallant cavaliers of Charles I., as it was of the fearless horsemen of Cardigan's light brigade.

# APPENDIX.

## APPENDIX I.

### A LIST OF THOSE REGIMENTS OF TRAINED-BANDS AND AUXILIARIES OF THE CITY OF LONDON, WHICH WERE ENGAGED AT THE FIRST BATTLE OF NEWBURY.

*Extracted from a MS.\* by Richard Symonds (author of the " Diary of the Marches of the Royal Army"), entitled :—*

"THE ENSIGNES † OF Yᴱ REGIMENTS IN Yᴱ CITTY OF LONDON
BOTH OF TRAYNED BANDS AND AUXILIARIES.
TOGEATHER WTᴴ THE NEAREST NUMBER OF THEIR TRAYNED SOLDIERS,
AS THEY MARCHED INTO FINSBURY FIELDS, BEING THEIR LAST GENERALL
MUSTER.
TUESDAY, SEPTEMB. 26, 1643.
ANNO PESTIFFERÆ REBELLIONIS."

---

THE RED REGIMENT OF TRAYNED-BANDS.

This Regimt· was not at yᵉ generall Muster in ffinsbury ffeilds.
Musketts     |     Officers about
Pikes     |     The Totall
Came from Newbery on Thursday, Sep. 28, 1643.

Collonel Isaack Pennington, Vsurper Maior, 1643.
Colonels Captayne Richard Verner.
The limitts of this Regimt·
    Cornhill, Lumbard-street, Fenchurch, the vpp. pt. of Grace Church Street, &c.

Lieut. Col. Robt. Dauies
    a Slop-maker for Seamen neare Billingsgate

Srieant Maior Tho. Chamb'laine.    A viol'a Merchant, liuing neare Lenden hall.

1. Capt. Thomas Player
    a hosyer and wholesaleman for narrow wares, liuing vpon new ffish street hill.

2. Capt. Chr. Whichcott, a merchant
    Colonel of the Greene Regimt· of Auxiliaries about Cripplegate.

3. Capt. Wᵐ· Manby, clerke of Leathersellers hall.

4. Capt. Joseph Vaughan, displaced.

---

\* Harl. MS. No. 986.
† The Ensigns or Colours of Regiments and Companies, given in the MS. are not reproduced here.

# PLAN
## OF THE
## FIRST BATTLE OF NEWBURY,
### Sept. 20th 1643.

## THE FIRST BATTLE OF NEWBURY.

THE YELLOW REGIMENT OF TRAYNED-BANDS.

This Regt. marched 2d into ye feild at ye generall Muster aforesaid and consisted of

| | | |
|---|---|---|
| Muskets | .. | 506 |
| Pikes | .. | 448 |
| Officers about | .. | 070 |
| The Totall | .. | 1024 |

Collonel Thomas Adams, Alderman, he was not at Newbury.
Collonel's Captayne Edw. Clegatt.
Limitts of this Regimt.
pt. of Thames Street, beginning at St. Magnus Church and reacheth to Bread Street, Dowgate, Walbrooke, ffriday street and part of Watling Street, &c.

Lieut. Col. Francis West, A Silke man liuing in Bread street.
This West was Colonel of this Regimt. at Newbery. Capt. Edw. Stoning was his Capt.-leiut. there, and shott in the heele and dyed at Reading and buried [there].

Srieant Maior Wm. Vnderwood, a Tobacco Seller in Bucklers Bury.
Capt. Rich. Hacket preded this Vnderwood in this Regimt. but left them refusing their oath of Associacon and is now in his Maties Service.

Garlicke hill and Queene Hithe Company.

1. Capt. Edw. Bellamy
    a Vintner at the Rost on ffleetbridge,
    a ffishmonger in Thames Street neare the Bridge.
Capt. Rich. Hacket was Capt. of this Company.

2. Capt. John Booker
    Register to ye Com'issioners of Banckrupt,
    Liuing in Wallbrooke.

3. Capt. Geo Dipford, a lyn Merchant.
    a Linnen Drap' neare Bow Church in the Ch. yard,
    Cheape Side Company agt. the Standard.

St. Antsokins Bow-Lane, &c. Company.

4. Capt. William Coleson.
    he wth his Company carried the Statues in the Church of All-hallowes to ye Parliam.
A Dyer liuing neare Dyers hall in Thames in Little All-hallowes p'ish. tenant to N.E.H.

---

THE BLEW REGIMENT OF TRAYNED-BANDS.

This Regimt. was not at this Muster but came from Newbery on Thursday, Septemb. 28, 1643.

It was the biggest Regimt. of ye Trayned bands 1400 of them at Brainf. or Turnha' greene.

The limitts of this Regimt. is Colman Street, The Stocks Lothbury, Old Jewry, pt. of Cheape side.

Collonel John Warner Alderma'.

Collonels Captayne Thomas Juxon a Sugar baker liuing in St. Thomas Apostles, most violent slayne at Newbery in this Manner, his horse was shott by a Can'on bullet in the forehead, being stun'd wth the blow, ran wth him violently right on into his Maties Army where

APPENDIX. 79

the horse fell downe dead, and he was mortally wounded and left dead, but the body of y<sup>e</sup> Army leauing the place left him too, and by that time he recouered his sences and was carried to London, and dyed w<sup>th</sup>in four dayes. His estate was neare Godalming in Surrey where he lived.*

Lieut. Col. Mathew ffoster.
Vintner at the Shipp behind the Exch. put out himselfe, but tooke the oath of Assoc. taken by the Capt. of the Citty for opposing all forces raysed w<sup>th</sup>out consent of P.

S<sup>r</sup>ieant Maior Owen Roe, a Mercer in Cheape side.

1. Capt. Mathew Sheppard. Merchant, a Sugar baker p'ner w<sup>th</sup> Juxon afores<sup>d</sup> in St. Thomas Apostles.
2. Capt. ffrancis Roe, brother to Owen Roe, one of these Roes liues in Colman street.
3. Capt. Robt. Mainwaring, of y<sup>e</sup> Custome hovse. Liuing in Aldermanbury.
   Hath a Troope of horse besides and quitted this Capt.

THE RED REGIMENT OF AUXILIARIES.

Colonel Thomas Atkins
Alderman.
Colonels Captayne or Capt. Leftenant,
Geo. Mosse.

The limitts of this Regm<sup>t.</sup>
Aldgate, Marke Lane, Tower street, Billingsgate, &c.

Leuit. Colonel Randal Mainwaring
his shop is In Cheape side neare Ironmonger lane by Col. Towse. Was Colonel of the Red Reg. of Auxiliaries and w<sup>th</sup> them at Newbury.

PRISONERS REMOVED OUT OF ELY HOWSE, 1643.

| | |
|---|---|
| Mr. William Ingoldsby, of Walton in Com' hertf. Cl : | S<sup>r</sup>ieant Maior Tucker Carried the Prisoners |
| Mr. Walt. ffarr Essex | out of Ely howse to the |
| Mr. John Scriuener, Com' Suff. Esqr. | Ship [on the Thames], |
| Mr. Hen. Wilford Esq. | was slayne at Newbery, |
| Mr. Hopestill Tilden, Jurate of Sandwich.† | Sep: 1643, his head |
| Mr. Sam' Daniell of Bulmer in Essex Recusant | shott off. This Tucker went out |
| Mr. ——— Tilyard | Colonel of this |
| Mr. Hall of Horney | Regim<sup>t.</sup> at Newbery. |

* Captain John Juxon was buried at St. Laurence Pountney, London, 16 Oct., 1643. He died of wounds received at the Battle of Newbury, being Captain of a Regiment of the Trained-Bands. He was born 10 Feb., 1609-10, and was eldest son of John Juxon, Citizen and Merchant-Taylor of London (son of Ralph Juxon, and an uncle of Archbishop Juxon). He married a daughter of George Langham, Citizen and Merchant-Taylor of London, an officer in the Parliament's service, and left three sons, John, Thomas, and George.

† Mr. Hopestill Tilden was baptized at Tenterden, Kent, 1 May, 1588, and was a younger brother of Nathaniel Tilden, Mayor of Tenterden, who emigrated to New England in 1635, and was ancestor of Mr. Tilden who "ran for" the Presidency of the United States in 1876. Hopestill Tilden settled at Sandwich, where he was in business as a Grocer, and was for many years one of the Jurats [equivalent to Alderman] of that Borough. He was buried in the Church of St. Mary, Sandwich, 19th December, 1661.

1. Capt. Willm' Tomson.
   This Tomson was leiftenant Colonel of this Regmt. at Newberry.
2. Capt. Edw: Hooker.
3. Capt. Lawrence Bromfeild.
4. Capt. Richard Hunt:
   a Confectioner in Bearebinder lane : slayne at Newbery quondam
   S'uant to Capt. Ditchfeild.
   This Hunt was 3d. Capt. at Newbury.

The Ensigns or Colours of the Blue and Orange Regiments of the Auxiliaries are given by Symonds, without any names of officers.

Total of the Trained-Bands and Auxiliaries engaged at Newbury.

TRAYNED BANDS.

Red Reg : S'ppose it recruted .................... 1000
Yellow Reg : Mustered .......................... 1024
Blew Reg : Suppose it recruted, and at most ...... 1000

AUXILIARIES.

Red Reg.
Blew Reg.    } Suppose they all 3 recruted } 3000
Orenge Reg   }   and to consist of ........ }

NOTE.—Until the reign of Queen Anne, every "Company" in a Regiment carried a "Colour." Those used by the Trained-Bands at this time were of the same colour as the name of the Regiment denotes : thus the Red Regiment bore a red flag. The devices on each were different in the several Regiments. The Colonel's Colour was perfectly plain ; the Lieutenant-Colonel's had the red cross of St. George on a white ground in the first quarter ; the remainder were similar, with the addition of a number of devices, such as a diamond, a trefoil, ball, or other such device, corresponding to the number of the Company. The Sergeant-Major [Major] had one such mark ; the Senior Captain two, and so on. 'History of the Hon. Artillery Campany,' by G. A. Raikes; pp. 139—140.

## II. THE ATTACK ON ESSEX'S REAR THE DAY AFTER THE FIRST BATTLE OF NEWBURY.

It is difficult at times to reconcile local traditional history and names with the probable course of events gathered from other and more trustworthy sources. Now, near Theale is a narrow winding lane (leading *north* from the main Reading road) to which has been assigned the name of "Deadman's Lane," and this has been described by several writers as the spot where this encounter took place, and somewhat in verification of this tradition, a sword,[*] portions of horse-trappings, &c., have been found in the adjacent fields ; but a glance at a map will prove at once that this "affair" had nothing whatever to do with the pursuit after the battle of the 20th.

[*] While inspecting the ground near Deadman's Lane a few years since, the writer was informed that in removing a bank in the immediate neighbourhood, a sword had been dug up, and this he was fortunately able to secure. The sword is a straight cut-and-thrust blade, much worn by repeated grinding; the fighting sword of a gentleman, from its lightness and finish. The hilt is of the ordinary pattern of the 17th century. This relic was presented to the Rev. A. Clutterbuck, when rector of Englefield.

## APPENDIX. 81

It is quite clear that, after having driven the King's forces into the town of Newbury and to some extent across the Kennet, the Earl of Essex would endeavour to keep that obstacle, the river, between him and the enemy as long as possible ; and only cross it to gain the main road by Reading to London, which ran along the north bank of the Kennet, *i.e.*, on the *enemy's side* of the river, when fairly beyond all danger of being disturbed by the King's troops from the direction of Shaw House.

It is well known that Essex after the battle advanced by Greenham Common *en route* for Reading and London, and it is evident he must have marched by the old winding roads through Aldermaston to the point of passage at Padworth and so by Theale. This line of march would leave Deadman's Lane on the left, and there would be no object whatever in going down it, unless the force had unaccountably lost its way. On this ground alone, therefore, it is improbable that any fighting took place there on this occasion.

Further, Sergeant-Major Foster, of the trained-bands, says that when on the march towards Reading, Prince Rupert overtook the army " in the narrow lanes about 1½ mile from the village of Aldermaston," and after the skirmish they marched unmolested to Theale, where they arrived at 10 o'clock.

Again, the 'Mercurius Britannicus'* says:—"Whereupon we marched toward Reading (to gaine quarters to supply our want of victuals) and when we had marched 6 or 7 miles, the enemy's horse having got an advantageous passage, which our horse endeavouring to cleere, charged them, *and in a narrow lane neere Sir Humphrey Forster's house*, part of our foote were disordered neere into a route by our own horse, for relief of which Col. Middleton alights from his horse and draws out 60 musqueteers, which he valorously led up first to relieve a stout cannoneer of ours, who with three men made good his station where he had charge of three case of drakes, against all the enemy's horse, the King's horse were beaten off and 80 slain in the place with the loss of 10 of ours." The 'Mercurius Britannicus' is never very particular as to accuracy in numbers.

This is evidence enough that Deadman's Lane had nothing to do with the march on London, as the lane is five or six miles from the village of Aldermaston, which is definitely named.†

A probable explanation of the finding of the sword and other articles near Deadman's Lane, is that some other fight occurred here during

---

\* From Tuesday, the 19th September, to Tuesday, 26th September, 1643.

† The following extract from the parish register of Aldermaston, tends to show that Essex and his men passed through that village, the soldier buried in the church-yard having most probably died on the march.

" 1643 September 23, a Parliament souldier kill'd at Newbvry."

There are also two antecedent entries (as follow)

" 1643 May 13, a Parliament souldier being a German."

" 1643 August 29, Wm. Hill, a Parliament souldier."

In moving the ground for the purpose of making a vault in Padworth Churchyard some years since, the remains of several male bodies were found promiscuously thrown into a large grave, which, from certain indications, were supposed to be those of soldiers who fell in some affray in the neighbourhood.

L

Parliamentary times—such as appears by the following letters to have taken place the previous month, August, 1643.

(No. 1). Letter from the Earl of Essex to Col. Goodwin.

Sir,—Understanding from Col. Ven* that som hors heave nowe quartered at Veal 3 myls from Reading, I resolved to send som hors to visit them, which Collonel Dalbeere desired to perform, as much [as] I know I have sent you, by which you may perceive it was no great matter for a great body of hors to tack som hors of a brocken troupe that quartered themselves at Wikeham against orders, and if the enemy had not taken the payns to have carried the leiftenant away I had called him to a Marshall's Court.† I am, your attached friend, ESSEX. Kingston, 13 Aug., 1643. (Tanner MSS., Bibl. Bodl. v. 62-1, No. 254).

(No. 2). Letter from Col. Dalbier to the Earl of Essex.

"According to orders marcht from Kingston to the quarters of my regiment at Cobham, and gave orders for the several troops to march to Bagshot, where with Capt. Pym's troop, I arrived about 7 o'clock: the troop consisted of 40 men, in all about 100 men, passed from Bagshot 10 at night with a guide who brought me to Swallowfield, where I took another guide who brought me to Burfield Bridge, which was a little after break of day, when, and no sooner, did I hear the enemy was got at Theale, which made me the greater dilligence to get them unaware, which indeed we did, for we found them without guard onely ready to goe away, not knowing anything of our entering the town, there was some 5 or 6 kill'd and so many or more sorely hurt: 26 of horse brought to this Castle prisoners, among which is the Captain who commanded, Lieut., Cornet, Quarter-master, and some Corporals, the rest are troopers. My men hath gotten about 40 horses, but very poore, insomuch that in all the matter is no great value. I am both weary and sleepy, and my horses tyred, which makes me stay here this night. I shall, however, if it please God, come to your Excellency to relate the business more at large. J. DULBIER." Windsor, 13 Aug., 1643. (Tanner MSS., Bibl. Bodl., A. 62-1, No. 235).

---

III. THE PRESENCE OF QUEEN HENRIETTA-MARIA AT THE BATTLE.

It has been stated by some writers that the Queen herself was present at the First Battle of Newbury, but this is not borne out by the follow-

---

* Col. Venn, who before joining the army had been a silkman in Cheapside, was Governor of Windsor Castle, which was garrisoned for the Parliament soon after the breaking out of the war. Prince Rupert made an unsuccessful attack upon it in the autumn of 1642. The Castle continued in the hands of the Parliament during the whole war, and in 1648 became the prison of the unfortunate King, who, as Heath expresses it, kept his sorrowful and last Christmas here. Col. Venn was one of the King's judges.

† The latter part of this letter evidently refers to other proceedings in Buckinghamshire, in which the Parliamentarians had the worst of it.

APPENDIX. 83

ing letters* written by her Majesty, when at Oxford, to the Duke of Newcastle.

Harl. MS. 6988, fo. 157.

Oxford. ce 23, Sept.

Mon cousin ce porteur est demeure sy a propos quil vous portera la nouuelle de la victoyre que nous auons eue sur les rebelles de quoy je vous en voye la relation : et quoy que se n'aye pas estte vne totalle desfait neaumoins sest vne fort grande victoyre il est vray que nous y auons perdu quantite de honneste gens : qui y ont fait des meruueilles je vous assure que nos gens que jay amene auec moy n'ont pas mal fait tellement que lon peut dire que nostre armee du north a ayde a la dcsfaite je suis sy lasse non pas de mestre batue, mais de en auoir ouy parler, que je finiray en disant que je suis constamant,

Vostre fidelle amie,
HENRIETTE MARIE R.

A Mon cousin le Marquis de Newcastel.

Harl. MS. 6988, fo. 158.

Oxford ce 7 Octobre.

Mon cousin jl y a sy longtamps que je nay reseu de vos nouvelles que je commance a croyre que vous nous croyes ysy tout morts : se que nous ne sommes pas ; sest nous qui tueons le autres : nonobstant les grandes rejouisances faits a Londre Il trouent que ils ont perdu leur armee : il y a beaucoup des fammes des citisiens de Londre qui vienent chercher leur maris a Newbery, disant que Mr. desex leur a dit quils estoit la en garnison : du depuis le Roy : tout batu quil est a en voye vne garnison a reading et son exselance ne les a point ampeches tout les jours jl vient des forces du parlement trouuer le Roy : jl m'est ariue vn malheur au quel je crois vous prandres part : Watt Monteque est pris a rochester par le parlemant venant ysy auec l'ambassadeur de france : il a voulu saduanser devant et a estte reconguu et pris : je croy que lambassadeur ne veut point venir quil ne lait encoire : jl y a vn chose que je desire sauoir de vous de vant que de la faire :

| *Marquis Hertford* | *Groume* | |
|---|---|---|
| 174 | a desire destre 15· 17· 27· 45. | |
| *de stoule* | | *du King of England.* |
| 22· 50 35· 62· 44· 7· 5· 8. 48. 35. 62. 23. 8. 66. | | 5· 63· 189. |
| | *quite* | |
| sela estant jl fault quil 52· 62· 27· 45· 8· 68. | destre. | 22. 35· 63. |
| *Gouerneur* | | *de Prince Charles* |
| 64· 8. 50. 40· 10· 63· 51· | | 5· 7· 239. tellement que il en fault 55. 42· |
| *Estre vn autre* | | *de P. Charles* |
| 8. 48. 45· 50· 8. 62. 41. 17. 62. 45. 50. 8. | | au pres 5· 8· 239. ce que |
| *Queene* | | *vous* |
| 260, ne veut pas sans premierement sauoir sy. | | 63. 35. 63· 48. |
| | *la rauoir* | |
| 66· 4· 70 voules 23. 18. 50· 17. 62· 35. 27. 50. | | se que jay cru auec |
| *vous* | *auez* | *pas* |
| lamploy que 64· 35· 63 48. | 17· 62· 8· 48. | ne se pouroit 33· 17· 48. |
| *accorder* | | |
| 17· 11 35· 50· 5· 8· 51. neanmoins : je attandrap vostre responce : et sy | | |
| | | *deux* |

---

* One of these letters is partly written in cipher, as will be seen; and some deciphered words appear to have been intercalated in the original.

vous tombes days la mesme opinion que moy: jl y a 5· 8· 62· 48.
*Places*
autres 33· 23· 17· 11· 8· 49· que je desire sauoir la quelle vous sera
plus agreable : nayant rien tant dans ma pancee que de vous faire voir
et a tout le monde lestime que je fais de vous : sest pour quoy mande a
moy franchement et comme a vne amie, comme je fais a sette heure a
*Chambellan ou gentilhomme de la Chambre du lit*
vous : se que vous desirez *11· 31· 17· 40· 13· 8· 23· 24· 18· 40· 5· 35·*
*62· 27· 17· 41· 45· 28· 23. 31· 35· 42· 44·,7· 5· 8· 24· 17· 11· 31· 19·*
*43· 13· 50· 7· 5· 62· 24· 28· 45·* sy jauois voulu aler par seremonies
je vous lorois fait escrire par vn autre : mais sela est bon la ou jl nia
pas vne estime comme jay de vous : et comme se sy est escrit auec
franchise je demande vne responce de mes me : et que vous me croyes
comme je suis veritablement et constamment,
Vostre fidelle et bien bonne amie,
HENRIETTE MARIE R.
A Mon cousin le Marquis de Newcastel.

The Marquis of Newcastle was at this time in the North, and a few
days previously writes as below to Prince Rupert, congratulating him
on his (questionable) success at Newbury :—
"May it please your Highness. God give you joy of your late great
victory, which I am confident the rebels will never recover: so that
upon the matter one may salute the King, King again, and only by
your hand, Sir, * * * * Your Highness's most faithful obliged
servant, W. NEWCASTLE.
"Cottingham, 6 Oct., 1643."

In the 'True Relation of the Late Battel neere Newbury,' the Prince
of Wales is also reported to have been present at the fight, but he had
been probably sent off with an escort from Faringdon to Oxford,
where the Queen, his mother, was then staying.

---

## IV. A CASE OF WITCH-MURDER AT NEWBURY.

[It is only for the sake of illustrating the thoughts and actions of the times
referred to, that the following account of a heartless and superstitious murder is
here given, with the grossly illiterate form retained, in which the brutality,
credulity and ignorance of the day produced it as a catchpenny sheet for the vulgar.]

"A MOST
"CERTAIN STRANGE AND TRUE DISCOVERY OF A
"WITCH
"Being taken by some of the Parliamentary Forces, as she was sliding
"On a small planck board and sayling on it over the River at Newbery,
"Together with the strange and true manner of her death, with the
propheticall
"Words and Speeches she used at the same time.
Printed by John Hammond 1643.

[A very rough woodcut of the conventional "witch" is printed with the title.]

"Many are in the belief that this silly sex of Woman can by no
meanes attaine to that so vile and dammed a practice of sorcery and
Witchcraft in regard to their illeterateness and want of learning, which

many Men of greate learning have become. Adam by temptatation toucht and tasted the deceiving apple so some high learn'd and read, by the same Tempter that deceived him hath bin ensnared to contract with the Devil as for example in the instancing a few English, Bacon of Oxford, Vandermast of Hollande, Bungy of Germany, Fostus of the same place, Franciscus the English monke of Bery, Doctor Blackleach and divars, others that were tedious to relate of, but how weake Woman should attain unto it many are incredible of the same and many too are opposite of opinion gainst the same, that giving a possibility to their doubtings that the malice and inveterate malice of a woman entirely devoted to her revengefull wrath frequenting desolate and desart places and giving way unto their wicked temptation may have commune with that world roaring Lion and covenant and contract upon condition, the like hath in divars places and tymes been tried at the assises of Lancaster, Carlile, Buckingham and elsewhere, but to come to the intended relation of this Witch's and Sorceresse's doings as is manifestly and credibly related by Gentlemen, Commanders and Captaines of the Earle of Essex his Army.

"A part of the Army marching thro' Newbery some of the Souldiers being scattered by reason of theyre loytering by the way in gathering Nuts, Apples, Plummes, Black berries and the like, one of them by chance in climbing up a Tree being pursued by his fellows or Comrade in Waggish Merriment jesting one with another espied on the river being there adjacent a tall lean slender Woman as he supposed to his amasement and great terrour treading of the water with her feete with as much ease and firmnesse as if one should walk or trample on the earth, wherewith he softly calls and beck'ned to his fellows to behold it and with all possible speed that could be to obscure them from her sight, who as conveniently as they could they did observe, this could be no little amasement unto them you may think to see a Woman dance upon the water, nor could all their sights be deluded, though perhaps one might, but arriving nearer to the Shore they could perceive there was a planck or deale overshadowed with a little shallow water that she stood upon which did beare her up, anon rode by some of the Commanders who were eye-witnesses as much as they and were as much astonished as they could be, still too and fro she fleeted on the water, the boord standing firm about upright, indeed I have both heerd and read of many that in tempests and on Rivers by casualty have become ship-wrack'd or cast over-boord where catch'g empty Barrells, rudders, boords or plancks have made good shift by the assisting providence of God to get on shore, but not in this woman kind, when as little thinking who perceived her tricks, or that she did imagine that they were the last she should ever show, as we have heard the Swan sings before her death, at last having been sufficiently upon the water he that deceived her alway, did so then, blinding her that she could not see at her landing the ambush that was laid for her, coming upon the shore she gave the boord a push, which they plainly perceived and crossed the river, they searched after her, but could not find her she being landed. The Commanders beholding her gave orders to lay hold on her and bring her to them straight, the which some were feerfull, but some being more valorous than other some, boldly went to her and siesed upon her by the armes demanding what she was, but the woman no whit replying any words unto them they brought her to the Commanders to whom, tho' mightily she was urged she did reply as little, so consulting with themselves what should be done to her, it being so apparently appear'd she was a Witch, being lothe to let her goe and as loth to carry her with them, so they resòlved with themselves to make a shot at her, and gave orders to a couple of their Souldiers that were approv'd good marksmen to charge and shoot her strait, which they purposed to doe, so setting her strait again a Mud Banke or wall two of the Souldiers according to their command made ready when having taken aime, gave fire and shot at her, as thinking sure they had sped her, but with a deriding and loud laughter at them she caught theyre bullets in her hands and shewed them, which was stronger testimony than the water that she was the same that their imagination thought her so to be, so resolving with themselves if either fire or sword or halter were sufficient to make an end of her, one let his Carbine close to her breast, where discharging, the bullett back rebound'd like a ball and narrowly it missed his face that was the shooter, this so inraged the Gentlemen that one drew out his sword and manfully [!] ran at her with all the force his strength had power to make, but it prevayled no more than did the shot, the Woman still, tho' speechless, yet in a most contemptible way of scorn still laughing at them, which did the more exhauste their furie against her life, yet one amongst them had heerd that piercing the temples of the head it would prevayl against the strongest sorcery and quell the force of Withcraft, which was allowyd for trial, the Woman hearing this knew that the Devil had left her and her power was gone, whereupon she began aloud to cry and roare, tearing her haire and making piteous moan, which in these words expressed were, And is it come to passe that I must dye indeed, why then his Excellencie the Earle of Essex shall be fortunate and win the field, after which no more words could be got from her, wherewith they immediately discharged a Pistoll underneathe her eare at which she strait sunk downe and dyed, leaving her legacy of a detested carcasse to the wormes, her soule we ought not to judge of, though the evills of her wicked life can scape no censure. FINIS."

V. THE DISCOVERY OF THE COFFIN AND REMAINS OF THE VAULT OF ROBERT DEVEREUX, THIRD EARL OF ESSEX, IN THE CHAPEL OF St. JOHN THE BAPTIST IN WESTMINSTER ABBEY, JUNE, 1879.*

The only entry of this burial in the Register of Westminster Abbey says that the Earl of Essex was buried "in St. John Bap. Chapel in a vault on the right side of the Earl of Exeter's monument, 19 Oct. 1646."

There is also a memorandum that a certain burial took place "neare ye Earle of Essex."

Probably no monument to him was erected, for there is no note of one. The memorandum of 1685, quoted above, renders it very probable, however, that his gravestone then existed.

This obscurity has always been unsatisfactory; but no attempt to throw light on the subject has ever been made until the present year,

---

* From an account of the operations which led to this discovery, prepared by Mr. Henry Poole, Master Mason of Westminster Abbey. Inserted with the courteous approval of the late Dean Stanley, D.D.

when a descendant of the Devereux family proposed to Dean Stanley to have an examination in St. John the Baptist's Chapel.

The existence of a vault having been inferred from the memoranda, it was thought there would be but little difficulty in finding it; and, under the order of the Dean, the search was made early in June. It began in the ground south of the Exeter tomb, where there was found the wall of the vault built by Baron Hunsdon, now partly under the Exeter tomb; and southward was found the marble coffin of an Abbot of the fifteenth century. The south-west corner of the Chapel was found to be filled with coffins, laid side by side and in piles, without any sign of a vault.

As regards the Earl's burial all this labour was fruitless, and with a feeling of disappointment the search was hopelessly given up.

On returning to the Chapel the next day for the purpose of closing all up, there was seen the angle of a lead coffin, which lay low down in the earth, at the extreme south-west corner of the area. It appeared to be a coffin of more than usual importance from the form of the soldering of the sheet-lead. The earth above the coffin was cellular and loose, and so allowed the hand to pass through towards the place of the coffin-plate. This was done, and a loose plate was felt and brought out. On partially clearing off the corrosion, the name of Robert Devereux, Earl of Essex, was seen, and the discovery was achieved.

The coffin had the appearance of being one of a number of common burials, and without a vault; but its position at the very bottom induced further examination. Then it became evident that the coffin had been once enclosed in a beautifully wrought vault of stone, which had been, not many years afterwards, wholly demolished to give room for interments over the coffin and by the north side of it.

The coffin lay on the original stone floor of the vault, and it seemed never to have been disturbed. Besides the floor, there remained a part of the south wall, but all the other three walls and the arch over them had disappeared.

After the disheartening abandonment of the search on the previous day, the pleasure arising from its successful resumption may be conceived.

The brass inscription-plate of the coffin was now flattened and attached to a small slab of marble, and laid on its place on the coffin.

The Dean directed the coffin to be enclosed within a new vault of stone, utilizing what remained of the old vault, and finally, that on the top of the covering should be laid a slab of marble thus inscribed:—

"This vault, shattered by later interments, was opened for the purpose of ascertaining the grave of the Earl of Essex, in June, 1879, and was then restored."

The vault was formerly and finally closed on the 19th June, in the presence of the Dean, Mr. Evelyn P. Shirley, of Lower Ettington, near Stratford-on-Avon, Mr. Knight Watson, secretary of the Royal Society of Antiquaries, and Mr. Doyne C. Bell, secretary to the Privy Purse.

From the nature of the fine white Purbeck marble gravestone which lay over the vault of the Earl, it is thought to be his original stone, once engraved with his inscription, and referred to in the memorandum of 1685. In 1710 was buried the wooden coffin which was found pressing on the Earl's coffin, and then, perhaps, the vault was demolished, and the Earl's inscription was smoothed out and superseded by that of "Mary Kendal." All this seemed to warrant the erasure of the inscription of that lady, and its renewal in smaller characters below the middle of the slab.

The upper part of the marble slab is now occupied by the inscription and the shield of arms of the Earl's coffin-plate, of which it is a facsimile, but twice-and-a-half larger.

The vault of the Earl has been spoken of as one of excellent work. Its construction, shape, and finish are very much like those of the beautiful vault which King Henry VII. built for his Queen Elizabeth of York, under their magnificent tomb.

It may be well to note here that the entry quoted in the first sentence of this notice is erroneous. The public prints of the day give the date of the funeral "on Monday, 22nd October," whereas the Abbey Register says "October 19." Such errors are not infrequent in that Register.*

## VI. BIOGRAPHICAL NOTICES OF OFFICERS AND OTHERS
MENTIONED IN CONNECTION WITH THE FIRST BATTLE OF NEWBURY.

### § 1. ROYALIST OFFICERS.

PATRICK RUTHVEN, EARL OF FORTH. Great-grandson of William, first Lord Ruthven, ancestor of the Earls of Gowrie, by his second wife, Christian Forbes. Created an English peer with the title of the Earl of Brentford, 27th May, 1644; had been made Field-marshal by the King at Coventry, and succeeded Lord Lindsey as General-in-chief after the battle of Edgehill. "An experienced commander," says Sir Philip Warwick, "and a man of naturall courage, and purely a soldier, and of a most loyall heart (which he had many occasions to shew, before the war was ended, and which his Country-men remembered, for they used both him and his Widow with all extremity afterwards)." He had seen service in Sweden under Gustavus Adolphus, in Denmark, Russia, Livonia, Lithuania, Poland, Prussia, and Germany. In England alone the number of his wounds had equalled that of the battles in which he had exposed himself. "At Edgehill," says Lloyd, "he modelled the fight." He was at Brentford and Gloucester, in both the fights at Newbury, at Cheriton, and at Cropredy Bridge, near Banbury. He had been shot in the head, in both arms, the mouth, leg, and shoulder; and, as if all this had not been enough for his scars and his story, the catalogue was finished by a fall from his horse that broke his shoulder. He survived to wait upon Charles II. in exile; and, returning to his native country, died near Dundee in 1651, and was buried in the parish church of Monifieth. By his wife Clara Barnard, who survived until 1679, he left three daughters, the eldest of whom married a gallant cavalier, Thomas Ogilvy (second son of the first Earl of Airlie), who was killed at Inverlochy, under

---

* On submitting the foregoing to the late Colonel Chester, the Editor of the 'Westminster Abbey Registers,' he could not accept Mr. Poole's conclusion, but was inclined to maintain the accuracy of the entry in the Register. He pointed out that in the year 1646, the 22nd of October did not fall on Monday, but on Thursday; while the 19th was really Monday, and that, as the "public prints of the day" were certainly wrong either as to the day of the month or the week, the balance of proof is in favour of the Register.

Montrose, in 1645; the second married Lord Forrester, by whom she had five children, who all assumed the name of Ruthven; the third married Major Pringle, of Whitebank, whose descendant is the present representative of the Earl of Forth and Brentford.

PRINCE RUPERT. Son of Frederick V., Elector Palatine, by Elizabeth, daughter of James I. The Prince came over from Holland to the assistance of the King, his uncle, about the time of the raising of the royal standard at Nottingham. "He possessed in a high degree that kind of courage which is better to attack than defend, and is less adapted to the land-service than that of the sea, where precipitate valour is in its element. He seldom engaged but he gained the advantage, which he generally lost by pursuing it too far. He was better qualified to storm a citadel, or even mount a breach, than patiently sustain a siege; and would have furnished an excellent hand to a general of a cooler head." Prince Rupert died, unmarried, at his house in Spring Gardens, 29th November, 1682, and was buried in Westminster Abbey.

SIR JOHN BYRON. Sir John Byron, K.B., M.P. for the town of Nottingham in the reign of James I., and for the county of Nottingham in that of Charles I. A faithful adherent of, and gallant officer under the latter King. Sir John commanded the corps of reserves at the battle of Edgehill; and the victory of Roundway Down, 5th July, 1643, wherein Sir William Waller was routed, was chiefly owing to his skill and valour, having at the head of his regiment charged Sir Arthur Hasilrigg's cuirassiers, and after a sharp conflict, in which Sir Arthur received many wounds, compelled that impenetrable regiment (as Lord Clarendon writes) to fly. Sir John Byron having given such proofs of his courage, and his six brothers at that time following his loyal example, he was in consideration thereof advanced 24th October, 1643, shortly after the first engagement at Newbury, to the dignity of a Baron of the realm, by the title of Lord Byron of Rochdale in the Co. Palatine of Lancaster, with limitation, in default of his own male issue, to each of his brothers. He was twice married; but dying in 1652 issueless, the barony devolved upon his brother Richard. Lord Byron's letter to Clarendon, frequently quoted in the text, was written while in exile, and is dated "St. Germains, December 10, 1647."

LORD WILMOT. Henry, 2nd Viscount Wilmot in Ireland, was created, 29th June, 1643, Lord Wilmot of Adderbury, co. Oxon, in the English Peerage. He was further advanced to the Earldom of Rochester, 13th December, 1652. He died at Dunkirk in 1659, and was succeeded by his only surviving son John, the better (but not so favourably) known Earl of Rochester. Lord Wilmot "ordered the horse at Newbery first Battel (being Lieutenant-General under Prince Rupert) in so convenient and spacious a place (Downs have been pitched upon as the most commodious Scene of a Horse Engagement), advising them by no means to be drawn into any uneven streight places; with so strict an eye upon all advantages and opportunities, and in such Ranks, that one Troop might be *in subsidiis* assistant to another, and no part stand naked or fail in the singleness of its own strength, but that one may second another from first to last, being aware of Livies charge upon *Cajus Sempronius, (Pugnavit incaute inconsulteque non subsidiis firmata acie non equite apte locato)*." (Lloyd's 'Memoires,' pp. 465-6.)

EARL OF CARNARVON. Robert Dormer, eldest son of Sir William Dormer, Knt., by Alice, daughter of Sir Richard Molyneux, Bart., of Sefton, co. Lancaster, and grandson to Robert Dormer, created a baronet by King James I., June 10th, 1615, and Baron Dormer, of

## THE FIRST BATTLE OF NEWBURY.

Wing, co. Bucks, succeeded to the Barony on the death of his grandfather in 1616, and was created Viscount and Earl of Carnarvon by Charles I. in 1628. It appears to have been on the question of Strafford's impeachment that he first joined the party in public affairs which he proposed to espouse, by using his utmost endeavours to save the life of that statesman. When the Buckinghamshire men were, in 1642, incited by Hampden to rise in opposition to established authority, he used all his influence to restore order in that county, where his estates chiefly lay, and combined with other loyalists in raising and arming forces for the King. He attended Charles to York, signed the famous declaration of June 10th, and was one of those royalists who were excepted from the first Indemnity. He distinguished himself in every action in which he was engaged, and particularly at the battles of Edgehill, Lansdown, and Roundway Down. Lord Clarendon speaks of him as an excellent officer, invaluable to the King for the strict discipline he maintained, beloved by the soldiers for his justice, and so scrupulous an observer of his word that nothing would induce him to continue in the army of the west after Prince Maurice, who commanded it, had violated the articles of capitulation made with the towns of Weymouth and Dorchester. Like his noble compatriots Sunderland and Falkland, Carnarvon fell in the first battle at Newbury, and his name is commemorated on the monument erected on the field where he gave his life for the King he had served so well. His death has been variously described. Clarendon states that the Earl, having charged and routed a body of the enemy's horse, and coming carelessly back by some scattered troopers, was by one of them, who knew him, run through the body with a sword; of which he died within a hour. In Sir Roger Manley's 'History of the Rebellion,' his death is thus related:—"There was a little hill five hundred paces from the town, which the Cavaliers had possessed and fortified with guns. Essex perceiving it, and having no other way to pass, he himself with his own regiment and that of the general's guards attacks it bravely, being as bravely received by the royalists, Stapleton with his own regiment and that of the general's guards, charging the Earl of Carnarvon, was repulsed, but the Earl, pursuing too far, was killed by a shot in [at] the head of his own men; a person no less remarkable for his fortitude and fidelity to the King, than for the nobleness of his extraction." The context shows that Sir Roger refers to the Wash as the hill fortified with the King's artillery.\* Lloyd, in his 'Memoires,' gives this account:—"The Earl receiving Sir Philip Stapleton with his regiment of horse and Essex his life guard with a brisk charge and pursuing them to the foot, when a private hand put an end to his life, and in breathing out his last he asked 'whether the King was in safety?'" It is further stated in Fuller's 'Worthies' in Bucks (p. 141), that as he lay dying on the heath a certain nobleman asked him if he had any request to prefer to the King, assuring him that it would be punctually fulfilled. "No," he replied, "I will not die with a suit in my mouth, but to the King of Kings." In Defoe's 'Memoirs of a Cavalier,' which, though woven into a romantic story, is written with apparent fidelity of statement, it is said:—"The Earl of Carnarvon was brought into an inn at Newberry, where the King came to see him. He had just life enough to speak to his Majesty, and died in his presence. The King was exceedingly concerned for him and was observed to shed tears at the sight. We were indeed all of us troubled at the loss of so brave a

---
\* The traditional spot where Lord Carnarvon probably fell is marked on the Plan.

## APPENDIX.  91

gentleman, but the concern our royal master discovered moved us more than ordinary. Everybody endeavoured to have the King out of the room, but he would not stir from the bed-side, till he saw all hopes of life gone." The body of the Earl was conveyed under guard to Oxford, and buried in the chapel of Jesus College, but was removed to the family burial-place at Wing, near Leighton Buzzard, and re-interred August 3rd, 1650. While on its way to Oxford, the funeral cortége is stated to have been attacked by a body of Parliamentary horse, and the Earl's jewels and plate taken. The following interesting anecdote relating to the Earl was communicated, in 1759, by Mr. James Pettit Andrews, F.S.A., to Edward Rowe Mores, in reply to his queries for a parochial 'History of Berkshire.' "A person now alive has formerly had much conversation with an old soldier (who dy'd forty years ago) about the Particulars of that Battle, but they gathered nothing strikingly new from him. There were not many years ago, persons who remember'd Ld. Carnarvon riding thro' Newbury with his sword drawn and jocosely taking measure of a gate (thro' which he propos'd bringing Essex as a prisoner) to know whether it was wide enough for the Parliament General's horns. The same persons soon after saw Carnarvon's body brought across a horse like that of a calf." The "horns" no doubt allude to Essex's unfortunate matrimonial relations. Lord Carnarvon married Anne Sophia, daughter of Philip Herbert, 4th Earl of Pembroke and Montgomery (from whom the present Lord Carnarvon paternally descends), and left an only child, Charles, his successor, who dying without male issue, the earldom became extinct, and the Barony of Dormer devolved on a distant kinsman, in whose posterity it remains.

HENRY SPENCER. First Earl of Sunderland, son of William, 2nd Lord Spencer, of Wormleighton, by Penelope, eldest daughter of Henry Wriothesley, Earl of Southampton, was born in 1620. After a few days' visit at Oxford, Lord Sunderland joined the army as it was on the point of engaging at Newbury. The Earl having no command in the army, attended upon the King's person under the obligation of honour, bringing, according to Lloyd, £15,000 and 1,200 men to his Majesty. He married the beautiful Lady Dorothea, daughter of the Earl of Leicester, by whom he had one son, Robert, his successor, lineal ancestor to the Duke of Marlborough and Earl Spencer, and one daughter, Dorothy, married to Sir George Saville, Bart., afterwards created Marquis of Halifax. The following letter was written by Lord Sunderland to his wife, Lady Dorothea (Waller's Sacharissa), a few days before the battle of Newbury, in which he was killed:—"Since I wrote to you last from Sudley, we had some hopes one day to fight with my Lord Essex's army, we receiving certain intelligence of his being in a field convenient enough, called Ripple Field, towards which we advanced with all possible speed; upon which he retired with the body of his army to Tewkesbury, where, by the advantage of the bridge, he was able to make good his quarter, with 500 men, against 20,000. So that though we were at so near a distance as we could have been with him in two hours: his quarter being so strong, it was resolved on Thursday, that we seeing for the present he would not fight with us, we should endeavour to force him to it by cutting off his provisions; for which purpose, the best way was for the body of our army to go back to Evesholme, and for our horse to distress him : upon which I, and many others, resolved to come for a few days hither, there being no probability of fighting very suddenly, where we arrived late on Thursday night. As soon as I came, I went to your father's, where I found Alibone, with whose face I was better pleased than with any of the ladies here. This expression is so much a bolder thing than charging my Lord Essex, that should this letter miscarry and come to the knowledge of our dames, I should, by having my eyes scratched out, be cleared from coming away from the army from fear: where if I had stayed, it is odds I should not have lost more than one. Last night very good news came to Court, that we, yesterday morning, fell upon a horse quarter of the enemies, and cut off a regiment, and that my Lord of Newcastle hath killed, and taken prisoners, two whole regiments of horse and foot that issued out of Hull; which place he hath great hopes to take ere long. By the same messenger, last night, the King sent the Queen word that he would come hither on Monday or Tuesday; upon one of which days, if he alter his resolutions, I shall not fail to return to the army. I am afraid our sitting down before Gloucester has hindered us from making an end of the war this year which nothing could keep us from doing if we had a month's more time which we lost there, for we never were in a more prosperous condition. Before I go hence, I hope some body will come from you, howsoever, I shall have a letter here for you. I have taken the best care I can about my economical affairs; I am afraid I shall not be able to get you a better house, every body thinking me mad for speaking about it. Pray, bless Popet for me and tell her, I would have writ to her but that upon mature deliberation I found it to be uncivil to return an answer to a lady in another character than her own which I am not yet learned enough to do. I cannot by walking about my chamber call anything more to mind to set down here and really I have made you no small compliment in writing thus much for I have so great a cold that I do nothing but sneeze and mine eyes do nothing but water all the while I am in this posture of hanging down my head. I beseech you to present his service to my lady who is most passionately and perfectly yours." They never met again! The day after the battle, the body of the Earl was removed from Newbury, and subsequently interred in the family burial-place at Brington, Northamptonshire.

LORD FALKLAND. Lucius Cary, Viscount Falkland, born at Burford, about 1610. He was the eldest son of Sir Henry Cary, of Berkhampstead and Aldenham in Herts, and of Elizabeth, daughter and sole heiress of Sir Laurence Tanfield, Chief Baron of the Exchequer.* Sir Henry was raised to the peerage of Scotland, November 10th, 1620, by the title of Viscount Falkland, and died in September, 1633, when his son, Lucius, inherited his title and estates. Lord Falkland's reputation for talents, genius, and general literature, by which he was distinguished, may be inferred from several addresses made to him on the occasion of his leaving England in the expedition against the Scots in 1639 with the Earl of Holland, particularly by the poets Waller, Cowley, Ben Jonson, and Suckling, neither of whom would have dared

---

* In Burford Church is a stately monument to Sir Laurence Tanfield and his lady, with their effigies at full length in the habit of the period; and at their feet Lord Falkland, their grandson, who fell at Newbury, is represented in armour, kneeling, with his back towards them; and his helmet was formerly suspended over the tomb. (See 'Gentleman's Mag.' lxi. p. 896. 'The tour of the Captaine, Lieutenant, and Ancient,' Lansdown MS. No. 213.) It is said that when the Earl of Essex and his troops lay in Burford Church, June 6th, 1644, they took down the pennons and flags over Tanfield's monument and wore them for scarves. The Manor of Burford was sold by Lord Falkland to Speaker Lenthall, in 1634.

to satirize a man of his character by vain adulation and false praise. Cowley's poem commences with these lines:—

> "Great is thy charge, O North; be wise and just;
> England commits her Falkland to thy trust,
> Return him safe; learning would rather choose
> Her Bodley or her Vatican to lose.
> All things that are but writ or printed there,
> In his unbounded breast engraven are;
> There all the sciences together meet,
> And every art does all his kindred greet."

And in Waller we find this passage:—

> "Ah! noble friend! with what impatience all
> That know thy worth, and know how prodigal
> Of thy great soul thou art, longing to twist
> Bays with that ivy, which so early kist'
> Thy youthful temples; with what horror we
> Think on the blind events of war and thee!
> To fate exposing that all-knowing breast
> Among the throng as cheaply as the rest."

He was chosen Member of Parliament for Newport, April, 1640, and again in November of the same year. He distinguished himself by his speeches in Parliament on the subject of ship-money, episcopacy, &c. In January, 1641-2, Lord Falkland was sworn of the Privy Council, and became one of the principal Secretaries of State. He followed the King to York, and supported the Royal cause by his pen and his sword until his death. He fought at the battle of Edgehill, and attended the King at the siege of Gloucester. At the First Battle of Newbury, he served in the front rank of Lord Byron's regiment, and whilst charging the enemy he received a musket shot in the stomach, and fell dead from his horse. The body of Lord Falkland was not found before the day after the battle, when it was discovered, says John Aubrey, the Wiltshire antiquary, "stript, trod upon, and mangled, and could only be identified by one who waited upon him in his chamber, by a certain mole his lordship had upon his neck." * The same morning a letter had been sent to Essex by Rupert, as follows:—

"We desire to know from the Earl of Essex, whether he have the Viscount Falkland, Capt. Bertue [the Hon. Henry Bertie, brother to the Earl of Lindsey], and Sergt.-Major Wilshire † prisoners, or whether he have their dead bodies, and if he have, that liberty may be granted to their servants to fetch them away.

Given under my hand at Newbery this 21 Sept. 1643.
RUPERT."

The body of Falkland, having been recovered, was placed across the back of one of the royal chargers, and mournfully escorted down the hill by a detachment of the King's own troop, and gently laid in the old Town Hall. The following morning the corpse was removed to Oxford, thence next day to Great Tew, and interred in the chancel of the parish church of St. Michael, as the register thus records:—

"THE 23RD DAY OF SEPTEMBER, A.D. 1643, THE
RIGHT HONOURABLE SIR LUCIUS CARY, KNIGHT,
LORD VISCOUNT OF FALKLAND,
AND LORD OF THE MANOR OF GREAT TEW,
WAS BURIED HERE."

No monument marks the spot, for fear, it is thought, of desecration

---

* Letters, vol. ii., pt. 1, p. 346.

† There were three or more Wilshires, Wilsheers, or Wiltshires, engaged in the Civil War, and it is difficult to determine the identity of the "Sergt.-Major Wilshire," mentioned in Prince Rupert's letter.

at this troubled period. Lady Lettice was buried at Great Tew, February 27th, 1646, leaving behind her a reputation for virtue and piety.

Another version, however, of the temporary disposal of the body of Falkland and the other Lords killed at Newbury is furnished by a MS. in the possession of F. D. Hibbert, Esq., of Chalfont House, Gerrard's Cross, entitled 'John Saunders, His Book, 1712. The account of my travels with my Mistress.' * From this the following is an extract :— "Augt. ye 1. She went in ye Alesbury coach, and I on ye outside, we din'd at ye Crown at Uxbridg, and went that night to Sr Richard Holford's house in Lincoln's Inn Fields, whar we ware welcomely receiv'd, but found my Lady in aweful condiscion. We stayed there till ye 11 of August, then my Mrs. went with Sr Richd. and Lady in their coach, and I on ye outside for Avebury, we sat out on Tuesday, and din'd that day at Mr. Bolding's at ye Crown at Slow, one mile from Winsor, I saw ye Castle as I past ye road. I lay that night at ye Bare, at Reading, which is a large town, and four churches in it, it is a good place for trade, ye river of Thames comes to it, it is . . . . miles from Slow. Ye 12 we din'd at Mr. Phillips at ye Bare in Spinumlands, in Nuberry parish, whare was ye great fight in ye sivil wars, four noble Dukes [Lords] thare killed and carried into that very house where I dined, it is . . . . miles from Reading. As I first [came] near Nuberry I see ye fields where many brave English men weare killed, and much blood was spilt there." This statement does not interfere with the accuracy of the tradition already referred to ; for it is more than probable that the bodies of all the more important personages who fell during the battle were first received at the Town Hall for identification, and as a temporary measure, and were then individually transferred to other places previous to their final interment, or transmission to the places selected for that purpose. Falkland's body may well have been brought first to the official centre of the town, and then have been moved to the Bear Inn on the Oxford Road, where it was placed in a shell or coffin and prepared for its final removal.

It is not difficult to fix the position of the Bear Inn, and Mr. John Tanner's evidence on the point is amply sufficient to establish the fact. In a letter received from him, he states, " I have referred to the papers I wished to see and I find that my impression is correct, namely, that the premises now occupied by Mr. Adnams, Mrs. Fidler, and Mr. Hunt (on both sides of the gateway) were the Bear Inn." These buildings are situated on the north side of the London and Bath road at Speenhamland. Mr. Tanner then goes on to say, " In a deed dated 29th September, 1757, the premises now in the occupation of Messrs. Forster and Abel (which were then known as the Elephant Inn) are described as adjoining to the Chequers Inn on the West, and the *two messuages or tenements (formerly the Bear Inn)* on the East. These two messuages or tenements were in 1757 in the occupation of John Awbrey and Francis Sheppard, who were, I think, brewers. From Mr. Sheppard they have come down to Mr. E. J. Alderman the present owner.

"It is not many years since in making some alterations in the garden at the back, some skeletons, and I believe, cannon balls were dug up. I heard many years since that the Bear Inn was shut up for some time,

---

* Sarah, youngest daughter of Samuel Trotman, Esq., of Siston Court, Gloucestershire, and Bucknell, Oxon, died in 1684, the wife of the **Rev. Dr. Hickes, rector of Whimple, Dorsetshire.**

and probably never again opened as an Inn, in consequence of a murder supposed to have been committed, if I remember right, in some altercation between the mistress and her cook; one or the other of them was thrown down stairs and killed."

Dr. Pordage, rector of Bradfield, a celebrated enthusiast, placed by Baxter at the head of the Bœhmenists, was tried at the Bear Inn, Speenhamland, in 1654, before the Commissioners of Berks, appointed by an Ordinance of the Lord Protector Cromwell and his council for ejecting "Scandalous, Ignorant, and Insufficient Ministers." The Commissioners at the first sitting consisted of Mr. Fettyplace, chairman, Mr. Samuel Wightwick, Mr. Samuel Dunch, Major Fincher, Major Allin, Mr. Evelyn, Mr. Angell Bell, Mr. Mills, Mr. Cox, and Mr. Stroude, with Mr. Woodbridge, rector of Newbury, Mr. Christopher Fowler, vicar of St. Mary's, Reading, Mr. Hughes, Mr. John Tickell, of Abingdon, and other ministers, as assistants. The Commissioners sat at the Bear Inn, Speenhamland, on October 5th, October 19th, and November 2nd, 1654, and at the Bear Inn, Reading, on November 22nd and December 7th. Sentence of ejectment was pronounced the day following the last sitting. The case is given *in extenso* in State Trials, vol. ii., pp. 217, 259.

The night previous to the battle, Lord Falkland slept at the house of a Mr. Head, in Cheap Street, and early next morning, by his express wish, the sacrament was administered to him by Dr. Twisse, the then Rector of Newbury, in the presence of Mr. Head and his whole family, who attended at Lord Falkland's especial request. The room which tradition points out as being the scene of Falkland's last communion is in a house now known as No. 1, Falkland Place, and contains a curious cupboard fitted into a recess, concealed by a panel. The cupboard is of mahogany, and the shell-like ornament at the top and the mouldings are gilt.

EARL OF LINDSEY. Montague Bertie, 2nd Earl of Lindsey, K.G. This nobleman being with his gallant father at Edgehill, when he received his death-wound, voluntarily surrendered himself prisoner in order to be near and attend him. The Earl's second wife was Bridget, daughter of Edward Wray, Esq., by Lady Elizabeth Norreys his wife, only daughter and heiress of Francis, Earl of Berkshire and Baron Norreys, of Rycote, and widow of Sir Edward Sackville, who was engaged at Newbury fight. By this Bridget the Earl had a son James, who became Lord Norreys in right of his mother, and was created Earl of Abingdon, also a daughter Mary, married to Charles Dormer, 2nd Earl of Carnarvon, and two other children. Lord Lindsey commanded the King's life-guards in several of the considerable battles that were fought in the course of the Civil War, and was wounded in that of Naseby. He died at Campden House, Kensington, the 25th July, 1666.

EARL OF NORTHAMPTON. James, 3rd Earl. This nobleman, while a commoner, and M.P. for the co. Warwick, having voted, in 1641, against the bill for attainting the Earl of Strafford, his name was amongst those called *Straffordians*, in the list posted up in the Old Palace Yard; and subsequently, with other members, he was expelled the House. He was afterwards distinguished with his gallant father (who fell at the battle of Hopton Heath) in the ranks of the cavaliers; and on the magnificent entry of Charles II. into the city of London, 29th May, 1660, he headed a band of two hundred gentlemen attired in grey and blue. The Earl married first Isabella, daughter and co-heir of Richard, 3rd Earl of Dorset, by whom he had one surviving daughter, Alathea, who married Sir Edward Hungerford, Bart. On her death without issue in 1678, her great fortune devolved upon her cousin, John, 3rd Earl of Thanet. The Earl married secondly Mary, daughter and heiress of Baptist Noel, Viscount Camden, by whom he had three sons and two daughters.

EARL OF NOTTINGHAM. Sir Charles Howard, 3rd Earl. He died 26th April, 1681, when the Earldom of Nottingham expired.

EARL OF CLEVELAND. Thomas Wentworth, Earl of Cleveland, and Lord Wentworth of Nettlestead, 1625. Lord Cleveland was especially prominent at the Second Battle of Newbury, where he was instrumental in saving the life of the King. On the death of the Earl, 25th March, 1667, the Earldom of Cleveland became extinct, but his grand-daughter, Henrietta Maria, succeeded to the Barony of Wentworth. She was the only child of his only son, Thomas, Lord Wentworth, who served his Majesty throughout the war, but died before his father, and was buried at Toddington, Beds., 7th March, 1664-5. As the Baroness Wentworth she is best remembered from her unhappy connection with the Duke of Monmouth. She died 23rd April, 1686, when the title reverted to her aunt, her father's only sister, Lady Anne, wife of John, 2nd Lord Lovelace ; and at her death, 7th May, 1697, it passed to her grand-daughter Martha, wife of Sir Henry Johnson, and at her death, in July, 1745, without issue, it reverted to Sir Edward Noel, 6th Bart., and at his death in 1774, passed to his son Thomas, at whose death in 1815, it fell into abeyance, which terminated, 12th November, 1856, in favour of Lady Byron, widow of the Poet, whose grandson, Ralph-Gordon-Noel Milbanke, is now 11th Baron Wentworth.

EARL OF HOLLAND. Henry Rich, Earl of Holland, captain of the King's guard, and general of the horse in the expedition to Scotland, was much in favour with James I. In the latter end of the reign of James, he was sent ambassador to France, where he negotiated the treaty of marriage between Charles and Henrietta Maria. His handsome person, gallant behaviour, and courtly address, are thought to have made an early impression upon the heart of that princess, of whom he is known to have been a distinguished favourite. His conduct was so various with respect to the King and Parliament that neither party had the least regard for him, if they did not look upon him as their enemy. Lord Holland with the Earls of Clare and Bedford had left the Parliament and joined the King, shortly before the battle of Newbury, Colonel Blagge, the governor of Wallingford, receiving the converts at the castle, and forwarding them with an escort of honour to Oxford. The three Earls subsequently returned to the Parliament. In 1648 Lord Holland once more adopted the royal cause ; and having received from the Prince of Wales (afterwards Charles II.) a commission as general, and the Queen, who was in Paris, promising money, he joined with the Duke of Buckingham, his brother Lord Francis Villiers, and a few others of high rank, in a rash and feeble effort for the King at Kingston-on-Thames. Being surrounded by a superior body of the Parliament horse and foot, he fled with Colonel Dalbier and about a hundred horse to St. Neots, where he was taken prisoner at an inn ; he was then confined in Warwick Castle, and afterwards in the Tower. He was tried by the so-called "High Court of Justice," and, by the casting vote of the Speaker, sentenced to be executed. Lord Holland was beheaded at Palace Yard, 9th March, 1649, upon the same scaffold as the Duke of Hamilton and Lord Capel. The Duke of Buckingham managed to escape at Kingston, but his handsome and brave brother, the young Lord Francis Villiers, was killed. He behaved with signal

APPENDIX. 97

courage, and, after his horse had been shot under him, stood with his back against a tree, defending himself till he sunk under his wounds. The initials of his name were inscribed on the tree, and remained until it was cut down in 1680. The names "King Charles' Road" and "Villiers' Path" at present alone commemorate the scene of this fight, which was one of the last struggles made for the King, then a prisoner in the Isle of Wight.

EARL OF BEDFORD. William, 5th Earl of Bedford, son of Francis, 4th Earl, elected a Knight of the Garter, 1672, and created, 11th May, 1694, Marquis of Tavistock and Duke of Bedford. His Grace married Anne, daughter and sole heiress of Robert Carr, Earl of Somerset, by his too celebrated countess, Frances Howard, the divorced wife of Essex. Sir John Russell, a younger brother of William, 5th Earl of Bedford, was also engaged in the First Battle of Newbury.

EARL OF CLARE. John Holles, 2nd Earl, who succeeded his father on his death, 4th October, 1637. He married Elizabeth, eldest daughter and co-heir of Sir Horatio Vere, Lord Vere of Tilbury. He lived in retirement during the Commonwealth. Lord Clarendon says of him:— "He was a man of honour and courage, and would have been an *excellent person* if his heart had not been set upon keeping and improving his estate; he was weary of the company he kept, and easily hearken'd to the Earl of Holland, in any consultation how to recover the King's authority, and to put an end to the war." The Earl died the 2nd, and was buried 23rd January, 1665-6, at St. Mary's, Nottingham.

EARL OF CRAWFORD. Ludovic Lindsay, the "Loyal Earl" of Crawford. The name of this nobleman does not occur in the list of prominent royalist leaders engaged at the First Battle of Newbury, page 42, but his participation in this fight is proved by references given by the late Lord Lindsay in his 'Lives of the Lindsays,' vol ii., p. 64, where an interesting memoir of Earl Ludovic will be found.

JOHN, LORD BELASYSE, second son of Thomas, 1st Viscount Falconberg, created Baron Belasyse of Worlaby, co. Lincoln, 27th January, 1644-5. He was buried in the churchyard of St. Giles's in the Fields, 14th September, 1689, and his loyalty to his King is perpetuated by the following inscription copied from the monument now on the outside of the church. "This monument was erected in the year of our Lord 1736, by the pious direction of the honourable Dame Barbara Webb, wife of Sir John Webb, of Cranford Magna in the county of Dorset, baronet, and the honourable Catharine Talbot, wife of the honourable John Talbot, of Longford in the county of Salop, esquire, surviving daughters and co-heirs of the right honourable John, Lord Belasyse, second son of Thomas, Lord Viscount Fauconberg, in memory of their most dear father, his wives, and children. Who, for his loyalty, prudence, and courage, was promoted to several commands of great trust by their majesties King Charles I. and II., viz., having raised six regiments of horse and foot in the civil wars, he commanded a tertia in his Majestie's armies at the battles of Edge-hill, Newbury, and Knavesby; at the sieges of Reading and Bristol; and afterwards, being made governor of York, and commander-in-chief of all his Majestie's forces in Yorkshire, he fought in the battle of Selby, with the lord Fairfax. And being lieutenant-general of the counties of Lincoln, Nottingham, Derby, and Rutland, and governor of Newark, he valianlty defended that garrison against the English and Scotch armies, till his Majesty came in person to the Scotch quarters, and commanded the surrender of it. At which time he also had the honour of being general of the King's horse-guards; in all which services during the war, and

N

other achievements, he deported himself with eminent courage and conduct, and received many wounds, sustained three imprisonments in the Tower of London ; and after the happy restoration of Charles II., he was made lord-lieutenant of the east-riding of the County of York, governor of Hull, general of his Majestie's forces in Africa, governor of Tangier, captain of his majestie's guard of gentlemen pensioners, and first lord commissioner of the treasury to King James II. He died the 10th of September, A.D. 1689, whose remains are deposited in this vault." The remainder of the inscription refers to his marriages and issue.

GEORGE, LORD DIGBY. Son and heir of John Digby, 1st Earl of Bristol, summoned to Parliament in his father's barony of Digby, June 9th, 1641. At the Restoration he was made Knight of the Garter, and died in 1676. The title became extinct on the death of his only son in 1698.

LORD JERMYN. Henry Jermyn, created Baron Jermyn, 8th September, 1643, and Earl of St. Albans, 27th April, 1660. He was Master of the Horse to Queen Henrietta, and one of the Privy Council to Charles II. In July, 1660, he was sent Ambassador to the Court of France, and in 1671 he was made Lord Chamberlain of His Majesty's household. He died unmarried, 2nd January, 1683-4, when the earldom became extinct, but the Barony, by limitation of the patent, devolved on his nephew.

LORD PERCY. Henry Percy, youngest son of Henry, 9th Earl of Northumberland, and brother of Algernon, 10th Earl. He was Governor of Jersey at the breaking out of the rebellion, but returned to England, raised a regiment of horse, and was constituted General of the Ordnance. He attended the King throughout the whole of the war, and was created Baron Percy of Alnwick, 28th June, 1643. He afterwards followed Charles II. into exile, and was appointed Lord Chamberlain of his Household. Died in Paris, unmarried, in April, 1652. His brother Algernon took an active part against Charles I., but was entirely free from any participation in his death, and subsequently promoted the Restoration.

LORD CHANDOS. George Brydges, son of Grey, 5th Lord Chandos, by Lady Ann Stanley, daughter and co-heir of Ferdinando, 5th Earl of Derby, succeeded as 6th Lord Chandos on the death of his father, 10th August, 1621, being then only a year old. He died at his house near Covent Garden (on the site of the present Chandos Street) 1st February, 1654-5, and was buried with his ancestors in the chapel of Sudeley. Leaving no male issue, the title passed to his brother William. "His Castle, at Sudeley near Winchcomb in Gloucestershire," says Lloyd, "b:ing besieged by *Massie*, with 300 *musqueteers* and three *companies of dragoons*, and two *sakers*, after a long siege, several assaults and batteries, when they were almost smothered by the smoke of hay and barns burned about the house, yielded *Jan.* 1642. A loss revenged by my Lord at *Newbury, Sept.* 20, 1643, when with the Earls of *Caernarvon* and *Northampton*, the *true* Heir of his father's valor, commanding His Majesties' Horse there, the King said, Let 'Chandois *alone*, his *errors are safe.*'" (Lloyd's 'Memoires,' p. 366.) It is related by the Rev. Alex. Jacob, chaplain to Henry, second Duke of Chandos, in his 'Complete English Peerage,' that Charles I. was so sensible of the advantages that had accrued to his army during this battle by the example exhibited by Lord Chandos, as well as the personal service performed by this nobleman, that he offered to create him *Earl of Newbury;* but his lordship, who had espoused the King's cause from motives of honour and justice, refused that distinction till he should have deserved it more by having a principal share in the re-establishment of His Majesty upon the throne. Lord Chandos was immediately descended from Richard Brydges, of West Shefford, near Newbury, who married Jane, daughter of Sir William Spencer, of Wormleighton, ancestor to the Duke of Marlborough and Earl Spencer. James, the first Duke of Chandos, purchased the Shaw Estate of the representatives of the Dolman family, and frequently resided at Shaw House, which figures so conspicuously in connection with the Second Battle of Newbury. His second duchess, but third wife, Lydia Catherine, died at Shaw House in 1750, and was buried in Shaw Church.

LORD MOLYNEUX. Richard, 2nd Viscount, succeeded to the title on the death of his father in 1632. He actively supported the interests of Charles I., and with his brother Carlyll raised two regiments of horse and foot, with which they served during the course of the war. Lord Molyneux was in the battle of Worcester. He died soon afterwards, leaving no issue by his wife Lady Frances Seymour, eldest daughter of William, Marquis of Hertford, and the honours devolved upon his brother Carlyll, 3rd Viscount, who was outlawed by Parliament for his exertions on behalf of the Charleses. The Viscountcy of Molyneux is now held with the Earldom of Sefton.

HON. HENRY BERTIE. Son of the 1st Earl of Lindsey, and brother to Montagu, 2nd Earl, who was also engaged at Newbury. This gallant young nobleman fell in the early part of the fight, and his body, like that of his comrade Falkland, was not found till next day. He is mentioned in a letter written by Prince Rupert to the Earl of Essex, printed elsewhere (see Falkland). His body having been embalmed, was temporarily placed in a vault at All Saints' Church, Oxford, and was afterwards removed and interred in the chancel of Wytham Church, near the grave of his comrade the Hon. Edward Sackville.

SIR CHARLES LUCAS. Son of Thomas Lucas Esq., next brother to John, who was afterwards the first Baron Lucas of Shenfield, co. Essex. His family was one of the most distinguished in the kingdom for its valour and its sufferings in the royal cause. "He carryed 2000 horse to assist His Majesty, with whom we finde him eminent both for his directions and execution about the hill near *Newbery* and *Enborne Heath*, which he maintained with one regiment well disposed and lined with musqueteers, and a drake, with small shot against the gross of *Essex* his army, the leading-man of which he pistolled himself in the head of his troop, giving close fire himself, and commanding others to do the like." Lloyd's 'Memoires,' p. 475. Sir Charles was at the head of those loyalists who, in 1648, shut themselves up in Colchester, and defended it against the army of Fairfax for three months. When the garrison yielded to the enemy, their ammunition was reduced to a barrel and a half of powder; and their provisions to two horses and one dog. Sir Charles Lucas met with cruel treatment for his resolute defence of this place. He, and his friend Sir George Lisle, were ordered to be shot to death the same day on which the Parliamentary army entered the town. He begged a day's respite to prepare for death, but his request was refused, and he was executed August 28th, 1648. He died with the courage of a soldier and a christian. His faithful servant, who was a sorrowful spectator of his death, with great earnestness begged the executioner of his master to dispatch him also, as his life was become "his torment." The bodies of the two friends, Lucas and Lisle, were interred in a vault in the north aisle of St. Giles's Church, Colchester. At the Restoration a large flat marble slab was laid over their grave, at the expense of Lord Lucas, with the following inscription:—"Under this marble lie the bodies of the two most valiant cavaliers Sir Charles Lucas and Sir George Lisle, knights, who, for their eminent loyalty to their Sovereign, were, on the 28th August, 1648, by command of Sir Thomas Fairfax, (the General of the Parliament Army) in cold blood barbarously murdered." In Lord de Grey's 'Memoir of Sir Charles Lucas,' a tradition is related that George Villiers, Duke of Buckingham, who married Fairfax's only daughter, applied to Charles II. to have this inscription erased. The King mentioned it to Lord Lucas (the brother of Sir Charles), who said that he would obey his Majesty's commands if his Majesty would allow the following to be substituted:—"Sir Charles Lucas and Sir George Lisle were barbarously murdered for their loyalty to King Charles the First, and King Charles the Second ordered the memorial of their loyalty to be erased." Thereupon the King ordered the inscription to be cut more deeply than before. Whitelock, in a few words, expresses the grief of heart the King suffered for the catastrophe of his two brave soldiers. He says, "At the sight of a gentleman in deep mourning for Sir Charles Lucas, the King wept."

SIR GEORGE LISLE. Son of Cave Lisle, of Compton Darvill, co. Somerset, had his military education in the Netherlands. He commanded the 'forlorn hope' of foot at the first battle of Newbury, and signalized himself upon many occasions in the Civil Wars; particularly at the second battle of Newbury, where the King, who was an eye-witness of his bravery, knighted him on the field of battle. He did gallant service at Cheriton fight near Alresford, at Naseby, where he and Lord Bard commanded the left tertia of foot, and was Governor of Faringdon when Sir Robert Pye made an unsuccessful attack upon the garrison in 1646. In 1648 he rose for his Majesty in Essex, and was one of the royalists who so obstinately defended Colchester, and who died for their defence of it. Sir Charles Lucas was the first executed; as he fell, Lisle ran and kissed him, and immediately standing up: "Soldiers," he exclaimed, "come nearer; you are too far off." "Rest assured," they replied, "we'll hit you." "Comrades," answered Lisle, smiling, "I have been nearer and you missed me;" and he fell by the side of his friend.

SIR EDWARD WALDEGRAVE. Son of Sir Edward Waldegrave, Bart., of Staninghall, Norfolk. He died at Oxford, and was buried at St. Mary's Church in that city, 8th December, 1644.

SIR LEWIS KIRKE. Second son of Gervase Kirke, gent., merchant, of London, and of Dieppe, in France, and of Greenhill, in the parish of Norton, co. Derby, by Elizabeth, daughter of John Gowding (or Goudon) of Dieppe. He was born about 1600, and commanded one of the ships in the expedition to Newfoundland and Canada in 1626, under the chief command of his elder brother, Captain (afterwards Sir) David Kirke. He afterwards joined the Royal cause, and became a distinguished cavalier. He was knighted at Oxford, 23rd April, 1643, and was subsequently Governor of Bridgnorth; at his death he was one of the Band of Gentleman-Pensioners. He survived the Restoration; and his Will, in which he described himself as of the Savoy Parish, co. Middlesex, dated 21st August, 1663, was proved 7th October following, in the Prerogative Court of Canterbury, by his brother and nephew, both named John Kirk, father and son, to whom he left the reversion of his estate after the death of his wife. His widow, Dame Elizabeth, by whom he left no issue, did not long survive him, as she was buried at St. Giles' in the Fields, 20th December, 1663. Her maiden name was Haines, but she was a widow when she married Sir Lewis Kirke, and her first husband's name has not been ascertained.

SIR WILLIAM VAVASOUR. Son of Sir Thomas Vavasour, of Haslewood, in the county of York. Commander-in-chief of the Gloucestershire forces, engaged at Marston Moor, 1644, where his brother Thomas was slain. Being disgusted with the miscarriage of that great battle, he left the King's service and went over to Hamburgh. Afterwards he joined the Swedish service, and was killed under the walls of Copenhagen, 1658 or 1659.

SIR THOMAS ASTON, of Aston, in Cheshire. Created a Baronet by King Charles I., 25th July, 1628, and was subsequently in the Civil Wars a zealous supporter of the Royal cause. He died of wounds received at Stafford, 1645. He was a relative of Sir Arthur Aston, Governor of Reading, slain at the storming of Drogheda, Ireland, 1649.

SIR ANTHONY MANSEL, Governor of Cardiff, son of Sir Francis Mansel, Bart., of Trimsaren, co. Caermarthen.

SIR EDWARD STRADLING, of St. Donat's, Glamorganshire. Third Baronet. This gentleman, who, like his father and uncles, was a zealous and active Royalist, brought a troop of horse to the assistance of the King at Newbury, and after the loss of that day, retired to Oxford, where he died of consumption. He was buried in Jesus College Chapel, 21st June, 1644.

SIR MICHAEL WODEHOUSE. Governor of Ludlow. He had been sometime page to the Marquis of Hamilton, had served in Ireland, whence returning early in 1643, he was preferred to be Sergeant-Major-General of the army of Prince Charles, and to the command of his life-guards. (Webb's 'Civil War in Herefordshire,' vol i., p. 387.)

SIR JACOB ASTLEY. This distinguished soldier, more especially referred to in the account of the Second Battle, was father of Sir Bernard Astley. He served in the Netherlands under Prince Maurice and his brother Henry, and afterwards under Christian IV., King of Denmark, and Gustavus Adolphus, King of Sweden. He was ever in action during the Civil War, and for his signal services he was created Baron Astley of Reading, co. Berks, 4th November, 1644. The title became extinct on the death of his grandson, Jacob, in 1688.

SIR JOHN FRECHVILLE. For the services rendered by Sir John Frechville to the royal cause, and on his petition to the King, a warrant was signed by Charles I., at Oxford, 25th March, 1644, for his creation as a peer by the style of Lord Frechville of Staveley, Musard, and Fitz-Ralph. The preamble of the patent takes notice of the loyalty of the said Sir John Frechville, and his eminent services against the "rebels" at Kineton, Brentford, Marlborough, Newbury, and many other places, where he had received several wounds.

SIR JOHN HURRY, frequently styled "Urry" and "Hurrey," but always "Hurry" in his own signatures, was a Scotch mercenary, who had previously served in Germany under Lord Forth. He led the attack on Reading under Hampden, and did good service for the Parliament at Edgehill, and under Waller. Shortly before the battle of Chalgrove-field he threw up his commission of colonel of horse in the Parliamentary army, and gave the information which led to the successful attack on the Parliament's troops on that occasion, and to the death of Hampden. Hurry was allowed to convey the news to Oxford, and was knighted by the King. He was engaged at the first battle at Newbury, at Marston Moor, where he was second in command under Goring, who led the left wing of horse, and took part in several other actions while in the King's service. Shortly before the second battle at Newbury, when the King was on his march from Cornwall, intending to retire into winter quarters at Oxford, and while the armies of Waller, Manchester, and Cromwell were being concerted with the view of bringing the King to an engagement, Hurry consummated another act of baseness. Having represented to the King that he wished to retire to the continent, he obtained a pass for that purpose, and with the avowed object of providing greater security for his passage, he tried to obtain another pass from Sir William Waller, who refused to grant it, and sent him up to the Committee of both Kingdoms. Hurry underwent a lengthened examination before the Committee, and endeavoured to make his peace with the Parliament by betraying the weak and impoverished condition of the King's army which he had recently left, and by the promise of bringing over "a greater soldier than himself." On the 10th November following, Sir Henry Vane, one of the Committee, presented several letters to the Commons from the Earl of Manchester, Sir William Waller, and Sir William Balfour concerning Hurry's "coming in," but on account of his former inconstancy his services do not appear to have been accepted, and he was permitted to leave the kingdom. (See Common's Journals under date.) In the interim we find him present at the second battle of Newbury, where he charged at the head of the forlorn hope, and afterwards employed in endeavouring to persuade Sir John Boys, his old ally, to yield up Donnington Castle—a proposal, it need hardly be said, without effect. He was afterwards appointed to a command in the Parliament's army in Scotland; and was defeated by Montrose at Alderne, 10th May, 1645. Finally, he changed sides a third time, and joined his previous opponent Montrose, 7th May, 1646, at Duthel upon the Spey. He was taken prisoner by Ross of Balnagown, in an encounter with the Covenanters, Montrose being captured shortly after, and was hanged, with his leader (Montrose), Sir Francis Hay, Col. Spottiswode, and about forty more of the Marquis's followers at Edinburgh, 21st May, 1650. Hurry's colours were azure or deep blue, with the Thistle of Scotland, as usually represented, leaved, &c., of gold, flowered, proper, around which in letters of gold, "✠ NEMO ME IMPUNE LACESSIT;" fringe argent and azure. The motto is that of the Order of St. Andrew, to whose badge, *The Thistle*, it has reference.

BERNARD BROCAS, of Beaurepaire, near Sherborne St. John, Hants. He was one of the sons of Thomas Brocas (son of Sir Pexall Brocas) by Elizabeth, daughter of Robert Wingfield, of Upton, co. Northampton. The Brocas family, of Beaurepaire, near Sherborne St. John, in the church of which parish many of them are buried, is one of the oldest in England, and only in 1873 broke up from their ancient moated mansion where they had lived for 800 years. For 300 years they had been hereditary Masters of the Royal Buckhounds, which office passed out of their hands shortly before the Great Rebellion. Twice over in the history of their tenure of Beaurepaire they were ruined by their adherence to the cause of their Sovereign; first, when Sir Bernard Brocas, son of the more famous Sir Bernard, (buried in Westminster Abbey, and described in the 'Scrope and Grosvenor Roll' by Sir Harris Nicolas) was executed by Henry IV., in 1400, for his share in the conspiracy to restore Richard II.; and secondly, at the Great Rebellion. Thomas Brocas, the head of the family at the latter period, not only lost a large part of his property at Windsor, Eton, and other places, in the King's cause, but some of his sons. Bernard, concern-

APPENDIX. 103

ing whom the tradition of the family is that the incident mentioned at p. 68 took place at Newbury, was the fifth son; Robert, the eldest, is said to have lost his life at Oxford; and Thomas, the second, is said to have been killed at the battle of Worcester, and to have been found with the Brocas banner wrapped round his body. What was left of the Brocas estates passed, about the time of the Restoration, through Jane, the daughter and sole heiress of the said Robert, the eldest son of Thomas Brocas, to her husband, Sir William Gardiner, Bart., of Roche Court, Fareham, Hants, that property having come to the Brocases with Mary des Roches, in the time of Edward III.; but in 1678 Beaurepaire was made over by Sir William Gardiner to the son of the said Thomas Brocas (the younger), killed at Worcester, and remained in his family until 1873. The Gardiners still remain at Roche Court.

COL. ST. JOHN. Edward, third son of Sir John St. John, of Lydiard Tregoze, co. Wilts; nephew of Sir Oliver St. John, Viscount Grandison. Sir John had three sons killed in the King's service, viz. :—William, his second son, under Prince Rupert at the taking of Cirencester; Edward, above mentioned, at Newbury; and John, his fifth son, in the north. In the first edition of this work it is stated that Col. St. John fell in the first action at Newbury, his name occuring in a contemporary list of the slain, but it is evident from the inscription on his monument in Lydiard Tregoze Church, viz., April, 1645, that this could not have been the case. He most probably died from the effects of wounds received in the second battle fought in the preceding October. In the St. John pedigree given in Edmondson's 'Baronagium Genealogicum,' the words occur after the name of Col. Edward St. John "killed at Newbury," and the inscription on his monument infers that he fell in action. On the pedestal of the monument in Lydiard Tregoze Church, supporting the full size statue of Col. St. John, in armour, gilt, is a bas-relief representation of a troop of cavalry, in marching order, four abreast, with a trumpeter and an officer in front, and at either end a variety of emblematical trophies are represented.

COL. EDWARD VILLIERS. Youngest son of Sir Edward Villiers, kt., by Barbara, eldest daughter of Sir John St. John, of Lydiard Tregoze, co. Wilts, kt., and younger brother of the Viscount Grandison. He was knighted 7th April, 1680, and the following year became Knight-Marshall of the Royal Household. He died in 1689, and was buried in Westminster Abbey, July 2nd.

COL. WILL. LEGGE. Son of Edward Legge, vice-president of Munster. He eminently distinguished himself by his faithful attachment to the King and his son Charles II. He was engaged in both battles of Newbury, and it is said that the night after the first action, Col. Legge being in attendance on the King in his bed-chamber, his Majesty presented him with a hanger (a short curved sword) with agate handle set in gold, which he had that day worn, and would have knighted him with it had he consented. The hanger was kept in Col. Legge's family till the house at Blackheath was robbed in 1693. Col. Legge died in 1672 at his house in the Minories, London, granted him by Charles II., and was buried with great pomp in the adjoining Church of the Holy Trinity. He was the direct ancestor of the Earls of Dartmouth.

COL. RICHARD. Lloyd, in his 'Memoires,' thus notices this Royalist officer:—"Col. Richard, a Kentish gentleman of good personal valour (under the good old Earl of Cleaveland) both at Newberry in the Newberry fights, where he exceeded his command; at Sherburn, where he exceeded expectation, (upon the surrender of which place he was taken prisoner) and at Colchester where he exceeded belief." The name of

## THE FIRST BATTLE OF NEWBURY.

"Richard" is possibly a mistake or mis-spelling, and intended for "Colonel Richaud," who may have been a son of Sir Peter Richaut, of Aylesford, Kent, knighted at Whitehall, 30th April, 1641. The name is variously spelt. In the list of Knights it is "Rickhard," and one of Sir Peter's sons wrote his name "Riccard."

COL. DANIEL O'NEILL. Lieutenant-Colonel of Prince Rupert's regiment of horse; afterwards Groom of the Bedchamber to the King. "The Honourable Col. Oneal, the onely Protestant of his family; its a question whether gaining more honor by his hard service about *Gloucester*, and in both the *Newberries* with King *Charles* the First, or by his assiduous Negotiations and Messages posting from place to place (in *Holland*, where he was warned to the Countess of *Chesterfield*, in *France*, where he was welcome to the best *Cavaliers*, and *Germany*) for King *Charles* the Second, especially in the various Occasions, Opportunities, and Revolutions, 1659, at *Fontarabia, Scotland, Flanders, England*, &c., that made way for his Majesties' Restoration, who let him to farm the Post Office. He died 1664. Its more to be called an *Oneal*, than an Emperor in *Ireland*." (Lloyd's 'Memoires,' pp. 664-5.)

COL. MORGAN, of Weston, in Lancashire, who raised a troop of horse for the King at his own charge: his estate was seized by the Parliament and bestowed on the son of "King Pym."

COL. THOMAS EURE. The evidence as to the identity of this officer is conflicting, but he appears to have been the son of William, 6th Lord Eure.

COL. RICHARD PLATT. Among the State Papers, Domestic Series, vol. lxxxiii, Pub. Record Off., is a petition from Veronica, widow of Col. Richard Platt, to King Charles II., for a portion of the sum allotted for such sufferers. Her husband, she says, spent a fair estate in raising troops for the late King, and was slain at the first battle of Newbury, and she, a Venetian, is left in great necessity. Shortly after, a warrant anthorises a £100 to be paid the said Veronica Platt out of the Privy Seal Dormant.

There is also a petition, in the same series, from the widow of an artilleryman named Clarke, whom she describes as "gunner to the late King," and states he was slain at Newbury battle, that herself and children had been turned naked out of doors at Weymouth during the Protectorate, whipped out of the town, and her goods, worth £300, taken by Col. Sydenham. Mrs. Clarke appears to have found a second martial husband, who, she mentions, "has been a prisoner amongst the Turks," and prays a Tidesman's place for him in the Custom House, and some reparation for her losses and sufferings.

COL. CHARLES GERARD. Son of Sir Charles Gerard, knt., of Halsall, co. Lancaster. He had been brought up from his youth in the profession of arms upon the usual scene of European warfare, the Netherlands; and joined his Majesty King Charles I. at Shrewsbury soon after he had raised the royal standard, and became eminently distinguished among the Cavaliers:—first, at Kineton or Edgehill, where he received some dangerous wounds, and soon after at the taking of Lichfield, the first battle of Newbury, and the relief of Newark. General Gerard then accompanied Prince Rupert into Wales and acquired high reputation by his victories at Cardiff, Kidwelly, and Cærmarthen, and for his success in taking the Castle of Cardigan and other fortresses, and reducing the strong garrison of Haverfordwest, with the Castles of Picton and Carew. In consequence of such gallant services, he was made by the King Lieutenant-General of his horse,

APPENDIX. 105

and elevated to the peerage as Baron Gerard * of Brandon, 8th October, 1645. His Lordship after the Restoration was created 21st July, 1679, Viscount Brandon and Earl of Macclesfield; but in the time of James II. he was committed, with the Earl of Stamford and Lord Delamere, to the Tower, and condemned to death, but pardoned. He lived to see the Revolution, and in fact to witness, says Banks, "three singular occurrences in the annals of English history [he might have characterised them as the three *most* singular], 1st, the deposition and decapitation of King Charles I.; 2ndly, the Restoration of his son; and 3rdly, the Revolution and total expulsion of the royal family so recently restored." Besides his Lordship, there were of his family the following persons actively engaged upon the royal side in these unhappy conflicts:—

His Brothers { Edward Gerard, a colonel of foot, wounded in the first battle of Newbury.
Sir Gilbert Gerard, slain near Ludlow.

His Uncles { Sir Gilbert Gerard, governor of Worcester.
Ratcliffe Gerard, Lieut.-Colonel to his brother.
This gentleman had three sons,
Ratcliffe.            } All in the
John, put to death by Cromwell. } battle of
Gilbert, created a baronet.     } Kineton.

(Burke's 'Dormant and Extinct Peerage,' pp. 229-30.) Charles, Earl of Macclesfield, died 9th January, 1693-4, and was buried in Westminster Abbey.

COL. THOMAS RAWDON. The eldest son of Sir Marmaduke Rawdon, who took a gallant part in the defence of Basing House, and in 1645 was made Governor of Faringdon, which he held for the King with distinguished bravery. Col. Rawdon fought in the battles of Newbury, and accepted many dangerous commissions for the service of the King. Having thus become a marked man he fled from the persecution of the ruling powers, and took refuge with a kinsman and younger brother in the Canary Islands. Some time afterwards he returned to England, and died at Hoddesdon, co. Herts, in 1666. Buried at Broxbourne, 30th August, æt 54. (See 'Life of Marmaduke Rawdon of York,' Camden Soc., 1863.)

COL. PINCHBECK. Of Leicestershire. Received his death-wounds at the First Battle of Newbury.

CAPT. THOMAS BAGEHOT. At the Restoration Capt. Bagehot applied for re-admission to the place of Groom of the King's Chamber in ordinary, which he held under the late King; and recounts his services at Newbury. (State Papers, Domestic Series, vol. xxii.)

CAPT. BASIL WOODD. Son of Basil Woodd, LL.D., Chancellor of St. Asaph and Rochester, and High Commissioner. In a petition presented by Capt. Woodd at the Restoration, he states:—"I have received several shots in my head, and one in my arm, which troubles mee many times. Several horses were shott under mee, one at Roundway-down, another at Newbury fight." Two other sons of Dr. Woodd

---

*His Lordship was first created Earl of *Newberry*, but the title was changed to *Macclesfield*. [The late Col. Chester, the editor of the 'Westminster Abbey Registers,' says that he cannot find any authority for this statement made in 'Burke's Extinct Peerage.' Charles Fitzroy, natural son of Charles II., by the Duchess of Cleveland, was created *Baron of Newbury*, Duke of Southampton, &c., in 1675, four years before, and it does not seem likely that the title shoult have been duplicated. It is quite possible, however, that "Earl of Newbury" was the title first selected, and that the alteration was made before the patent passed the Great Seal ?]

O

served the King, one of whom fell at Preston ; a daughter married the brave Col. Bowles who was killed in Alton Church, 1643. Basil Thomas Woodd, Conyngham Hall, Knaresborough, great-great-great-grandson of Dr. Basil Woodd, has in his possession the Star of the Mantle of the Order of the Garter, traditionally held as the parting memorial given to Capt. Basil Woodd by Charles 1. on the morning of his execution.

CAPT. CLIFTON. Francis Clifton, son of Sir Cuthbert Clifton, of Westby, Lancashire.

CAPT. NEWMAN. See note, p. 28.

GEORGE PORTER. This royalist adherent is mentioned in 'A perticular Relation of the Victory gotten at Newberry the 20th of September 1643, by His Majesties Forces over the Rebells,' written by Lord George Digby, as being wounded in the battle, while serving as a volunteer in the King's army. He was most probably the eldest son and heir of Endymion Porter, Esq., Groom of the Bed-chamber to Charles I., by Olive, 4th daughter and co-heir of John, Lord Boteler. He was comptroller of the King's Post in 1640 (but must have then been very young), and compounded for his estate 23rd March, 1645-6, by a fine of £1000. Subsequently he became a Groom of the Bed-chamber to Charles II. He married Diana, daughter and co-heir of George Goring, Earl of Norwich, and widow of Thomas Covert, of Slaugham, Sussex, by whom he had, with other issue, George, his son and heir, who was Vice-Chamberlain to Catherine, Queen of Charles II., and a daughter Mary, who married Phillip, 2nd Viscount Strangford. He died 11th December, 1683, aged 63. "Loyal bloud," says Lloyd in his 'Memoires,' "like *Harvies* went round the *Porters* from the highest to the meanest, 26 of the name having eminently suffered for his Majesty."

CAPT. GWYNNE. Was a retainer in the household of Charles I. before the commencement of the Civil War, and employed in training the children of that unfortunate monarch to military exercises. He natur-ally engaged in the royal service, and seems to have distinguished himself by his personal courage and activity. After the execution of the King, he followed the banner of his son (Charles II.) in the most difficult enterprises in which it was displayed. Gwynne was with Montrose in his last unhappy attempt. He afterwards served under the Duke of York in the fight before Dunkirk, and other actions in Flanders. At the Restoration he appears to have experienced his share of the neglect with which Charles II. treated the old cavaliers.

§ 2. PARLIAMENTARY OFFICERS AND OTHERS.

EARL OF ESSEX. Robert Devereux, Earl of Essex, was only son of the unfortunate favourite of Queen Elizabeth, and inherited much of his father's popularity. He acquired, in the Low Countries, a great reputation as a soldier; a kind of merit that was despised by James I., and overlooked by Charles. His courage was great, his honour was inflexible; but he rather waited for, than sought opportunities of fighting; and knew better how to gain, than improve a victory. When he took the command of the Parliamentary Army, he was better qualified than any man in the kingdom for that post; but was soon eclipsed by

APPENDIX. 107

a new race of soldiers, who, if not his superiors in the art of war, went far beyond him in spirit and enterprise. He died the 14th of September, 1646, and his death helped to open a way for the ambition of Cromwell. An account of the discovery of the burial place of the Earl appears on page 86.

LORD ROBARTES, OR ROBERTS. John, Lord Robartes, 2nd Baron of Truro, co. Cornwall, created. Viscount Bodmin and Earl of Radnor, 1679. "That which in the first place crownes all his actions, was the fierce and famous battell at Newberry, where this noble lord lead on the battell in his owne person, charging the maine body of the King's army with such resolution, as did inliven the London Brigade to second and relieve them suddenly: yet notwithstanding this noble champion stood to the fight, and lead up other souldiers, and incouraged them, and so continued untill the enemy retreated with great losse of men and armes." (Ricraft's 'Survey of England's Champions,' 1647.) At the Restoration he was well received by Charles II., and appointed a Privy Councillor, Lord Privy Seal, and Viceroy of Ireland. He died at Chelsea in 1685. Dr. Calybute Downing, the famous Puritan divine, Rector of West Ilsley, near Newbury, was chaplain to Lord Robartes' regiment.

LORD GREY OF GROBY. Thomas Grey, son of Henry, 2nd Lord Grey, created Earl of Stamford, 26th March, 1628. He was one of the King's judges, and his signature appears on the warrant of execution.

SIR JOHN MEYRICK. He had served in the royal army, and was knighted by the King, but he deserted to the Parliament, and was made Sergeant-Major-General by the Earl of Essex, and afterwards, at the siege of Reading, appointed General of the Ordnance, being superseded in his former office by the famous Skippon, by order of Parliament. Sir John Meyrick's Will was proved in 1659.

SIR PHILIP STAPLETON. Inherited "but a moderate estate in Yorkshire, and, according to the custom of that country, had spent his time in those delights which horses and dogs administer." A Member of the Long Parliament; joined in the prosecution of Strafford; opposed the self-denying ordinance, 1644. Withdrew beyond sea, and died at Calais as soon as he landed. "Was denied burial upon imagination that he had died of the plague." ('Peacock's Army List,' p. 25.) His Will was proved in 1647. Stapleton's cuirassiers were called "Essex's Life-Guard," and corresponded to Lord Bernard Stuart's cavalier troop.

SIR WILLIAM CONSTABLE. Son and heir of Sir Richard Constable, of Flamborough, co. York, Kt., by Anne, daughter and heiress of John Hussey, of Driffield. He was knighted by the Earl of Essex, in Ireland, in 1599, and created a Baronet, 29th June, 1611. He had been Colonel of a Regiment of Foot, and some time Governor of Gloucester, and was one of the signers of the death-warrant of King Charles I. His Will, dated 13th December, 1654, was proved 18th July, 1655, by his relict Dame Dorothy, who was the eldest daughter of Thomas, first Lord Fairfax. He left no issue, and the title became extinct. He was buried in Westminster Abbey, but, not only were his remains exhumed after the Restoration and thrown into the common pit in the churchyard, but his estates were especially excepted in the general pardon subsequently granted by King Charles II. His relict died 9th March, 1656, and was buried in the Church of St. Mary Bishophill Senior, York.

SIR WILLIAM BROOKE. It is very probable that this Parliamentary officer fell at the first battle of Newbury, as on the 28th September,

## THE FIRST BATTLE OF NEWBURY.

**1643**, the day that public thanks were given to certain members of the Commons engaged at Newbury, it was ordered that Sir Philip Stapleton should bring in an Ordinance "for the sequestring and disposing of the Michaelmas rents of *Sir Wm. Brooke*, to the use of his Lady and family; and for the sequestring of the estate if it descend to Sir John Brooke." The Ordinance for "sequestring the estate of Sir Wm. Brooke, who lately died in the service of the Parliament," was assented to by the Commons on the 9th of October following, wherein Sir John Brooke is referred to as "now in actual arms against the Parliament." Sir William Brooke was the only son of George Brooke (3rd but 2nd surviving son of William Brooke, 5th Lord Cobham, and younger brother of Henry, 6th and last Lord Cobham of the first creation). George Brooke was attainted and executed as a participator in "Raleigh's conspiricy," 5th December, 1603. He left issue, by Elizabeth his wife, daughter of Thomas, Lord Burgh, or Borough, one son, William. This William was restored in blood, and was created a Knight of the Bath at the coronation of King Charles I., in 1625. He married twice, but left issue only three daughters, and therefore left no direct heir male. Sir John Brooke (son and heir of Henry, younger son of George, 4th Lord Cobham) was in 1645, created Lord Cobham—the old title having expired in 1618, by the death of Henry, 6th Lord, while under attainder. This Sir John Brooke appears to have been the next male heir of Sir William, and accords with the statement in the Commons Journal.

SIR WILLIAM BALFOUR. Of the family of Balfour, of Pitcullo, co. Fife, Scotland, gentleman of the King's privy-chamber, and Lieutenant of the Tower of London. Though he had great obligations to the Court, he made no scruple of attaching himself to its most violent opponents. He was turned out of his office as Lieutenant of the Tower a little before the breaking out of the Civil War, and was succeeded by Col. Lunsford. At the battle of Edgehill, Sir William Balfour commanded the reserve, and did eminent service. He led also the right wing of horse at the Second Battle of Newbury. His Will was proved in 1661.

SIR SAMUEL LUKE. Governor of Newport-Pagnell in 1645. The supposed original of Butler's 'Hudibras,' and author of the 'Journal of the Siege of Reading,' printed in Coate's history of that town.

MAJOR-GENERAL SKIPPON. Philip Skippon was Sergeant-Major-General of the Parliamentary army, Major-General of the London militia, and Governor of Bristol. After the passing of the "self-denying ordinance," he was preferred to the same post in the army that he held before; to which he was thought justly to be entitled on the ground of merit. He was president of the Council of War under the Earl of Essex, and both in the cabinet and the field approved himself an excellent soldier. He commanded the infantry at the battle of Naseby, where he exerted himself with his usual intrepidity. "Magnanimous Skippon," says May, "was grievously wounded, yet would not forsake the battle; but with all possible endeavours performed his part, till the victory was obtained." He was a zealous republican, and went the greatest lengths with that party. His name frequently occurs as a member of the House of Commons in the Interregnum. He was also one of Cromwell's Council of State, and had £1,000 a year in lands of inheritance assigned him by the Parliament for his services. The Duke of Buckingham's estate at Bletchley was given to him, on that nobleman's forfeiture; but at the Restoration it reverted to its right owner. Skippon's colours were:—"From the dexter corner blue clouds and

## APPENDIX. 109

therefrom issuing a naked arm and hand proper, holding a sword proper, hilted or, before this, paleways, a book closed and clasped or; beneath these, on two lines in writing ' Ora et pugna. Juvat et juvabit, Jehovah ; ' fringed gold and argent." (Prestwich's ' Respublica,' p. 38.)

MAJOR-GENERAL DEANE. The well-known Parliamentary General-at-Sea. He was the eldest son of Edward Deane, of Pinnock, co. Gloucester, Esq., by his second wife, Ann Wase. (For an elaborate and admirable account of him and his career, consult his 'Life,' by the Rev. John Bathurst Deane, published by him in 1870.) He was killed during the naval engagement with the Dutch on the 2nd June, 1653, when only in his 42nd year. He married at the Temple Church, 21st May, 1647, Mary, daughter of John Grimsditch, of Knottingley, York, Esq., who survived him, and married at St. Bartholomew the Great, London, 2nd January, 1654-5, Col. Edward Salmon, another well-known Parliamentarian. Colonel [he is described as "Colonel" in the Register] Deane's remains were ignominiously exhumed after the Restoration, and, with those of others equally eminent in maintaining the honour of the British flag, thrown into a common pit in the churchyard. His Will, dated 31st March, 1653, was proved 20th January, 1653-4, by his relict. He left two daughters, Mary and Hannah. The stupid stories propagated by his political enemies as to his vulgar origin and early career, have been abundantly disproved by his recent biographer; and posterity is already doing justice to his memory.

LIEUT.-GENERAL MIDDLETON. See Appendix to the Second Battle.

COL. ARTHUR GOODWIN. Of Upper Winchendon, co. Bucks. The intimate friend and neighbour of John Hampden, and his colleague in the representation of the County of Bucks in the Long Parliament. Like him, he held a command under the Earl of Essex, and was quartered at Aylesbury in the first campaign. The following letter from Col. Goodwin to his daughter Lady Wharton, is exceptionally interesting from the circumstances under which it was written :—" Deere Jenny,— I am now heere at Hampden in doinge the last duty for the deceased owner of it, of whome every honest man hath a share in the losse, and therefore will likewise in the sorrowe : In the loss of such a friend to my owne particular, I have no cause of discontent, butt rather to bless God that he hath not accordinge to my deserts bereft me of you, and all the comforts deerest to me : All his thoughts and endeauours of his life was zealously in for this cause of Gods, w$^{ch}$ he continued in all his sickness, even to his death ; for all I can heere the last words he spake was to mee, though he liued six or 7 howers after I came away as in a sleepe: truly Jenny (and I know you may easily be persuaded to it) he was a gallant man, an honest man, an able man, and take all, I know nott to any man liueinge second, God now in mercy hath rewarded him. . . . I have writt to London for a black suite, I pray let me begg of you a broad black Ribbon to hange about my Standard. . . . . . I would we all lay it to heart, that God takes away the best amongst us, I pray the Lord to bless you. . . . Y$^r$ ever, deere Jenny, most affectionate father, A$^r$· Goodwin. Hampden, June 26, 1643."* Col. Goodwin did not live very long after the death of his friend Hampden, but the exact date of his death cannot be ascertained. His Will was proved 11th November, 1644, by Philip, Lord Wharton, and Jane his wife, daughter of the deceased.

COL. EDWARD MASSEY, OR MASSIE. Major-General. Originally an active Parliamentarian, and the celebrated Governor of Gloucester

---

* Carte's MSS., Letters, Bibl. Bodl. v. 103, No. 40.

during its siege; subsequently as active a Royalist, and, in the words of Clarendon, "looked upon as a martyr for the Presbyterian interest." He was the fifth son of John Massie, of Coddington, Cheshire, by Anne, daughter of Richard Grosvenor, of Eaton.

COL. SHEFFIELD. Younger son of the Earl of Mulgrave.

COL. JOHN MELDRUM. There appears to have been two eminent military men of this name, both Scotchmen, and both named *John*, who are often confounded in contemporaneous history. *Sir* John Meldrum, who was knighted at Windsor 6th August, 1622, was undoubtedly the one who took part in the memorable actions at Newark, Hull, Scarborough, &c., and received his death-wound at the last place. His Will, dated 24th May, 1645, was proved 2nd June, 1647. The Meldrum named in the list of Parliamentary Officers who fought at Newbury was no doubt *Colonel* John Meldrum, who was killed at Alresford, Hants. His name occurs in the List of the Parliamentary Army in 1642, as Lieutenant of the Second Troop of Horse, under the general command of William, Earl of Bedford; and he evidently obtained rapid promotion. As the Battle of Bramdean (or Cheriton) Heath, near Alresford, took place on the 29th March, 1644, and his nuncupative Will was made on the 8th of April following, it is probable he was mortally wounded on that day; or, the two dates may be identical, allowing for the difference between Old and New Style. The Will states that he was "very much wounded." It was proved 16th November, 1648, by his relict Jane, then a minor, who, in 1655, petitioned the Parliament as the widow of the "eldest colonel of horse in the late army," slain at Cheriton fight. She has waited seven years for the arrears of her husband without receiving anything whatever, and is starving, applies for aid "among other distressed widows whom God has put it into your heart to relieve." Col. Meldrum's remains were included amongst those of other eminent Parliamentarians which were exhumed after the Restoration, and thrown into a common pit in St. Margaret's churchyard.

COL. NORTON. See Appendix to the Second Battle.

COL. DALBIER. A Dutch engineer and Quarter-Master-General in the Parliamentary army. "It was from Dalbier," says Heath, "that Cromwell first of all learnt the mechanical part of soldiering; and who helped him to drill his Ironsides." We find Dalbier's name mentioned in the old Chronicles as early as 1628, when it was proposed that he and Sir William Balfour should raise 1000 German horse for the English expedition against France, a project, however, not carried into effect. He appears to have entered the Parliament's service soon after the breaking out of hostilities, and distinguished himself by his valour and conduct on many occasions. He was at the battle of Edgehill, at Brentford fight, and several minor actions in 1642. In the month of May, 1643, he was a prisoner for debt in the King's Bench, but by some means obtained his liberty, whereupon a suit was commenced against Sir John Lenthall, the Governor, for permitting his escape. The proceedings were stayed by the order of the Commons; Dalbier having become "a great officer in the army." He was engaged in the first battle of Newbury, at Cheriton Down, near Alresford, 29th March, 1644, where he was wounded, and served with Essex in Cornwall, where he narrowly escaped being taken prisoner. In May, 1645, he was under accusation and restraint, but was released, and took part the same year in the battle of Naseby, the capture of Winchester Castle and Basing House, where he was second to Cromwell in command, and received the thanks of Parliament for his services. He

APPENDIX. 111

conducted the final siege of Donnington Castle, which was surrendered to him, on Articles, 30th March, 1646. Being left out of the New Model Army and dissatisfied with his treatment, he joined the rising of the Earl of Holland, and was killed in an Inn at St. Neots, Huntingdon, July 5th, 1648.

CAPT. HUNT. An officer in one of the city regiments of trained-bands, slain in the First Battle of Newbury. The 'Mercurius Aulicus' of October 1st, 1643, has the following notice of Captain Hunt:—"A confect. maker, in St. Mary, Woolnooth. This Hunt was the first that committed sacrilege in his own parish church (after John Pym's orders for defacing of churches), pulling down the cross from the King's crown over the font, lopping off the hands and pulling out the eyes from the tombs and monuments, cutting off the cherubim's wings placed upon the arches, and (which both Christian and Jew will abhore) blotting out the dreadful name of God as it stood over the commandments, in Hebrew, Greek, and Latin. In this Hunt's pockets were found his watch, his commission from the rebels, an assessment roll of his neighbours at Hackney parish, besides £16 in money, which the souldier had who stript off his Buff."

CAPT. FRANCIS ST. BARBE. He was fourth and youngest, but second surviving son of Henry St. Barbe, Esq., of Ashington, co. Somerset, and Broadlands, Hants. His name occurs in the list of killed in the first engagement at Newbury.

CAPT. HAMMOND. This was probably the same Capt. Hammond who was engaged in the Second Battle, at Shaw, and the King's gaoler at Carisbrooke Castle.

CAPT. CHARLES FLEETWOOD, afterwards the distinguished Parliamentary general, the son of Sir William Fleetwood, cupbearer to King Charles I., and comptroller of Woodstock-park. On the breaking out of the war between King and Parliament, young Fleetwood declared for the latter. He commanded a regiment of cavalry in 1644, and held the rank of Lieut.-General at the battle of Worcester, to the gaining of which, by Cromwell, he largely contributed. He married the Protector's daughter after the death of her first husband Ireton, and was appointed commander of the forces in Ireland in 1652. He strongly opposed Cromwell assuming the title of King in 1657; and was soon after superseded in Ireland by Henry Cromwell, the Protector's youngest son. On the death of Cromwell, he concurred in the appointment of Richard as his successor, but soon after joined in inducing him to resign, and thus paved the way for the Restoration. He died 4th October, 1692, and was buried in Bunhill Fields.

CAPT. CHARLES PYM. Only surviving son of John Pym, of Brymmore, in the county of Somerset, M.P. for Tavistock, one of the most celebrated actors in the eventful drama which terminated in the execution of Charles I. Capt. Charles Pym commanded a troop of horse in the Parliament's service, and was a member of the Parliament of 1640, and of the Pensionary Parliament of 1661. He married Catherine, daughter of Sir Gilbert Gerrard, Bart., of Harrow-on-the-Hill, and was created a Baronet, 14th July, 1663. He died about 1672. His only son Charles succeeded as second Baronet, but died unmarried, being killed in a tavern brawl in Old Fish Street, London, 4th May, 1688, and was buried 8th May at Harrow-on-the-Hill, when the title became extinct. The family estates passed to his sister Mary, who married Sir Thomas Hales, second Baronet, of Bekesbourne, Kent.

WILLIAM TWISSE, D D., Rector of Newbury. The son of a clothier at Newbury, whose father had immigrated from Germany. He was born at Speenhamland about 1575, in a house said to have stood in the Lamb-and-Castle Yard. He was educated at Winchester and Oxford, became a Fellow of New College, 11th March, 1597-8, and was presented to the living of Newbury in 1620 by the Prince of Wales, afterwards Charles I. Twisse was appointed Prolocutor of the Assembly of Divines under the Commonwealth; but on account of his age and infirmities he was soon unable to attend the sittings of the Assembly, and in a few months was taken ill and laid upon his bed, where he lingered for about a year, and died July 20th, 1646. His funeral in Westminster Abbey was attended by most of the members of the House of Commons and the whole of the Assembly of Divines, but his remains were included among those disinterred after the Restoration. His Will, dated 9th September, 1645, with a codicil, 30th June, 1646, was proved 6th August in the latter year. He would seem not to have been so reduced in circumstances as the accounts of him usually represent, for, besides other not inconsiderable legacies, he bequeathed his manor of Ashampstead, Berks, to trustees for the benefit of his younger son. He left four sons and three daughters, but his wife, Frances, daughter of Barnabas Colnett, of Combly, Isle of Wight, had predeceased him. There is a portrait of Dr. Twisse in the vestry of Newbury Church, which appears, from the Churchwarden's accounts, to have been either painted by, or purchased of, one Richard Jerome, in 1647, a year after Twisse's death, at a cost of one pound fifteen shillings. The following is the entry in the Churchwarden's book:—

"1647.—Paid to Richard Jerome for Dr. Twisse his picture. 1. 15. 0."

Dr. Ward, the antiquary, mentions this picture as having been much damaged by cleaning, in 1745.

ROBERT CODRINGTON. The author of the account of the battle, originally printed in 1646, from which extracts have been taken, was second son of Robert Codrington, Esq., of Codrington, co. Gloucester. He was elected Demy of Magdalen College, Oxford, 29th July, 1619, when he was about 17 years of age, and took his M.A. degree in 1626. After that he travelled into several foreign lands, and at his return lived a gentleman's life, first in Norfolk, where he married, and finished his life in London by the plague in the year 1665. He published many pieces on different subjects in his life-time, and left several manuscripts prepared for the press. Though Codrington plainly declares himself a Parliamenteer, his history, so far as it goes, is the least exceptionable and the most comprehensive of any writings on the same subject, in those times; for, besides the character of his hero, the Earl of Essex, he gives us the general opinion, and the ground of the first part of the Civil War; and seems to relate the natural facts without aggravation. He always speaks of the King's Majesty with respect, ascribing the ill-conduct of his affairs and bad success to the wickedness and heat of the counsels he received; and heartily wishing a good and lasting reconciliation and peace between the King and his Parliament. ('Life and death of Robert, Earl of Essex,' Harleian Miscell., vol. i., pp. 211, 212.)

APPENDIX. 113

VII. EXTRACTS FROM THE CERTIFICATES OR RETURNS OF THOSE PERSONS WHO, PURSUANT TO AN ORDER OF THE HOUSE OF COMMONS, MADE THE PROTESTATION IN THE COUNTY OF BERKS, 30TH JULY, 1641.

This Protestation was reported and agreed to in the Commons, and ordered to be made by every member of that House, on the 3rd May, 1641. It was agreed to by the Lords, and ordered to be made by every member of their House on the following day. Subsequently it was resolved that the Protestation is fit to be made by every one, and that that person soever who shall not make the same is unfit to bear office in the Church or Commonwealth, and that it is "A Shibboleth to discover a true Israelite."

The Protestation runs as follows:—I, A. B., do in the presence of Almighty God promise, vow, and protest to maintain and defend as far as lawfully I may with my Life, Power, and Estate, the true *Reformed Protestant Religion* expressed in the Doctrine of the *Church of England* against all Popery and Popish Innovations, within this Realm, contrary to the same Doctrine, and according to the duty of my allegiance to His Majesty's Royal Person, Honour, and Estate, as also the Power and Privileges of Parliaments, the lawful Rights and Liberties of the Subjects, and every Person that maketh this Protestation in whatsoever he shall do in the lawful Pursuance of the same; and to my power, and as far as lawfully I may I will oppose and by all good Ways and Means endeavour to bring to Condign Punishment all such as shall, either by Force, Practice, Counsels, Plots, Conspiracies, or otherwise, do anything to the contrary of any thing in this present Protestation contained, and further, that I will in all just and honourable ways endeavour to preserve the Union and Peace betwixt the Three Kingdoms of England, Scotland, and Ireland: and neither for Hope, Fear, nor other Respect, shall relinquish this Promise, Vow, and Protestation.—LORDS JOURNAL, IV. 234.

The extracts following are made from the original returns preserved at the House of Lords, by permission of Sir William Rose, K.C.B., Clerk of Parliaments.

BRIMPTON PARISH—Mr. Thos. Bird (minister) and parishioners.

CHADDLEWORTH PARISH—Thomas Nelson, Thomas Tipping, John Blagrave, and several members of the Bartholomew and Pocock families.

CHIEVELEY PARISH—Richard Nixon (vicar), John Money, Laurence Money, Richd. Pocock, sen., Richd. Pocock, jun., Edward Aubery, sen., John Aubery, jun., John Dolman, jun.; Gyles Smith, and Peter Holdways, churchwardens; Edward Paty, and Richard Chaulk, overseers; Stephen Butler, constable.

COMPTON PARISH—Richard Hasell, Minister, Richard Pottinger, sen., Richard Pottinger, jun., Robert Ffetiplace.

ENBORNE PARISH—Edward Blandy, Mr. William Elk, jun., George Mathews, John Mathews, William Lovelock, Bartholomew Hasell, Wm. Elk, Rector of Enborne; Mr. Philip Hedd and Edward Bromley, Churchwardens; Paul Hunt, High Constable. But Wm. Holmes, Sen. above 4 score years old and deaf and feeble; and John Holmes, jun., a

P

simple young man and lame; and Wm. Plantin, 3 score and 12 or above, and infirm and decayed both inwardly and outwardly in mind and all other means, and Saml. Lyford, and John Warner, poore disabled men, and Francis Belcher, a yonge swageringe stranger who hath lately at Newtown married Margaret Nalder, and is now living with his wife at Enborne, have not made protestation.

FRILSHAM—The Protestation taken in the public congregation and signed by Samuel Watkins, pastor there, Richd. Smallbone, Luke Hore, and members of the Fisher, Pocock, Newbery, Chamberlain, and other families.

GREENHAM ( a Tything of Thatcham)—All most willingly took the Protestation, not one refusing. John Howes, John Warde, Thos. Barnes, James Osgood, Edward Kiggill, Thos. Collins, sen., Thos. Collins, jun., Wm. Hawkins, Jno. Degweede, Jno. Pocock, Joseph Hickman, John Hickman; Simon Ffarant, Curate; Thos. Osgood, constable; Thos. Knighton, churchwarden; Edward Green, overseer; Thos. Parker, tythingman.

HAMSTED-MARSHALL—Thomas Slocock, Jo. Slocock, Ric. Slocock, and others. All the residents in the parish signed, except Wm. Bunn now four score, and Thos. Pary who is in Wiltshire and has not had warning, both are good protestants and would not refuse to sign the protestation. Saml. Paine, curate; John May and Thos. George, churchwardens. The names of Baker, Dore, Bartholomew, Harding, Lovegrove, Tubb, Holmes, Crooke, and Toms appear as residents in the parish at this time.

HAMSTED-NORRIS—Wm. Moore, vicar. Protestation signed by the Palmer, Dore, Boseley, Matthews, Abery, Goddard, Marriner, Kimber, and Howse families. The following refused, Henry Prince, Andrew Prince, Richard Brabrooke, Esq.

WEST ILSLEY—John Head, minister, &c.

EAST ILSLEY—Joseph Warner, minister, &c. Refusals—John Boulton, Henry Lipeat, recusants. Signed, Giles Pocock, Jo. Ambrose, churchwardens; James Pottinger, constable.

INKPEN—Richard Money the elder, Richard Money the younger, John Brickenden, rector; Wm. Kirke, Ffortunatus Hambling, churchwardens; Humphrey Banks and William Bayley are from home.

KINTBURY—Sir John Dorrell, John Dorrell, Esq., Alex. Browne, John Gunter, Robert Elgar, John Elgar, Robt. Field, Wm. Hazell, Robt. Ffidler, Richd. Blandy. *Wallingtons*—Sir Jno. Kingsmill, Charles Gunter, Marmaduke Gunter. *Inglewood and Balsden*—Thos. Lowder, Thos. Webbe, Willm. Webbe, James Choke. *Tything of Holt*—Willm. Nalder, James Nalder, — Faithfull; Francis Allen, vicar; Edwd. Butcher, Robt. Field, churchwardens; Thos. Mountigue, Jas. Wiggins, overseers.

LECKHAMSTEAD—Giles Hatt, Richd. Blagrave, Henry Blagrave. Signed also by parishioners of the name of Adnams, Head, Maskell, Selwood, Whistler, Wernham, Buckeridge, &c. Henry Greetham, clerke, Giles Spicer, constable, Richd. Hatt, overseer, John Spicer, Edwd. Averill, churchwardens.

MIDGHAM—John Tull, absent, Thos. White, Thos. Bird, absent at court, Thos. Prior, curate, Thos. Tull, Richd. May, churchwardens.

NEWBURY—Willm. Pearse, maior, Willm. Twisse, rector, Timothy Avery, gent., Richd. Tomlyne, Esq., Richd. Avery, gent., Richd. Waller, gent., Hugh Hawkins, gent., John Houghton, gent., John Cooke, gent., John Wheatly, curate, John Barksdale, gent., John Edmonds, Gabriell Cox, Richd. Holwell, Edd. Trenchard, Esq., Henry

APPENDIX. 115

Trenchard, gent., Thos. Knight, Adam Head, John Hamblin, Joell Dance, Richd. Cox, John Bruce, Mr. Dunce, Esq., Philip Weston, Wm. Waller, Wm. Bew, John Merryman, gent., Nathaniel Hempsteed, Edwd. Blandy, Ed. Avery, James Purdue, Thos. Pearse, John Dibley, Francis Norris, Willm. Smart, John Waulter, Thos. Wilson, Joseph Gilmore, Alexdr. Gilmore, sen., Alexdr. Gilmore, jun., George Cowslade, Thos. Cowslade, Richd. Shaw, John Mundy, gent., Thos. Virtue, Thos. Sansum, Wm. Curteis, Joseph Nalder, W. Arundell, W. Nash, Mr. E. Lovelock,gent., Wm. Goddin, Richd. Bowyer, Thos. Jemmett, John Hoare, Thos. Somersby, Thos. Gray, &c., &c. No refusals to sign the Protestation in the parish of Newbury, Wm. Twisse, rector, Briant Linch, Ralph Kingham, churchwardens. The Protestation taken before Humphrey Dolman and Roger Knight, two of His Majesty's Justices of the County of Berks, 1641.

PEASEMORE—Ed<sup>d</sup>. Lyford, rector, John Stampe, gent. Signed also by Dew, Bew, Drew, Tanner, Fisher, Aubery, Garlick, Hide, Caulcott, Hatt, Clark, Harding, and others.

SHAW-CUM-DONNINGTON—Francis Rowland, sen., Francis Rowland, jun., Wm. Bosley, Thos Dolman, Richd. Money, John Blagrave, John Nalder, John Graye, Richd. Kinge, Wm. Portlucke, Mr. Griffin Doncastle, and Mr. Richard Smith, of Grange, John and Robt. Hastinges, Gyles Stampe, John Royston, rector, Roger Whatley and Wm. Snowswell, churchwardens, Thos. Shipton, John Norcroft, and John Challis, overseers of Poore.

LITTLE SHEFFORD—John Prime, rector. With the exception of the Rector, none of the parishioners could sign their names, but all put their "mark."

GREAT SHEFFORD—Jo. Nixon, rector. Geo. Browne, Esq., Elleanor Browne, his wife, Elleanor Browne his daughter—These desired a long time to consider, which was refused. George Browne son of Geo. Browne, aforesaid, and Morrice Jonathan, servant—would sign in all except the part against Popery. Anne Cooper, Anne Northover—professing themselves simple maidens requested time to consider on the part of religion. Elizbh. Wylder, Ursula Wylder, widow, daughter of said Elizabeth—absolutely refuse to sign the Protestation. John Arundell, constable and churchwarden.

SPEEN—Thos. Castillian, Esq., Jo. Barker, and others, John Barker, minister.

WASING—Thos. Walker or Walthen, rector.

WELFORD—Hinton, Esq., and others, John Mundy, clerk.

WINTERBORNE DANVERS in the parish of Chieveley—Henry Greetham, clerk, Laurence Head, Thomas Kimber, and others.

## VIII. LIST OF THE SEQUESTRATORS OF THE ESTATES OF "DELINQUENTS, PAPISTS, SPYES, AND INTELLI- GENCERS," FOR THE COUNTY OF BERKS; APPOINTED UNDER ORDINANCE OF THE LORDS AND COMMONS, APRIL 1ST, 1643.

Sir Francis Pile, Bart. (1); Sir Francis Knollys, jun., Knt. (2); Peregrine Hobby (3); Henry Marten (4); Roger Knight (5); Henry Powl (6); Thomas Fettiplace (7); and Tanfield Vachell (8), Esquires.\*

(1). SIR FRANCIS PILE, second Baronet. Sat for the County of Berks in the second Parliament of 1640, succeeding on the disablement of Mr. John Fettiplace in 1646. The first of the family who was created a baronet was Francis, of Compton-Beauchamp, who received that honour from Charles I , 12th September, 1628, for his services to the Crown. He married Elizabeth, daughter of Sir Francis Popham, of Littlecote, knt., and dying in 1635. he was succeeded by his eldest son, the member for the county above mentioned. The baronetcy became extinct 4th May, 1761, on the demise of the 6th baronet.

(2). SIR FRANCIS KNOLLYS, JUN., second son of the famous Sir Francis Knollys, K.G., Treasurer of Queen Elizabeth's household and captain of the Guard, who received from his royal mistress the grants of Whitley Park (the Abbot's park mentioned by Leland as being at the entrance to Reading town), and the manor or farm of Battle, which also belonged to Reading Abbey. Sir Francis resided at the Abbey- house of Reading at the period of the Civil War. Captain Symonds, who was at Reading in 1644, described the dining-room at the Abbey- house as having the arms and initials of Queen Elizabeth, for whose reception it was probably fitted up. Sir Francis, jun., the sequestrator, sat for the county of Berks in the Parliaments of 1614-25, and for Reading in those of 1625-26-28-40 until his demise in 1645.

(3). PEREGRINE HOBY, son of Sir Edward Hoby, of Bisham, co. Berks, who received the honour of a visit from Queen Elizabeth at Bisham, in 1592, who, when Princess, had spent part of three years here, under the guardianship of Sir Thomas Hoby. Edward, the son of Peregrine, was created a baronet 12th July, 1666, a title which became extinct on the death of the Rev. Sir Philip Hoby, fifth baronet, June 29th, 1766.

(4). HENRY MARTEN. The Regicide. Son of Sir Henry Marten, of Longworth, near Faringdon, Dean of Arches, Judge of the Prerogative Court and of the High Court of Admiralty, who was esteemed the first civilian of the age. His "ungodly son," as Wood calls him, represented the county of Berks in the Parliaments of 1640-40, and was governor of Reading in 1642, but on the approach of a party of the King's horse Marten quitted the town and fled with his garrison. After the Restora- tion, Marten surrendered on the Proclamation, and was tried at the Old Bailey. He was found guilty, and petitioned for pardon, which he obtained on condition of perpetual imprisonment. He was first con-

---

\* This Committee sat at Reading Abbey.

APPENDIX. 117

fined in the Tower, but soon removed to the Castle at Chepstow, where he was incarcerated twenty years. Marten was buried in the Church at Chepstow, and over his remains was placed a stone with the following inscription, the acrostic epitaph being written by himself.

"Here
Sep. 9, in the year of our Lord 1680,
Was buried a true Englishman,
Who in Berkshire was well known
To love his country's freedom, 'bove his own,
But living immured full twenty year,
Had time to write, as does appear,
HIS EPITAPH.
H ere or elsewhere (all's one, to you, to me,)
E arth, air, or water, gripes my ghostly dust
N one knows how soon to be by fire set free
R eader, if you an oft tryed rule will trust,
Y ou'll gladly do and suffer what you must.

M y life was spent in serving you, and you,
A nd death's my pay (it seems) and welcome too;
R evenge destroying but itself, while I
T o birds of prey leave my old cage, and fly,
E xamples preach to th' eye, care then, (mine says)
N ot how you end, but how you spend your dayes."

Carlyle gives the following characteristic notice of Henry Marten in his 'Oliver Cromwell's Letters and Speeches,' (vol. iii., p. 168). "Harry Marten is a tight little fellow, though of somewhat loose life: his witty words pierce yet, as light-arrows, through the thick oblivious torpor of the generations; testifying to us very clearly, Here was a right hard-headed, stout-hearted little man, full of sharp fire and cheerful light; sworn foe of Cant in all its figures; an indomitable little Roman Pagan if no better:—but Harry is not quite one's King either; it would have been difficult to be altogether loyal to Harry!"

(5). ROGER KNIGHT, of Greenham. See *Appendix* to Second Battle.

(6). HENRY POWLE. Of the family of Powles of Shottesbroke. This Henry Powle was High Sheriff of the County of Berks, 8 Car. i, 1633. Mr. Powle's younger son Henry sat for Windsor in the Convention Parliament of 1688, over which he presided as Speaker, became Master of the Rolls, 13th March, 1689-90, and died 21st November, 1692. He married, in 1679, Frances, Countess Dowager of Dorset, relict of Richard Sackville, 5th Earl of Dorset.

(7). THOMAS FETTIPLACE, of Fernham, near Faringdon.

(8). TANFIELD VACHELL, of Coley House. M.P. for Reading in the second Parliament of 1640 (Long Parliament), succeeding to that seat on the demise of Sir Francis Knollys, jun., knt., in 1645. King Charles was at Coley House in May, 1644, which at this time belonged to John Hampden in right of his second wife, Letitia, daughter of Sir Francis Knollys, brother to William, Earl of Banbury, and widow of Sir Thomas Vachell. "Mr. Tanfield Vachell whom the King made Sheriff of Berks in 1643, and who left his service and went to Rebellion, whose house on the south side of the town was newly built upon the old priory and now pull'd down, is cousin and heir to yᵉ said Sir Thomas Vachell, his uncle. 'Tis reported in Reading an old story of Vachell, yᵗ would not suffer yᵉ Abbot of Reading to carry the hay through his yard, yᵉ Abbot after many messengers, sent a Monk, whom Vachell in fury kill'd, he was forced to fly, and his kin after adopted the motto, 'It is better to suffer than revenge.'" (Symond's 'Church Notes,' Harl. MSS., 965, Mus. Brit.)

## IX. THE COMMISSIONERS FOR RAISING MONEY AND FORCES WITHIN THE COUNTY OF BERKS, AND FOR MAINTENANCE OF GARRISONS WITHIN THE SAID COUNTY, FOR USE OF PARLIAMENT, APPOINTED JUNE 27TH, 1644, were:—

William Lenthall, Speaker and Master of the Rolls (1), Sir Francis Knollys, Knt., Sir Francis Pile, Bart., Sir Robert Pye, sen. (2), Sir Benjamin Rudyerd, Knt. (3), Richard Whitehead, Edward Dunch (4), Henry Marten, Peregrine Hoby, Tanfield Vachell, Daniel Blagrave (5), Major-General Richard Browne (6), William Ball, John Packer, sen. (7), Robert Packer (8), and Cornelius Holland (9).*

(1). WILLIAM LENTHALL (the Speaker of the Long Parliament), of Besilsleigh, co. Berks, who purchased this property of the Fettiplaces, in 1634. The old mansion, which was a magnificent structure surrounded by a quadrangular court, is now destroyed except a picturesque portion of the offices and the massive stone pillars of the gateway. Cromwell and other distinguished characters of the day were frequent guests at Besilsleigh. The elder branch of the Lenthalls became extinct at the decease of William Lenthall, a gentleman of the Privy Chamber to Charles II., M.P. for Wallingford in 1680. The family is now represented by Edm. Kyffin Lenthall, Esq., of Besilsleigh.

(2). SIR ROBERT PYE, SEN. Soon after the commencement of the Civil War the house of Sir Robert Pye, sen., at Faringdon, was garrisoned for the King. His son, Sir Robert Pye, jun., was a prominent member of the Parliamentary party; and ultimately was equally zealous for the restoration of Charles II., who appointed him one of his equerries. Sir Robert Pye the elder died in 1662. His son Robert, who married a daughter of John Hampden, died in 1701, within a week of the death of his wife. His great-great-grandson was the poet laureat Henry James Pye.

(3). SIR BENJAMIN RUDYERD, KNT., of West Woodhay, near Newbury, descended from the Rudyerds of Rudyerd, co. of Stafford; third son of James Rudyerd, Esq., of Hartley, co. Hants, by Margaret his wife, daughter and heiress of Lawrence Kidwelly, of Winchfield, in the same county, esquire. Sir Benjamin was born on St. Stephen's day, 1572, in the parish of East Woodhay, Hants, and educated at the public school, Winchester, and St. John's College, Oxford. By the influence of his patron, Sir John Harrington, afterwards Lord Harrington of Exton, preceptor to the accomplished but unfortunate Princess Elizabeth, Rudyerd soon obtained a favourable reception at the court of King James I. and in the above-mentioned noble family, distinguished alike by their talents and piety, he, no doubt, received those lessons of moderation which so greatly distinguished his whole political career. From that family, too, he chose a partner in the joys and sorrows of his life, in the person of Elizabeth, one of the two daughters and co-heiresses of Sir Henry

Harrington, next brother to John, first Lord Harrington of Exton. On the 9th March, 1617, Rudyerd was appointed to the then high and distinguished office of Surveyor of His Majesty's Court of Wards and Liveries, and on the 30th of the same month, King James honoured him with the degree of knighthood. Upon the differences arising between King Charles I. and the Parliament, Sir Benjamin was one of the several members of both houses who did all they could to persuade the Parliament to an accommodation, and warned them of the miseries of a civil war. On the abolition of the Court of Wards and Liveries in 1647, £6,000 was voted to Rudyerd, and so great was the esteem of the House towards him that they further voted him a part of the forfeited estates of the Marquis of Worcester as a reparation for the loss of his office, but notwithstanding these marks of favour, he was heartily disgusted with the disloyal attempts of the Independents, and he stood to his post to the last moment advocating moderation and deprecating destruction. In December, 1648, Rudyerd and other well affected members of the Parliament having been beaten on the 4th instant, question, " whether the King's answers to the propositions of both Houses were satisfactory," on the 6th, the question was varied by the King's friends, among whom Rudyerd stood prominently forward, in the hope of further averting the progress of the rebellion, and making a happy peace with the Sovereign, then a prisoner. It was now put in these terms, "that the answer of the King to the propositions of both Houses are a ground for the House to proceed upon for the settlement of the peace of the kingdom," which was carried by a majority of 129 to 83. Such an unexpected occurrence threw Cromwell and the Parliamentary generals into the greatest consternation, and the result was the well-known *coup d'état*, when all the obnoxious members were seized as they arrived at the House: one of the victims on this occasion was Rudyerd, then 76 years of age, who was thrown into prison with the rest. It appears Rudyerd did not remain in confinement any length of time, as the Journals of the House of Commons record his release from the Gate-house shortly afterwards, owing, it is said, to the influence of Mr. Prynne. Sir Benjamin then retired to his house at West Woodhay, built for him by Inigo Jones, and spent the remainder of his days in the quiet to which his mind must have been a stranger while engaged in the political struggles of the times. Sir Benjamin died at West Woodhay on the 31st May, 1658, aged 86 years; a few months only before the death of Cromwell. He was buried in the Church at West Woodhay, where in Ashmole's time there was "a neat black marble monument" to his memory, with an epitaph said to have been written by Sir Benjamin in his younger days. It is printed in Ashmole's 'Collections,' and in the 'History of Newbury,' p. 289. The only son of Sir Benjamin married one of the five daughters and co-heirs of Sir Stephen Harvey, of Morton Murrell, in the co. of Warwick (created Knight of the Bath at the coronation of King Charles I.), and by this connection Mr. Rudyerd was brother-in-law to the celebrated Speaker Lenthall. Mr. John Rudyerd, the ingenious designer of the Eddystone Lighthouse erected in 1701 and which stood until destroyed by fire in 1755, was a descendant of Sir Benjamin.

(4). EDMUND DUNCH. Member for Wallingford in the Parliaments of 1628-40, and for the County in the Parliaments of 1654-56. His return to the Long Parliament was declared void. Mr. Dunch, High Sheriff of the County, 9 Car. 1, 1632-3, was the son of Sir William Dunch, who married Mary, daughter of Sir Henry Cromwell, and aunt to the Protector. In 1658 he was created a baronet, and afterwards called to the Upper House by the title of Baron Burnell, of which he was divested at the Restoration; he died in 1678. Edmund Dunch, grandson of "Baron Burnell," married a daughter and co-heiress of Col. Charles Godfrey, Master of the Jewel Office, by Arabella Churchill, sister to the great Duke of Marlborough, and one of the mistresses of King James II., when Duke of York, by whom she had four children. This marriage is somewhat remarkable, as Mrs. Dunch being half-sister to the legitimate children of James II., the blood of the Cromwells and Stuarts was thereby commingled. On the death of Edmund Dunch in 1719, without male issue, his family became extinct.

(5). DANIEL BLAGRAVE, of Southcote, one of the regicides, was third son of Anthony Blagrave, Esq., and nephew of the eminent mathematician who built Southcote Manor-house. He represented the borough of Reading in Parliament; and, as a reward for his services to the Commonwealth, received the office of "Exigenter" in the Court of Common Pleas, worth annually at that time £500, and was made Master in Chancery. He was likewise Treasurer of Berkshire, and one of the County Committee, who were authorized to remove all "inefficient" ministers, in which office he distinguished himself by his vexatious persecution of the clergy. The emoluments of his office in the Common Pleas, it is supposed, enabled him to purchase the King's fee-farm-rent of the valuable Manor of Sonning and some other estates; and, having kept in with every form of government during the Interregnum, he obtained a seat in the Convention Parliament of 1658. At the Restoration, finding the danger which threatened him, he fled the kingdom, and, retiring to Aix la Chapelle, died in 1668 in an obscure condition. John Blagrave, nephew of the above and son of Anthony Blagrave, by Dorothy, daughter of Sir Thomas Dolman, of Shaw, was one of the gentlemen of Berks who had assisted in the Restoration, and qualified to be made a knight of the proposed Order of the Royal Oak. This family of the Blagraves, of Bulmarsh Court and Southcote, became extinct in the male line on the demise of John Blagrave, Esq., in 1787, and is now represented through the female line by J. H. Blagrave. Esq., of Calcot Park.

(6). RICHARD BROWNE. Major-General of Oxfordshire, Berkshire, and Buckinghamshire. Was an eminent citizen of London, a warm advocate for the presbytery, an excellent officer in the field, and had no small influence in the Parliament. He attended the Earl of Essex when he first marched against the King; and had a considerable hand in defeating the Royalists near Worcester and at Edgehill. He took Arundel Castle by storm, and, seizing on Abingdon, bravely defended it against the whole force of the garrison at Oxford. In a sudden sally from Abingdon he surprised and took Bellasith House, which was strongly garrisoned by the royal party, and found in it a good supply of provision. He was one of the Commissioners deputed to receive the King from the Scottish army, when,'" perceiving the great advantage His Majesty had in his disputes with their politicians and divines, and probably penetrating the designs of the Independents, he returned to his allegiance, and ever after inflexibly adhered to it." He was much in favour with Charles II., whose Resident he was in Paris before the Restoration, and was soon after created a baronet, having before received the honour of knighthood. He had the command of the City Militia, and was Lord Mayor of London in 1660. His only daughter

APPENDIX. 121

and heiress espoused John Evelyn * during her father's residence in France.
(7). JOHN PACKER, of Donnington Castle. } See Appendix to the
(8). ROBERT PACKER, his son. } Second Battle.
(9). CORNELIUS HOLLAND, M.P. for Windsor. One of the King's judges. Once servant to Sir Harry Vane, by whom he was preferred to be Clerk of the Green Cloth to the King, whose death-warrant he ultimately signed. Winstanley in his 'Martyrology,' and the author of a work entitled 'The History of the King Killers,' concur in representing this regicide as a man of great depravity. In a pamphlet entitled 'The Mystery of the Good Old Cause,' it is stated that "Holland made himself a farmer of the King's feeding-grounds at Crestlow, in Bucks, worth £1,800 or £2,000 per annum, at the rate of £20 a year, which he discounted. He possessed Somerset House a long time, where he and his family nested themselves. He was keeper of Richmond House, which served for his country-retreat. He was also commissary for the garrison at Whitehall and the Mews, and he had an office in the Mint. It is supposed he gave £5,000 to each of his ten children!"

## X. SHIP-MONEY.

"Ship-Money," a word, says Lord Clarendon, "of a lasting sound in the memory of this kingdom," indicates a project which in its progress made the dissensions between King and Parliament irreparable, and in its consequences led to the misery of eleven years of almost uninterrupted Civil War.

Schedules were prepared, and sent to each Sheriff, containing the list of all the counties, cities, and corporate towns, and the proportions in which each was rated, to the end that each district and community might be made aware that the contribution was enforced impartially. These Schedules present a view of the comparative wealth and importance of those places, which is remarkable in the contrast it affords with their respective conditions in present times.

DISTRIBUTION OF SHIPS, WITH THEIR TONNAGE, NUMBER OF MEN, AND CHARGE, AND THE SUMS SET ON THE CORPORATION TOWNS IN THE COUNTY OF BERKS.

(From Sir Peter Temple's MS. Papers—Stowe, given in the Appendix to Lord Nugent's 'Life of Hampden.')

| | | TONS. | MEN. | CHARGE. |
|---|---|---|---|---|
| Berkshire County | One Ship of | 320 | 128 | £4000 |
| Town of Windsor | | | | 100 |
| Borough of Newbury | | | | 100 |
| Borough of Reading | | | | 220 |
| Borough of Abingdon | | | | 100 |
| Borough of Wallingford | | | | 20 |

Portsmouth was assessed at £60; Bath £70; Preston £40; Stafford

---

* Cowley in his 'Garden,' addressed to this worthy gentleman, compliments him upon his taste for horticulture and books, and his happy choice of a wife, who had, as he expresses it,
"The fairest garden in her looks,
And in her mind the choicest books."

Q

£30; and Liverpool £25. Such a disproportion to the present wealth of some of these places shows what great changes have been produced since that date in their relative commercial importance.

PETITION OF THE GRAND JURY OF THE COUNTY OF BERKS AGAINST SHIP MONEY, &c.*

To the King's Most Excelent Matie.

The Humble Petition of your Maties most Loyall subjects the Grand Jury Impaneled 11 July, 1640, to serve at the generall assizes holden for the County of Berks, in the behalfe of themselves, and the rest of the Countie. Sheweth, That whereas your Petitioners have been of late yeares and still are much burthened with sundry grievances of divers natures deriving ther authority from yr Maje but being directly contrary to yr Maties Lawes established in this your kingdom, the chief of these presenting themselves in a schedule hereunto annexed, for redresse, whereof, as your petitioners hoped, your Matie was graciously pleased about the midle of Aprill to assemble the great Councell commonly called the High Court of Parliament, and about three weeks after to dissolve it, for want (as it seemes to your petitioners) of a goode agreemente betwixt the two houses. Neverthelesse since the said dissolution to express such a fatherly care of your Poor people, that yr Matie has vouchsafed by a Printed declaration to invite them to the poureing out of their complaynts unto your Princely eare. It may therefore please your most Excellt. Matie to take the sayd particulers into your tender consideration, to give your Petitioners such ease therein, as in your Royall Wisdome shall be thought fitte. And whereby it may appeare to all your Maties Subjects, and especially to thos of yr Maties most honorable Privy Councell, and your Officers and Ministers of Justis, that yr Matie is resolved to continue unto them all their rights and Liberties which they desired by ther Petition of Rights and wer confirm'd by yr Matie the 3rd yeare of your rayne. And your Petitioners as they are bound shall continue to preserve the length and happinesse of yr Maties sayd raigne by ther prayers and all other actions, of zeal and duty.

A Schedule of such grievances as most oppresse the Countie.

1.—The Illegall and insupportable charge of Ship mony, now the 5th yeare Imposed as high as ever, though the subject was not able to pay the last year, being but a third.
2.—The new tax of coal and conduct mony, with the undermeanes used to enforce the payment of it by messengers from Counstable.
3.—The compellinge sume freemen by imprisonment and thretnings to take peoples mony, and others for feare of the like imprisonment to forsake ther houses and habitations hideing them selves in woods, whereby ther families are obliged to be maintayned by the parishes, and harvest work undon for want of Labourers.
4.—The Infinite number of monopolies upon every thing allmost the Countrymen must bye. Besides the easterne part of this Countie, wher your Maties fforest of Windsor is, is particularly burthened with immeasurable inroades of the deare, which if they shall goe on soe for five years will leave neither foode nor roome for any creatures in the fforest.

---

* Addl. MSS., Brit. Mus., No. 24064, f. 9.

APPENDIX. 123

With rigid execution of forest lawes in ther extremitye, with the exaction of the Imoderate fees by som officers under the Ld.Cheef Justis in Iyre [Eyre].*

## XI. STATE OF PUBLIC FEELING IN THE COUNTY IN 1643.

That the County of Berks was generally favourable to the Parliament may be inferred from the following extract of Members returned to the Long Parliament, compiled by Professor Masson, and introduced in his 'Life of Milton.'

(The Shire and four Boroughs)     No. of Members.
Parliamentarians .. .. 5
Royalists .. .. .. 2
So unstable as meanwhile
  to have changed sides .. 1
Non-effective .. .. 2
                            10

The Royalist element in the County is indicated by the following list of those who faithfully attached themselves to the interest of the King, and compounded for their estates, which had been sequestered by the Parliament.

|   |   |   | £ | s. | |
|---|---|---|---|---|---|
| Appleyard, Charles | Wargrave | | 0003 | 10 | 00 |
| Bunbury, Thomas † | Reading | Dr. | 0117 | 00 | 00 |
| Braxton, Anthony | do | | 0100 | 00 | 00 |
| Bishop, Richard | | Esq. | 0385 | 00 | 00 |
| Bricket, Thomas | Shinfield | | 0012 | 08 | 08 |

---

* Lord Falkland felt and spoke strongly upon the extra-judicial opinion the Judges had given at Charles' request, on the King's right to Ship-Money. "No meal undigested," he said, "can lie heavier upon the stomach than that unsaid would have lain upon my conscience." He complained that the judges, "the persons who should have been as dogs to defend the flock, have become the wolves to devour it;" that they had exceeded their functions, "being judges of law and not of necessity, that is, being judges and not philosophers or politicians;" that to justify the plea of necessity, they have "supposed mighty and eminent dangers in the most quiet and halcyon days, but a few contemptible pirates being our most formidable enemies;" they also, "supposing the supposed doings to be so sudden that it could not stay for a Parliament which required but a forty days' stay, allowed to the King the sole power in necessity, the sole judgment of necessity, and by that enabled him to take from us what he would, when he would, and how he would." He especially declaimed against the Chief Justice (at this time Lord Keeper) Finch, who importuned the other judges, "as a most admirable solicitor, but a most abominable judge." * * * "He it was who gave away with his breath what our ancestors have purchased with so long expense of their time, their care, their treasures, and their bloods, and strove to make our grievances mortal and our slavery irreparable." * * * "He who hath already undone us by wholesale," [and now as Chancellor] "hath the power of undoing us by retail."—Corderoy and Phillpott's 'King and Commonwealth,' p. 83, and authorities there quoted.

† Thomas Bunbury, D.D., Vicar of St. Mary's, Reading.

# THE FIRST BATTLE OF NEWBURY.

|  |  |  | £ | s. | d. |
|---|---|---|---|---|---|
| Choke, Francis † | Avington | Knt. | 0572 | 00 | 00 |
| Clifford, Richard | Shalbourne | Gent. | 0145 | 10 | 00 |
| Davis, John | Pangbourne | Knt. | 0382 | 10 | 00 |
| Dicus, Hugh | Reading |  | 0060 | 00 | 00 |
| Fartham, John | do |  | 0002 | 13 | 04 |
| Forster, Sir Humphrey | Aldermaston | Bart. | 1000 | 00 | 00 |
| Gwynn, William | Sunning-hill | Gent. | 0112 | 15 | 00 |
| Gardiner, Roger | Whitewalton |  | 0015 | 13 | 04 |
| Hide, Humphrey | Kennington | Esq. | 0538 | 00 | 00 |
| Hide, Humphrey | Kingston Lisle | Esq. | 0610 | 00 | 00 |
| Hall, Thomas | Windsor | Gent. | 0020 | 00 | 00 |
| Hamlyn, Henry | Reading | Gent. | 0033 | 06 | 08 |
| Herbert, Edward | Bray | Gent. | 0166 | 13 | 06 |
| Langton, William | Stanwick | Esq. | 0111 | 00 | 00 |
| Langton, George | do | Gent. | 0008 | 06 | 08 |
| Lovelace, Lord John | Hurley |  | 6057 | 07 | 05 |
| Milton, Christopher * | Reading |  | 0080 | 00 | 00 |
| Mason, Robert | Hidden | Esq. | 0522 | 00 | 00 |
| Neville, Richd. | Billingbere | Esq. | 0877 | 00 | 00 |
| Peacock, John | Cumnor | Gent. | 0140 | 00 | 00 |
| Porter, William |  | Gent. | 0681 | 00 | 00 |
| Reeves, Thomas | Reading | Esq. | 0160 | 00 | 00 |
| Sawyer, Edward | Dudcot | Gent. | 0091 | 00 | 00 |
| Stonehouse, Sir Geo. | Radley | Bart. | 1460 | 00 | 00 |
| Stafford, Edward | Bradfield |  | 0848 | 00 | 00 |
| Thomas, John | New Windsor |  | 0022 | 13 | 04 |
| Tyle, Richd. | Warfield | Yeoman | 0032 | 10 | 00 |
| Worktop, Thomas | New Windsor | Gent. | 0160 | 00 | 00 |

This list must not be supposed to specify the whole of the losses of the Berkshire Gentry on this occasion, as there is no doubt that those who were actively concerned forfeited their whole property, not being allowed to compound.

Among the Recusants in the neighbourhood who suffered severely for their religious principles were the Eystons of Hendred (a family who have now held property in the County for over 500 years), the Perkinses of Ufton Court, Brownes of Gt. Shefford, and the Dancastles of Well-House and the Grange, in the parish of Shaw. The name of Gabriel Coxe who, while Mayor of Newbury, received the King at his house, occurs in the catalogue of persons reported to be Papists.

---

† Sir Francis Choke, of Avington, was Lieut.-Colonel of Sir Faithful Fortescue's regiment raised for the King.

* Christopher Milton. This was the brother of the great poet, John Milton, Cromwell's Latin Secretary. "He entered as a student of the Middle Temple, of which House he became an ancient Bencher, and kept close to that study and profession all his life-time, except during the Civil Wars of England, when he adhered to the Royal cause, and became obnoxious to the Parliament by acting to the utmost of his power against them so long as he kept his station at Reading in Berkshire, and therefore, as soon as that town was taken by the Parliamentary forces, he was obliged to quit his house there and steer his course according to the motion of the King's army. When the war was ended, and his composition made through his brother's interest with the then prevailing powers, he returned to his profession," 'Collection of the Works of Milton,' 1738.—Bodleian Library.

APPENDIX. 125

XII. AGREEMENT BETWEEN CHARLES I. AND THE COUNTY OF BERKS RESPECTING A CONTRIBUTION TO BE LEVIED FOR THE SUPPORT OF THE KING'S ARMY.

THE AGREEMENT MADE BETWEEN HIS MAJESTY AND THE KNIGHTS, GENTLEMEN, FREEHOLDERS, AND INHABITANTS OF THE COUNTY OF BERKS FOR THE BETTER PROVISION AND ORDERING OF HIS MAJESTIE'S ARMY, AND A DECLARATION OF HIS MAJESTY'S GRATIOUS ACCEPTANCE THEREOF, AND HIS ROYAL PROCLAMATION COMMANDING THE DUE OBSERVANCE THEREOF IN ALL PARTS.

Printed by His Majestie's command at Oxford, Oct. 19, by Leonard Lichfield, Printer to the University, 1643.

At a Councell of Warre Held the 13 October, 1643, His Majesty being present.

This day the High Sheriffe, Gentlemen, and Freeholders of the County of Berks did present to His Majesty their agreement, on the behalfe of all the inhabitants of that County, which was in this manner following:—

FIRST.—They doe agree to pay by way of Loane, during the space of a Moneth, a weekly contribution of 1000*l*. by the week, towards the maintenance of the King's army out of that County, to be proportionately laid upon all parts of the County (except the hundreds of Riplesmere, Bray, Cookham, Benhurst, and Wargrave, lying within the Forest division, which are left to His Majesty to dispose of), to beginne from the 29 September now last past, to be levyed and rated upon the Lands, Rents, Annuities, Parsonages, and Tythes, and Personal estates of the inhabitants of the whole County (except before excepted) in such manner, and according to such proportions, as by the ancient and usuall course of the severall parts of the County rates laid upon the County have been rated and levyed.

That the one halfe of the said 1000*l*. by the week shall be paid in mony, and the other halfe in provisions, and for the provisions they shall be of such sorts as the souldiers shall desire at the rates hereunder written, vizt.

Oates to be rated at 20<sup>d.</sup> the Bushell.
Beanes and Pease at 3<sup>d.</sup> the Bushell.
Hay at 5<sup>d.</sup> the Todde.
Grasse for a horse at 3/- the Week.
Straw at 10/- the Load.

And so after those rates for a greater or lesser quantity. But it to be alwaies at the election of the parties paying, to pay the whole rate in mony if they so please.

That, if any losse or damage shall happen to any of the inhabitants either in their horses or other cattell or in any of their provisions or other goods by any of the King's souldiers, such losse or damage shall be repayed and recompensed to the party suffering out of the said weekly Loane.

That all the provisions to be delivered according to this agreement shall be delivered at the Towne of Abingdon on Friday in every week, or at such other places as shall be mutually agreed upon, and the delivering to bee on such daies in every week, as shall be likewise agreed upon, to the hands of the Collectors or Commissaries to be to that purpose appointed, who shall then also receive the mony to be paid according to this Agreement, and Books shall be kept wherein shall bee set what shall be paid in mony and what and how much in provisions, and from whom, and by whom the same is paid, that so the defaulters may also appeare, and be proceeded against accordingly for such their default.

That the Defalcations or Reparations to be made to any according to this Agreement shall be held good, and allowed of whensoever it shall be set downe and allowed under the hands of any three of the Commissioners named in the Commission for setling of this Contribution. And if the losse or dammage amount to more than the party damnified in his own particular should pay for the week, then the Reparation to be made up and repayed to the party grieved by the High Constable or Collector of that part of the County, upon warrant under the hands of any three of the said Commissioners allowing the same aforesaid, and if any Hundred, Parish, or particular Person, shall make default of payment, that Hundred, Parish, or Person, so making default shall be left to the care and discretion of the Commander of that part of the King's army next to the place where such default shall be, and for the supply of whom that part shall be allotted.

That no manner of free-quarter or billetting shall be taken by or for any Horse or Foot Souldiers, nor any Taxe, Charge, or Imposition whatsoever shall be laid upon or required from any inhabitant of this County, without present payment for the same in mony, as they shall agree by consent, except only for House room according to the quality of the person Billeted, and of the Person in whose House he is so Billeted, and except for fire and candle, such as the Master, Mistris or Dame of the Family use for themselves and their own family.

That no Women, Boyes, or Children following the army be admitted from henceforth to have House room, unlesse it be by consent, and by composition with the owner of the House for the same.

That the High Constables in every Hundred respectively be the immediate Collectors both of the Moneys and Provisions from the Inhabitants paying the same, and they to pay the same over to the High Sheriff of the County, or such as he shall appoint, at the times and places before mentioned, and they to pay or deliver the same to such officers of the army as shall be appointed to receive and distribute the same unto and amongst the Souldiers.

And because the said weekly summe of a 1000*l.* was formerly laid upon the whole county, whereof the five Hundreds above mentioned were parcell, It is now ordered that such summe of mony, parcell of the said 1000*l.*, which the said five Hundreds should have borne and are now excepted as aforesaid, shall by the Rule of proportion bee rated and layed upon the rest of the County.

That these agreements be setled by order of the Councell of Warre, and entred with the Secretary of the Councell to the end that all Commanders, Officers, and Souldiers may take knowledge of and observe the same.

# APPENDIX.

And it is further desired by the County, and on their behalfe, that the Lords and others, His Majesty's Commissioners, would by their order, as much as in them lyeth, confirme the same, and give life to the execution thereof, and that His Majesty by his Royal Proclamation will be pleased to command the due execution and observance thereof, in all the parts thereof. And His Majesty having perused these agreements, and declared his gratious approbation thereof, now according to the request made on behalfe of the County, the Lords and others His Majesty's Commissioners doe order—That they will be ready to give their best assistance that these agreements shall be duly observed that they will constantly meet in the Audite-house there to receive the complaynts of the County if there shall be cause, and as there shall be cause to recommend the Redresse of what shall be amiss in any part, either to the King's Majesty or the Councell of Warre, if the Lords themselves shall not have the meanes otherwise to redresse the same. And to the end that the County may have a convenient opportunity on all occasions to present their complaints when there shall be cause, they doe with one consent make choyce of William Hynton, Esquire, one of the gentlemen of His Majesty's Privy Chamber and one of the Inhabitants amongst them, to performe the good office for them from time to time, which His Majesty doth very well approve.

All which His Majesty doth very well approve of, and doth command to be printed and published, in every Church and Chapellry of the County to the end that notice being generally taken thereof, all persons of all qualities, whom it doth or may concerne, may apply themselves to the performance thereof.

And further His Majesty being desirous that so good a worke may not perish in the execution which is the life of all good actions, doth by his Royal Proclamation declare—That he doubteth not, but the Inhabitants of this County will on their parts observe the same, and will continue it as long as the necessity shall continue, which His Majesty will, by all possible meanes he can, endeavour to shorten and ease, for he doth strictly charge and command, That on the part of the Souldiers, the same be duely observed. And that if any Souldier of what quality soever presume to breake those agreements or to offend contrary to the same, every such offender shall be severally proceeded against, according to the quality of his offence, that by the exemplary punishment of some, others may be warned and deterred from committing the like. His Majesty being resolved, as on the one side to punish those who will not be admonished according to the due course of justice, so on the other side, to reward those who have and shall deserve well by their good examples, according to their severall qualities and deservings, as soone as it shall please God to enable Him thereunto.

Given at His Majestie's Court at Oxford, the 17 day of October in the Nineteenth yeare of His Majesty's Raigne, 1643.

# THE
# SECOND BATTLE OF NEWBURY.
OCTOBER 27TH, 1644.

## CHAPTER I.
### INTRODUCTORY.

ALTHOUGH the return of Essex to London, and the King's retirement to Oxford, after the First Battle of Newbury, terminated the campaign of 1643 as regards the two principal armies on either side, these movements did not put an end to the military operations of the year; a ceaseless war of skirmishes and sieges being continued, with varied success, in other parts of the kingdom.

In the autumn of 1643, the Earl of Manchester having reduced Lynn after a vigorous resistance for three weeks, drew his forces into Lincolnshire, where he was joined by Cromwell as his Lieutenant-General, and by Sir Thomas Fairfax. On the 11th of October they were attacked by a strong body of Royalist cavalry at Winceby, near Horncastle, where the King's troops were utterly beaten and Lincolnshire was recovered for the Parliament. The siege of Hull was raised by the Marquis of Newcastle on the 12th; and, on the other hand, the Earl of Manchester succeded in taking the strong garrisons of Lincoln and Gainsborough.

Although not an event of any material importance, an incident occurred at Newbury about this time which may be introduced in this, its chronological position, simply on account of the locality of the circumstance. In the month of November, Lord Saltoun, who had been employed in obtaining contributions in aid of the Royal cause from the English Catholics in France, was intercepted at Newbury, with several companions, while on his way to the King at Oxford. They had landed on the coast of Sussex; and Sir William Waller, having notice of their arrival, had sent out a body of horse under Captain Gardiner, commonly styled the Mayor of Evesham, who succeeded in capturing the whole party. Lord Saltoun was the bearer of dispatches of importance from the

French court, and had in his possession when taken a considerable sum of money, with which he had intended to raise two troops of horse in the western counties. After detention for some time at Farnham Castle, the prisoners were at length sent up to London to be dealt with according to the pleasure of the Parliament.*

On the 19th January, 1643-4, the Scotch auxiliary forces consisting of about 18,000 foot, 3,000 horse, and between 500 and 600 dragoons, under the command of Alexander Leslie, Earl of Leven, marched into England as adherents of the Parliament. This contingency Charles had long foreseen; and the entrance into the field of these levies raised in his own name, but contrary to his proclamation, turned the scale of fortune against him. From this time the King's affairs began to decline, and the arms of the Parliament were almost everywhere victorious.

In the depth of that inclement winter, Sir Thomas Fairfax moved across from Lincolnshire, and, joining the forces of Sir William Brereton from the county of Leicester, appeared suddenly before Nantwich and forced the besiegers, under Lord Byron, to retire with heavy loss; more than half of Byron's force of 3,000 foot, chiefly newly raised Irish auxiliaries, were reported as either slain or captured. Nantwich was the only town in the county-palatine of Chester which had remained firm to the Parliament from the beginning to the end of the Civil War, and this defeat inflicted a very severe blow on the King's cause; the Irish levies, on whom he had mainly depended to enable him to take the field in the spring, being almost annihilated.

Royalist disasters now followed each other in rapid succession.

Early in the year 1644 (29th March) the King's forces under Lord Hopton were defeated in the " battle of Cheriton " by the Parliamentary Generals Waller and Balfour, at Bramdean Heath, near Alresford. Hopton retired to Basing, and next day to Reading, with considerable loss, the gallant Sir John Smith (who had rescued the royal standard at Edgehill), Lord John Stuart, brother to the Duke of Richmond, besides some other officers of note, and about two hundred soldiers, being killed on the King's side. On this occasion the army of the Parliament also suffered severely, and lost an excellent and experienced officer, Colonel John Meldrum, who fell mortally wounded. Waller soon after obtained possession of the City of Winchester without difficulty; but the garrison

---

* Godwin's 'Civil War in Hampshire,' p. 75.

at the Castle, under Lord Ogle, notwithstanding, held out for the King.

In the north the two Fairfaxes came upon Colonel Bellasis, Governor of York, at Selby, on the 11th of April, when the Colonel and the majority of the King's party were made prisoners and a considerable quantity of war *materiel* and military supplies were taken.

A few advantages gained by the Royalists in Cheshire, Staffordshire, Nottinghamshire, Sussex, and other parts did not compensate for such multiplied losses as these, still the King was not despondent, but remained hopeful that the war might take a more favourable turn.

When active military operations recommenced late in April, 1644, the Parliament had no less than five armies afoot. That of Fairfax and the auxiliary army of the Scots, in Yorkshire; that of Lord Essex, then being recruited in London after its successes at Gloucester and Newbury; that of Waller, which had been reinforced after its expulsion from the west; and, lastly, the army supported by the associated eastern counties, consisting of 14,000 men, under the command of Manchester and Cromwell.

From these extraordinary preparations the Parliament seem to have intended to have brought the war to a speedy termination, all endeavours made by the King towards an honourable peace having apparently been tried and abandoned as impracticable.

At this time the King had two large armies in the field. His own, consisting of 10,000 men, and the northern division, under Prince Rupert and the Marquis of Newcastle, of 14,000 men; and there were in addition several considerable forces scattered throughout the country, while regiments of English and Irish troops were landed from time to time in Wales and elsewhere.

Understanding that Waller's object was to march towards the west, early in April Charles concentrated his forces at Marlborough. On the 10th of this month his troops, consisting of 6,000 foot and 4,000 horse, met at Aldbourne Chase, or Goring Heath, where they were reviewed by the King "to his great satisfaction"; and it was resolved that every effort should be made to bring Waller to an engagement. It was, however, afterwards deemed prudent not to carry out this resolution, and the army was ordered to quarter in Newbury, which was the most suitable station in regard to the important garrisons of Reading, Wallingford, and Oxford, and where the movements of the Parliamentary forces could be better observed and opposed.

About the 10th May, Essex and Waller marched from London, each at the head of 10,000 men. As soon as the former had reached Windsor and the latter had encamped at Basing, the King advanced from Newbury, where his army had been quartered for nearly a month, to Reading, and caused the defensive works of that town to be demolished in order to augment his forces by the troops of the garrison, amounting to 2,500 men, all seasoned veterans. This having been accomplished, the King removed to Oxford, and hearing that Essex and Waller had orders to invest that city, he did his utmost, by completing the fortifications and re-victualling the garrison, to anticipate and, if possible, frustrate the hostile intentions of the Parliament.

Meanwhile the Parliamentarian armies pushed on and occupied Reading, Newbury, and Abingdon, which last the Royalists had likewise abandoned on Essex's approach; thus becoming masters of the whole of Berkshire except Donnington Castle, Faringdon, and Wallingford.

The news which Charles had heard was well founded; for Essex and Waller having joined their forces on Blewbury Downs, the 24th May, were advancing in opposite directions for the purpose of shutting him up in Oxford, and if not reduced by starvation, his army was to be engaged, and the person of the King was to be secured should he attempt to escape.

Towards the end of May Oxford was almost entirely invested, and Charles, being apprised of the design of the Parliament, and realising the extreme danger he was in, decided to leave the city. In order to facilitate his escape and draw off the attention of his pursuers, he first dispatched a party of horse and foot with cannon towards Abingdon, then held by Waller's army. On the night of the 3rd of June, Charles, accompanied only by some of his chief attendants and his guard of cavalry, marched out of the north gate of the city to the rendezvous outside the walls, where the main body of his troops awaited him; hence he passed unperceived between the two hostile camps. The force which accompanied the King on his march consisted of 3,000 foot and 4,000 horse, the remainder of his army being left behind in Oxford for the defence of the city during his absence. He proceeded by rapid marches to Worcester, and thence across the Severn to Bewdley; but he was as yet uncertain where to steer his course, being, as Clarendon pathetically expresses it, "hunted as a partridge upon the mountains, and knowing not whither to resort, or to what place to repair for rest." So soon, however, as the King heard that the two Parliamentary Generals

## THE SECOND BATTLE OF NEWBURY.

had separated, and that he should therefore have only one to contend with, he retraced the road he had followed in his flight from Oxford, and returned to Burford after a perilous march of seventeen days. Having reinforced his army by about 4,000 men from the garrison of Oxford, Charles determined to seize the opportunity of fighting Waller before he could be assisted by the other army under Essex, then on its way to the west.

After a series of well-executed manœuvres, Charles engaged and defeated Waller on the 29th of June, at Cropredy Bridge, on the banks of the Cherwell, near Banbury; the brunt of the battle being borne by the Earl of Cleveland on the one side, and by Middleton, Waller's Lieutenant-General on the other.

Three days after on the plains of Marston Moor, about seven miles from York, was fought the most decisive battle that had yet taken place. It was obstinately disputed between the largest armies that were engaged during the course of the war, nearly 50,000 men being present in the field. The battle was won by the division of the Parliamentary army commanded by the Earl of Manchester and Cromwell, in conjunction with the Yorkshire forces under Lord Fairfax and his son Sir Thomas, and with those of the Scots under the Earl of Leven and Major-General David Leslie, an able and dashing cavalry officer.* The result of this contest was most disastrous to the King's interests. The Marquis of Newcastle, enraged at seeing the King's army defeated through what he considered Prince Rupert's precipitate conduct, suddenly determined to quit the country, and, embarking at Scarborough two days after the battle, crossed over to Hamburgh, accompanied by his brother Charles and his two sons, General King (Lord Ethyn), Lord Fauconberg, Lord Widdrington, the Earl of Carnwath, Sir Edward Widdrington, Sir William Vavasour, Sir Francis Mackworth, Sir Charles Cavendish, Sir William Carnaby and his brother Francis, and about eighty other Royalists of rank.

Shortly after this disaster to the Royal army, Manchester, Fairfax, and Leven, with their combined forces besieged York, which surrendered to the Parliament on the 20th July; and the King thus lost all hold upon the north.

It is not within the scope of this brief *résumé* of the military occurrences between the First and Second Battles of Newbury

---

* David Leslie, afterwards Lord Newark, (no relation of Alexander Leslie, Earl of Leven), was a son of Patrick Leslie, Commendator of Lindores, and grandson of the Earl of Rothes.

to enter upon the irreconcilable jealousies and divisions which distracted the Parliamentary camp, and to which this great victory had given rise. The subject has been ably treated elsewhere. It will be sufficient to turn now to the events that followed the Royalist defeat and culminated in the Second Battle, which like its forerunner, bears the name of Newbury.

The first report concerning the issue of the action at Marston Moor reached the King at Evesham on the 5th of July. The messenger, however, had left the field while the victory inclined to the King's party, and it was not until the 12th that Charles heard the fatal result of the battle. The almost total destruction of his northern army confirmed the King in his determination to follow in pursuit of Essex before other reverses might occur. Encouraged by easy conquests, Essex had advanced further and further into the west, unaware of the dangers gathering behind him. In three weeks he had raised the siege of Lyme, taken Weymouth, Barnstaple, and Tiverton; and had dispersed, almost without a blow, the Royalist troops which attempted to stop him. He was in sight of Exeter when he heard that the King, having defeated Waller at Cropredy Bridge, was rapidly advancing against him, and collecting on the way all the forces he could command. A council of war being immediately called, it was put to the question whether they should go on and entrench themselves in Cornwall, or return, seek the King, and offer him battle. Essex was of the latter opinion; but several of the officers (among whom was Lord Robartes) possessed large estates in Cornwall, the rents of which had long been in arrear, and they relied on this opportunity to obtain payment from their tenants. They therefore opposed any idea of going back, asserting that the people of Cornwall,\* who were oppressed by the Royalists, would rise at the approach of the army, and that Essex would have the honour of dispossessing the King of this loyal county, hitherto his firmest support. Essex allowed himself to be persuaded, and, having sent to London for reinforcements, entered Cornwall, where he soon found himself pent up in a desperate position.

---

\* During the Civil War the mainstay of the throne was in the west and north, especially in Wales, Devon, and Cornwall. The famous Generals Grenville, Godolphin, Trevannion, and Slanning were called "the wheels of Charles's wain." They were, says Prince in his 'Worthies of Devon,' all slain at or near the same place, at the same time, and in the same cause.

## CHAPTER II.
## ATTACK ON DONNINGTON CASTLE.

To send Waller to his comrade's relief, with a newly equipped army, was then the strenuous effort of the Parliament; and as, to complicate matters, Prince Rupert was sure to move southward, it became a necessary part of their plan that Manchester's army should come out of its quarters in the eastern counties, and follow Waller's route westward.* Colonel Middleton was also dispatched with a force of 3,000 or 4,000 horse and foot to harass the King's rear. He had orders to reduce, on his way, Donnington Castle, the residence of Mr. John Packer, which on account of its commanding the great road by which the western trade was carried to London, had been garrisoned and fortified by order of the King shortly after the First Battle of Newbury the previous year, and Colonel Boys appointed its governor. The following Commission † is without subscription, but undoubtedly refers to the appointment of this staunch supporter of the Royal cause to the command of the fortress:—

"Charles R. Trusty and well-beloved, we greet you well. Whereas we have thought fit, for the defence and security of this part of our County of Berks, to leave a sufficient number of soldiers in Donnington Castle, we have made choice of your foot and of the dragooners of Sir Robt. Howard.‡ Wherefore our will and pleasure is that you forthwith repair with the said forces unto the said Castle, there to continue and keep the same for our use, and to command all the officers and soldiers therein as you shall find fit for our service. And for your so doing, these shall be your sufficient warrant. Given under our sign-manual at our Court at Newbury this 22nd Sept. 1643."

As to the supplies, it is recorded that "Donnington Castle hath three Hundreds out of which he (the Governour) weekly receives contribucion, viz<sup>t.</sup>, Kimbry [Kintbury] Eagle 20 parishes, Faire-Crosse 14 parishes, and Compton 8 parishes, besides Newbery is in too. These found him beds and

---

* See 'Manchester's Quarrel with Cromwell,' Camden Soc., pp. 58-59.
† Warburton's 'Prince Rupert,' vol. ii. p. 314
‡ Sir Robert Howard, fourth son of the Earl of Berkshire, was knighted by the King at Cropredy Bridge, June 29th, 1644.

DONNINGTON CASTLE.
OUTWORKS OF DEFENCE.

## ATTACK ON DONNINGTON CASTLE.

weekely payment for the building the workes, which cost about £1,000. Faire-Crosse Hundred paid about £60 per weeke."* The main element of defence of this little fortress was its massive gate-house, with barbican and portcullis, and the extensive series of earthworks constructed by Boys, and thickly planted with his heaviest guns. The remainder of the structure with its subordinate towers and curtain walls had, as Camden says, "windows on all sides, very lightsome," and was incapable of withstanding an artillery attack at a short range. It was more especially owing to the brilliant heroism, skill and dash displayed by Sir John Boys and his small garrison, whose daring deeds and chivalrous adventures appear almost incredible, that the old Castle became a post of such strategic value, and was so long and obstinately maintained against the almost overwhelming numbers and organised efforts of their powerful but unsuccessful antagonists.

The operations of Middleton before Donnington Castle are mentioned in the following terms in 'The True Informer' from Saturday, August 10th, to Saturday, August 17th, 1644. "On Monday, July 29th, Lt.-Genl. Middleton came before Donnington Castle with between 3,000 and 4,000 horse and foot. At their entrance into Newbury they took divers of the stragglers of Donnington Castle, and on Wednesday morning drew up both horse and foot against the Castle, and without summons fell on a barn,† wherein the Governor of the Castle had placed some musquetiers, which our guards gained, beat the enemy, and took divers of them prisoners, after which the General sent a summons to the Governor, in these words:—
'Sir, I demand you to render me Donnington Castle for the use of the King and Parliament. If you please to entertain a present treaty you shall have honourable terms. My desire to spare blood makes me propose this. I desire your answer. JOHN MIDDLETON.' 'Sir,' answered Boys, 'I am instructed by His Majesty's express commands, and have not yet learned to obey any other than my Sovereign. To spare blood, do as you please, but myself and those who are with me are fully resolved to venture ours in maintaining what we are entrusted

---

* Symond's 'Diary,' p. 144. Sir John Boys appears to have been well off for supplies, as in the month of July, 1644, we find he was able to spare "four score and seven oxen," for the garrison at Oxford, which were sent from Donnington Castle Park and put into Christchurch meadows.—MS. Accounts of Captain Henry Stevens, Commissary-General in His Majesty's army, in the possession of his descendant the Rev. Thomas Stevens, late Warden of Bradfield College.

† A portion of the walls of this barn is still standing on the south-west side of the Castle farm-yard; and formed part of the original out-buildings of the Castle.

with, which is the answer of JOHN BOYS. Donnington Castle, July 31, 1644.' After this answer received, the said Lieutenant-General drew up his foot with scaling ladders and other provisions, dividing themselves into three several places, at last the enemy fired the barne, whereupon our soldiers who were in it came forth, and the rest, in regard that they had not great pieces to batter the Castle, retreated with the loss of 6 common soldiers and a Lieutenant, concerning whom the Governor of the Castle (considering he had gott a great prize, though he lost three persons) sent a Drum to the Lt.-Genl. with this message. 'For Lt.-Generall Middleton. Sir, Christian charity requires me to give you notice that I have many bodies of yours, which I cannot accommodate with Christian burial, as likewise many of your wounded men which I know not how to dispose of. This I thought good to give you notice of, that you might take some course for them accordingly. Your Servant, JOHN BOYS. Donnington Castle, July 31, 1644.' To which message the Lt.-Generall sent this answer—'I conceive no inherient holinesse to be in any place or buriall, for all earth is fit for that use. In that you say you have no accommodation for our wounded men, who are your prisoners, if you please to exchange them, quality for quality, I shall take it a curtesie done to, Sir, Your Servant, JNO. MIDDLETON.'" On the following Monday morning, the Castle being "recommended" by the Parliament to Major-General Brown, Governor of Abingdon and Commander of the Forces of the Associated Counties of Oxon, Berks, and Bucks, Middleton proceeded to join Essex in the west. On his way he was met and routed by Sir Francis Doddington and Sir William Courtenay, and compelled to retreat to Sherborne in Dorsetshire, where he fell upon a party of the King's horse, and, putting them to flight, repaired his credit by this unexpected and opportune success.

CHAPTER III.

## THE ARMIES OF THE KING AND PARLIAMENT.

Manchester with his army arrived at Huntingdon on the 8th of September. By that time, however, the fate of Essex in Cornwall had been decided. Before relief could reach him he had been obliged to make his own escape by sea to Plymouth, on his way to London, leaving the mounted troops, under Sir William Balfour, to cut their way eastward as they could, and his foot, under Major-General Skippon, to negotiate terms of surrender, which were agreed to on September 1st. The news of Essex's defeat reached Manchester at Huntingdon, whence on the 8th of September, he wrote to the Derby-House Committee,* expressing his condolence over the sad event,—"The Lord's arm," he adds, "is not shortened, though we be much weakened. I trust he will give us a happy recovery. I shall with all speed I can, march in observance of your former orders." He was now instructed to march westward for Abingdon with all possible expedition, and to send advertisement of his progress as he advanced.

The activity and firmness of the Parliament at first caused the King to slacken his movements. He addressed a pacific message to the Houses; and, for three weeks, contented himself with appearing before Plymouth and Lyme, which did not surrender. Towards the end of September, however, he learnt that Montrose, who had long since promised him civil war in Scotland, had at last succeeded, and was already obtaining one triumph after another. In a fortnight he had gained two battles (at Tippermuir, September 1st, and at Dee Bridge, September 12th), occupied Perth, taken Aberdeen by storm, raised most of the northern clans, and spread fear to the very gates of Edinburgh. On hearing this news, Charles flattered himself that the disaster of Marston Moor was repaired, that Parliament would soon find in the north a powerful adversary, and that he himself might without fear proceed to follow up his successes in the south. He resolved to march upon London; and, to give his expedition a popular and decisive appearance, a proclamation, sent forth in every direction at the moment of his departure, invited all his subjects of the south and east to rise in arms, choose officers for themselves, and joining him on his way, march with him to summon the Parliament at length to accept peace.†

Prince Rupert on the 3rd of October had left the King for Bristol; and the latter promised not to engage until the Prince returned to him with reinforcements of Langdale's and Gerrard's troops. On the 11th, however, the pressing necessities of his four gallant garrisons at Basing, Donning-

---

* The Derby-House Committee consisted, for the English Parliament, of seven selected Peers and fourteen selected Commoners. Essex, Manchester, Waller, and Cromwell were of the English part of this Committee. Derby House, Cannon Row, Westminster, being the meeting-place of the Committee, it received the name of the "Derby-House Committee."

† The proclamation is dated from Chard, September 30th, 1644. 'Rushworth,' vol. ii. 3, 715. Guizot's 'Hist. Eng. Reform.,' p. 244.

ton, Portland, and Banbury, induced him to put his army in motion; and on that day he thus writes to his nephew from Blandford:—

THE KING TO PRINCE RUPERT.

"Nephew,      [In cipher.]
I am advertised by a dispatch from Secretary Nicholas that the Governours of Basing, Banbury and Donnington Castle, must accommodate in case they be not relieved within a few days. The importance of which place and consequently [illegible] hath made me resolve to begin my march on Tuesday towards Salisbury, where, Prince Rupert may rely upon it, the King of England shall be, God willing, on Wednesday next, where I will desire Prince Rupert to come with what strength of horse and foot you can, and the two demi-cannons, many of my men being unarmed. I have sent to Bristol for musquets which I desire Rupert to speed to me. I desire to hear daily from you, and particularly when you will be with me, and which way you will march, and how strong you can come to

Your loving Uncle and most faithful friend,
Blandford, 11th Oct. 1644.      CHARLES R."*

If everything had happened as the King anticipated, he might have arrived in London before the Parliament's forces could have joined to form a new army; but his troops, instead of increasing on their march, as Charles had supposed, daily diminished: their pay was long in arrear; the men were half-starved, and in want of shoes and stockings; sickness had disabled many; desertions were numerous; and he was obliged to make frequent halts in towns, to wait for money and other necessaries, which he found would not be supplied when he had gone.† Owing to these delays, the King did not reach Salisbury till the 15th of October, six weeks after the surrender of the Parliamentarians at Lostwithiel; and, instead of proceeding toward London, as was at first intended,

---

* Warburton's 'Prince Rupert,' vol. iii. pp. 26-27.

† The King's army about this time consisted of 5,500 foot and 4,000 horse. (Clarendon, vol. ii. p. 541.) The Royalist forces, being supported by voluntary contributions, were poorly paid, whereas the pay of the Parliament was very good, especially that for the officers; but soon after the breaking out of the War an ordinance was passed, wherein it was enacted that all officers of the Earl of Essex's army, whose pay amounted to 10s. a day and upwards, should only receive half their pay, the other half being postponed until the troubles should be over. Horses at this time were valued at about £4; they had been as cheap as 30s. and 50s. Oats were 1s. 6d. a bushel, and 12s. a quarter; peas and beans 2s. a bushel. Hay 5d. the tod; and grass-feed 2s. 6d. a week. In 1655 wheat was 33s. and malt 20s. a quarter.

THE ARMIES OF THE KING AND PARLIAMENT. 139

he decided to direct his march to Oxford, relieving his distressed garrisons on the way. Before this could be accomplished, however, he had to meet the combined army of the Parliament at Newbury.

While Charles was advancing from Cornwall, news had come to Oxford that the gallant old Marquis of Winchester—

"He who in impious times untainted stood,
And midst rebellion durst be just and good,"

was so hard pressed at Basing that he must surrender in ten days if no relief came. Sir Arthur Aston, the governor at Oxford, declared that the dangers of the relief were more than any soldier who understood command would expose himself to, and that he could not suffer any of the small garrison under his charge to be hazarded in the attempt; but Colonel Gage, who had lately come from the English regiment in Flanders, a worthier servant than whom the King did not possess, offered to take the command, and hoped to give a good account of it, if the Lords then at Oxford would enlist their servants, and raise a good troop or two of horse. Colonel Hawkins' regiment, having opportunely come into Oxford, was raised to 400 by volunteers, and, with 250 horse, was placed under Gage's command. With this small force he threaded his way through bye roads to Wallingford and Aldermaston, and thence to Basing, where, on the 14th of September, he attacked and beat off the besiegers, levied arms and provisions in Basingstoke and the neighbouring villages, relieved the garrison, and then, though the whole country was up, came back to Oxford on the sixth day with 100 prisoners; having lost in the expedition only two officers, Captain Sturges, of the Queen's Lifeguard, and Cornet Stonor, of the Wallingford troop, with nine others, and about forty or fifty slightly wounded.* It was agreed on all sides that a more soldierly action had not been performed during the war. Colonel Gage was knighted for this and other gallant services, in the Presence Chamber at Christ Church, Oxford, November 2nd, 1644; but the brave Colonel did not long enjoy his

---

* Walker's 'Hist. Discourses,' p. 95. Gage's force crossed the Kennet by a ford near Burghfield Bridge (the Bridge itself having been previously broken down), and forded the Thames near Pangbourne. In the year 1839, in digging a grave in the nave of Ewhurst Church, on the Basingstoke road, near Kingsclere, the remains of two soldiers, with portions of military ornaments, were found at a shallow depth. These interments had the appearance of having been hastily conducted, and were supposed to have been the bodies of officers slain in a skirmish in the neighbourhood during the operations before Basing.

distinction, being slain at Culham Bridge, near Abingdon, the following January.

When the King arrived at Salisbury (15th October) he was informed that the Parliament had made preparations to intercept his march; that Waller with his troops lay at Andover; that Manchester had advanced as far as Reading with 5,000 horse and foot, and 24 pieces of ordnance; and that the London Trained-bands, consisting of the Red and Blue regiments of the City of London, the Red regiment of Westminster, the Yellow regiments of Southwark and the Tower Hamlets, making in all about 5,000 men, commanded by Sir James Harrington, were beginning their march to join him. The Earl of Essex's army, newly organized and equipped, was near Portsmouth, as well as those troops returning from the west under Colonel Middleton; and these were expecting orders to join the other forces.

Had Charles used this information, and hastened his march to Oxford, he might have brought this year's campaign to a conclusion, which would have been the most reasonable thing for him to have done, because he had received letters from Prince Rupert, in which he stated that it was impossible for him to bring up his troops so soon as the King expected. If such a determination had been formed, Donnington Castle and Banbury might both at a seasonable time have been relieved. But misfortune always attended the movements of the unhappy monarch. He was too easily led. John Milton thus describes the King's fatal peculiarity:—" Whether with his enemies or friends, in the Court or Camp, he was always in the hands of another; now of his Wife, then of the Bishops; now of the Peers, then of the Soldiery; and lastly of his enemies: for the most part, too, he followed the worse counsel, and most always of the worser men." In this instance Lord Goring who did not wish Prince Rupert to join in these operations, urgently advised the King to march against Waller, who was at that time with about 3,000 horse and foot at Andover, and at some little distance from the bulk of the Parliament's forces. A Council of War was held, and the King at last yielded; the ostensible object being to cut off Waller before he could effect a junction with Essex and Manchester, and thus the more readily to advance the relief of Basing and Donnington Castle.

The cannon which the Royalists had taken from Essex in Cornwall had been left at Exeter. The larger guns then with the forces were ordered to be sent to the garrison at Langford House, near Salisbury; the remainder of the artillery and baggage-waggons were placed at Wilton House. The Royal

## THE ARMIES OF THE KING AND PARLIAMENT. 141

army was drawn up in Clarendon Park, and guards were posted at all the entrances to the City of Salisbury, to prevent information of the King's purpose being spread about. This succeeded so well that the Royalists reached within four miles of Andover before Waller had any notion of their movements. On the enemy's approach he drew out his whole force, as though disposed to fight; on perceiving the King's strength, however, he drew back into the town, leaving a body of cavalry to make good his retreat; but the King's troops charged furiously, and effected a complete rout, pursuing the Parliamentarians through the town of Andover, giving no quarter. Waller, nevertheless, made good his retreat to Basingstoke. "It was a greate mercy of God," he says in his 'Recollections,' "when the King came upòn me with his whole army at Andover, and I had nothing but a mere body of horse and dragooners with me, I made a faire retreate to Basingstoke."

This affair is thus recorded by Captain Symonds, who was then with the King's army. "Friday, 18 Oct., 1644. His Majestie, &c., left Sarum and marched towards Andevor, Waller's forces being then in Andevor, Generall Goring raysed a forlorne of horse, consisting of about 200 gentlemen, who were spare commanders of horse, beate them out of Andevor, took Carr, a Scot colonel, and another captain, a Scott, that died, who a little before his death rose from under the table, saying he would not dye like a dog under a table, but sate downe upon a chayre, and ymediatly dyed of his wounds. Tooke about 80 prisoners, followed the chase of them two miles, who all ran in great confusion. Had not night come so soone, it might have made an end of Waller's army for our intention was to engage them, but they disappointed our hopes by their heeles."*

The condition of Waller's force at this time appears to have been quite as deplorable as that of the King's army. Writing from Shaftesbury to the Derby-House Committee, on the 27th September, he says:—"Our wants are so extreme, that a major of horse hath been forced to borrow six pound to pay for the shoeing of his Horse. I am sorry we are so inconsiderable to the House. This last night and this morning it was in discourse that the officers should send in a petition to the Parliament for the supply of their wants." Referring to the question as to which of the Generals should take the command after the three armies were united, he adds:—"I doubt not but that the Earl of Manchester and myself will agree well

---

* Symonds's 'Diary,' p. 141.

enough about that, but I am so heartily weary of this war that I shall submit to anything that may induce to the dissipating of it." Addressing the Committee on the 20th of October from Basingstoke, he has even worse tidings to communicate as to his difficulties in obtaining supplies and clothing for his men. "Your poore creatures," he writes, "are so pittifull an object that the like is not to be seene in England. . . . . It is no little griefe to us that our poore dragoones goe naked this weather. O that they might be thought upon for clothes. We can but enforme them it is not in our power to help them." Worse still, his men were daily deserting, and in the absence of regular supplies, the discipline of the troops was considerably shaken. No time was lost by the Parliament in attending to Waller's requirements, and the next day eight hundred suits of clothes were ordered to be sent to clothe Sir William's "naked" dragoons, together with forty loads of cheese and biscuit dispatched to Farnham Castle to be apportioned between the armies.

Cromwell, who had been in the neighbourhood of Banbury, and present at the latter part of the siege with a detachment of horse, joined at Reading the army of the Earl of Manchester, who for more than a fortnight had been lying idle there, finding excuse after excuse for not marching further west. On the 16th October, the Earl, after a consultation with Waller, marched from Reading to Basingstoke, and on the 21st his forces, united with those of Essex and Waller, near Basing, consisted of about 11,000 foot and 8,000 horse and dragoons.* Such a force, both in respect of numbers and composition, had not as yet been formed under one leader since the commencement of the war. To the chief command of this army, magnificent for the period, the Earl of Manchester, in the absence of the Earl of Essex, was nominated. Cromwell retained as before the rank of General of Horse. The whole, wound up to the highest pitch of enthusiasm, prepared to advance against the King.

The Derby-House Committee had by this time sent two of their number, namely the Scottish representative, Sir Archibald Johnston, of Warriston,† and the English, Mr. John Crewe,

---

\* "That after this conjunction, wee being at Basing, neare 11,000 foote and about 8,000 horse and dragoones, and the King with not above 10,000 horse and foote." Cromwell's evidence from the 'Information against the Earl of Manchester'; Public Record Office.

† Afterwards Lord Registrar of Scotland, and "one of Cromwell's Lords." He was one of the most unrelenting of the enemies of Montrose, who, when some others proposed more merciful measures, insisted upon his suffering the whole punishment described by the sentence, and even jeered him as he was preparing for execution.

THE ARMIES OF THE KING AND PARLIAMENT. 143

to see that all possible advantages should be taken against the enemy, and to prevent any contention between the chief officers as to the command, and other matters. These two civilians met Manchester at Basingstoke, and that their presence tended to allay the ill-humour and murmurings among the Parliamentary leaders, we may gather from the words of Baillie, who was then in London as a Scotch Commissioner to the Westminster Assembly of Divines. In a letter to his cousin, he says:—" The emulations and quarrells among all these three armies, both Generalls and inferiour officers, were formidable; yet such was the diligence and wisdom of the Chancellor and others that Warriston and Mr. Crew going down from the Committee of both kingdom's did move all the three Generalls and their armies, to joyn cordialie against the enemie."*

At this time a difference of opinion existed in the Parliamentary camp as to the best course of action. Cromwell and some of the other generals urged a direct interception of the royal army; but Manchester, who seemed disposed to give the King every chance, resolved to march back to Reading, with the object (as he states in his defence) of making the attack from the north, or left bank of the Kennet. Cromwell's evidence partly bears out this view. "On Tuesday, 22nd Oct., it being agreed (as we thought) to march towards him [the King] or to interpose betwixt him and Redding, about Aldermaston Heath, and our horse marching before to the heath, our foot struck down to Swallowfield, and thence next day to Redding, as if we had declined to fight, and thus making fower days march from Basingstoke to Newbery (which might have been little more than one t'other way), wee gave the King opportunity to have got cleare to Oxford (if hee would) without fighting; and, staying there, he had thereby time to fortify himself against our approaches to Newberry.†

Manchester further states in his 'Narrative of the Campaign': "For the subsistence of the armies at Basingstoke it was concluded to march to Redding, and so come uppon the

---

Retributive justice, however, willed that he himself should suffer an ignominious death thirteen years after, on the very spot where Montrose was executed. He had been attainted at the Restoration, and fled, but was seized in France about two years after, brought over and executed at Edinburgh. This "stern and sullen Puritan" was a very active opponent of the King's interests, and was suspected of a secret correspondence with the English regicides.

* Baillie (Robert), the 'Letters and Journals of' Bannatyne Club, vol. ii. p. 237.
† Cromwell's evidence, from the 'Information against the Earl of Manchester.' State Papers, Public Record Office.

other side of the Kennett uppon the enemy, and to forse the King to fight, notwithstanding the enemy being in their strengthe. My Lord of Essex beeing in Redding leaft sicke."

Nor were the Royalists at all clear as to the strength and intentions of the Parliamentarians, as the following extract from a letter to Prince Rupert from Lord Digby shews:—
"Wee may promise ourselves a very happy conclusion of this summer's warre, for now we know the worst of the Rebells forces. Essex, Manchester, and Waller, and the Trained Bands newly come out of London, were all joyned yesterday, and by all intelligence of those who hath seen them at their rendezvous do not muster in all [cypher] foot and [....] horse, of which the only considerable ones are Cromwell's. His Majesty, over and above what your Highness knows of, hath [here the forces are enumerated in cypher]. It seems the Rebells begin to apprehend themselves too weake to encounter us, for our intelligence this morning is that they have retreated to Reading. Believe it is for their feares, and the distractions in London are soe great, in all probabilitie it will be fatall to them. Yours, &c., GEO. DIGBYE. Newbery, 23 Oct., 1644."*

The easy success of the King's army in the affair with Waller at Andover so raised the spirits of his troops that they were eager to engage the combined forces of the Parliament; but, as Clarendon remarks, the King wisely did not seek the opportunity. It was, however, resolved to attempt the relief of the closely besieged garrisons of Donnington Castle, Basing, and Banbury before going into quarters at Oxford for the winter; and, for this purpose, orders were dispatched for the guns and baggage, which had been left at Langford and Wilton, to be at once sent forward.

On Saturday, the 19th of October, the King marched from Andover to Whitchurch, where he was to remain until Lord Brentford, who was behind, and the Earl of Cleveland, who had been detained with the siege of Portland, should come up with the remainder of his force. The following day (Sunday) a party of horse was dispatched to relieve Donnington Castle; and the next night a spy in the service of the Parliament returned to the camp with the following intelligence:—"His Majesty's army was in Whitchurch all Sunday night; and that town was full of soldiers, both horse and foot, but their train of artillery was not there, only some few wagons belonging to Officers. That their train stood on Andover downes, within two miles of Whitchurch or there-

* Addl. MSS. Brit. Mus., No. 18980.

abouts. The King was last night at Whitchurch, but by some reported to be at Winchester, and by others at Andover. The last night, about 8 of the clock, went out about 4,000 horse out of Whitchurch to give an alarm, and returned this morning about break of day. [This was the party which was sent to relieve Donnington Castle.] Yesterday it was ordered that the train should be drawn up to Whitchurch Downes, but was hindered by the wet weather, and so staid two miles short. And that this day [Monday] the rendezvous was to be kept upon Sevenborough [Seven Barrows]*: the drums beat up at Whitchurch at break of day. This day about 8 o'clock there stood at Whitclear [? Whitway or Highclere] a great body of horse, as he conceiveth to be 2,000, on this side Sevenborough. That about 12 o'clock there were going to Kingsclere some empty carts, accompanied with some troops of horse, which carts he supposed were to carry provisions that were summoned to be brought to Donnington Castle. [These apparently were the empty carts returning from the Castle.] That it is generally reported the King quarters at Donnington the next night. Carriages were warned at Bawgus [Baughurst] and the parishes adjacent, to appear this morning at Whitchurch. From Newbury, that great provisions of victuals are made, and all towns adjoining, for the army, which is expected there this night. That a great party from Oxford and Wallingford is to be there to meet the King's forces this night." †

By Monday, the 21st October, the whole army had advanced as far as Kingsclere, which, being mid-way between Basing and Newbury, was considered a suitable place from which to attempt the relief of the former garrison. This position, however, having been found too much exposed for an army threatened by an enemy so much superior in cavalry, the embarrassed Royalists, after a night's halt, proceeded on their march to Newbury; a general rendezvous being appointed on Red Heath, on the south side of the town, the head-quarters of the horse being in the town of Newbury, with an advanced post on the Lambourn at Welford.‡ On the King's arrival at the camp on Red Heath, he was welcomed by Colonel Boys, who received the honour of knighthood from his Majesty

---

* Part of a Cuirassier's breastplate of the Caroline period was turned up by the plough near the Seven Barrows, a group of ancient British tumuli, in the year 1881.

† 'The Parliamentary Scout,' 24 to 31 Oct., 1644.

‡ "The manor belonging to Mr. Hinton *jure uxoris*; a faire habitacion, com. Berks." Symonds's 'Diary,' p. 143.

T

for his valiant defence of Donnington, and was made Colonel of the regiment which he had before commanded as Lieut.-Colonel to Earl Rivers, who was nominally the chief governor of the Castle.

A messenger having brought to the King at Newbury intelligence of the exhausted condition of the garrison at Banbury, Lord Northampton was dispatched on Thursday, 24th October, from the camp with 1,500 horse for the relief of the Castle, which for thirteen weeks had been gallantly defended by the Earl's brother, Sir William Compton. That night he quartered at Farnborough, and the next day near Woodstock, where the Earl was joined by Colonel Gage with a regiment of foot and some horse from Oxford. Thence the united force advanced to Banbury, routed Col. Fiennes, and raised the siege. The very day after this service had been so well performed, Colonel Sir John Hurry, who has been mentioned as a renegade, seized the opportunity to consummate a second act of treachery. Under pretence of retiring to the continent, he obtained leave to withdraw from the Royal army (in which, it is probable, he considered his services not sufficiently valued); and, availing himself of his pass, hastened to the Earl of Manchester's camp and betrayed the unprovided condition and diminished numbers of the King. The immediate consequence of this intelligence was the Second Battle of Newbury.

CHAPTER IV.

SIEGE OF DONNINGTON CASTLE.

Meanwhile, after the departure of Middleton, Colonel Horton (Lieut.-Colonel of Lord Wharton's regiment), who is described as Adjutant-General to Major-General Brown, was left to blockade Donnington Castle. Having effectually guarded all the avenues leading to the stout little stronghold so that no succour could get to its relief, he summoned Boys to surrender, but met with defiance. Accordingly, having received reinforcements from Abingdon, Windsor, and Reading, he commenced to lay close siege to the Castle, and raised a battery "at the foot of the hill towards Newbury." *
In a twelve days' cannonade he beat down three of the south towers and part of the curtain-wall. Having received another

---

* Traces of this battery can still be discerned in the meadows on the south side of the road leading from Donnington to Speen. It is shown on the Plan.

## THE SIEGE OF DONNINGTON CASTLE.

contingent, Horton then summoned the Governor a second time, in the following terms:—"Sir, We have formerly testified our clemency in tendring you quarter upon your surrender of the Castle for the use of the King and Parliament, and now again we, being desirous (notwithstanding our increase of powers) to manifest our mercy, do hereby once for all freely offer yourself and men free quarter in case you yield the Castle, for the use aforesaid, before Wednesday next at 10 of the clock in the forenoon, and further we here testifie (in the presence of God) that if this our favour be not accepted and the Castle surrendered, there shall be no active man amongst you have his life, if God shall ever please to yield them to our mercy. Yours, JEREMY HORTON." To which Colonel Boys replied:—"Sir, Neither your new addition of forces, nor your high threatning language, shall deter me, or the rest of these honest men with me, from our loyalty to our sovereign, but we do resolve to maintain this place the uttermost of our powers, and for the matter of quarter, yours may expect the like on Wednesday or sooner if you please. This is the answer of, Sir, Your servant, JNO. BOYS."

Upon this second denial, Manchester himself came to Newbury on Friday, October 4th, and, getting another refusal, resolved to storm the Castle on Wednesday, October 9th; but his men not being willing for the work, the proposed assault was abandoned, and Manchester returned to Reading, giving orders, however, for the siege to be continued. This was conducted with ordnance of a fairly heavy calibre. Symonds, in his 'Diary,' thus refers to the garrison at this time:—"The men within the Castle were the Earl of Rivers' regiment, about 200, and 25 horse, 4 peice of cannon. The enemy made a great open battery, with their hundreds of 36lb bullets, toto a 500 and odd bullets, most of them 36lb., some 6lb, some 12lb." Doubtless there were other guns used by besiegers and the besieged; and it may be interesting here to give some particulars as to the capacity of the artillery at this period,* thus—

|  | Bore. | Weight. | Weight of Shot. | Point Blank Range. | Extreme range. |
|---|---|---|---|---|---|
|  | IN. | LBS. | LBS. | PACES. | PACES. |
| Cannon Royal | 8½ | 8000 | 66 | 800 | 1930 |
| Culverin | 5¼ | 4500 | 17½ | 200 | 2500 |
| Demi-culverin | 4 | 3400 | 9½ | 200 | 2500 |
| Saker | 4 | — | 7 | 170 | 1700 |
| Minion | 3½ | 1000 | 4 | 150 | 1500 |
| Drakes | Carried a ball from 4 to 6 lb., and were used as light field-artillery. | | | | |

* See Monson's 'Tracts,' p. 342.

There were also guns termed "Basilisks" after that mythic creature; they were 48-pounders. Such a one is called "a warning piece" in Vicars' account of the siege of Bristol. "Falcons" with 6lb. shots, and "Falconets" with 3, 2, and 1lb.; "Peteraroes" for throwing stones, &c.

We incidentally obtain some information as to the size of the projectiles of this period from an order for stores entered in the Commons' Journals 9th October, 1645, shortly before the taking of Basing House. The following items are specified:—Whole-Cannon English shot of 63lbs. weight. Demi-Cannon shot 32lbs. weight. Granado shells 13in. and 10in. diameter, and "One Great Mortar Piece." The latter was a ponderous piece of ordnance of terrible destructive power and exceptional calibre, its use being almost exclusively restricted to siege operations. One of these monster mortars is mentioned as having been brought into requisition at the siege of Donnington Castle, when seventeen shells were fired from it by the besiegers under Colonel Dalbier. Some further reference to this "Mortar-Piece" is made in the account of the last days of the siege of the Castle. At the siege of Gloucester the besiegers shot, besides granadoes, great stones from their mortar-pieces, and red-hot iron balls of 18lbs. and 22lbs. weight. A granado of 80lbs. weight is mentioned as having been shot from a mortar-piece at the siege of Basing. Also logs bound with iron hoops. Cross-bar shot was also used, *i.e.*, shot with iron bars crossing through them, sometimes standing six or eight inches out at both sides, very useful in demolishing the enemy's palisading, &c.

The day after Manchester's departure the besiegers removed their guns "to the other side of the Castle," that is, to Snelsmore Heath. Here the trenches constructed by the Parliamentarians are still very distinctly traceable, as shown on the Plan. The line of fire from this position was somewhat oblique; which to some extent accounts for the preservation of the towers of the Gate-house. An attempt was made to approach the walls by saps, * but, this being perceived by Boys, the garrison made a sortie, and beat the enemy out of their trenches, killing the chief in command of the party and many soldiers: and they brought away the "cannon-baskets,"† with a large quantity of arms and ammunition. Though much disheartened, the Parliament-

---

* "Saps," that is trenches made under cover from the fire of the enemy's place, behind a mantelet or stuffed gabion. Mantelets on wheels were used during the Civil War.
† Gabions.

THE SIEGE OF DONNINGTON CASTLE. 149

men went on their approaches, and continued bombarding the
Castle until Friday, 18th October; and then, hearing of the
advance of the King's army, they drew off their ordnance and
retired. In nineteen days (twelve at Speen and seven at
Snelsmore) they had spent over 1000 rounds on the impregnable little castle with very little hurt to its defenders.
Horton and his men retired towards Abingdon, and the
Windsor force to Newbury; while Manchester's detachment
fell back on Reading. The 'Mercurius Aulicus' of October
15th, 1644, contains some curious information as to the siege
and defence of the Castle. The following is an extract:—
"Such was Col. Horton's great mercy that the day before the
Governor and his men were to dye (in case they did not surrender) they sent Master Fogge, Horton's Chaplain, with a
letter which Fogge had procured from Mistris Fleetwood, in
Newbury, to her husband, Dr. Fleetwood,* Chaplain to Earl
Rivers' regiment (to whom Col. Boys is Lt.-Col.), and this
letter Fogge brought to Dr. Fleetwood in the Castle, wherein
Mistris Fleetwood wrote—'that if the Castle did refuse Col.
Horton's mercy, they were all lost men,' and therefore desired
her husband and the rest to prepare themselves (and indeed
so they did) to shew themselves gallant men. This letter,
you must know, the poor gentlewoman was forced to write to
her husband, tho' Fogge had the wording of it, and to make
the pageantry more complete, Col. Horton pretends a great
unwillingness to let any such letter passe into the Castle, and
therefore sends this note to Fogge, on purpose also to be
communicated;—' Mr. Fogge, At the earnest sute of Mrs.
Fleetwood I am instructed to permit the passage of this letter
into the Castle by your hands, hereby requiring you to testifie
to all therein (if the Governor will permit it) that if they
please to come forth before tomorrow at 9 o'clock in the forenoon they may have faire quarter, otherwise according to my
solemn vow they may expect no favour. JEREMY HORTON.'
This poor preaching was easily discerned by Col. Boys, who
read it and scorned it." The 'Mercurius Aulicus' adds that

---

* Dr. James Fleetwood, son of Sir George Fleetwood, was made
D.D., in 1642, at Oxford by the King's special command for the good
services he had done him at the battle of Edgehill. Upon the Restoration he was the first person that was sworn Chaplain-in-Ordinary to
Charles II.; when he was also made Provost of King's College, Rector
of Anstey in Hertfordshire, and of Denham in Bucks. In 1675 he was
consecrated Bishop of Worcester. He died in 1683, in the eighty-first
year of his age There was also a James Fleetwood, S.T.P., Rector of
Shaw, near Newbury, shortly after the Restoration, which living he
resigned in March 1660-61.

"Manchester also gave orders to an unfortunate brother to Col. Boys (who was a Captain in Manchester's army) to write to the Governor, to assure him that, if he would surrender the Castle, he should not only have all honourable conditions, but freely be admitten to his house, and possess his estate quietly in Kent ; * and, if he would come forth and capitulate, he should do it safely ; if not, [to demand] that his brother might be permitted to come to him into the castle, to inform him further of his Lordship's intention. To whom the Governor made answer :—That neither the Earl of Manchester and all his forces should deter him from his fidelity and loyalty to his Sovereign, neither would he entertain any manner of parley concerning the delivery up of the place, which he was resolved to maintain to his last drop of blood."

A letter, written by Chaplain Fogge,† respecting the siege, is given in the 'London Post' of October 23rd, 1644. It is to this effect :—" Sir, These are to certifie to you that Sir Miles Hobart's regiment is here at Newbery, where we had almost brought Donnington Castle down to the ground by the active endeavours of General-Adjutant Colonell Horton. But Lieut.-Gen. Brown called him and his force away, and the gunnes are taken off and carried to Reading, and here is only one regiment and some of Col. Montague's, and 2 or 3 troops of horse ; yet we keep them in the Castle, and if we might have gunnes and furniture, I would undertake we could have the Castle in a week. * * * The town of Newbery and the county adjacent cry out they must fall if we go and let

---

* Sir John Boys' estate was at Bonnington in Kent : it was seized and sequestrated by the Parliament.

† When Prince Rupert took Bolton, and put so many to the sword, the Rev. Robert Fogge had a narrow escape. Having set his man to wait with two horses at a certain place, he determined, if the town was taken, to ride for his life ; but when he came thither, the man and his horse were gone. He happened, however, to meet with another horse, or else he would have been killed, for the Prince had a particular aim at him. In the war-time he married his second wife, who proved to be a papist. Her sons were in the King's service, and much enraged against their father-in-law. One of them sent him a challenge. He took his sword under his coat and met him, and so humbled the young man that he was glad to be reconciled. Fogge died at Nantwich in April, 1676, aged 80. (Palmer's 'Nonconformists' Memorial,' vol. ii, p. 604.) Fogge's son Rowland subscribed to the Declaration in 1665, and ultimately became Dean of Chester. One of the Rev. Mr. Fogge's family, a certain Captain Fogge, directed the plundering of St. George's Chapel, Windsor. The numerous gold vessels, which the munificence and piety of successive Sovereigns and Knights-of-the-Garter had here consecrated to religious uses, were said to have been exquisitely wrought and to have weighed 3580 ounces.

POSITION OF THE ROYALISTS. 151

the Castle stand. I wish the Committee were well informed concerning it. I dare say it is a place of such consequence as they would not lose the opportunity to gayne it, considering it is sore battered, and one breach in it that many may enter abreast. Truely two or three fire-balls or granadoes shot into it would make it ours. The Lord guide the state and be with you and us all.* Yr humble servt., R. F." [Robert Fogge]

CHAPTER V.

POSITION OF THE ROYALISTS.

Before proceeding further, it will be necessary to give an outline of the position of the Royal army on the morning of Saturday, the 26th of October. The Royalist strength is said by the 'True Informer' of October 26th, to have been about 13,000, " whereof 7,000 foot are most of them very poore for want of cloaths, which is provided for them, but are not used for fear they should run away, or should be lost in battle." Charles despised his late antagonist, Waller; and, having little apprehension of an attack, was ignorant of the strength of the enemy gathering around him. He remained quietly at Newbury, resolving to await the Earl of Northampton's return from Banbury, in order to relieve Basing. But the Earl's absence together with that of the troops under Prince Rupert, who was detained at Bristol endeavouring to raise a sufficient force to come to the King's assistance, frustrated this plan. Upon the near approach of the Parliamentary army, Charles, finding it too late to attempt a retreat to Oxford, was compelled to fight, contrary to his promise and inclination. He determined, however, as in the former action, to act only on the defensive. On Friday, 25th October, he therefore drew his army into " the fields between Donnington Castle and Newbury," thinking it wisest to await an attack, and to try the issue of a general action, on ground of his own selection; his judgment in this instance being seconded by an intimate knowledge of a locality where the year before he had met the same enemy. It is not difficult to fix the position occupied by the Royal army at this time. (See Plan.) The fields above-mentioned were the scene of the principal part of the fighting after the Royalists were subsequently driven from Speen Hill. They extend on the west to the old high-

* This letter is given in Colonel Columb's admirable little book, 'Donnington Castle: a Royalist Story,' p. 141.

way from Hungerford, now called "the Backway," on the
north to the River Lamborne, and on the south to the hamlet
of Speenhamland. The general appearance of the neighbourhood has been much changed since the period of the Battle.
In maps of the seventeenth century the old gabled houses in
the Broadway appear quite in the fields. A house still standing in the London Road is said to have been the
Manor-house; and in the old maps an avenue of trees is
shown leading up to it from the direction of the Marsh. A
range of buildings near, erected on the site of the Lamb-and-
Castle Yard, marks the traditional birth-place of the famous
Dr. Twisse. Newbury Marsh, opposite, was formerly quite
open to the old highway to London, which, going somewhat
northward, passed Shaw brick-kiln, and joined the line of the
existing road to Thatcham near the Turnpike Gate, which
was removed a few years since. The original road from
Shaw House to Newbury is said to have crossed the river
Lamborne westward of the fish-pond, and entered Speenhamland nearer the town than the present road, as indicated on
the accompanying Plan of the Second Battle.

A reference to the Plan will show that the Royalists occupied
an advantageous position in and about the town of Newbury, protected on one flank by the River Kennet, and in some degree
covered by the guns of Donnington Castle on the other. They
strengthened their front with breastworks and entrenchments,
and occupied in force several houses and gardens, which
extended conveniently beyond the town. One house in particular (Shaw House), the residence of Sir Thomas Dolman,
stood in a most convenient situation, a little in advance of the
chief breastwork. In addition to this, there was a row of
smaller houses* to the east of the present Rectory, which
were turned to the best advantage for the purposes of defence.
All these, as well as the gardens of Shaw House, which they
strengthened by thick embankments, were filled with troops,
under the command of Sir Richard Page. At every window,
battlement, and parapet, musquet and pike were ready for
service; all the hedges and ditches swarmed with skirmishers;
and every convenient mound was surmounted with one or
more pieces of artillery. Sir Jacob Astley and Sir George
Lisle kept the passage of the Lamborne at Shaw. Sir Thomas
Hooper and Sir John Brown were placed with a strong body
of horse and foot in the fields by the little hill on which the
Water-tower now stands; around it a work was cast up, and

---

* These houses, called the "Hop Gardens," were removed some
years ago, and several cannon balls were found imbedded in the roofs.

SHAW HOUSE.

## POSITION OF THE ROYALISTS.

they occupied this as well as the hedges and lane (Long Lane), and the old orchard above it. Colonel Thelwall with his Reading brigade, held the gardens, and formed the reserve. Sir Bernard Astley's troops lay around an entrenched house in the park at Shaw, "between Shaw and Newbury."[*] Every house in the village of Shaw was occupied and fortified by the Royalists. In one respect alone, however, and that a very essential point, their line on this side was weak. A hill (Clay Hill and the adjacent elevated ground), little more than a musquet-shot in their front, offered to an assailant every facility for the secure and undiscovered formation of columns of attack; and the result of the coming action proved that against that solitary defect in his position, all the other advantages possessed by the King could not avail.

Prince Maurice, with his brigade of Cornish horse and two brigades of foot and artillery, was posted in the village of Speen below Speen Hill. On the heath above, hastily constructed works had been thrown up by the Royalists; and here were stationed part of the Cornish foot and the Duke of York's regiment, commanded by Sir William St. Leger, with five pieces of artillery. The ground on which the King's left thus rested is evident enough at the present day, though the name of "Speen Hill" has been in later times wrongly applied to the well-known suburb between Newbury and the village of Speen. Speen Hill proper, the eminence referred to in the various narratives of the Battle, is the hill rising from the village of Speen towards Benham Park. The heath above, a portion of which still remains uncultivated, at that time extended over the now enclosed fields for some distance; on the west it skirted the Roman road from Speen to Cirencester by the way of Wickham and Baydon, and on the south the present Bath road. Sir Edward Walker thus refers to it:—"At the entrance of the Heath, between two Hedges we cast up a work which cleared the Heath and all the fields to the North even to the river [Lamborne]; to the South, within the hedge, there was one narrow field, and from thence a perpendicular descent into a Marish [Speen Moor] between that and the River Kennet. This was our position, wherein, had the traverse been finished and made down to the Marish, altho' we were inferior in number, yet we should have sufficiently provided

---

[*] This entrenched house formerly stood at the south-east angle of Shaw Park: but was pulled down many years since. Considerable remains of the earthworks still exist in its vicinity, and are marked on the Plan.

154 THE SECOND BATTLE OF NEWBURY.

to have withstood their force."* Mid-way between Newbury and Speen, Sir Humphrey Benett's brigade of horse was drawn up. † Lastly the King with the main body of the horse and artillery, was stationed in the fields between Donnington Castle and Newbury; and this was nearly the centre of his position.

Strong guards were placed on the south of the town, and detachments of horse guarded the outlying passages of the Lamborne at Bagnor and Boxford to check any advance upon the fords. Owing, however, to the want of a sufficient strength of cavalry, diminished by the loss of three of his best regiments which had been despatched to Banbury, the King was at this time overmatched in his favourite and usually most serviceable arm. He also had no effective reserve to support the scattered infantry, and was thus deprived both of the power of checking hostile reconnoitring parties and of obtaining intelligence of his opponent's operations.

CHAPTER VI.

## MOVEMENTS OF THE PARLIAMENTARY ARMY.

The following letters, read in the House of Commons at the time, will supply all necessary information concerning the movements of the two divisions of the Parliamentary army under Essex and Manchester, after they had returned to Reading,‡ and are interesting on account of their precision and the local particulars they contain :—

"My Lords and Gentlemen,
The King's foote quartered last night at King's Cleer seven

---

* 'Hist. Discourses,' p. 111.

† Sir Humphrey Benett's Brigade of Horse consisted of the undermentioned Regiments. Symonds's 'Notes,' Harl. MS., No. 986.
1. Reg. Col. ...... Bennet, High-Sheriff of South$^n$· had 9 troops in the field, almost full, but [only] 2 colo$^{rs}$· [colours].
    Lieut.-Col. ...... Verney, son to Sir Edm. V., who was slayne at Edghill.
    S$^{rt}$· Maior Richard Aldworth.
    Capt. Mr. Rob$^{t}$· Smyth, brother to Colonel Smyth, who was taken prisoner, w$^{th}$ S$^r$ Alex. Denton, at Hilsden Howse, Com. Buck.
2. Reg. Sr. Geo. Vaughan, Colonel, ⎫
    Sr. Robt. Welsh, Lieut.-Colonel, ⎬ 80.
    but [only] 2 Troopes. ⎭

‡ D'Ewes's 'Diary,' Harl. MS. 166, fol. 139.

miles from here. A great body of Horse went towards them the last night, a party of which commanded by Captain Ffincher one of Sir William Waller's captaynes went soe neare them that they took sixty prisoners, some of them being officers.

My Lord of Manchester last night gave notice to the Committee at Reading, and desired them to send it to Abingdon, that a great body of our Horse marched toward them the last night, and that our army marcheth to-day, if they can withstand a storme. We hope they will be in noe danger. The whole army now marcheth away. Wee rest,

My Lords, your humble Servants,
A. JOHNSTON. JO. CREW.

Basingstoke, Octobr. [22] 1644."

"My Lords and Gentlemen,

My Lord Generall [Essex] quartered all night at Bradfeild six miles from Reading. My Lord of Manchester's forces, which had the van quartered at Bucklebury upon Intelligence that the King's army continued at Newbery. This morning about 10 of the clocke the Horse and Foot are all drawne out upon Bucklebury heath 4 miles [it is about 5 miles from the site of the Parliamentary camp] from Newbery, great bodies of the enemyes Horse are in view, but whether to face or engage we know not. Our resolution if they will not stand their charge [is] to pursue them. My Lord Generall hath had upon him some indisposition for divers daies, which hath been more encreased by his striving with it, hee would not be persuaded from marching yesterday, and was resolved to have marched to-day, but not taking his rest last night hee is is growne feverish and was forced to goe back to Reading on a feather bed layd in his Coach, here will be much want of his presence, wee shall conceale his absence as much as we can, and hope that those which are here will make all the supply that they can by extraordinary diligence.

Wee remain, my Lords, your humble servants,
ARCHIBALD JOHNSTON. JO. CREW.

Bucklebery Heath, 25 October, 1644.

Since the wrighting this Letter it was thought fit at a Counsell of Warre held upon the Heath that we should march to Thatcham 2 miles from Newbery [3 miles]. Wee have now intelligence that the enemye's Horse and Foote are drawne up betweene Newbery and Denington Castle. This night we are to marche beyond Thatcham either to the right or left hand as the feilds shall be most advantageous. Our officers continue very unanimous and our soldiers are very cheerfull upon their going on towards the enemy."

On the following day the two Parliamentary Commissioners wrote from Thatcham to the Derby-House Committee to the following effect :—

" My Lords and Gentlemen,

Yesterday upon Bucklebury Heath wee received your letter, which gave us hope that the army will shortly receive the provisions which you have sent. The newes of Newcastle came very seasonably to us, which much encouraged the souldiers, and so affected them that many of the regiments went presently of their own accord to solemn prayer. The army about an hower before night came within a myle and within view of the enemy, who was drawne forth in a body in a place of advantage neere Newbery. Our dragoones and theirs fired upon one another for two howers, twenty of our horses were killed, but not one of our men lost. A captain of our Horse, who came up in the vann, was shott in the thigh, six o'clock in the evening. It was resolved last night that the field should be viewed by the chiefe officers early this morning. It will be an advantage to us to set upon his army on this side Newbery, because wee shall be betwixt the enemy and our provisions ; and to fall upon him on the other side, because we shall be betwixt the enemy and Prince Rupert, who is dayly expected with additional forces, the ground not having been viewed they could determine nothing herein. Being informed by those that came from London that they met many souldiers going homewards, wee renew our desire that some exemplary punishment may be inflicted upon them.

Wee remaine, your Lops. humble servants,

W. JOHNSTON. JO. CREWE.

Wee have had a faire night (blessed be God), and hope for a faire day." *

The Parliamentary force under Manchester and Waller encamped in Sir Humphrey Forster's park at Aldermaston †

---

\* Letter-book, Derby-House Committee, Public Record Office.

† Sir Humphrey Forster's estates were sequestered by the Parliament ; and in his proposition to compound Sir Humphrey pleads that his estate lies in the King's quarters, and is subject to every motion and change of the war, and hath been equally possessed by both sides, whereupon all the stock is taken away, the walls of the park and the fences broken, and damage done by the soldiers to the value of £8000 : that his children have been in want, and himself hath subsisted ever since by borrowing. That he has a family of nine children, and his eldest son, who has been a Captain in the Parliamentary service, has a considerable amount of pay not yet paid to him. Sir Humphrey concludes by stating that he has voluntarily taken the covenant, and found six men for the defence of Reading. (State Papers ; Domestic Series, Public Record Office.) In a petition to the Parliament from

on October 23rd and 24th, and the next morning (Friday 25th) they crossed the Kennet at Padworth, and came to the rendezvous on Bucklebury Heath, as will be seen by the correspondence, having with them three days' provisions.

Here they were joined by the other division, which had been under the command of the Lord-General, the Earl of Essex; and the two columns being thus concentrated prepared for action. At mid-day they appeared in the fields between Thatcham and Shaw, on the east side of Newbury, where some sharp encounters soon ensued between advanced parties of the Parliamentary horse and the cavalry outposts of the Royalists, but without serious loss on either side.

According to local tradition, a considerable engagement between the cavalry outposts of the two armies took place in the fields between Dunston Park and Red Field, to the west of the village of Thatcham. The bodies of the slain are said to have been buried in a meadow forming part of "Mortimer Farm," on the east side of a road known as "Lawrence's Lane," which leads from "Three-Chimney Lane" to Bucklebury Heath.

Meanwhile Essex himself was not fated to take part in this second trial of strength with the Royalist forces near Newbury. His illness did not diminish on his return to Reading, where he remained alone, despondent and inactive. Informed of this, Parliament charged a joint-committee of the Lords and Commons to wait on him, and "renew the assurance of its trusting affection." "This was not," says Whitelock, "(as was given out) a piece of Courtship, but, I think, real, and there was cause enough that it should be so, the General having so highly deserved from them: yet there were some had designs against him, and were desirous to remove him from his *command*, because they were jealous, that he was too much inclined to peace, and the favouring of the King and his party. I think I know as much of his mind as others did, and always observed him to wish for peace, yet not upon any

---

Lady Anne, wife of Sir Humphrey Forster, dated April 17th, 1645, she states that, on account of Sir Humphrey's harsh treatment, she has long lived at a distance from him, and that when he became a delinquent the Committee for sequestrations made several orders for petitioner's maintenance out of his estates, and on the 21st March last, after full hearing, ordered that she should enjoy the fifth part of his goods and estates. She prays that in the ordinance for clearing him of his delinquency a special proviso may be inserted, securing her a fifth part of his estate, as formerly ordered, or that some other provision may be made for her maintenance. The proviso was ordered to be inserted. ('The Lord's Journal,' VII, pp. 384 and 420.)

dishonourable or unjust terms; he was a Lover of Monarchy and Nobility, which he suspected some designed to destroy, together with Gentry, Ministry, and Magistracy, which humour then began to boyl up; but he resolved to support them, and wanted not advice to that end. But the jealousies upon him (who was a most faithful and gallant man and servant to the publick) gave him great trouble in his thoughts, and they did work so high with his enemies, that some gave out he was by private intimation to forbear engaging in this Service; and for certain he was not in it." *

There can be no doubt therefore of the cause of the Earl's absence from the Second Battle; and the following letter written by him to the Derby-House Committee in reply to their address further corroborates this view.

"My Lords and Gentlemen,

It is a comfort to mee in this sad tyme of mine affliction, in minde and body, to see that I am continued in your care, being at this present soe uselesse a servant to ye State. The particulars of my disease, I shall crave pardon that I deferre the accompt of it till Doctor St. John's, old Mr. Bowden of Reading, and Langley my owne Chirurgion shall set downe the trew state as much as they can perceive of it as yet, only thus much, I think it has been much occasioned (the inconveniency I am like to suffer) by striving soe long with it; thinking it the greatest worldly misfortune that would have befallen mee at this present, but it is God's doing, and I must with all humility submitt to his pleasure—soe acknowledging your Lordship's great favoure in sending hither, I rest, my Lords,

Your Lordships' most humble servant,
Reading, 27 Oct., 1644."                              Essex.

The absence of the Earl of Essex was carefully concealed from the troops, as it was known that he exercised a powerful influence in rousing the enthusiasm of his own regiments, and imparting additional spirit to the whole army. All went on favourably; and it was encouraging to find that during the night of the 25th the detached parties of the King's troops posted on the height which overlooks Shaw House and the town of Newbury were withdrawn, and that the soldiers of the Parliament occupied the position from which the Royalists had been dislodged by their advance.

The site of the Parliamentary Camp was on an extensive tract of elevated table-land, stretching from Clay Hill for a

---

* Whitelock's 'Memorials,' p. 103.

considerable distance towards Ashmore Green and Cold Ash Common. It is now called, from the gravelly character of the land, "The Stones." Skirting this plateau on the west, is an escarpment, which forms a continuous natural rampart, in some places so well defined as to have the appearance of an artificial work. The meadows below the southern edge are now known as "Runaways." Donnington Castle stands out boldly in front of the camping ground. On Clay Hill, near "Red Field," is still to be seen part of an extensive entrenchment or breastwork, which helped to defend the Parliamentary front. It is about twelve feet wide by eight feet deep, and originally extended along that face of the hill which has since been to a great extent removed in the process of digging clay. The ditch has been partially filled in; and the workmen in removing the earth have found many cannon-balls, bullets, and other relics of warfare, including scores of the well-known tobacco pipes of the Caroline period. Wood-ashes have also been found in heaps beneath the surface in many parts of the higher ground, indicating the remains of the camp-fires around which the soldiers of the Parliament bivouacked.

## CHAPTER VII.

### PRELUDE TO THE BATTLE.

When it was known in London that the two armies were at last in the presence of each other, the shops were closed, the people rushed to the churches, and a solemn fast was ordained, to seek the blessing of the Lord on the coming battle.*

In the absence of Prince Rupert, the King again led his own army, assisted by his nephew Prince Maurice, the old Earl of Brentford acting as Lieutenant-General, and Lord Goring being in command of the Horse. Amongst his Majesty's more prominent supporters present in the engagement were:—The Duke of Richmond and Lennox, the Earls of Cleveland, Lindsey, Newport, Berkshire, Rivers; Lords Hopton, Capel, Colepepper, Bellasis, Digby, Herbert, Bernard Stuart; Sir Jacob Astley, Sir Bernard Astley, Sir Wm. Bronkard, Sir Edward Walker, Sir Wm. St. Leger, Sir Anthony St. Leger, Sir John Cansfield, Sir Richard Page, Sir John Owen, Sir Thomas Hooper, Sir George Lisle, Sir

---

* Rushworth, 'Hist. Collections,' II. 3, 719—720.

John Brown, Sir John Grenville, Sir Humphrey Benett, Sir Henry Gage, Sir Richard Lane, Sir Thomas Bassett, Sir Joseph Wagstaffe, Sir Charles Lloyd; Colonels Gerard, Ashburnham, Markham, Leke, Topping, Thornhill, Thelwall, Legge, Fielding, Hamilton, Bovel, and Capt. Symonds, the Diarist, who was also present at the subsequent relief of Donnington Castle.

On this occasion the Parliament was represented by many of its most eminent and foremost leaders. Among those whose names have been more prominently handed down to us as associated with this action and its concurrent incidents may be mentioned the following:—The Earl of Manchester, Sir William Waller, Sir William Balfour, Sir Arthur Hesilrige, Sir James Harrington, Sir John Hurry (who has now changed sides), Major-General Crawford, Major-General Skippon, Major-General Holbourne, Lieut.-General Oliver Cromwell, Lieut.-General Middleton, Lieut.-General Ludlow, and Colonels Berkeley or Barclay, Norton, Ingoldsby, Pindar, Birch, Hooper, Jones, and Capt. Robert Hammond.

The early morning of Saturday, 26 October, was devoted by the Parliamentarians to the pushing of a reconnaisance. This the Royalists endeavoured to interrupt by sending out bodies of musqueteers to skirmish, while both parties kept up a smart cannonade; the Parliamentarians from a battery which they had established on the summit of Clay Hill; the Cavaliers from the lower ground in the vicinity of the town. For some time the firing produced little effect on either side, but towards evening the Royalists brought two of their guns round to the south of the River Lamborne, at Woodspeen; and these they so planted as to enfilade the enemy's line as far as a bend on Red Field exposed it. The Wiltshire regiment of cavalry in particular, commanded by Col. Ludlow, which was on the slopes towards the Lamborne, suffered severely, and was compelled to shift its ground. Ludlow's cousin Gabriel Ludlow, who had distinguished himself at Wardour Castle, here received his death-wound.

This incident on Red Field is thus related by Ludlow: *— "My Regiment being that day on the Guard, received the greatest Damage; amongst others my Cousin Gabriel Ludlow, who was a Cornet therein, and who had behaved himself so well in the Defence of Warder-Castle, was killed: He died not immediately after he was shot; so that having caused him to be removed out of the reach of their Guns, and

---

* 'Memoirs of Ludlow,' vol i, pp. 129-130.

procured a Chirurgeon to search his wounds, he found his Belly broken, and Bowels torn, his Hip-bone broken all to shivers, and the Bullet lodged in it; notwithstanding which he recovered some sense, tho the Chirurgeon refused to dress him, looking on him as a dead Man. This Accident troubled me exceedingly; he being one who had expressed great Affection to me, and of whom I had great hopes that he would be useful to the Publick. In this condition he desired me to kiss him, and I not presently doing it, thinking he had talked lightly, he pressed me again to do him that favour; whereby observing him to be sensible, I kissed him : and soon after having recommended his Mother, Brothers, and Sisters to my Care, he died."

A portion of Ludlow's regiment was commanded by Major Wansey, a prominent man for the Parliament in Wiltshire, who, "in order that the whole regiment might not be lost in one engagement, had secured himself in the rear of all." Here Ludlow found him in the evening after the battle on the 27th, when darkness compelled the combatants to retire.

Finding the King so strongly placed, protected by Donnington Castle, the Kennet, and the Lamborne, the Parliamentary generals held a Council of War on Red Field. It was then resolved to divide their force into two columns. Waller and Cromwell, with all the horse and foot which had lately been under the leadership of Essex, and four regiments of Trained Bands, under Skippon (one regiment had been left in garrison at Reading), were to make a flank march, and attack the Royalists' position on Speen Hill; while Manchester and Crawford with about 3000 foot, and a body of 1500 or 1800 horse under Ludlow, made a demonstration from the hill at Shaw. It was further agreed, that, as soon as the latter body should, by hearing the discharge of cannon, understand that their comrades at Speen Hill were engaged, Manchester should force the passage at Shaw; and thus, if both sides succeeded, they would completely encompass the King and have him at their mercy. The attention of the enemy was meanwhile to be diverted from the main body of the Parliamentarians while making the flank march, by continuous attacks on their position at Shaw, until the signal was given from the Speen side for the main blow to be struck.

These matters are thus referred to in the documents of the period. In Cromwell's 'Evidence'* it is stated that "On Saturday, October 26, when we came up to Redhill Field,

* From the 'Information against the Earl of Manchester;' State Papers, Public Record Office.

within shot of Shawe, and found the passes of the river soe possest against us, it was agreed that the Lord-General's and the City foote, with the greatest part of the horse, should march about by Boxford and attempt to breake in upon the enemy on that side by Speene, and that his Lordship, with his owne foote and about 1500 horse, should stay behind at Shawe side, and fall on there at the same instant that he should perceive the other part to fall on at Speene (which was already in his viewe)."

The news of a body of Parliamentarians being on their march to Speen Hill appears to have been brought to Lord Digby at Newbury on the Sunday morning;* but, owing to the numerical weakness of his army, it was not possible for the King (who had from the first determined to stand on the defensive), to dispatch at that time a force to oppose Waller's march, and at the same time to keep Manchester (whose numbers had been over-estimated) in check at Shaw. It seems, however, somewhat surprising that notice was not given earlier to the Royalists at Speen of Waller's march. Clarendon states that they were taken unawares. The King had indeed sent a body of troops, about 500 in number, under Sir John Douglas, to guard the pass of the River Lamborne at Boxford; where they made but a feeble resistance when the enemy appeared in such superior numbers.

Acting on the decision of the Council of War, on Saturday evening the right wing of the Army of the Parliament, under Waller and Cromwell, began their march towards Speen Hill, the route taken being apparently by the Old Bucklebury road, and Cold-Ash, to the Hermitage road, thence by Prior's Court and through the village of Chieveley to North Heath, where they halted for the night.† Early next morning (Sunday) they were on the move; and, marching as rapidly as the heavy and hilly roads would admit, by Winterbourne‡ church and woods, they passed the village of Boxford. Fording the

---

* Letter from Lord Digby to Prince Rupert, dated Newbury, 27 Oct., Addl. MSS., Brit. Mus., No. 18980. So also—"They learn'd in the morning (Sunday) our greatest force was a-marching toward Spen Hill:" 'Narrative of the Earl of Manchester's Campaign;' State Papers; Public Record Office.

† "On Saturday the greater part of the Parliamentary forces retired to *Chieveley*, and quartered there that night in the open fields." Oldmixon, 'History of the Stuarts,' VI., p. 262. The same route is stated in Rushworth's 'Hist. Collections,' II., 3, 724.

‡ "While the Cannon play'd from the Hill [Clay Hill] they drew the rest of their army through Winterbourne towards Boxford to have girt in His Majesty." "Mercurius Aulicus," Monday, 28 Oct., 1644.

## PRELUDE TO THE BATTLE.

River Lamborne at the latter place, as already noticed, they met with only slight opposition from the Royalist outpost here stationed to defend the passage. Crossing the Newbury-and-Wantage road, they proceeded by High-street Lane to Wickham Heath, which they gained at the cross-roads.

There is sufficient evidence in a letter from the two Parliamentary Commissioners, addressed to the Derby-House Committee,* to support this opinion as to the route taken. They state that "Yesterday the forces which went from Thatcham towards Newbury, by the way of Wickham Heath and were there drawne up, set upon a worke and breastworke, well-guarded with ordnance, horse, and foote, which commanded all the wayes which lead to that side of the field betwixt Newberry and Dennington Castle, where the King's army was drawne up."

They "passed the river," says Clarendon, "which was not well defended by the officer appointed to guard it, with horse and foot, very many of them being gone off from their guards, as never imagining that they would, at the time of day, have attempted a quarter that was thought the strongest of all. But having thus got the river, they marched in good order, with very good bodies of foot winged with horse, toward the Heath."†

"About which time the Earl of Essex's forces [those recently under his command], all Waller's, and part of Manchester's horse, pursued their design of falling on the quarter at Speen, of which we had notice from Dennington, from whence their motion was discovered. And had Sir John Douglas actively opposed them (who was the day before sent with 300 horse and 200 foot beyond Dennington Castle to that end), they could not so easily have passed the river." ‡

The distance from North Heath to Speen Hill (the "Heath") is about 7 or 8 miles as traversed by the Parliamentarians: and this, considering the bad roads, was a fair four hours' march for such a large body of troops, who were not allowed to proceed altogether unmolested; for upon the high ground, they had been perceived by the garrison at Donnington Castle, and Sir John Boys had despatched a small body of horse to intercept them. These made a sharp attack on their rear; but, soon recovering from this slight interference, the Parliamentary Generals pushed on, and shortly approached the outworks of the Royalists; but it was

---

\* 'Letter-Book, Derby-Ho. Com.,' No. 59, Public Record Office.
† Clarendon's Hist. of the Rebellion,' II., p. 547.
‡ Walker's 'Hist. Discourses,' p. 111.

nearly one o'clock before the artillery and the rear came up, and about three o'clock in the afternoon before the army was deployed for battle.

CHAPTER VIII.

MANCHESTER ATTACKS SHAW.—ACTION AT SPEEN.—ATTACK ON SHAW HOUSE.—RETREAT OF THE KING.—ROLL OF KILLED & WOUNDED.

Leaving Waller and Cromwell arranging the preliminaries of battle on Speen Hill, we will return for a moment to Manchester's force left on the hills at Shaw. As soon as it was daylight, on Sunday morning, which at this season (27th October) would be about seven o'clock, Manchester commenced the attack on the royalist post at Shaw, by despatching a body of 400 musqueteers to assault the entrenched position at the south-east angle of Shaw Park, crossing the Lamborne by a temporary bridge thrown over the river at the foot of Clay Hill the previous night.* They advanced at a quick pace over the meadows at what is now the back of Shaw Crescent, and favoured by the unevenness of the ground, and the haze of the early autumnal morning, were almost unperceived until they surprised the guard at the works covering the passage of the river and the house at Shaw. Without a moment's hesitation the Parliamentarians furiously assailed and mastered the party at the breastworks; but, their impetuosity carrying them too far, they were checked by a charge from the royal cavalry under Sir George Lisle and Sir Bernard Astley near Shaw House; and, being without adequate support, they were driven back with great loss. To add to their discomfiture, in attempting to regain the temporary bridge and retreat on their main body, they came into collision with a reserve of their own men, who were tardily coming to their support; and in the mêlée many fell by the swords of the pursuing cavaliers, and numbers were drowned in the river in endeavouring to reach the opposite bank. In this the first onset about 40 prisoners and 100 stand of arms were taken by the royalists. This affair is

---

* Near the Lamborne, as indicated on the Plan, where the Parliamentarians crossed the river in this attack, several skeletons were found some years ago. In Redfield, also, on the removal of a bank, about 40 years since, three skeletons were discovered lying side by side.

thus alluded to by the contemporaries.—"My Lord of Manchester commanded a party of 400 musqueteers to falle over the little river which passes by Dunington Castle, over a bridge, which most dextrously hee commanded the night before, to prepare for the diversion of the King's forces from goeing to Spen Hill, where they learned in the morneing our greatest force was a marching, which accordingly was done, and if those who weare commanded had not exceeded theire commission, [they] would have had greate victory; and as it was they tooke two workes from the enemy wherein they tooke a captayne and severall prisoners, and advanced too farr without order, and were repulsed, to the greate greife of the Earle of Manchester."* "Sunday, as soone as day, they put over a tertia of foot over a bridge they made in the night, intending to surprize one of our guards. But the guard retreated to the next; and joyned, fell upon them, being nothing considerable in number, made their two bodyes retreat, killed some, tooke about 40 prisoners and a 100 armes: then they lay quiet till 3 afternoone, onely our cannon and theirs playd." † Again :—"Sunday, October 27. Some of Manchester's Forces and London Trained Bands ‡ crossed the River Kennet [Lamborne] between the Hill and Newbury, and did some Execution on those who kept the Pass against them. But Sir Bernard Astley, coming to Rescue, forceth the other over the River." §

After the unsuccessful attempt to pierce the Royalist line at Shaw, no further effort, with any vigour, was made by Manchester until the pre-concerted signal informed him that Waller's force had fallen on at Speen Hill. The interval until four o'clock was occupied by warm skirmishes between the two parties, accompanied by an active interchange of artillery fire. Manchester, busy with his preparations for advancing in force, rode to and fro, and spiritedly addressed his men, while his Chaplain, Simeon Ashe, ‖ offered up fervent prayers for their success.

---

* 'Narrative of the Earl of Manchester's Campaign ;' State Papers ; Public Record Office.
† Symonds's 'Diary,' p. 145.
‡ The greater part of the Trained Bands were with the right wing.
§ Baker's 'Chronicle,' p. 579.
‖ Simeon Ashe, Manchester's Chaplain, was author of 'A True Relation,' &c. Dr. Calamy speaks of him as a man of great sanctity, who went seasonably to heaven at the very time he was cast out of the church. He was buried on the eve of St. Bartholomew's day, 1662. Simeon fell under the obloquy of the Cromwellians: and he had a considerable share in the restoration of Charles II, whom he went to congratulate at Breda.

## THE SECOND BATTLE OF NEWBURY.

The right wing of the Parliamentary Army, having successfully accomplished their flank march, were now on this Sunday morning, whilst the bells of the neighbouring churches were sounding for divine worship, preparing for the contest. Waller was in chief command; Sir William Balfour led the right wing of horse; Lieut..General Cromwell the left; Major-General Skippon, the foot. Their men were rapidly placed in position on the high ground between the Wickham Road and Stockcross, overlooking on their right the Kennet Valley and the scene of their triumph the preceding year. At the same time, the Royal trumpets rang out "To arms!" The scattered troopers, many of whom, in fancied security, were engaged in foraging for their horses, galloped back to their comrades; but before their ranks could be well formed, a shout of revenge "for the business in Cornwall"\* was heard along the Parliamentary line, the red, white, and blue colours were unfurled,† and the "forlorn hope" of 800 musqueteers came on with unshrinking courage. These were veterans who had lately served under their brave old leader Essex, and were now led by Lieut.-Col. Lloyd, with Hurry for his Major, nephew of the notorious renegade Sir John Hurry. They were supported by Colonel Aldridge's brigade, consisting of his own, Davies's, Fortescue's, and Ingoldsby's regiments. Essex's old regiment was sent up as a support on the right, where the Trained Bands were already engaged, and urged on by the excitement which prevailed, they rushed pellmell into the Royalists' entrenchments. A desperate fight ensued; the blood of the Cavaliers was up; and, fighting hand to hand, they slaughtered their assailants in heaps, as they mounted the bank, and the ditch was soon filled with the dead and dying. Major Hurry, bravely leading the "forlorn-hope" (his colonel having already been struck down), fell mortally wounded. The gallant Col. Gawler, who had done good service for the Parliament in many a bloody field, dropped lifeless from his horse, pierced by a royalist bullet. For a moment the enemy was repulsed; but determined to carry a

---

\* It is said that the Cornishmen behaved with great inhumanity to the Parliamentary soldiers who fell into their hands on the surrender of Lord Essex in Cornwall.

† "Col. Aldridge, blew colours with lyons rampant or. Col. Davies, white colours, Citty, London." Symonds's 'Diary,' p. 66. Col. Ingoldsby's colours were "gules, a scroll in three folds, its parts making two C's conjoined and endorsed, on which these words 'Pro Deo et Republica,' fringed sable with gules and argent." Prestwick's 'Respublica,' p. 36.

## ACTION AT SPEEN.

position so necessary in effecting a junction with Manchester, he renewed the attack. An hour's hard fighting succeeded; and then bringing all their energy to bear on this point, in the midst of a storm of shot from the gallant defenders, and from the guns at Donnington Castle,* the Parliamentary soldiers again came to the charge. Forward! was the word; and, despite the resolute resistance of the brave but outnumbered Royalists, they fought with a calm determination that nothing could withstand. The King's troops at last gave way. Flushed by this temporary success, their opponents pressed forward with increased impetuosity. Again a stirring cheer arose from their ranks, and making a dash at the guns they had lost in Cornwall, now deserted by their late captors, who fled at headlong speed down the hill, "they clapped their hats on the touch-holes, and embraced them with tears of joy."† The forces of Prince Maurice in the village of Speen, unable to stand against the overwhelming numbers of the Parliament, stayed the tide for a time, but at length yielded to superior force. Driven from their position to join in the retreat with the remnant from the Heath, they fell back disorganised on the main body of their horse and artillery in the fields "between Speen and Newbury," and hastily endeavoured to reform their broken ranks.

The Royalists were cleared from off the Heath. The guns‡ lost at Lostwithiel, thus regained, were limbered up and sent to the rear, together with those which had been planted at the foot of the hill. Waller now launched his cavalry in pursuit of the retreating enemy, and avenged in merciless slaughter the cause of the Parliament. Well might the Commissioners write, "Wee desire to give God the glory of this victory, it being His worke and upon His day;"§ while Waller exclaimed, like the Fifth Harry, in the fulness of his gratitude,

"O God, Thy arm was here!
And not to us, but to Thy name alone,
Ascribe we all."

Great was the panic among the Cavaliers at this moment. They "threw down their arms, and ran away, crying 'Devils!

---

\* Letter from the Two Commissioners to the Derby-Ho. Committee, 27 Oct., 1644.

† Ludlow's 'Memoirs,' p. 130.

‡ "We tooke 9 good brass pieces, six of them being sakers, which we left behind in Cornwall." (Skippon's Letter to the Derby-Ho. Committee.) The other three guns were with Prince Maurice.

§ Letter from the Two Commissioners to Derby-Ho. Committee, 28, Oct., 1644.

## THE SECOND BATTLE OF NEWBURY.

Devils! They fight like Devils!' For ours gave no quarter to any they knew to be of the Cornish."* Following up this advantage, while Waller fell on the Royalists' rear in their retreat from Speen Hill, Sir William Balfour, with the right wing of horse, swept round under the hill, on the south side of Speen Church, skirting the Kennet, and, having gained "the large field" between Speen and Newbury, where stood the King, with the young Prince of Wales and many of his attendants, he made a spirited attack upon the royal guard.

It is evident that for a short time the King and his staff were in imminent danger; for a whole brigade of Royalist horse, at the first shock, outnumbered to a great degree and already demoralized by increasing panic, reeled and wavered, and at length, giving ground to the advancing host, put spurs to their horses, and fled in disorder towards the town of Newbury.† The King, dismayed at the sight, vainly endeavoured to restrain the flight of his retreating squadrons, and lead them on again; but the authority of command was gone, and he found himself surrounded by the enemy. At this crisis Sir John Cansfield,‡ with two troops of the Queen's regiment, gallantly galloped forward to the support of his royal master. Lord Bernard Stuart and his life-guards gathered round the King; and rapidly wheeling round, to get more ground, they rushed valiantly with the troopers of Sir John against the eager enemy. A deadly strife ensued; many a horse ran riderless over the fields; the Parliament men were dispersed; and the King was rescued. The brave cavaliers, however, too ardent in their enthusiasm, always led away by the same fault, pushed on too far. The calm old Skippon, not less cool than daring, permitted them to continue the pursuit until their impetuosity carried them within a few yards of his infantry, when, at a signal, the musqueteers and pikemen furiously assailed them, and

---

\* Vicar's 'Parl. Chron.' Lond., 1644.

† Sir Edward Walker, (Hist. Discourses, p. 112), relates that the body of royalist cavalry which had given way at Speen, were speedily forced back into action by the guard posted at Newbury Bridge. It has been thought the river Kennet was not bridged in the town at that period, but an application from the Mayor and certain inhabitants of Newbury to the Council of the Prince of Wales, afterwards K. Charles I., dated March 1, 1623, is extant, requesting assistance towards repairing the Bridge at Newbury, which had suddenly toppled over into the river the preceding 8th of February. Tanner MSS., Bodleian Lib., No. 314, fol. 214.

‡ The motto on Sir John Cansfield's banner was from the 101st Psalm,—" Fiat pax in virtute tua."—Estrenne's 'Mottos and Devices.'

gathered round the King; and rapidly wheeling round, to get more ground, with the troopers of Sir John they rushed valiantly against the eager enemy. A deadly strife ensued; many a horse ran riderless over the fields; the Parliament men were dispersed; and the King was rescued. The brave cavaliers, however, too ardent in their enthusiasm, always led away by the same fault, pushed on too far. The calm old Skippon, not less cool than daring, permitted them to continue the pursuit until their impetuosity carried them within a few yards of his infantry, when, at a signal, the musqueteers and pikemen furiously assailed them, and they were forced to retire, exposed to a galling and destructive fire.

At this moment Cromwell, with the left wing of horse, well in hand, came upon the scene, and made for Sir Humphrey Benett's cavalry brigade, stationed on the south-west side of Speen Fields towards Newbury, which was without doubt the weakest point in the Royal line. In ten minutes Sir Humphrey's steel-clad troopers, panic-struck at so vigorous a charge, and taken at a disadvantage, were completely overpowered, and had well nigh been annihilated had not Lord Bernard Stuart and his guards secured their retreat on Shaw. Cromwell now advanced "towards the north side of the field," in the direction of Donnington; but he was met by Lord Goring, with the Earl of Cleveland's brigade, who charged with telling effect on the leading squadrons, and forced them to retire over a hedge. Goring's troopers leaped the obstacle in pursuit, but Skippon, once more rallying his battalions, drove him back in turn, routed and dispersed, with considerable loss. The gallant old Earl of Cleveland, at the head of his regiment, allowed his courage to carry him too far ahead of his men; and, his horse falling under him, he was taken prisoner.*

"The Knight is left alone, his steel-cap cleft in twain,
His good buff jerkin crimson'd o'er with many a gory stain:
Yet still he waves his banner, and cries amid the rout,
'For Church and King, fair gentlemen! spur on, and fight it out!'"—*Praed.*

The battle on the Speen side of the Royalist position had now raged three or four hours; the sun had set, and the night was fast closing in, yet the contest was continued in

---

* "Drawing up (with General Goring) his brigade, at the east side of Spiene, in the Second Newbury fight, to secure the King's guards, in much danger, with such old English valor (telling his men they must now charge home), that he scattered the enemy, till too far engaged and overpowered he was taken prisoner, as the King himself was like to be." Lloyd's 'Memoires,' p. 570.

broken order, but for the most part with unabated spirit. At last all formation was lost; and it would be tedious, if not impossible, to continue the narration of what had now become mere skirmishes in the dark, friend and foe being commingled. The fighting gradually ceased, and both parties occupied themselves in drawing together their scattered forces.

This is borne out by Cromwell who states in his Evidence against the Earl of Manchester that "Wee on the other side [Speen], haveing gayned most of the hedges toward Newberry feild, did cease and drawe our men together to avoyd confusion in the darke by that scattered way of fighting."

The darkness of the night, until the moon rose, was advantageous to the dispirited Royalists, many of whom escaped under its cover who would otherwise have been killed or taken prisoners.

As there was considerable rivalry between the leaders in this battle, discrepancies in the various accounts of the action are very marked. Thus, Manchester, whose hostility to the future Protector was well known, gave it as his opinion before the House of Lords\* that "On that day there was no service at all performed by Cromwell." But this is not at all likely; and personal dislike must have warped the Earl's mind. Oliver was not a man to stand idle when any fighting was to be done; and in the despatch of the Two Commissioners he is expressly mentioned as having done great service,—an assertion far more likely to be true than that of his comrade in the fight.

We turn now to the course of the action at Shaw. About four o'clock,† Manchester heard the distant firing on Speen Hill, and beheld from the eminence with joy and thankfulness the hasty, disorderly retreat of the enemy towards Newbury. Animated with this encouraging sight, says his Chaplain, Simeon Ashe, the Earl prepared to descend to the more difficult work of forcing the strong position at Dolman's house.

For the purpose of carrying this important post, Manchester divided his force into two columns, to assault the house at two different points; the right to attack on the north-east side by the garden; and the left, which was somewhat the larger

---

\* November 28, 1644; also in the 'Narrative.'

† Cromwell, in his charge against Manchester, says, that the Earl would not allow his men to fall on until half-an-hour after sunset; but this differs from other accounts of the battle, whether Royalist or Parliamentarian, which state that Manchester made his attack not later than 4 p.m.

ATTACK ON SHAW HOUSE. 171

body, to attempt it lower down at the foot of the little hill by the village of Shaw. (See the Plan.)

Suddenly, under cover of an active cannonade along their whole line, a dark and terrible mass of steel-clad men moved down from behind the protecting eminence of Clay Hill.

"Compactly move the blocks of spears,
"In 'back,' and 'breast,' and steel cap bright;
"And on each flank,
"In eight-deep rank,
"With lighted match, the musqueteers."\*

The "battle-march" of the Puritan warriors was a solemn psalm pealing from their fierce array.† The royalist guns thundered a refrain. Preserving the greatest order, the Parliamentary battalions steadily descended the steep hillside to meet again, for the second time that day, their equally brave, and no less devoted antagonists.

It was evident that the eager and excited soldiers of the Parliament, who felt that they had been too long held back, brooked no further suspense, and the foremost lines of the right column immediately advanced on the garden side of Shaw House. The Royalists had all the advantages of position; every accessible point being well protected in all directions, both by cannon and musquetry; and, full of confidence, they received the enemy with a tremendous volley, poured in from behind the hedges of Long Lane.‡ Though for the moment amazed and staggered, Manchester's men withdrew not an inch; and the first shock was no sooner overcome, than they rushed boldly forward, to be again driven back. Again and again were they led on, and as often repulsed; but, seconded by a strong body of Ludlow's cavalry, they once more fell on, and this time with some effect. The cavaliers sent forth another and telling volley from behind their breastwork on the little hill where the Water-tower § now stands; but, nothing daunted, the Parliamentarians advanced, and drove out the foremost musqueteers from their cover. They now received a check; for Sir John Brown, with the Prince of Wales's regiment, caused terrible havoc in their ranks, the Royalist fire being maintained with

---

\* 'Donnington Castle,' by Col. Columb, R.A., p. 157.
† Clarendon's 'Hist.' iv. p. 548.
‡ Several cannon-balls have been found in the banks of Long Lane.
§ The ground around the Water-tower has the appearance of having been artificially raised for defence, particularly on the eastern side of the mound  To the north-east of the road to Donnington from Long Lane, also, there are evident indications of entrenchments. The ramparts are still well defined in the gardens of Shaw House.

great coolness. Still the assailants pressed on; pike met pike, sword clashed with sword; the one party endeavouring to gain the hedges and entrenchments, the other resolutely opposing them. Many fell at the foot of this hillock: but not one put a foot on it, except as a prisoner. Again reinforced with a fresh body of horse, this gallant band returned to the charge, and almost reached the garden-wall,* while others penetrated even to the lawn in front of the house. Sir John Brown, for a time compelled to give way, prudently fell back on the reserve in the garden. Meanwhile Sir Richard Page, with his leather guns, and 400 musqueteers in the dry moat, did considerable execution.† Ludlow's cavalry recoiled, wheeled about, and retreated, followed by Sir John Brown; and many a brave trooper fell, never more to draw sword again in cause of Parliament.‡ The foot,

---

* There was formerly a sunken road in front of this wall, with a raised bank on each side. When the roadway was diverted some years ago, and the present wooden fence erected, several human skeletons were met with; and a 6lb cannon-ball was found firmly imbedded in the brickwork. More recently, in the latter part of the year 1882, five human skeletons (two of which were headless), apparently those of young men, were discovered in the course of excavating the ground for the purpose of erecting new greenhouses on the north-east side of the terrace and yew-tree hedge at Shaw House to the west of the Water Tower, and just within the line of the old road above mentioned. There can be little doubt that these were the remains of soldiers who fell during the attack on the garden, above described. The tibia of a horse was found with a portion of the human bones.

On the Lawn in front of Shaw House are four iron guns, about 5ft. 9in. long, with 8½ inches bore, said to have been left by the Parliamentarians, as memorials, when the house was given up to its owner, Sir Thos. Dolman, but there is nothing in the character of these pieces of ordnance to directly establish their connection with the time of Charles I. Several mementoes of the Civil War are preserved at Shaw House—suits of armour, an iron cap or head piece, a cloak said to have been worn by Oliver Cromwell, cannon and musket balls, &c. Here are also to be seen a pair of cavalry kettle-drums reported to have been part of the spoil of the battle-field in 1644. They consist of two large copper shells or basons rounded at the bottom, 21 and 19 inches in diameter across the heads respectively, and each have triangular stands affixed to them. In the absence of any marks or other distinguishing characteristics, their identification with the time of Charles I. rests on verbal tradition only.

† See Capt. Gwynne's 'Mil. Mem.' ch. xiii. The portable leather gun was made of the toughest leather, and bound with metallic hoops. A strong horse could carry two of them through miry roads. They could be discharged only 7 or 8 times. Col. Wemys is commonly supposed to have been the inventor; but the original inventor was Gustavus Adolphus, who employed them at the battle of Leipsic, Sept. 7, 1631. See 'Mil. Mem. of Col. John Birch,' Camd. Soc., 87, 88.

‡ Ludlow's 'Memoirs,' p. 131.

however, soon rallying, advanced towards Thelwall's reserve, who brought his men boldly forward. Without waiting to return their fire, the Parliament men rushed in upon the Cavaliers and gallantly fought to the death. Even by their enemy's admission they struggled heroically; but the odds were against them, for they were able to do little against an enemy sheltered by walls and earth-works. Thus, though twice reinforced, and bravely led forward, twice they were repulsed; and, abandoning all hope of penetrating this well defended place, they gradually retired out of fire, to Clay Hill, leaving one of Crawfurd's colours and two "drakes" in the hands of the successful defenders of the royal stronghold.*

Simultaneously with the attack on the garden, Manchester's left column made a vigorous assault, by the village of Shaw, on the north side of the Lamborne, towards the front of Shaw-house; but Sir George Lisle stripped to his shirt, and therefore (says 'Mercurius Aulicus') mistaken for a witch † by the Parliamentary soldiers, burst at once, with his fiery cavalry, into the very heart of Manchester's infantry, and scattered them "like spray before some storm-driven ship." No pause was made,—no mercy shown by the excited troopers,—the whole mass was swept up Clay Hill,‡ pursued by the enraged cavaliers, who hewed down the fugitives by scores. It is said that they only escaped total destruction through the devoted heroism of Ludlow's men, who sacrificed themselves by moving forward to cover the retreat. So great

---

* The loss of these "drakes" (light field guns) was stated by the Earl of Manchester to have been the fault of Capt. Hammond, who is previously mentioned in the list of wounded at the first battle of Newbury, and as probably the Col. Robert Hammond who was afterwards the King's gaoler at Carisbrook. Further investigation shows that this was the case. He was nephew to Dr. Henry Hammond, chaplain to the King, and to Col. Thomas Hammond, one of the Regicides, and was appointed Governor of the Isle of Wight in September, 1647. After the King was beheaded, Col. Hammond was sent over to Ireland or went there with Cromwell, and died of a fever at Dublin, 24 Oct. 1654.

† " At the last Newb'ry Battle, in the sight
Of Majesty, he led the Foot to fight,
Strip'd to his Shirt, that others might descry
His Actions, and Example take thereby;
From whence the frighted Rebels gave it out,
That a white Witch was seen to fly about
The Royal Army scowring to and fro,
Where'er the Contest did the hottest grow."
'Hist. Grand Rebell.' By Henry Ward. Vol. ii, p. 432.

‡ Walker's 'Hist. Disc.' p. 113.

was the execution that Clarendon states 500 men were left dead on one little spot of ground.*

The moon was now up. Manchester had received a reinforcement of horse, expected earlier in the day; and he resolved to make another and final effort. However skilful and daring the attempt, it was foiled by the pluck of the Royalists, who stood their ground, and again compelled their assailants to retire.

It has often been a matter of surprise that Shaw House should have suffered so little, considering that a series of violent attacks were made on it by the Parliamentarians, but this seems easy of explanation. Firstly, only the eastern end of the House is turned towards Clay Hill, on the slope of which the enemy's guns must have been posted. Next, between the latter point and the building rises a hillock, on which the Water-tower now stands, and this very materially sheltered the house from view and injury. Thirdly, there were no heavy siege-guns brought against it, as at Donnington Castle. Further, it was concealed by trees, in most cases stout enough to stop shot from light field-guns, and was surrounded by high fences and a thick rampart. Thus we need not wonder that it escaped unscathed.†

These important fights, at Speen and Shaw, constituted the last great action between the two parties here. Whatever its ultimate results may have been, at first each army seems to have fancied itself worsted. The Parliamentarians had been repulsed, and had suffered severely at Shaw; but their right wing at Speen had been completely successful. The King, on the other hand, who had been a witness of his ill fortune on the Speen side, and unaware that at Shaw the tide of war had turned in his favour, considered his position no longer tenable, and determined to act at once on the resolution he had taken in the morning, in anticipation of an unfavourable issue, namely, to retreat on Wallingford. Orders were accordingly dispatched to Prince Maurice, Lord Goring, Lord Hopton, Sir Jacob Astley, and the other commanders, to draw off their men to Snelsmore Heath.‡ Battalion after

* Clarendon's 'Hist.' II. p. 548.

† A shot-hole in a shutter in one of the eastern rooms of the House is registered by a brass plate as having been made by a bullet when the King was standing close by. When this could have occurred is difficult to determine.

‡ Snelsmore Heath formerly extended over the whole of the now-enclosed fields between Donnington Castle and the present Common. At the time of the Civil War there were one or two cottages standing between the Common and the Castle, which Sir John Boys burnt to prevent their being occupied by the enemy.

battalion began silently to quit its ground, and march in the direction of the rendezvous; while the guns and heavy stores were conveyed by a circuitous route to Donnington Castle. Charles, at the earnest entreaty of his friends, who perceived the utter frustration of all his hopes, now thought of providing for his own safety; and, having sent for his guard, amid a troop of fugitive horsemen made good his escape to Donnington Castle, deciding to proceed to Bath, where he might by his presence hasten the Welsh and Northern forces which his nephew Prince Rupert was then getting together for his assistance. After half-an-hour spent in the Castle with Sir John Boys, in whose care he left his wounded, baggage, artillery, and ammunition, the King, with the young Prince of Wales, the Duke of Richmond, the Earls of Lindsey, Berkshire, and Newport, Lord Capel, and others, and accompanied by a guard of about 300 horse, hurried from the scene of his overthrow, and by about four o'clock in the afternoon of the next day reached Bath (having ridden over fifty miles, as Symonds says, "sans rest"),* where he met Prince Rupert, and informed him of the sad disaster.

Prince Maurice ably conducted the retreat of the army, and, notwithstanding the great superiority of the enemy in cavalry, he got to Wallingford by way of Compton without hindrance the next day, and then quietly went on to Oxford. The Parliamentarians, who remained on the ground all night, awoke in the morning to find the King was gone! Waller and Manchester appear to have been entirely ignorant of each other's success or failure until the next day. Simeon Ashe says,—"The next morning, as soon as we had in the field, near the bodies both of friends and foes which lay in the field, made our addresses to God both by praise and prayer according to the present affecting providences, we march'd over the river [Lamborne] to Newbury; and all this time we neither met with, nor heard of our friends at Speen."†

The losses on both sides, in killed, wounded, and prisoners were heavy. Sir Edward Walker‡ gives the following list of the "hurt and wounded" on the Royalist side :—King's Life-guard, 29 common soldiers; Prince of Wales's Regiment, 69 common soldiers, 2 Captains, 2 Lieutenants, 1 Ensign, 1 "Sarjant;" Sir Jacob Astley's Regiment, 16 common soldiers; Col. Bellasis' Regiment, 25; Col. Bowles' Regt., 23; Col. Dalton's Regt., 22; Col. Owen's Regt., 14; Col. Harford's

---

* Symonds's 'Diary,' p. 146.
† 'A True Relation,' &c.
‡ Harl. MSS., No. 6804; 92.

Regt., 13; Col. Dyve's Regt., 14; Col. Blagg's 6 common soldiers: in Sir Gilbert Gerrard's "Tertia," "9 officers slain," 22 "shott;" 100 "soldiers slain," 116 "shott," "41 sicke and unable to march:" in Lord Harbert's 5 "Readgements," 2 Captains, 1 Ensign, 45 common soldiers, "11 sicke men; my Ld. Harbert hath taken care to send these into Bristol:" in Lord Grandison's Regt., "5 common soldiers, 2 sicke men, 11 men killed:" in Col. Charles Gerrard's Regt., the Lieut.-Col., 2 Captains, 2 Lieutenants, 9 Ensigns, 7 "Sarjants," 78 common soldiers. Col. Sands' [Sandys'] Regt., 26; of Lord River's Regt.,....; of the Lord-General's Regt., 74; Soldiers hurt and not able to march, 351; of Col. Chas. Gerrard's Regt., 78; altogether 529, and 59 Officers hurt, total 588.

It is difficult from the above account, to summarize the number of those actually killed and of those only wounded; but the King's loss was evidently much greater than some of the Royalist writers represent; for each party sought to reduce its own loss and augment that of its opponent. Sir Edward Walker, in his 'Discourses' says there were not above 100 common soldiers slain; and Clarendon follows him; Sir Roger Manley, a zealous champion in the Royal cause, goes so far as to say "5000 men were slain on the King's side;" while Whitelock, the Parliamentary writer, reduces the number to 200 slain and 300 prisoners. The following royalists are mentioned as having been killed in this engagement:—Sir William St. Leger, M.P., son and heir of Sir William St. Leger, a Privy Councillor, and Lord-President of Munster in 1629; Lt.-Cols. Leke, Houghton, Topping, and Jones (killed on the little hill where the Water tower now is at Shaw); Majors Trevellian and Knyvett; Captains Whittingham, Catelyn, Wolfall, Philpot, and Mildmay (eldest son of Sir Humphrey Mildmay); also Mr. Barksdale, a volunteer. This loyal gentleman was a member of an old Newbury family, one of whom (Mr. Thomas Barksdale) gave an acre of land to the Parish of Speen, the rent thereof to pay for a sermon at Speen Church every Easter-Tuesday. Of the wounded were—the Earl of Brentford, shot in the head; Sir John Grenville, Sir John Campsfield, Sir Edward Waldegrave, Lt.-Col. Page (shot in both thighs and in the arm); Major Alford, shot in the thigh; Capt. Wells, wounded severely; fell into the hands of the enemy and died in prison, Lieut. George Hume, or Haines; and Mr. Stephen Knight, "chief clerk of the Avery" to the King. In his petition for restoration to the office, shortly after the return of Charles II., Mr. Knight pleads that he was severely wounded at Newbury in the last battle, and subsequently plundered of all he possessed, and that his family were turned out into the streets.

That the prisoners captured by the Parliamentary Army were numerous, appears in the contemporary papers.* It seems that many of the persons here enumerated belonged to the neighbourhood, and their descendants still reside in the locality. Some five or six hundred "stragglers" were subsequently taken prisoners by the Parliamentarians when they entered Newbury. Of these, the 'Weekly Account' in the succeeding week (from Oct. 31 to Nov. 4, 1644), reports—"The Letters from Sir William Waller confirm the taking of a great store of arms and many prisoners since the late victory near Newbury; but most of the men, being poore country-fellows (that were forst [forced], and offered to take the covenant not to fight any more against the Parliament), they were left to their election, whether they would fight for the Parliament, or depart to their own dwellings, upon which many of them made choice of the Parliament's service."

*Of Lord Cleveland's Brigade*, taken prisoners were—Lord Cleveland, Captain Philpot,† Lieut. Harper, Lieut. Roane, Cornet Whealand, Quarterm<sup>r.</sup> Ironmonger, Quarterm<sup>r.</sup> Campion, Quarterm<sup>r.</sup> Nicholas, Mr. John Percy, and 38 Troopers of the same Brigade.

*Of Col. Astley's Regiment*—11 officers and troopers.

*Of Lord Hopton's Brigade*—Capt. Elmes, Quarterm<sup>r.</sup> Simon Court, Edward Phillips, Henry Dimmock, Hugh Pope, "Gentleman of Armes," besides divers troopers.

The following were also taken prisoners—Colonel Philpot, Capt. Mildmay,‡ Capt. Nevet [Kynvett],‡ Mr. Richard Nishton, Mr. John Curtis, Mr. Edward Archer, and "divers other Gentlemen of Armes and Reformadoes,‖ of these many of them are officers, the rest gentlemen;"—Mr. John Champion, Mr. George Edmons, Mr. Henry Leonard, Mr. John Edge, Mr. John Goare, Mr. John Williams, Mr. William Bartholomew, Mr. James Lovelock, Mr. Henry Atkins, Mr. Thos. Poply, Mr. Thos. Holden, Mr. James Fant, Mr. William Dormer, Mr. Thos. Plant, Mr. John Aldred, Mr. John Petty, Mr. Michael Franklin, Mr. James Champion, Mr. John Farnaby, Mr. Robert Hill, Mr. Henry Coard, Mr. Peter Holway, Mr. Thos. Compton, Mr. George Huntley, Mr. Richd. Thebon, Mr. Cornelius Owen, Mr.

---

* 'Perfect Occurrences of Parliament,' from 25 Oct. to 1st Nov. 1644.
† Died of his wounds.
‡ Both died of wounds.
‖ "Reformadoes" were officers who, having lost their men, were continued on whole or half-pay.

Thos. Greenfield, Mr. Richd. Painter, Mr. John Hobbs, Mr. Edmond Card, Mr. John Davis, Mr. Wm. Halen, Mr. Edwd. James, Mr. Joseph Hitchcocke, Mr. Robt. Kinder, Mr. Daniel Stout, Mr. William Wood, Mr. John Hill, Mr. Wm. Banister, Mr. Richd. Cornewell, Mr. Thomas Turke, Mr. Wm. Eiles, Mr. Peter Smith, Mr. Richard Whiston, Mr. Daniel Dongway, and Mr. Henry Vincent.

The estimates of the losses on the side of the Parliament, likewise vary most considerably, Sir Roger Manley leads off with 2503 as the number actually killed. Clarendon, comes next with 1000; and Carte gives the same. On the other hand, the Parliamentary Commissioners, in their report to the Derby-House Committee, dated from Newbury, the day after the battle, state, "Major Skippon guesseth that the number slaine, on both sides, [*i.e.* of the Parliamentary forces engaged at Speen and Shaw] were between two and three hundred." Little reliance can be placed on these statements, which were made for party purposes. The average of these figures would give about 1000, which is probably a fair calculation.

Very few names of Parliamentary Officers who fell in this battle have been handed down to us. Col. Gawler, Lt.-Col. White, Captains Willet, Talbot, and Charles D'Oyley, of the Earl of Essex's Life-Guards, were killed at Speen (the latter, it is said, by the hand of Sir Humphrey Benett); and Cols. Norton, Berkeley, Lloyd, and Lieut. George Haines, are mentioned as wounded.

In an original letter, containing a brief account of this battle, from Col. Norton to his friend Richard Major of Hursley, the Colonel says—"We killed some men of note, and lost some, amongst w$^{ch}$ was Lieut.-Col. Knight, sonne to John Knight, who was to me much lamented by my L$^d.$ Man[che]ster and many others, and died w$^{th}$ y$^e$ reputac'on of as gallant a man as any in all y$^e$ army and as much beloved; truly I am sorry for himselfe, and not lesse for poor John Knight's sake; but as he lived to be a good christian soe he died like a good souldier. Many we had wounded; amongst y$^e$ number I receaved a faier admonition (by musquet-shott in my legge) for medling where I had noe charge, but I thanke God, my bone was to hard for y$^e$ bullett, and I hope I shall be upon both legges againe ere it be long. I could not help it; for I thought there was need when I engaged myselfe to lead up Col. Ludlowe's Regiment, his horse having broken his bridle, soe y$^t$ he was faine to quit." [Here the remaining part of the sentence, probably with some others, is lost, the paper having failed at the fold.]

## ROLL OF KILLED AND WOUNDED.

Endorsed:—"Coll. Norton, 22 Octob., 1644. Newbery battaile." (Major* Letters and Papers, British Museum.)

Sir Wm. Waller, it seoms, had a narrow escape in this engagement. To this he thus refers in his note-book,† in which he was in the habit of making daily jottings:—"At the second Newbury fight, when I fell on with my troopes by way of Speene Field and were there mingled with the enemy, I had a great deliv'rance, for one of the adverse party coming behind me, and being ready to fire his pistoll in my reines, in that instant one of my life-guard killed him, or otherwise in all probability he would have killed me.

O God, the Lord, the strength of my salvation, thou hast covered my head in the day of Battle!
The Angell of the Lord encampeth round about them that feare his worde, and delivereth them."

The greater number of the slain found a grave near where they fell, while many of those who died of their wounds in the town of Newbury were buried in St. Nicholas' churchyard. The Churchwarden's accounts from 23 Aug., 1644 to 20 Sept., 1645, containing the following list of payments in connection with these interments:—

Given at Vestry, 20 Sept. 1645. Account passed by William Nash, Mayor.

| | | | |
|---|---|---|---|
| Paid for a shroud for a Soldier, carrying him to Church | 0 | 0 | 8 |
| Carrying Soldier and cleaning the Church | 0 | 5 | 0 |
| Carrying Soldier and making a great grave | 0 | 4 | 0 |
| Carrying a Soldier to Burying | 0 | 1 | 4 |
| Shroud for a Soldier | 0 | 3 | 4 |
| Carrying and Burying 3 Soldiers | 0 | 3 | 0 |
| Coffin for a Lieutenant | 0 | 7 | 0 |
| For Carrying, Burying Soldier | 0 | 1 | 2 |
| For Carrying another Soldier to Burying | 0 | 1 | 0 |
| Burying 2 Soldiers more | 0 | 2 | 0 |
| Burying 6 Soldiers more | 0 | 5 | 6 |
| Shrouds for Soldiers | 0 | 3 | 6 |
| Carrying a Soldier and Burying | 0 | 1 | 0 |
| Digging Graves for Soldiers | 0 | 4 | 0 |
| Burying 3 Soldiers more | 0 | 4 | 6 |
| Ditto 4 ditto | 0 | 6 | 6 |
| Digging Graves | 0 | 2 | 2 |
| Burying 2 Soldiers | 0 | 3 | 5 |
| Ditto 2 ditto | 0 | 3 | 0 |
| Burying a Soldier | 0 | 1 | 6 |
| Digging 19 Graves and cleaning the Church | 0 | 4 | 0 |
| Burying a Soldier | 0 | 1 | 6 |
| Ditto ditto | 0 | 1 | 6 |

* Dorothy, daughter of Mr. Richard Major, married Richard Cromwell, the Protector's eldest son. When the old house at Hursley was pulled down some time in the last century, a seal was found, supposed by the artist Vertue, who saw it, to have been the identical seal of the Commonwealth, which the Protector took from the Parliament.

† Sir W. Waller's 'Recoll.,' C. 45 a; Brit. Mus.

## CHAPTER IX.

## MILITARY MOVEMENTS AFTER THE BATTLE.

Heavy as the combined losses were, they did not prevent the speedy resumption of hostilities. Though the battle had been somewhat indecisive, inasmuch as the King's army had escaped by way of Donnington to Oxford, and the King himself to Bath, Manchester soon took steps to reap the full fruits of the battle, which he claimed as a victory. Early on Monday morning the 28th October, when the Parliamentarians found that the King was really gone, a Council of War was called at Speen. It is asserted that Cromwell, on that occasion, not doubting as to the state in which affairs stood, repeatedly requested leave to push on with his cavalry and overtake the retreating royalists; but he was peremptorily restrained by the General-in-chief; and, as Cromwell brought a charge to this effect against Manchester in the House of Commons, the statement is probably true. Waller also wrote from Newbury, on the 30th of October, to the Derby-House Committee, advising immediate action, "after the great trouble with which the three armies were got together; and if ever victory could be followed with advantage this is one," when after much time had been wasted in an angry discussion, Manchester reluctantly consented that Waller, Cromwell, and Hesilrige, with the horse (about 6000 strong) which had been engaged on the Speen side of the battle, should march in pursuit. With this force the Parliamentary Generals reached Blewbury, without firing a shot; and then finding that the enemy had got clear over the river at Wallingford many hours before, it was judged both hazardous and useless to pursue further; and the troops were accordingly quartered in Blewbury, Hagborne, Chilton, Harwell, and the neighbouring villages. Meanwhile a letter having been sent by Manchester from Newbury, desiring the return of the force, the three Generals came back to Newbury, where they had an interview with the Earl. They then pressed earnestly to have the whole army marched speedily into quarters beyond Oxford (about Witney, Burford, and Woodstock), where the King's troops had already begun to rally. That being denied, they requested that two or three thousand of the foot then quartered in Newbury should march to join the horse at Blewbury. Manchester could not however be persuaded to stir until the Saturday following (November 2nd), on which day he started with a portion of his infantry, and in two days managed to get as far as Harwell, which same distance, Cromwell says, the Earl on his return "dispatcht in one." Arriving at Harwell, Manchester refused to proceed further until he had received instructions from the Committee in London; his excuse being the badness of the roads and other impediments. The two commissioners, Lord Warriston and Mr. Crew, proceeded from Harwell to London to represent matters in person to the Derby-house Committee: but on Tuesday (November 5th), the day before the directions of the Committee were received, Manchester appointed a rendezvous for the next morning on Compton Downs, four or five miles back towards Newbury. The whole body of horse under Cromwell on Tuesday night lay on Chilton plain, and the following day moved to Compton, and joined Manchester, who had by this time, much to his satisfaction, received orders from London not to divide his army, but to march back to Newbury and endeavour to take Donnington Castle. Siege-pieces and ammunition were dispatched to him for that purpose. Consequently the entire force retraced their steps, reaching Newbury on the 7th of November. From Cromwell's statement to the Commons, it appears that he commended these Berkshire Downs as a suitable position "for lying in the King's way" with his returning army, and indeed this locality narrowly escaped being the scene of a bloody conflict between the two armies; for no sooner had Cromwell quitted Chilton Plain, than the royal forces took up their quarters on the same spot on the Downs where their enemies had encamped the preceding day. But as this is somewhat anticipating the course of events, it will be necessary to return to the proceedings of the King after his retreat to Bath.

When the King met Rupert at Bath, the Prince had with him about 400 horse and 600 foot, making, with the King's own troop and followers, about 1300 men. With this strength Charles and his nephew marched out of Bath on Wednesday, 30th of October, and quartered that night at Sherston near Malmesbury; next day they reached Cirencester, where the King received a letter from Sir Jacob Astley (created Baron Astley of Reading a few days after, at Oxford), informing him of the good condition of his army, with advice to his Majesty to advance speedily, and, with the additional forces then at his command, to march again to Newbury, disengage his cannon, and offer the enemy battle. From Cirencester the King marched to Burford, and by the way he met the Earl of Northampton, with those regiments which had relieved Banbury; and he also received the intelligence that General Gerard and Sir Marmaduke Langdale, with a force of 4000 horse and foot, would encamp that night at Stow-on-the-Wold. Whereupon, to give more ease to the troops, and to make preparations for his march to Newbury, the King left his force at Burford, and hastened with his guards and attendants, to Oxford, which he entered on the 1st of November, being received with great joy and acclamation, after his long absence of five months, during which time he had passed through and overcome many difficulties.

As soon as the King came to Christ-Church, Oxford, he conferred the dignity of Knighthood on Colonel Gage, who in his Majesty's absence had done well both in defence of that city, and in the relief of Basing and Banbury. Charles also gratefully thanked them embers of his Council, who had managed his affairs since his departure. This having been done, the succeeding days were employed in making preparations to take the field; a new train of artillery was expeditiously formed, and the whole army put into good serviceable condition.

---

CHAPTER X.

RENEWED ATTACK ON DONNINGTON CASTLE, AND RELIEF OF THE GARRISON.

Meanwhile, between the action on the 27th October and the King's return to Oxford, the Parliament's forces entered Newbury; and, with a strong body of horse and foot, surrounded Donnington Castle. They again summoned the indomitable Boys to surrender, assuring him this time, that if he did not instantly comply, they would not leave one stone upon another. "If so, I am not bound to repair it," was the Governor's scornful reply. Being urged a second and a third time, with the offer that he should be permitted to march out with all the arms, ammunition, and stores deposited in the Castle,—"Carry away," he said, "the Castle walls themselves, if you can; but, with God's help, I am resolved to keep the ground they stand on, till I have orders from the King, my master, to quit it, or will die upon the spot." An assault was consequently determined on, but the officer who led the storming party having fallen at their head, and great differences prevailing among the Generals, nothing further was at that time done. The Royalist journal, 'Mercurius Aulicus,' for Sunday, Nov. 17, 1644, gives the following account of some affairs as then reported;—"The

Rebells sped so ill at downright fighting that they now practise a new way of murther, for we are certainly advised from Donnington Castle, that when the Rebells close besieged the place, they hyred a souldier to poyson their Well on the north side of the Castle, which lay without the workes, between the Rebell's trenches and the workes. This souldier having informed the rebells that the Well was most necessary for the support of that garrison received his twenty shillings (for that was all this poor Rebell demanded), and in the night time conveyed the poyson down the Well, but next morning the commander (toucht it seems with the horror of the fact) sent a Drum with a letter to Sir John Boys to give notice what was done. The Governor returned thanks to their Commander, and at first fit opportunity drew 40 musqueteers out of the Castle, and in the face of the rebells cleaned the Well, taking out the bag of poyson, and digging it deeper. After which time we kept the Well in despight of the Rebells, and to make tryall whether or no the Well was truely poysoned, we tryed the experiment upon a Horse, which having drunk of it, swell'd and dyed within 24 hours." A Well in the position indicated has recently been discovered on the north-west side of the Castle, about 400 yards from the buildings. By the nature of the ground it is screened from the observation of an enemy posted on Snelsmore Common; so that the garrison could obtain water thence without exposure or difficulty.

At this time the Earl of Brentford, who had been wounded on the 27th, sought temporary shelter in the Castle, where his Lady attended him; and the Parliamentarians, hearing he was there, sent Col. Hurry to his old general, with large offers if he would give up the place, or induce Boys to do so,—a proposal rejected with indignation. On the 30th Oct., three days after the battle, Lord Brentford, having somewhat recovered from his wounds, obtained a guide to direct him by cross-roads to Bath, where he was anxious to rejoin the King and inform him of the safe retreat of the army to Wallingford. But he was pursued by a party of the enemy's horse, led by Col. Birch, and his Lady was taken prisoner. The general, however, managed to escape, owing as Skippon in his dispatch states, to one of their party unadvisedly sounding a trumpet near where he was reposing himself.*

---

* This episode is related in an interesting document printed by the Camden Society, entitled 'A Military Memoir of Col. John Birch.' That portion referring to the capture of Lady Brentford, is given in the APPENDIX.

On Wednesday, the 6th of November, the royal army was drawn out on Bullington Green, near Oxford, and inspected by the King, who found he had a force of 6000 foot and 5000 horse, with which to relieve Donnington Castle, and recover his ordnance and baggage that had been left there after the action of the 27th October. Prince Rupert consented without reluctance to supersede Lord Brentford as Commander of the King's forces; whilst the old General was solaced with the honorary post of Lord-Chamberlain to the Prince of Wales.

The following officers were amongst those who accompanied the King's army in this expedition:—Prince Rupert, Prince Maurice, the Earl of Northampton, Lord Wentworth, Lord Gerard, Lord Hopton, Sir Marmaduke Langdale, Sir Humphrey Benett, Sir Thomas Aston, Sir William Blakiston, Sir Henry Gage, Col. Blagge, governor of Wallingford, Col. Tucker, Col. Keck, Col. Neville.

On Thursday, Charles marched with his troops to Wallingford, and the day following, Friday 8th November, the army encamped on Ilsley Downs, while the King quartered with Bishop Goodman at West Ilsley Rectory.*

The march was resumed on Saturday morning towards Newbury; and the succeeding events of the day are thus stated in detail by Sir Edward Walker: †—"On Saturday our army marched in battalia, expecting some opposition. The van was led by his Highness Prince Rupert and General Gerrard. In this order we marched, and got possession of the heath on the backside of Dennington Castle,‡ from which a small force of the rebels might have kept us, the

---

* Dr. Godfrey Goodman then held the Rectory of West Ilsley, *in commendam*, with the See of Gloucester, of which he was deprived by Archbishop Laud in 1640 for refusing to subscribe to the Canons; but was restored upon his submission. He was sequestrated by the Committee of Plundered Ministers, for his tithes of West Ilsley. In a petition to the Protector Cromwell, the Bishop says that his "great losses were such as he thinks no man suffered more," and complains that a Mr. Humphrey Newbery, who was appointed by the Committee to supply his place at West Ilsley, came there with a body of soldiers and forcibly took possession of his Living and property. Dr. Goodman ultimately became a Roman Catholic, and died in that faith Jan. 19, 1655, and was buried near the Font in St. Margaret's Church, Westminster. He is said to have been concerned in the noble design of bringing the New River Water into London. The old Rectory-house at West Ilsley, an interesting Elizabethan building, was taken down about 35 years since.

† 'Hist. Discourses,' pp. 118, 119.

‡ Snelsmore Common. The King's route was by Chieveley and North-heath.

entrance into it being steep and the way very narrow,* and
then we must have gone about and fallen in by way of
Speene.† On that heath the army was drawn up about
twelve of the clock, and every one prepared to fight. Thence
in good order we marched by Dennington Castle, passing the
river at a mill, and two fords below it ‡ without any opposition, and thence drew into the large field between Speene
and Newbery, where the army was set in order. The rebels
in the interim drew a great body of horse and foot into the
other field towards Shaw, having made breastworks and
batteries on the backside of Newbery towards both these
fields, § resolving to keep the town, which was the reason
they gave us so easie a passage to the heath behind Dennington. About three in the afternoon we advanced within reach
of their cannon, which they discharged amongst us without
doing any hurt. Then a body of our horse charged another
of theirs in the lower field ‖ and routed them, pursuing them
almost to their breastworks; when the rebel musquetiers
placed in the lane between the two fields ¶ gave fire on our
horse and caused them to retreat (though without disorder).
In the interim we could discover a great body of their horse
on the hill on the south side of Newbury** almost at a stand
whether to come down or retire. The armys being now on
the point of being engaged, His Majesty advised with his

---

\* Bussock Hill.
† Through Winterbourne.
‡ Donnington Mill. The fords over the Mill-stream and the Lamborne. This mill was probably a dependency of the Castle in mediæval times.
§ These breastworks and batteries were in Newbury Marsh, then open to the fields above-described, at the back of Speenhamland. The remains of the earthworks still existing are shown on the Plan. They were but "sorry works" as Skippon describes them. In levelling portions of the Marsh for the purpose of planting trees, and improving the roadways, in March, 1883, a detached human skull and a number of bones were discovered in the soil. A small cannon shot, 1lb in weight, of the usual 17th century type, was likewise dug out at a depth of 4 feet below the surface. Cannon balls of a large size have also been found in other parts of the ground.
‖ The "lower field" is that nearest to Shaw Avenue.
¶ The "lane between the two fields," was the old road to Oxford, which followed about the same line as the modern highway from Newbury.
\*\* The body of horse seen on the hill on the south side of Newbury was that under Cromwell, in the meadows below the Wash, on the left of the Wash Road from the town. Manchester accuses Cromwell of not coming up with this body of cavalry until after the King had marched away; but Cromwell retorts that Manchester was "most ready to finde the danger or infeisibility of drawing out to interpose."

2 A

Council what was fittest to be done, who considering that he had already effected what he came for thither, which was to relieve Dennington (provisions being put in in the interim) that it was in his power to draw off his ordnance and ammunition thence; and that he had sufficiently regained the opinion and honour of the day, by passing his army over the river in the face of theirs, and offering them battel if they durst draw out, and withal considering how dangerous it might prove to force them to fight, having the advantages of breastworks and batteries and a town at their backs, it was unanimously concluded that we should draw off and attempt them no further. And to let them know that we did it not out of any apprehension, Prince Rupert sent a Trumpet [a "Drum" or "Trumpet" was equivalent to a flag of truce], to give them notice of our intentions, so that, if it had been their will, they might have fallen on our rear. But they suffered us quietly to pass with drums beating and trumpets sounding the same ways we came over the river. His Majesty lay that night in Dennington Castle, and all the army about him. In this action we lost one Captain of horse * and about fourteen Foot slain by their cannon in the retreat; and I believe the rebels lost twice that number."

Some traces of this skirmish were discovered in the year 1869, when two skeletons were found in a garden which occupies part of the site of the old Pelican Inn at Speenhamland. The skeletons were both perfect, and lay side by side, one on its back and the other on its face, and both in the direction east and west, about two-and-a-half feet below the surface. A piece of clothing, like a soldier's coat-trimming, some brass buttons, portions of accoutrements, and a pike-head, were found near the remains; also a gold ornament, somewhat like a brooch or fastening, a spur, the bone of a horse, and the bowl of a 17th-century tobacco-pipe. Scores of such pipes have been picked up in the neighbouring fields. There is little doubt that these were two troopers, most probably officers, "brothers in arms," who fell in the above mentioned skirmish, which took place over this very ground on Nov. 9th, 1644. Some fifty years ago a skeleton, having a large gash in the skull, was discovered, with a sword by its side, not far from the same spot; and more recently another skeleton was exhumed in the rear of the adjoining premises now used as a Brewery. The remains of three bodies, together with some cannon balls were also met with in digging gravel near the Castle-houses on Speen Hill.

---

* Capt. Fitzmaurice, of the Prince of Wales' regiment.

# MILITARY PLAN,

Shewing the position of the Royal Army in the fields between

## SPEEN AND NEWBURY,

on Saturday, November 9th 1644,
when the king relieved Dennington Castle.

From the Original by
### SIR BERNARD DE GOMME,
IN THE BRITISH MUSEUM,
Add. M.S., 16,370, fo. 60.

RIVER LAMBOURNE

Dennington Castle

Order of his Ma:ties Armen of 4200 Horse, and 3000 ffoote and Battalia upon this plaine before Newbury, Commanded by his highnesse Prince Rupert, the 9 October 1644 — at the Relieving of Dennington Castle,

## RENEWED ATTACK ON DONNINGTON CASTLE.

The position of the King's army in the "large field between Speene and Newbery," referred to by Sir Edward Walker, and quoted on the preceding page, as being the place "where the King's army was set in order" is indicated with much exactness on a contemporary military plan showing the forces in the field. This interesting addition to the subject has been obtained from the British Museum,* since the publication of the first edition of this work, and a copy of the plan is inserted in the present volume. The ground denoted as that occupied by the King's battalions, is in strict agreement with the written description which has been given, but it will be seen from the title on the plan that the draughtsman (stated on the endorsement at the back of the drawing to be Sir Bernard de Gomme) has written the date of the relief of Donnington Castle as being in October 1644, whereas it was on the following 9th of November. This plan appears to have been drawn from memory, and is not strictly accurate in some respects. The Church at Newbury is shown as being on the east side of the Bridge instead of the west, and the river Lamborne is denoted as the "Kennet Fluvius." The latter river is that crossed by the Bridge at Newbury.

Sir Bernard de Gomme or de Gomez, to whom we are indebted for this plan, accompanied Prince Rupert to England in 1642, as a military engineer, and is mentioned in a petition for the office of Surveyor General of Fortifications, dated Dec. 1660, as having served the late King (Charles I.), as engineer and quartermaster-general, of which place he had a grant, dated June 30. 1645, and confirmed by Charles II. at Breda, June 15, 1649. In March, 1661, he obtained a grant of the office of Engineer of all the King's Castles, &c. in England and Wales, the fee being fixed at 13s. 4d. a day, with order that he keep an exact account of all engines to be made by him, and of all disbursements of money. [Cal. State Papers, Domestic, Car. II., 1660-1.] In the third volume of Pepys's *Diary*, p. 90, sixth edit., there is a note about Sir B. de Gomme as being born at Lille in 1620, and having died in 1685, his place of burial being within the Tower of London.

A correspondent of a London Diurnal† communicates the following intelligence from the Parliamentary army, in connection with the return of the King to Donnington Castle:—
"Friday, Nov. 8.—This day the King designed a partie of 6 or 7000 horse and foot to relieve Dennington Castle and to

---
* Add. MS, 16, 370. A collection of coloured Plans of Fortifications, etc., temp Car. I. and II.
† 'Perfect Passages of each Daye's Proceedings in Parliament,' Nov. 6 to Nov. 13, 1644.

fetch away such things out of the Castle as were most materiall, vizt.—
1. The King's Crown, which His Majesty wore on some high dayes, and had carried and brought back from Exeter.
2. The Great Seale, and other Seales which the Lord-keeper had left also in the said Castle.
3. The King's writings and divers Writs of great consequence, which were also carried in thither.
4. Divers Jewells, much gould, silver, and other treasure, which was also in the said Castle.
5. That they should endeavour to bring away what artillery and ammunition they could.
6. To carry relief with them to the Castle.

"This party was at Wallingford, from whence they were to march to Dennington, and the Castle of Dennington doth so command all the fields between the Castle and Newbery, that it is not safe for our army to march out there; yet some guards of horse were still out and the enemy from the Castle play'd this day very fast, many cannon-bullets falling in Newbery.

"Saturday, Nov. 9.—This day there came intelligence that the night before the enemy in Dennington Castle had not only made shot with their cannon gainst Newbery, but made many flourishes, and at night made a great fire at the top of the Castle, so that the Earl of Manchester, Sir Wm. Waller, Lt.-Genl. Cromwell, and Sir William Balfour (to whom the charge of the armies for the present is committed) began to suspect the enemy coming that way, and so special care was taken for securing our armies in their quarters that night, lest the enemy should come on a sudden, that therefore their outguards should be ready, which was performed with a great deal of paines, care, and discretion, but more especially to oppose the enemy between Kingsclere and Dennington Castle, if they came, which was their direct way from Wallingford, and no other was probable.

"Tuesday, Nov. 12.—Besides that spoken of in the instructions to the King's forces, there was left in Dennington Castle about 18 small pieces of artillery carried into the Castle, besides 5 or 6 great pieces of ordnance that were planted on the works below, and good store of ammunition, some say 60 cart-loads, besides 30 cart-loads they took with them, what of this was carried away they will not tell us. But about 5 o'clock in the afternoon they retreated with what they had taken out of the Castle, and what they brought in is best known to themselves, but what they did was in a short time, and the great pieces lie still upon their works."

## RELIEF OF THE GARRISON.

To resume our narrative, on Sunday morning, the 10th of November, the King's troops were drawn up in marching order on the heath adjoining Donnington Castle, with so many of the guns which had been left with the garrison after the retreat on the 27th October, as they could conveniently take with them, attached to their train. All being in readiness, the King bade farewell to the gallant governor Sir John Boys, and looked, it may be imagined, with tearful eye on the shot-wrecked walls of Donnington, which had been maintained in his cause with such fidelity, and which was to himself so full of stirring memories of disaster and defeat, but never of dishonour. The trumpets gave a parting blast, answered by a hearty cheer from Boys' merry men on the Castle walls, as the King, accompanied by Prince Rupert and his retinue, led the vanguard over the heath. Soon, however, the sound of drums and trumpets died away, and the little company of heroes at the Castle were once more left alone.

From Snelsmore Heath the army marched to Winterbourne,\* where the troops were halted, it is said, to give thanks to God for their great success; the King, Prince Rupert, and the chief officers of his staff, attending divine service in the parish church. The route was then by Boxford and Shefford to Lamborne; and here the King took up his residence with Mr. Garrard;† the main body of the foot being quartered in the town, and the horse at Wantage and the intermediate villages. This is referred to in the following terms by a Parliamentary scout:—" Monday, 11 November 1644. The last night the King's head-quarters were at Wantage and Lamborne; and a part of the horse took off all the provision they could meet as they went along by Peesemoure and other villages, and intended to quarter this night

---

\* The Winterbourne estate at that time belonged to the Head family, one of whom was Lord Falkland's host at Newbury.

† The principal residence of the Berkshire Garrards was at Kingwood, about one mile from Lamborne, on the road to Marlborough by way of Ramsbury, and occupied a beautiful position on an eminence overlooking the neighbouring Valley. The old house (where a room in the east wing was long shown as "The King's Chamber") was taken down many years ago. The Mansion must have been of considerable extent, judging from traces of the foundations; and the remaining stabling attests to its having been of the Elizabethan character. The line of the avenue, leading from the high-road, and crossing the park, is still defined by a few trees here and there; and many other vestiges of former importance can be discerned. Queen Henrietta Maria was also at Kingwood, April 18th, 1644, on her journey from Oxford to Exeter. She had taken a farewell of the King a few days previously, never to see his face again. There are several memorials of the Garrards in Lamborne Church. Their arms were azure, a chevron engrailed ermine.

at Auburn and Ramsbury; and wee heare they intend to relieve Basing. That all the foot which lay at Lamborne marcht away this morning towards Auborne, where they had a rendezvous, and intended to quarter there that night, but there came a sudden allarm that the Parliament horse were coming after them, that they gave a command that they should march to Marlborough, and in the afternoone they march'd out of Wantage, having 2500 horse and many stragling foot. They report that a party of their foot was to winter at Marlborough, the rest to go to Winchester. The King is reported this night to bee at the army againe."*

It is time, however, to leave the King's army, and return to the opposite camp.

The Parliamentary Generals, upon the intelligence that the King was quietly marching away from Donnington Castle, rode to the top of Clay Hill, "to looke uppon the departing enemy," and then called the inevitable Council of War, which resulted in the customary wrangle, and in the usual inaction. But one of their officers, whose name is not recorded, determined to have one slash at the King before he was out of their reach; and, having got a few horse together, started in pursuit. His advance, however, having been noticed by Rupert, the Prince unobserved placed a body of his cavalry in a barn by the road-side, and let the pursuers pass; but the moment they reached the spot, the ambushed troopers came out from their hiding place and took the Parliament men "front and rear," so that, as Symonds records, 15 of them were killed and more taken prisoners. This was the only effort made to oppose or harass the King's march.

From Lamborne, the Lords Capel, Hopton, and Culpepper, with other officers, were sent on to Marlborough to provide quarters for the army, and to levy contributions on the inhabitants of the district for the support of the King's forces.

It was a matter of surprise to the Royalists that the enemy with a powerful artillery and a strong body of cavalry, did not force on an engagement, but, on the contrary, allowed the King's troops, after relieving Donnington Castle, to advance within gunshot of the town, which was strengthened with numerous field-works, and afforded every requisite security in case of a repulse. But Manchester was immoveable, and appears to have formed an intractable resolution of remaining inactive, which no argument nor remonstrance could influence or disturb.

Writing from Newbury on the 10th of November to the

---

* Sir Samuel Luke's Letter-book; Egerton MSS.

Committee at Derby House, the three Parliamentary commanders, Manchester, Waller, and Balfour, gave the following reasons for deciding against fighting. "It was impossible for us to hinder the King from takeing his traine out of the Castle, and to keepe the towne of Newberry, he comeing with soe considerable an army; for had we drawne up between the Castle and the King: the King had wheeled about and possessed the towne. Then the weather and want would have driven us to a retreat. The King would not only have his traine, but the towne as a quarter and Basing relieved, and that had beene ye best. Wee heare the last night he drew out some of his traine, and sent it to Wallingford; this morning early wee found him drawne up in battalia, with horse and foote, about a mile from the Castle. We drew out, intending to have falne upon the King's army. But considering his many advantages of ground, and the weather falling bad, following might breake our army; ye officers of ye foote complaining of lessening of their foote, and many hundreds of our horses being already dead, and the living very weake, and many of the troopers run from their colours. And being assured that upon our quitting Newberry, the enemy would forthwith take it, wee thought it fittest to returne to Newbury, where wee now are, watching the King's motions, and waiting your Lordships' further orders." *

Cromwell offers his own explanation of the matter in the following deposition :— †

"That the king's armie marching from Dunnington Castle and being drawen up on Winterborne heath, the army belonging to the Parlement drew out of the towne of Newberry and Newberry feild into Shawfeild about a mile from the king's army, and the Earle of Manchester with diverse of the cheife officers having viewed the same did a little after repayre into a cottage in or neere the said feild to consult what to doe, and amongst other debates it was urged by this examinante that if wee should beate the king's army it would hinder his affayres in France and might prevent the coming of French forces into this kingdome, which wee heard, was indeavoured; to which his lordshippe gave answer that he did assure them, meaning the councell of warre then present, there was noe such thing as any forces to be brought from France, which undertaking of his lordshippe this examinante wondered at, consideringe what hee, this examinante had heard concerning endeavours of that nature, and this examinante still pressing

---

* Letter Book, Derby-Ho. Com. Public Record Office.
† State Papers, Domestic Series, Public Record Office.

towards engagement his lordshippe urged further that hee was against fighting, giving this as his reason and saying that if wee should beate the king never soe often, yet he would be king still and his posterity; but if hee should beate us but once, we must be hanged, and our posterity undone, or words to that effect; to which this examinante replyed that, if this principle was true, it condemned all our former fighting as foolish, and was an argument against fighting for the future, and a ground for making a peace how dishonourable soever. "OLIVER CROMWELL."

The following extract from a letter, dated Newbury, 15th November, from the general officers, Manchester, Waller, Balfour, and Skippon, to the Derby-House Committee, is descriptive of the state of the Parliamentary army at this time, and shows how little able the people of Newbury and the neighbourhood were to bear further demands upon them :—

"The Horse are very unable for marching or watching, having been for a long time tired out with hard duty in such extremeatie of weather as hath been seldom seen, soe that if much more be required at their hands you will quickly see your cavalry ruined without fighting. The foote are not in better case, besides the lessening of their numbers through cold and soe much duty; wee finde wee have to encrease soe much upon them that wee cannot in duty conceale it from you, nor indeed with that christian consideration which we owe to them, whose extreame sufferings wee dayly looke upon, not, without a little sorrow. The places we are in not affording food or covering for them; nor is the condition of the people lesse to be pittied, who both in our horse and foote quarters are soe exhaust, that they have soe little left for themselves that wee may rightly feare a famine will fall upon them."

On Tuesday, 12th November, which turned out (says Symonds) "a miserable wett windy day," the King's army moved on from Lamborne to Marlborough, Charles quartering in the house of Lord Seymour* at the Castle. The army was encamped on the Downs at Fyfield, about two miles distant.

---

* Francis, Lord Seymour, was brother to the Marquis of Hertford, afterwards Duke of Somerset. It was this Lord Seymour who built the house at Marlborough, known in later times as the "Castle Inn," and which subsequently constituted the nucleus of the present famous School-house. The plans and elevations of this house were furnished by Inigo Jones, who was of the same political party as the Seymours, and then at the height of his fame as an architect. Ramsbury Manor-house is also said to have been built from designs by Inigo Jones; but this was the work of his pupil and nephew John Webb. The King quartered at Ramsbury Manor in April, 1644; where also Cromwell visited Lord Pembroke 12 July, 1649.

Charles remained five days at Marlborough, during which time he personally superintended the fortifications of the place; and he found that the fierce threats of his officers of the Commisariat department had so strongly impressed the terrified inhabitants of the district, that not only were the wants of the troops amply provided for, but a sufficient quantity of food and forage was left to supply some of his necessitous garrisons. The greater part of the hay and corn which the neighbourhood had just harvested was sent off, with a body of cavalry, to Worcester; and arrangements were made for re-victualling the garrisons at Donnington Castle and Basing.

The following warrant will show the manner in which these supplies were procured:—

"To the High Constables of Ramsbury Hund. and to each of them:

"These are in His Majestie's name to command you or either of you to charge, provide, and send in, out of your Hundred to my quarters at Andrew Goddard's House at Ogborne St. Andrew, near Marlbury, for the use of his Majestie, two and twenty hundred weight of bread, twelve hundred weight of cheese, three fat Beefs, tenn fatt Muttons, fower dosens of poultrie, forty bushells of oates, twenty bushells of beanns and pease, also you are straitly charg'd to bring in eight able and sufficient Teems with Carts for His Majestie's necessary service. Charging you and every one of you and every petty constable in your hundred not to presume the least neglect in the due and speedy execution hereof in every particular, and that all the said provisions and carts be brought in by three o'clock in the afternoone next Sunday, as you tender the good of His Majestie's service, your owne persons and estates. Given under my hand this 14th day of November, 1644. WM. MORGAN, Commissary.

"You or either of you are required to be there present, with a return of the names of those who shall refuse to perform what is charged upon them." *

Another warrant, dated at Marlborough, empowers the officers to seize all such "Physick and Chirurgery" in that town as shall be necessary for the use of the army, the owners to be paid out of the contributions from the district.

At a Council of War held at Marlborough on Saturday, the 16th November, it was decided that the relief-party to be sent to Basing should consist of 1000 horse, each trooper carrying before him a bag of corn or other provisions, and should march so as to reach there by a given time (communicated to the garrison), then each should throw down his sack, and make good his retreat as best he could. To effect this design, Hungerford was thought the most fitting place in which to

---

* Sir E. Walker's papers, Harl. MSS., 6802; 295. Many other interesting papers relating to the doings of the King's army at Marlborough will be found in the same collection.

2 B

quarter the army, and obtain supplies for the enterprise. Its conduct was entrusted to Sir Henry Gage, who had had such good success on a former occasion. Accordingly the advanced portion of the troops marched back to Hungerford, where they arrived the same evening, the King with the main body of the army following the next day, Sunday, November 17th.†
The royal forces being augmented by the arrival at Hungerford of 500 horse, which had been newly raised by Sir Francis Doddington in the West.

While the King was at Marlborough, the Parliamentarians, hearing of his intention as regards Basing, left Newbury with the greater part of their force, with the view (as Cromwell states in his "Charge against Manchester") of proceeding to Kingsclere, "for a more direct interposicion in the King's way to Basing, and that there we might fight with him upon the downes, if he came that way, and lye ready (if he should bend towardes Newberry) to repossesse it before him; and on those grounds onely and to that end was our remove agreed to in full Councell." "But," adds Cromwell, "being thus got out, and upon on our way to Kingscleare, having intelligence that the King was coming by Hungerford towardes Newberry, his Lordship [Manchester] would then neither go on to Kingscleare, nor return into Newberry, but upon new pretences (without the Councell of Warre) turn'd his course to Aldermarston (which was five miles homewards from Newberry, and seaven miles nearer home than Kingscleare). And, though Kingscleare was the knowne direct roade to Basing, yet he pretended to turn to Aldermarston with intent to goe directly to Basing, and that he would fight the King there which way soever he should come, if he attempted to releive it. This gave some satisfaction for present, but from Alder-

---

† "Sunday, 17º Novembris, left Marlingsborough, and that night the King lay at Hungerford, com. Berks, seven miles [10 miles] five myles [9 miles] short of Newbery, where the head-quarters of the enemy was. The King's troope at Chilton, a myle from Hungerford. Mr. Packer, who owes Denyngton, aud was secretary to the Duke of Buckingham, owes a pretty faire howse. A little on the left hand this daye's march, wee left Ramsbury, the faire seate of the Earle of Pembroke. Wee marched through a forest belonging to the Marques of Hertford."

\* \* \* \*

"Popham, descended of Judge Popham, owes a faire large seate, halfe a myle distant from this, [Chilton Foliot], the Manor of Littlecot, with a Parke." Symonds's Diary, pp. 152-3.

The King's quarters, while at Hungerford, were at the Bear Inn, where the rooms occupied by himself and his suite are still pointed out. It was at this same hostelry that William Prince of Orange received James II.'s Commissioners in Dec. 1688.

marston his Lordship would not be got to Basing (makeing excuses), but with much adoe being got out next day to Mortimer Heath, he would not be perswaded to goe on any further, alledging that many of his soldiers were run to Redding, and more would goe thither (being got so neare it); that (when he pretended for Basing) draweing the army to Aldermarston (which was cleare out of the way) he brought the soldiers soe neare Redding that they would be running thither, and then made their running thither an occasion to avoyde going to Basing at all, and at last to drawe all to Redding."

Manchester, in his 'Defence,' says—"So, uppon our intelligence of the King's remove from Marlburrow, it was supposed hee was marching to Basing, to releive it with his army, wee conceived it fitting to march that day to Oldermeiston, where wee continued uppon the feilds, and, if the enemy went to Baseing, to endevour to intercept him; and so at Oldermeiston, at a councell of warr, where the question was only, whether it was councellable to fight or not, and concluded by all, no man speaking so much against fighting as Cromwell, and so unanimously consenting not to fight, but to endeavour to hinder the releife of Baseing, or to withdrawe the forces, which weare lying before Baseing, and so to keepe our armies intire, dividing ourselves, the foote at Redding and Henly, and our horse all about Fernham, Okingham, Windsor, Maydenhead, and Stwins" [Staines].

Immediately after the Parliamentarians had left Newbury, the Governor of Donnington Castle, exasperated with the inhabitants for their refusal to afford succour to his garrison in any way, made a sally into the town "on the Lord's day," with the intention of seizing the Mayor and some of the principal inhabitants, and carrying them prisoners to the Castle, and demanding a ransom for their release. This design Sir John Boys nearly accomplished before an alarm was given, and a party of Parliamentary horse quartered in the town came to the rescue. A Parliamentary Journal[*] affirms that the party from the Castle went to the Mayor of the Town and pulled him out of his house, which they plundered, and that they "abused his whole family most shamefully;" and that they then went to the houses of eight or nine more chief persons in the place, dragged them also out of their dwellings, "abused their wives, children, and servants," and carried away great plunder; and that the

---

[*] 'Perfect Passages of each Day's Proceedings in Parliament,' Wednesday, Nov. 20, 1664.

gentlemen themselves were actually conveyed prisoners to Donnington Castle.

The Parliamentary forces being withdrawn from Basing, Sir Henry Gage's expedition for its relief was satisfactorily accomplished; and Sir George Lisle, with 1000 men, took an ample supply of provisions to Sir John Boys at Donnington Castle, and brought back "without let or hindrance" the rest of the spare and military stores, which had been left behind a few days previously. Both Donnington Castle and Basing having now been well cared for, the King decided to return to Oxford, with the intention, if practicable, of surprising the Parliament's garrison at Abingdon on his way.

On Tuesday, the 19th November, which was the King's birthday, the army marched from Hungerford to Great Shefford, his Majesty lodging for the night at the Old Manor-house. In his 'Diary,' Capt. Symonds the Royalist chronicler writes:—

"Tuesday, 19 November, the army marched. His Majestie lay at Great Shefford in the old manor howse of Mr. Browne, Esq., com., Berks; a parke belonging to it.\* This day in the march a soldger hangd for plunder, but the rope broke."†

Instances of occasional license attributable to the Royalist troops such as that recorded by the Diarist, frequently occurred in spite of the efforts of their officers to preserve strict

---

\* A considerable part of the old Manor-house at Great Shefford is still standing, and the chamber where Charles slept is known as "The King's Room" to this day; while the name of "The Home Park" attached to an adjacent field denotes the inclosure referred to by Symonds:—

The Brownes of Shefford were a younger branch of the ennobled house of Browne, Viscounts Montagu. Sir George Browne, knt. of Wickham, in Kent, eldest son of the first Lord Montagu married Eleanor, daughter and co-heir of Anthony Bridges, Esq., of Shefford, and was father of George Browne, Esq., of Caversham and Shefford, who, by his wife Elizabeth, second daughter of Sir Richard Blount, knt., of Mapledurham, had nineteen children; three of the sons fell in the service of Charles I. The eldest son, George, was made a K.B. at the coronation of Charles II, and dying in 1678, was buried at Great Shefford. The younger son, John, was created a Baronet, 19th May, 1665. This title became extinct in 1774, on the demise without issue of the 5th Baronet, Sir John Browne. The name of Mr. Browne of Shefford occurs in the list of those Royalists who compounded for their estates during the Usurpation, as follows:—

"Mr. Browne, of Shefforde, being proved a papist and in armes, his estate, worth £200 p. anum, was let at Micheallmas last at £70 to Mr. Browne's baley, and £1000 profered for his stock, and secueritie for the munies, was sould to his baley for £400 p."—Addl. MSS. No. 5508, Brit. Mus.

† Symonds's "Diary," p. 154.

discipline, and the testimony of a contemporary writer as to the character of the King in this respect is worth noting for its sincerity and the characteristic trait which illustrates it:—

"I never observ'd any great severity in y<sup>e</sup> King us'd either towards y<sup>e</sup> enemy when he had him in his power, or to y<sup>e</sup> soulgier in his own army, except only at Wing a house of my Ld. Carnarvon, where he command'd to be hang'd upon a sign post a soulgier for stealing a chalice out of y<sup>e</sup> Church."\*

Capt. Symonds, the diligent and observant antiquary, continues his entries under November 19th with the following interesting local notes:—

"Lord B. [Lord Bernard Stuart] and troope at Little Fawley, the neate and faire habitacion of the Lady Moore, wife to Sir Henry.—Painted over the Porch at Lady Moore's howse—†

"Argent, a moor-cock sable [Moore]. Motto—Regi et legi.

"The same; impaling, argent, a saltire engrailed gules, a chief azure, "TWITTYE," Suum cuique pulchrum.

"Champion all this part of Berks.‡

"He that built this howse was Sergeant Moore,§ temp. D. [? T] Egerton, Canc.: Sir Henry was his son. Nothing but Moore's coate in the church of Fawley."

On Wednesday, Nov. 20th, the King at the head of his troops marched to Wantage, passing the night at the house of Sir George Wilmot at Charlton; and on Thursday he went

---

\* Sir Henry Slingsby's "Diary."

† The picturesque old manorial mansion of the Moores of Fawley, where Lord Bernard Stuart and his aristocratic troop of the King's Life Guards were quartered, is a most interesting specimen of the domestic architecture of James the First's time, but has long been inhabited as a farm-house. It was built, as Symond's records, by the eminent lawyer Sir Frances Moore, Sergeant-at-Law, 1614-21, and although it has undergone considerable alteration at the hands of its successive owners and occupiers, most of its original characteristic features have fortunately been preserved.

‡ "Champion" *i.e.* champion land; not inclosed; downs and open fields.

§ Sir Francis Moore, who was born at East Ilsley in 1558, died Nov. 20, 1621, and was buried at Great Fawley. He married Anne, heiress of William Twitty, Esq., of Boreham in Essex, by whom he had several children. Henry the eldest, referred to by Symonds, was created a baronet in 1627, and was drowned, as recorded in the parish register of Fawley, 22 February, 1633: when his son of the same name succeeded to the title and estates. The latter is mentioned as being concerned in the Royalist Rising in Wilts in 1655. Sir St. John Moore, knt., brother to Sir Henry the second Baronet, was one of those persons designed for the knighthood of the Royal Oak by Charles II,—his estate being valued at £1,500 a year. On the demise of Sir Thomas, 6th baronet without issue, 10 April, 1807, the baronetcy became extinct.

on to Faringdon, where he supped and slept at the house
belonging to Sir Robert Pye. Sir Robert had purchased of
the Untons the manor and estate of Faringdon in 1622, and
upon the breaking out of the civil wars his house there was
garrisoned for the King. His son, Sir Robert Pye, jun.,
warmly supported the parliamentarian cause, and became a
colonel of horse in General Fairfax's regiment. Cromwell
made an unsuccessful attempt upon this garrison in the
month of June, 1645; and the following year, a second
attack equally unsuccessful, was attended with a singular
circumstance. Sir Robert Pye the younger, who had married
Anne, daughter of the celebrated John Hampden, heading
the assailants on his own father's house, then held by
Sir George Lisle; and did not hesitate to batter down its
walls. The church spire shared in the destruction, and the
damage done to the town by fire and shot during the siege
was estimated at the large sum of fifty-six thousand, nine
hundred and seventy-six pounds, four shillings, as appears
from a petition entered in the Commons Journal, 1 Sept.,
1648. Faringdon House was one of the last places which
held out for the King, being included in the Articles for the
surrender of Oxford in the month of June, 1646. At
Faringdon the King stayed a day to await the result of
Sir Henry Gage's expedition for the relief of Basing, and
to consider where to make his winter quarters. The question
of disposing of the army being a business which required
time for its consideration, was referred to Prince Rupert as
General of the King's forces. "And so," says Sir Edward
Walker, " His Majesty leaving his Army about Farringdon,
on Saturday the 23rd of November, attended by his Regiment
of Guard, and some other horse, marched toward Oxford,
passing not far from Abingdon, where some parties of the
Rebel's Horse drew out but durst not engage themselves.
About two in the afternoon, his Majesty came to his residence
in that city, where he yet continues with as much honour
and safety as the violence and oppression of so universal a
Rebellion will give him leave."

No sooner had the King left the army than Prince Rupert,
strong in the power of his own will, determined to make an
attack on the garrison at Abingdon; but the vigilant governor
Browne was not to be easily caught; and the Prince, having
lost several of his men, was glad to get back again to
Faringdon, little satisfied with the result of his expedition.
The King's army were then put into their winter canton-
ments, and Rupert joined the King at Oxford.

The Parliamentary historian, Oldmixon, the bitter opponent

of the Stuarts, with creditable candour, thus speaks of the
King's admirable conduct in this campaign. "If the same
courage and conduct had been shewn by the King in so good
a cause as that of King William at the Boyne, his fame and
his memory would have been equally glorious and immortal."

The disappointment in Parliament and in London generally
at the result of the Second Battle at Newbury was extreme.
The day after the news arrived of the engagement between
the two armies the monthly fast took place as usual (Oct. 30,
1644), as if there were no subject for rejoicing. Disagreeable rumours began to circulate: the victory, it was said,
might have been far more decisive; but discord had reigned
amongst the generals, who had suffered the King to retreat
without impediment, almost in the very face of the army, on
a bright moonlight night, when the least movement might
have prevented it. It was much worse when the news came
that the King had just reappeared in the neighbourhood of
Newbury,—that he had, without interruption, removed his
artillery from Donnington Castle,—and had even offered to
renew the battle, without the Parliamentary army quitting its
inaction. The clamour became general, and the House of
Commons ordered an enquiry. Cromwell had only waited for
this opportunity, to break out and report his complaint
against Manchester:—"It is to the Earl," he said, "all the
blame is to be imputed, ever since the battle of Marston
Moor; he is afraid to conquer, afraid of a great and decisive
success; but now, when the King was last near Newbury,
nothing would have been more easy than entirely to destroy
his army. I went to the General; I showed him evidently
how this could be done; I desired his leave to make the
attack with my own brigade; other officers urged this with
me, but he obstinately refused; saying only, that if we were
entirely to overthrow the King's army, the King would still
be King, and always have another army to keep up the war;
while we, if we were beaten, should no longer be any thing
but rebels and traitors, execrated and forfeited by the law."
These last words greatly moved Parliament, who could not
endure that any should suggest a doubt as to the legality of
their resistance. Next day, in the Upper House, Manchester
answered the attack; explained his conduct and his words;
and in turn accused Cromwell of insubordination, of falsehood, even of treachery; for on the day of the battle (he said)
neither he nor his regiment appeared at the post assigned
them. Cromwell did not reply to this charge; but renewed
his own accusations more violently than before.

It would be foreign to the design of this Memoir to devote much space to the elucidation of the notorious quarrel between Manchester and Cromwell, which has been so largely dealt with by recent writers.* "This great leading incident in the history of our Civil War," observes Professor Masson,† "brought to the surface and into direct antagonism principles of the very greatest significance in reference to the management of the war; and the triumph of the movement-party on that occasion led directly to the ruin of the royal cause." Indeed, it enabled Cromwell, by the exercise of extraordinary finesse, to bring forward and successfully carry through the Commons the "Self-denying Ordinance," which enacted—

"That during the time of this war, no member of either House shall have or execute any office or command, military or civil, granted or conferred by both or either of the Houses of Parliament, or any authority derived from both or either of the Houses, and that an Ordinance be brought in accordingly."

CHAPTER XI.

## THE NEW MODEL.

The "Self-denying Ordinance" was rejected by the Lords, but the Commons had found another way of effecting their great purpose of army reform, by requiring the Committee of both kingdoms to report at once on "The New Model of the Army," which they had been instructed to devise. This had been done on the 9th January, 1645; and by the 28th it had passed the Commons; and on February 15th, "The New Model Ordinance" became law. It was no longer of any use for the Lords to stand out against "The Self-denying Ordinance." That Ordinance, in fact, was already realized in the fabric of the "New Model;" and, accordingly, having been reintroduced into the Commons in a modified form, and having passed that House, it received the assent of the Lords on April 3rd, 1645. On the preceding day, the Earls of Essex and Manchester had simplified matters by formally resigning their military commands. The commander-in-chief of the New Model Army was to be Sir Thomas Fairfax, and

---

\* A letter from the Earl of Manchester, of much importance, as showing what were the grounds on which he quarrelled with Cromwell, has been recently (1883) published by the Camden Society, and is reprinted in the APPENDIX, (No. XII).

† Historical Preface to the "Quarrel between the Earl of Manchester and Oliver Cromwell."—Camden Soc., 1875.

the Major-General, or third in command, was to be Philip Skippon. The place of Lieutenant-General, or second in command, was at first left vacant, but Cromwell's name, exempted by special vote from the operation of the "Self-denying Ordinance," was soon inserted into the "New Model Army," in the post of Lieutenant-General, which had been purposely kept open for him. Thence, through successive stages, followed the rest of his career, ending in his Protectorship of the United Commonwealth of England, Scotland, and Ireland, with their Colonies and Dominions.

Professor Masson further remarks that the accurate student of English history will note that the termination of this famous quarrel between Cromwell and Manchester coincides in time with another great event, distinct from the new modelling of the army and the Self-Denying Ordinance, namely the Establishment of the Presbyterian system in England, the first definite votes for which, in the two Houses, were made in January, 1644-5.

It is worthy of record that the New Model Army,* consisting of 21,000 men—14,000 foot, 6000 horse, and 1000 dragoons, came to Newbury on its first march. On the 30th April, Fairfax advanced from Windsor (hitherto his headquarters) to Reading; and thence on May-day to Theale; and on the 2nd May, he quartered in the town of Newbury, where a meeting took place between him and Cromwell. At this interview the desirability of attempting an attack on Donnington Castle was considered; but the fortress had withstood so many assaults that it had the reputation of being impregnable; and, whatever the views of the two Parliamentarian generals on the subject may have been, they at all events did not make any attempt on the garrison.

The day that the Newly-modelled Army arrived in Newbury, intelligence was received that Lord Goring was advancing out of the West with a large body of horse and dragoons; his orders being to check Fairfax, and keep him separate from Cromwell; and finally to join the King's army, and enable it to meet the enemy in a general battle. Whereupon a party of horse was sent out the same night towards Hungerford and Marlborough to reconnoitre; and, meeting with a detachment of the Royalists, they took Col. Hacket

---

* The strictest discipline was observed in the New Model Army, and terrible punishments were summarily inflicted on offenders. While Fairfax's troops were at Newbury a soldier was ordered to have his tongue bored through with a red hot iron for notorious swearing and blasphemy; and other like examples of prompt and rigid severity for military offences are recorded.

and six other prisoners, without loss on their own side. This affair resulted very opportunely, as Col. Hacket, in order to conciliate his captors, gave the information that Goring intended early next morning to surprise Cromwell's quarters at Stanford-in-the-Vale and other places near Faringdon. Cromwell being at once warned of his danger, the attack was successfully repulsed.

Sir Marmaduke Rawdon, the gallant Governor of Basing, who had been recently superseded in his command of the garrison there on account of certain religious dissensions, and appointed Governor of Faringdon, was ordered to join Goring in this expedition against the Parliamentary forces under Cromwell. "On May-day, 1645, some 500 horse and foot cavaliers marched out of Loyalty House. As they were crossing the Kennet, between Thatcham and Newbury, they were attacked by Colonel Butler's Puritan regiment of horse, but succeeded in reaching Donnington Castle, where they were prudently refused admission by brave Sir John Boys, who was apprehensive of a siege. Fortunately for Sir Marmaduke Rawdon and his men, Fairfax's large army and about 32 guns did not reach Newbury until the following evening, so that they were able to pursue their march next morning, but were chased throughout the day by Colonel Butler, until about five o'clock in the afternoon, when they joined Goring's army near Lambourn. Col. Butler captured some prisoners, amongst them was a Commissioner of Excise, who had about £25 in his possession. Goring was on May-Day at or near Marlborough 'at dinner with his officers, roaring and drinking healths, and making themselves merry,' and he mustered his army at Marlborough on May 2nd. Some of his men had penetrated as far as Farnham, but were obliged to beat a hasty retreat towards Oxford, abandoning three guns and some ammunition."*

From Newbury Fairfax marched, on May 3rd, to the relief of the important town of Taunton, which was closely invested by the royalists, but stoutly held by Blake.

On the 7th May the King left Oxford and rejoined Prince Rupert, intending to raise the siege of Chester, or to give battle to the Scottish army,—Cromwell and Browne following and watching their movements. When this news reached London, the Committee of both Kingdoms sent an express ordering Fairfax to retrace his steps at once and invest Oxford, detaching a brigade for the relief of Taunton ; and the army returned to Newbury on the 14th May. Here,

* Godwin's 'Civil War in Hampshire,' p. 211.

FINAL SIEGE OF DONNINGTON CASTLE. 203

Fairfax remained three days to refresh his men and arrange his plans. The day following his entry into Newbury, he "faced" Donnington Castle, with a portion of his troops, and took ten officers and other prisoners. This, however, appears to have been little more than a mere exhibition of force; and on the 17th the New Model proceeded from Newbury to Blewbury, and encamped on the Downs two nights. By the 19th they had marched as far as Nuneham; the next day two miles further to Garsington; on the 22nd to Marston about a mile from Oxford, where Fairfax was joined by the Horse under Cromwell and Browne, and the city was invested; but, the artillery train being at Windsor, there was no means of undertaking a regular siege. Fairfax withdrew from Oxford on the 9th June, having received orders to go in search of the King and fight at all hazards. Before he set out, he sent an application to Parliament, signed by himself and sixteen colonels, for Cromwell, who was away in the Eastern Counties, to join him. The Lords deferred their answer, but the authorization of the Commons was prompt, and was accepted as sufficient. Fairfax immediately sent word to Cromwell; all the regiments hastened their march; and within a few days (on the 14th June) came the crowning defeat of the King at Naseby; and from that moment the issue of the war was practically decided.

CHAPTER XII.

FINAL SIEGE OF DONNINGTON CASTLE.

The Parliament during the spring and summer of 1645, had too important work on hand to be able to pay much attention to Donnington Castle; but in the autumn of that year it was determined to set about the siege in earnest. After the storming and surrender of Basing House (14th Oct., 1645). Cromwell strongly urged the House to curb the predatory incursions of Sir John Boys and the Governors of Wallingford and Faringdon, which so injuriously interfered with the trade between London and the West; and, for that purpose, he advised "a strong quarter" being made at Newbury. The Parliament consequently determined forthwith to reduce Donnington Castle, and the charge of this service they particularly recommended to Cromwell and Colonel Dalbier, both of whom were shortly afterwards in the neighbourhood of Newbury. Cromwell, possibly aware of the intrepid spirit which animated the governor and garrison at Donnington, seems to have weighed the chances of an assault, and to have decided against undertaking "such a knotty piece of business." He therefore went into Devonshire to join Fairfax. The matter, however, was not to be set aside; and it was resolved to accomplish the reduction of a fortress to which so much importance was attached; and to enforce the submission of its Governor, who had so often baffled and disappointed the attempts of his opponents. Instructions were accordingly sent to the Committees of the three Counties, Oxford, Berks, and Bucks, to unite their several forces for this purpose. The Committee of both Kingdoms conferred the command of the expedition (27 Oct.) on Colonel Dalbier, who was intrusted with the various duties of the siege, and authorised to proclaim martial law. Colonel Martin was appointed his second in command. Considerable sums of money were voted by both Houses* for the equipment and pay of the troops, and for providing all necessary *matériel* for the effective prosecution of the siege. Nothing was omitted that was considered necessary to ensure the success of the enterprise.

On the 6th Nov., Dalbier marched with the forces of the three associated Counties to Newbury, to meet the Hampshire contingent, which had been ordered to join him. The latter body were under the command of Colonel Thomas Bettesworth, High-Sheriff of Hants, "a gallant active man," whom we shall hear of again presently. Dalbier's force was subsequently further augmented by 200 foot furnished by the Committee of the County of Sussex; and five companies of foot and a troop of horse, by the County of Surrey. The last, which came from Farnham, were under Colonel Fielder, late Governor of the garrison in that town, the works there having been ordered to be "slighted." † A troop of horse also, which had been engaged at Basing, was sent by the County of Kent. Captain John Blagrave, of Reading, was promoted to the rank of Major of his regiment, and appointed to the command of the Berkshire detachment of horse, consisting of three hundred men. Captain Robert Voisey had the charge of the foot drawn out of the garrison of Windsor.

Notwithstanding all these reinforcements, Dalbier did not apply himself with zeal to effect a rapid reduction of the

---

* On the 4th Nov. 1645, £3000 was voted; on the 10th, £500; on the following 28 Feb. 1645-6, £2500, with £600 for the pay of the Kentish Horse employed in the siege.

† "Slighted" *i.e.* razed or levelled with the ground.

Castle; and, intelligence having reached him that the King had returned to Oxford, he at one postponed the siege and retired with his force to Aldermaston. He was aware of the character of the royalist Governor and the value of the defences, and considered an attack with the forces at his command difficult and hazardous. He decided therefore to remain at Aldermaston until he had collected the whole of his disposable strength, and had perfected his preparations. Unless his integrity be questioned, it is difficult to account for Dalbier's comparative inaction, considering that all the arrangements had been so carefully made, and that such a reasonable prospect of success presented itself; but possibly he had sufficient reasons to excuse himself, as his courage was undoubted. At this time the King's affairs were daily becoming more disastrous. While Fairfax was obtaining success after success in the West, the royal forces were everywhere being defeated and dispersed. What Dalbier's motives were it is impossible to say; he was, however, indisposed to make a vigorous and decisive attempt on the Castle; and, as will be seen from Captain Knight's relation of the siege, in the Appendix to this volume, it was not until the beginning of December that Dalbier again returned to Newbury. Much to his chagrin, he found on his arrival at Donnington that the whole of the houses in the village and adjacent places had been burnt by order of Sir John Boys, consequently he withdrew his infantry into Newbury, and quartered the horse in the immediate neighbourhood. The season of the year was very unfavourable for military operations, "the winter being very rude and viollente;" and as every place affording shelter or protection had been burnt or otherwise destroyed, Dalbier could not lay close siege to the Castle, as he had intended. Meanwhile the Parliament were asking what was being done before Donnington; and it is evident that they were not satisfied with the progress of affairs, and with Dalbier's lingering proceedings. Early in December a report was ordered to be made concerning Donnington Castle; and shortly afterwards the whole business was referred to the Committee of Hants, Surrey, Sussex, and Kent, and the Committees of the three associated counties of Oxon, Berks, and Bucks, with a request that they would represent their opinions to the House of Commons. These joint Committees presented their report on the 9th January following; and a letter was also read from Colonel Dalbier. Both of these were recommitted for further consideration.

Nothing of moment or of military interest occurred for some little time in connection with the siege of the Castle,

Dalbier remaining quiet in his quarters in Newbury. His intended operations against the threatened fortress were postponed until the Spring. Sir John Boys in the interval was vigilantly on the watch against any surprise from Dalbier's force, whose movements, from his position at Donnington, he could clearly observe. He therefore made every preparation against the inevitable assault, knowing full well that all depended on his own exertions, that no aid could be expected, and that the calamity which he had so long and honourably striven to avert must necessarily soon follow. But this did not discourage the gallant Governor, who laboured vigorously in restoring and enlarging the defences, provisioning his little garrison, and securing forage for the horses of his trusty band of forty troopers. "Such gallants were they," says Captain Knight, "that the enemy's horse never faced the Castle, but they received some loss." In fact every available means were employed that could secure the place and insure a successful resistance. Although the investment of the Castle had not yet actually commenced, the two parties were not altogether inactive, there bring a frequent "beating-up of quarters," and daring sallies by Sir John Boys on the Kentish regiment lying at Burghclere, Woodhay, and Balsdon House, near Kintbury, all of which are fully narrated by Captain Knight, who shared in the ever memorable defence already referred to.

In the month of March, Dalbier resolved to take more active measures, and commenced a regular investment. Having advanced within reach of the shot-riddled fortress, a "mortar-piece" was brought into requisition, the shells from which fell upon the ancient masonry with destructive effect, and in a few hours it came down in such masses that some of the garrison ran out into the works for shelter. The bore of this formidable piece of artillery must have been more than fifteen inches in diameter, judging from a fragment of one of the projectiles still preserved in the Castle.* The three counties of Oxon, Berks, and Bucks possessed one of these mortars, which is referred to in the "Commons' Journal" of January 19th, 1645, when it was proposed to employ this piece of ordnance against Belvoir Castle, an intention subsequently countermanded; and it was no doubt retained for service against Donnington Castle. The charge

---

* A short time since, in removing the roots of a fine and aged elm-tree which had been felled on the south side of the Castle, considerable portions of a shell of large size were discovered, the diameter of this projectile when entire being fully 15 inches. The remains of an iron vessel containing lead were also found at this spot, which had probably been used for casting bullets.

ordered by the House to be paid for the use and transport of this mortar was three hundred and fifty pounds, which would indicate that it was of unusual size and capacity, and its transit a difficult operation.

The concluding incidents of the last days of the siege are thus described in the "Weekly Account,' under date of Thursday, 26th March, 1646. "From Dennington we have received intelligence that Col. Dalbeer, drawing up close to the Castle to break the ground and intrench our men, the enemy at our beginning to break the ground sallied forth, took 50 prisoners, two colors, and some of the spades and pickaxes, but this retarded not the work, for since that time he hath shot divers granadoes into the Castle, fired the Barn and some other Outhouses, and done some execution on the main Fabrick, which hath brought the enemy to stoop and send out to desire a parley, which being refused the Governor hath sent to Oxford desiring to be satisfied in time whether he may expect reliefe, for otherwise he must be forced to a render on such conditions he could get, which his long standing out will in no way advance." The following week, Tuesday, March 31st, the correspondent of the same journal thus proceeds to inform its readers of the progress of events:—"I have already told you what execution Col. Dalbeer hath done against Dennington Castle, and of the Governour's sending to Oxford, I shall in this place give you the sequill; for it is this day certified that upon the messenger's going to Oxford Sir John Boys (Governor of the Castle) received not only assurance that he could expect no relief from Oxford, but further that there was a great defeat given to Sir Jacob Astley, which till now he seemed ignorant of. Hereupon the Governor stooping to play on such conditions as before he seemed to reject, a treaty was hearkened unto, and we understand this day by Mr. Packer's son, whose inheritance it is (and come from thence this day) that Col. Dalbeere is to have the possession thereof tomorrow at nine of the clocke. There are in the Castle about 200 common souldiers, divers pieces of Ordnance, and good store of Baggage."

The 'Moderate Intelligencer,' of the same date, informs its readers that "This day came the news of the Accord of Dennington Castle, which they are to surrender tomorrow: the granadoes made such work that the souldiers within knew not where to secure themselves, divers leaping over their works and craving quarter; the house will be preserved for that universally well spoken of gentleman and owner Mr. Packer."

A few days before the capitulation of the Castle, Colonel Dalbier, having intimation that a body of the King's horse were drawing towards Donnington from the garrison at Oxford, dispatched Colonel Bettesworth to intercept them. They were met between Oxford and Faringdon; and, after a very spirited encounter, the Royalists retired; but, on being pursued, eighty of the troopers were taken prisoners. On the previous Thursday, Col. Bettesworth had met with a reverse in another skirmish, four of his men being killed, and eleven others taken prisoners by the royalists.

Sir John Boys, who was shut up within the fortress, and ignorant of the state of affairs without, finding the old walls coming down about his ears, and his guns either dismounted or unserviceable, upon the return of the King's messenger with instructions to deliver up the Castle, surrendered it into the hands of Colonel Dalbier on the following conditions:—

ARTICLES AGREED UPON, MONDAY, THE 30TH MARCH, 1646,
FOR THE SURRENDRING OF DENNINGTON CASTLE.*

1. It is agreed upon, that Sir John Boys, knight, Governour of Dennington Castle aforesaid, shall march according to the Articles insuing agreed upon (that is to say) upon Wednesday morning next, being the first day of April, by 6 of the clock, the Governour, with all his Officers, Gentlemen, and Souldiers, are then to march out with Cullers flying and Drums beating, the Governour with 4 horses and arms, and every Field Officer with 2, and every Capt. 1, the Lieut.-Col of horse with two horses and arms, and the other officers and reformado officers of horse with 1 horse and arms apiece, 100 of the foot soldiers to march with their arms two miles, and the rest to march without, towards Wallingford, and then 50 to lay down their arms, and the other 50 to march with Cullers flying, drums beating, light matches, Bullets in their mouth, and Bandeliers fil'd with powder.

2. That if any officer or souldier in this Garrison hath been in the Parliament service, shall receive the equall benefit comprised in these articles.

3. That what officer or souldier late of this garrison shall desire to go beyond sea, shall have a Passe to go to London, or to what place they shall desire, within the Parliament's quarters, to procure the same accordingly.

4. That all Officers and Souldiers, late of this Garrison, who desire to go to their own Mansions or place of residence

---

* 'Perfect Occurrences of Both Houses of Parliament and Martiall Affairs, beginning Friday. the 27 March, and ending Friday, 3 April, 1646.'

SIR JOHN BOYS.
*From an original portrait.*

FINAL SIEGE OF DONNINGTON CASTLE. 209

and several dwellings, have a free passe to do so, without being molested or pressed to any oath, provided that they be engaged never to take up arms against the Parliament.

5. That there shall be a safe conduct granted to Wallingford accordingly.

6. That there shall be two Carts with teams, provided by the time appointed, the one to carry Sir John's baggage, the other to carry the Officers'.

7. That the Governor, Officers, and Souldiers, late of Dennington Castle aforesaid, shall at the time deliver up the Castle aforesaid to Col. Dulbier for the use of the Parliament, with all the Ordnance, Arms, Ammunition, and Provision therein (except what is before expressed), without embezzling the arms or ammunition, or demolishing the works.

8. That the prisoners now in Dennington Castle shall upon the signing of these articles be delivered forth and set at liberty.

9. That the wounded Souldiers of the Castle shall have liberty to be left in Newbury or elsewhere the Governour pleases, and to have present passes, that after their recovery they may go to their severall mansions or dwellings without interruption or molestation.

*Signed*   COLL. MARTIN,
           MAJOR RYNES,           } For COL. DULBIER.
           MAJOR COLLINGWOOD

           MAJOR BENNET,
           CAPT. OSBORN,          } For SIR JOHN BOYS.
           CAPT. GREGORY,

At the time of the surrender there were in the Castle 6 pieces of ordnance, about 20 barrels of gunpowder, with a proportionable quantity of match and other ammunition, and 140 men.

The field which tradition points out as that in which Dalbier was encamped, and where the treaty for the surrender of the Castle was negotiated, is still called "Dalbier's Mead." It lies on the eastern side of the Castle, and near the gardens and park of Donnington-Castle House.

The honourable and exceptional terms given to the gallant and faithful custodian of the Castle, Sir John Boys, bear witness that his unshaken loyalty to the King was acknowledged and admired even by his adversaries; and perhaps it would be impossible to find a brighter page in the whole history of these Civil Commotions than that which records the deeds of daring and devotion of this brave Cavalier.

2 D

By the time Donnington Castle had fallen, the King's cause was irretrievably lost; the wreck of his army, scattered about in the Western Counties, was either defeated and dispersed, or compelled to take refuge in those few towns which were still hostile to the Parliament.

In the Midlands the Royalists were equally unfortunate. On the 21st of March, 1645-6, a few days before the surrender of Donnington Castle, Sir Jacob (now Lord) Astley, having succeeded in collecting about 3000 men from the Royalist garrisons of Salop, Stafford, and Worcester, partially evacuated for that purpose, was on his way from the last mentioned place to Chipping-Norton, where he had arranged to meet Sir John Cansfield with 1500 horse and foot from the King's garrison at Oxford. But through some misinformation or delay, Cansfield's troops did not arrive at the proper time, and before Astley could obtain succour or withdraw, he was attacked by a considerable number of the Parliamentary forces under Brereton, Morgan, and Birch, at Donnington, a hamlet in the parish of Stow-on-the-Wold; and, after a gallant resistance, totally routed. The brave old soldier Lord Astley, Sir Charles Lucas, and most of the officers who were not killed, were taken prisoners. This was the last body of troops that appeared in the field for the King before the close of what is known as the "First Civil War."[*]

The important city of Exeter opened its gates to Fairfax on the following 13th of April, after sustaining numerous assaults, and a vigorous blockade for more than two months.

On the other hand, a succession of disasters now attended the Royalists on all sides; every day towns fell from their keeping, one after another, there being no longer a field force capable of offering any effective opposition.

Fairfax, having now swept all before him in the West, was enabled to lead his army back in triumph to besiege Oxford, which was now almost the only place of any strength that had not yielded to the Parliament. The smaller towns of Wallingford and Woodstock were already blockaded; and the King foresaw that his last strongholds must inevitably fall into the enemy's hands.

---

[*] It was on this occasion that Lord Astley is reported to have used the memorable and prophetic words which have been so often quoted: "Sir Jacob Ashley being taken captive. and wearyed in this fight, and being ancient (for old age's silver haires had quite covered over his head and beard), the souldiers brought him a drum to sit and rest himselfe upon; who being sate, he said (as was most credibly enformed) unto our souldiers: Gentlemen, yee may now sit downe and play, for you have done all your worke, if you fall not out among yourselves."— Vicar's "Burning Bush," p. 399.

FINAL SIEGE OF DONNINGTON-CASTLE. 211

The Parliamentary general, Fairfax, arrived at Newbury on the 27th April, 1646; and, after disposing of the troops which had been engaged with Dalbier at Donnington Castle, came the second time before Oxford. "Having observed the situation of the city," says Sir Roger Manley, "he made a large quarter capable of receiving three thousand men upon Hadington [Headington] Hill, which he also fortified very well; and drawing a line from thence round, he strengthened it with other forts, appointing the Colonels Raynsborough, Lambert, and Herbert to command them. Whereby the city was entirely shut up."*

Meanwhile, the King hearing that Fairfax had reached Newbury, within 25 miles of Oxford, and on the recommendation of Montreuil, the French envoy, determined to take the disastrous step of placing himself under the protection of the Scottish army. The guards being loosely kept by the troops round Oxford, Charles, disguised as a servant, was enabled to leave the city on the night of the 27th of April with little difficulty; his only attendants being Ashburnham and Hudson. After many perilous adventures he arrived at the head-quarters of the army then besieging the town of Newark-on-Trent, on the 5th of May; and soon discovered how fatal was the counsel of his advisers.

Woodstock surrendered on the 26th of April; Banbury on the 8th of May; and Newark was given up after a siege of six weeks, the following day. All motive for continuing the war was now at an end; and the King desirous of attaining a reconciliation with the Parliament, sent a warrant on the 10th of June, signed with his own hand, to the governors of all the remaining royalist garrisons in England and Wales, enjoining them to obtain honourable conditions and disband the forces under their several commands.

Oxford, the seat of learning and of loyalty to the King, where Charles had so long kept his court, was surrendered to Fairfax on the 24th of June; Lichfield capitulated on the 16th of July; Worcester, on the 23rd; Faringdon, included in the "Oxford Articles," on the 24th; and Wallingford Castle on the 27th, being one of the last of the garrisons in England that held out against the Parliament.†

It would be exceeding the limits to which the history of

---

* Manley's "Hist. of the Rebellion," p. 129.
† The last strong place in England which held out for Charles was Pontefract Castle, where, after the King's death on the scaffold, his successor was duly proclaimed by the garrison, which did not capitulate until six months later.

the Two Battles of Newbury legitimately extends to enlarge upon the many melancholy incidents which accompanied the few remaining years of the checkered life of the unfortunate King.

Betrayed by the Scots—his own countrymen, confined as a prisoner at Holdenby, Hampton Court, Carisbrook, and Hurst Castle, successively, he was finally brought to Windsor, and thence taken to London, where on the 30th of January, 1648-9, he met his death with fortitude and dignity on the scaffold erected before the banquetting house of Whitehall.

Whatever may be the political estimate of Charles's character, there can be no doubt as to his domestic virtues and the courage with which he endured his fate. Even his faults as a Ruler, and the errors of his Administration, were rather the effect of the school in which he had been trained than of any inherent tendency to despotism on his part. A professed believer in the Divine Right of Kings, he was conscientiously unable to bow to the rising tide of disbelief in such a creed. There was a point beyond which nothing could make him bend; and, if his conduct had always been as straightforward as his principles, he would have attained the summit of fame as a political and ecclesiastical martyr. But if he failed in many ways as a King, he at least died like one; and even his political opponent, Andrew Marvel, generously recognized his exemplary patience and equanimity in those familiar lines which form part of an ode addressed to Cromwell himself:—

> "He nothing common did, or mean,
> Upon that memorable scene;
> But with his keener eye
> The axe's edge did try:
> Nor called the gods, with vulgar spite,
> To vindicate his helpless right;
> But bowed his comely head
> Down as upon a bed."

His conduct in reference to the Battles of Newbury, as we have here traced it, illustrates both the virtues and faults of his character, from a military point of view; and if these pages have added anything to the vividness with which every feature of the English Revolution deserves to be studied, the labour expended on them will have been amply rewarded.

# APPENDIX.

## I.—THE KING'S MARCH TO NEWBURY.

OCTOBER, 1644.

*(From the 'Iter Carolinum.')*

Friday, 18 Oct to Andover. The White Hart. (Dinner in the field.) 1 night; 15 miles.
Saturday, 19 Oct. to Whitchurch. Mr. Brooke's.* (Dinner in the field.) 2 nights; 7 miles.
Monday, 21 Oct. to Kingsclere. Mr. Towers'.† (Dinner at Whitchurch.) 1 night; 5 miles.
Tuesday, 22 Oct. to Newbury. Master Dunce's‡ night's residence. (Dinner at Kingsclere.) 5 nights; 6 miles.

*(From Symonds's 'Diary.')*

Monday, 21 October. His Majestie, &c. left Whitchurch, the general rendesvous (sic) upon the Downe near Kingsmill's howse. §

---

* Whitchurch. The King when at Whitchurch Quartered at "The Priory," the house of Mr. Thomas Brooke, a staunch royalist, whose family had long resided at this place. There are several of their memorials in the Church. Mr. Brooke, who is said to have entertained Charles and his officers at the old Town Hall, was lay impropriator of the Rectory; but, being proved a "Delinquent" by the Parliament, his estates were sequestrated, and the Minister of his appointment expelled. The inhabitants of Whitchurch petitioned the Committee for Compositions sitting at Goldsmiths' Hall, to grant an increase of stipend, out of Mr. Brooke's estate, to the "Orthodox" minister, Mr. Bellchamber, whose income was only £14 a year, a quarter of malt, and a quarter of wheat. The Committee accordingly voted £50 a year for this purpose. The petition, which is preserved at the Record Office, is signed by Will. Pointer, Robt. Mills, Richd. Holloway, Will. Rolph, Will. Webb, Dan. Clarke, and others.

† Kingsclere. The residence of Mr. Towers was at Frobury Park, but one mile from Kingsclere. Part of the old mansion at Frobury is now occupied as a farmhouse, on the south side of which are the remains of the ancient chapel. A portion of the stone pulpit was in the building within the last fifty years; and at the present time the base of the font, which appears to be of local stone, does duty as a horse-block in the farm-yard. The house is partly surrounded by a moat, which probably also served as a fish-stew. Foundations have been met with in various parts of the grounds, showing that a building of considerable extent once existed here. Traces of a carriage-drive to the mansion from the Ecchinswell-and-Newbury road are discernible; the chief approach was, as at present, from the Kingsclere road on the south. In the "Lay Subsidy Rolls," Pub Record Office, $\frac{175}{550}$, 17 Car. I. 1641, Robert Towers is described as "of Frobury, Gent." and assessed as owner. This was most probably the gentleman who received the King. The property is now life hold, and reverts to Lord Bolton.

‡ See Appendix II.

§ At Sydmonton. Henry, second son of Sir Henry Kingsmill, of Sydmonton, was slain when fighting gallantly for the King at Edgehill, and was buried in the Churchyard of Radway. In Jago's Poem of "Edgehill," there is a print of this monument; but only the mutilated remains of the effigy now exist, and these are preserved in the tower of Radway New Church. In the Kingsmill Chapel, Kingsclere Church, there is a fine alabaster altar-tomb, with effigies of Sir Henry and Lady Bridget Kingsmill.

## THE SECOND BATTLE OF NEWBURY.

Tuesday, 22 Oct. The general rendesvous (sic) was upon Red Heath, neare Newbery. His Majestie knighted Sir John Boys upon the hill, the Governor of Dennygton Castle that was so much battered, and so often sett upon by all their forces at severall times. The King lay at Mr. Duns his howse in Newbery: the troope at Welford, the Manor belonging to Mr. Hinton, *jure uxoris*, a faire habitacion, com. Berks.

When the King's army was in Cornwall, the infantry was divided into three tertias, and every tertia should consist of three brigades, and thus they continued the marche backe againe.
First tertia was commanded by Colonel Blague, governor of Wallingford Castle; his regiment was there at Wallingford.
    Colonels:
        King' Life Guard.
        Lord Generall Ruthvin's.
        Sir Jacob Astley, Major Generall
        Colonel Sir Henry Bard.
        Duke of Yorkes.
        Sir James Penniman's.   Eldest Regiment of the Army.
        Lord Percies.
        Sir Lewis Dives
Second tertia was commanded by Colonel George Lisle.
    Colonels:
        Colonel Cha. Lloyd, Quartermaster Generall and Enginere Generall. (Ebor.)
        Colonel George Lisle's, which was Colonel Bolles.
        Colonel Thelwel's, Wales.
            Owen, raysd in Wales.
            Ewre, vulg. Euers.
            Blackwall, Nott.
            Gilby, raysd Ebor.
            Stradling, Wales.
            Vaughan's, Wales.
Third tertia commanded by Sir Bernard Asteley, son to Sir Jacob.
    Colonels:
        Lord Hopton's Regiment.
        Colonel Apisley.
            Talbot.
            Cooke.
            Courtney, &c.            (Sir Ja. Penniman told me.)
Prince Maurice his army marched by it selfe.
Colonel Sir James Penniman's regiment of ffoot, whiche was his cousin's Sir William P., first Lt.-Colonel to Sir William (sic).
George Symons, Leift.-Colonel now, was Major at first.   Ebor.
Major Will. Wyvell, Ebor
1 Captain, Richard Page, now Leift.-Colonel, Nov. 1644.
2 Captain, Fr. Lawson, Lincoln.
3 Captain, William Bridges, a scrivener in Chancery Lane, knighted at Leicester.
4 Captain, Fr. Bateson, Ebor.
5 Captain, Jo. Jackson, Ebor.
**6 Captain, Anthony Norton, Ebor.**
7 Captain, George Etherington, Ebor.
8 Captain, Robert Carington, Ebor.
**All raysd in Yorkshire, and came with the King from Yorke.**
            (Told me by Sir Ja. himselfe, 29 November, 1644.)

## APPENDIX.

## II.—THE KING'S STAY IN NEWBURY.

The late Mr. C. E. Long, M.A., the editor of Symonds' Diary, has suggested that the name of the King's host at Newbury during the few days he was here before the Second Battle, and which is written by Symonds "Duns," and in the 'Iter Carolinum' "Dunce," may have been intended for "Dunch"; but no record has been found of any branch of this extremely anti-royalist family having resided in Newbury. In the "Protestation Returns," given at page 115, the name of — Dunce,* Esq., of Newbury, appears written exactly as spelt by the careful compiler of the 'Iter Carolinum,' Garter-King-at-Arms, who adds "a night's residence." We are told by 'The True Informer' for the week ending Oct. 26th, that "His Majesty lay Wednesday night at Newbury, at one Mr. Weston's house, where he was on Thursday morning, it not being possible for him to get to Oxford, by reason of the great floods." If we can believe 'Mercurius Aulicus,' we are spared a deal of unnecessary investigation in endeavouring to identify the house where the King stayed, for that paper tells us *it was demolished!* The following is the version given by the Royalist chronicler—"Tuesday, Oct. 29, 1644, next morning after His Majesty's army was drawn off from Newbury, the Rebells very eagerly entered the town, where they quickly manifested their strength was much abated, but their malice as high as ever, for the first enquiry they made was for the house where His Majesty himself had lodged, and no sooner found it out, but instantly (like perfect Rebells) they layd the house flat with the ground, and if that was not sufficient to speake them the worst of Rebells, they took that very Bed whereon they guessed His Sacred Majesty had lyen, hacked the bed-poasts with their swords, cut and slasht the bedding, and scattered the pieces up and down the streets, evidencing themselves the most perjur'd, bloody, malitious covenantors, that sweare they fight for His Majestie's Person and Honour! and yet are wild because they cannot murther him, from whose mercies God Almighty still preserve him."

From the above accounts it appears quite clear that the King slept at Mr. Dunce's house on Tuesday night, and at Mr. Weston's on Wednesday night. (The latter was Mayor of Newbury the following year, 1645, and also in 1652.) In the 'History of Newbury' (p. 47), it is stated that a certain Mr. Hoar, a wealthy clothier,† who appears, from local records, to have been a person of good position in the town, gave up his house, on the west side of Cheap Street, for the reception of the King. The house was on the site now occupied by the residence appertaining to the Eagle Iron-works.

When the army, however, was drawn out from the town and stationed at Shaw, Donnington, and Speen, the King probably took up his quarters at Shaw House, placed at his disposal by Sir Thomas Dolman, then a youth, scarcely of age,—"which place," says Richard Blome in his 'Britannia,' published in 1673, "had the good fortune in the time of the late war to receive His Majesty and His Majesty now reigning" (Charles II., then Prince of Wales). At Shaw House a

---

* In the 'Subsidy Rolls,' Pub. Record Office, the name is spelt "Daunce," and also in a petition from the inhabitants of Newbury, 1625-6, in respect to the town's purchasing the manorial rights of the Crown. In Blewbury Church is a monument to the wife of Sir John Daunce, daughter of Thos. Latton of Chilton, near Ilsley. The name has gradually been reduced to "Dance."

† The 'Diary or Exact Journal,' Oct. 24 to 31, 1644, certifies that the King lodged "in a Cloathier's house," but does not mention the name of its owner.

brass plate is inserted in the wainscot of a room on the east side of the mansion, to commemorate an attempt made to shoot the King while dressing at the window. It was probably placed here by the zealous antiquary, Mr. Pettit Andrews, F.S.A., author of a 'Continuation of Henry's History of England,' who was born at Shaw in 1737, and contributed much valuable local information to Mores' 'Collections towards a Parochial History of Berkshire.' The brass plate is thus inscribed—
"The Hole in the Wainscot, which appears through the aperture of this plate, was occasioned by a ball discharged from the musquet of a Parliamentary Soldier at King Charles the First, while he sate dressing himself in this Projection. The ball was found and preserved during many years, but is now lost. This regicidal attempt seems to have been made on Oct. 26 or 27, A.D. 1644."

Then follows an extract from Blome, a portion of which is given above, and a quotation from Ludlow's 'Memoires,' vol. i. pp, 129 and 131.

On another plate on the opposite side of the window, a second record of the event is placed in a frame, in the centre of which is a medallion portrait of Charles I., with this inscription—

HANC JUXTA FENESTRAM<br>
REX CAROLUS PRIMUS<br>
INSTANTE OBSIDIONE<br>
SCLOPPOPETRÆ ICTUS TANTUM NON<br>
TRAJECTUS FUIT<br>
DIE OCTOB. XXVII. MDCXLIV.

The above tradition of the bullet is probably not to be wholly disregarded, although the reference to a "siege" of the house is a mistake. See p. 174.

Sir Thomas Dolman, who, as stated above, was the possessor of Shaw House when it was garrisoned for Charles I. After the last battle of Newbury his family adopted the following motto:—

"King and Law,
Shouts Dolman of Shaw."

It is traditionally reported that his motto arose through "King and Law," having been the password agreed upon the night prior to the battle, and that young Dolman announced it to the army by the command and in the presence of the King himself. It is also said that there was great slaughter in the garden, and that the King and Dolman fought side by side. Another story is that Dolman having forgotten the password, the King himself lustily gave it to the youth with direction to shout it to the soldiers, and that it had the immediate effect of causing such a volley of shot to be poured upon the Parliament men as routed them from Mr. Dolman's garden, and turned the battle on this side in the King's favour. From this circumstance the above motto was adopted by the family and is still retained. Mr. Dolman, who was knighted 2 February, 1660, was Clerk of the Privy Council, and M.P. for Reading in 1661. Sir Thomas Dolman was honoured by a visit from King Charles II., and his Queen, the Duke of York, (afterwards James II.), and many of the nobility, in the month of August, 1663, as appears from the following paragraph in *The Intelligencer* of September 7, 1663. "Thursday, August 27, that night their Majesties lodged at Sir Thomas Dolman's (about a mile from Newbury), where they were entertained, together with their royal highnesses, (and indeed the whole court) with a magnificence, prudence, modesty, and order to admiration, (their royal highnesses

APPENDIX. 217

and most of the court lodging in the town itself), a good part of that evening his majesty spent in viewing the ground, where one of the Newbury battles was fought: calling to mind more particulars, occurring then to his memory (himself having been present in the fight), than can be imagined."

Sir Thomas Dolman died 18 July, 1697, aged seventy-seven, and was buried in Shaw Church, where a memorial is erected to him.

## III.—RED HEATH AND RED HILL.

Many opinions have been given as to the locale of this Heath and Hill, mentioned by Sir Edward Walker, Symonds, and other writers as the spot where the King's army held their rendezvous on their arrival in the neighbourhood of Newbury, Tuesday, 22nd October, 1644; and where Col. Boys received the honour of knighthood from the King. Some have placed it on Greenham Common, others at Snelsmore; but the view now advanced is that the camping-ground was more probably on the Wash and adjacent Heath, where we still find the names of Red Heath and Red Hill (marked on the Plan).

It appears that the Royalists were surprised to find the Parliamentarians in such close proximity on Tuesday, 22nd October, on which day their whole army, according to Cromwell (a most exact narrator of the campaign), was in the neighbourhood of Aldermaston, on the way from Basingstoke, with the intention (as he thought) of intercepting the King by a direct advance towards Newbury. The Earl of Manchester, however, much to Cromwell's chagrin, who objected to such a retrograde movement, marched the next day to Reading, giving the Royalists an idea that they retreated to avoid coming to an engagement (see above, p. 143). When it was found that the enemy followed so closely on their track, the divergence from the direct route to Newbury from Kingsclere, and the holding-back of the main body of the King's army on Red Heath, may have been advised as a precautionary measure, in case the enemy should attack with his vastly superior force on the east side of Newbury; the King's position on the south of the town (which was occupied by a body of his horse), having the advantage of the River Kennet as a barrier to a surprise. Sir Edward Walker * mentions that "the King caused his army to be so quartered as to do but little duty, and yet to be secure from the rebels, who (it was thought) would not attempt us in that place, and whence his army could not conveniently remove till he had done his endeavours for the relief of Basing, and that the Earl of Northampton, with that additional strength he took with him to Banbury, was returned."

Again, a Parliamentary Journal of the 26th Oct. † tells us:—" The King's forces have pulled up Thatcham bridge [over the Kennet between Thatcham and Greenham Common] to prevent our forces, if they can, following after them. Our Pioneers are laying the Bridge

---

* 'Walker's Hist. Discourses,' p. 110.
† 'Perfect Passages in Parliament,' Oct. 26, 1644.

again, because the waters are too high to pass over the fords," intimating that the King's forces were on the south side of the Kennet. The 'Parliamentary Scout,' of the same date, is more explicit on the subject—"We were informed (it reports) that this day at night our armies were very near the King's; that we had declined the way of the Bridge, by which we should have entered on the south side of the King's powers, and that we had gone up by the Rivulet [the Lamborne] which runs by Donnington Castle, and had forded it above, and were got upon the north between Oxford and the King" [the hill before Shaw]. Another Diurnal* says—"The west was open to the King to bring in provisions: that he pulled up some bridges about Thatcham to hinder the advance of the Parliamentary forces, by reason of which it was considered His Majesty had resolved to retreat westwards." On the evening of the 27th October, a Spy informed the Scout-Master General [Sir Samuel Luke], that the King's army had arrived at Newbury on Tuesday, and were "quartered on the heath," the King and his chief officers lodging in the town, and that this day, about sun-setting, a party of horse left the camp to march to the relief of Banbury.†

The most precise delineator, however, of this disputed rendezvous is Capt. Gwynne, who, in his 'Memoirs,' ch. xi, says—"The second Newbury fight we drew upon the same ground the enemy fought us upon the first battle," in which the Captain was also engaged. Gwynne mentions, in the next chapter, that the King marched with his army from the camp "faire and orderly through the towne into the spacious Spinham-lands," clearly indicating that the troops advanced from the south side of Newbury. Further on, in ch. xv., Gwynne adds—"And the Messenger that came to the King at Newbury, and brought him intelligence that Banbury was besieged, might as well at the same instant told him that on the other side of the town were three armies [that] waylaid him, then perhaps he had thought fit to keep on the same side of the town he was on, and plant some of his great guns against the town's end and the river-side, and let the enemy which pursued him fall upon his cannons' mouth (if they liked it) rather than he did fall upon theirs, and if the King did approve of so doing, then he could easily march away that night and send to his army at Oxford and to the Earl of Northampton to come and meet him where he thought convenient."

From Kingsclere to Red Heath or Common the whole district was at that time one continuous heath, traversed by tracks and roads well enough adapted for the passage of an army, and enabling them to avoid the danger of marching through an enclosed country by narrow roads. There is apparently no reason why Greenham Common, had it been the rendezvous, should not have been correctly described, as even in "Domesday Book" it is called "Greneham;" and in all seventeenth-century maps and documents contemporary with the war it is properly designated; and, indeed, had the King's army been encamped here, their position could readily have been observed by the Parliamentarians on the corresponding heights at Shaw. The existence of the names "Red Heath" and "Red Hill" in the neighbourhood of the Wash certainly makes this locality more compatible with the narratives than other sites devoid of these distinctive appellations.

Cromwell, in his narrative, describes the field adjoining Clay Hill as

* 'Diary or Exact Journal,' Oct. 24 to 31, 1644.
† Sir Samuel Luke's Letter-Book, Egerton MSS.

"Red Hill field," and this has induced a consideration as to the site of the King's camp on the 22nd Oct. being on that side of the town; but this view does not prove tenable; for on the near approach of the Parliamentarians on Friday, this hill was occupied by a detachment of horse under Prince Maurice, but not in any strength.

IV.—DESCRIPTIVE ACCOUNTS OF THE SECOND BATTLE OF NEWBURY.

*From Sir Richard Bulstrode's "Memoirs and Reflections on the Reign and Government of King Charles I." (p. 117, et seq.)*

"I must not forget, that, after the defeat in Cornwall, the King staying sometime in the Western parts, Essex got together another army, and having joined with Waller and Manchester, was then so strong, that he hoped to take his revenge, and encompass the King, who was then going to Oxford, taking Newbury in his way. Essex, with his army, had made his rendezvous in Aldermarston Park, belonging to Sir Humphrey Foster; from whence he came more suddenly upon us than we expected, which put us into some confusion. They attacked us at the same time in several places, with different success, being much stronger than we; and when they could not prevail in one place. they attack'd us in another, hoping in the end to surround us: so that there was fighting at the same time in several places, in most of which the enemy prevailed, and we retired, and were upon the defensive in all parts. Upon the west side of Spine they pressed us very hard, where young Sir John Greenvil was posted upon a high rising ground with some foot and cannon, with a small retrenchment before him: General Goring being then on that side, and seeing the enemy intended to attack that place with horse and foot, to prevent which, he resolved to charge their horse with the Earl of Cleveland's brigade, which was then drawn upon that side, which was done accordingly. But the Earl of Cleveland engaging his person too far, was there taken prisoner, and then a great body of the enemy's foot advanced in good order upon Sir John Greenvil, forced him from that post, with the loss of some men and cannon, and himself wounded in the head with a sword in this action. Upon this success, the enemy pursued furiously, and the fight continued very hot, the enemy still advancing. Whereupon I was commanded by General Goring, to bring up the Queen's Regiment of Horse, which was then in reserve, commanded by Sir John Cansfield, who charged them so home, that he stopp'd their career, and obliged them to retreat, which gave some breathing time to our troops on that side; but in this action Sir John Cansfield had one of his legs shot and broken: and while we were fighting on that side of Spine, Manchester with his army, attacked Mr. Doleman's house at Shaw, below the Castle, where there was a sharp engagement all that afternoon, and the garden was warmly attacked, and as well defended, by the Collonels Lisle and Thelwall, with the help of Sir Thomas Hooper's Dragoons, and a little before the evening, Sir John Brown with the Prince's regiment of horse, charged the enemy so briskly, that he obliged them to retreat up the hill, with the loss of some colours, and two field pieces of cannon. Thus the fight continued on all sides till the night parted us. The King stayed in the field till midnight, that all our cannon were drawn off within the walls of Dennington Castle to their security, and then General Goring, with most of the army, marched that night towards Oxford, without any alarm from the enemy, who durst not follow us, and the King went to Bristol. The next day, after our retreat, Essex possess'd himself very quietly of Newbury, making little doubt of taking Dennington Castle, which was thrice summoned, and as often stormed, but without success; and finding it would be a work of time, and nothing was to be got there but blows, he retired with his army, and quitted Newbury; to which place General Goring soon came again, relieved the Castle with what was wanting, and brought off all our cannon."


*From the Diary of Sir Simonds D'Ewes, Bart. (Harl. MS. 166, fol. 139b., 141, 141 b.)*

[*The contractions in the originals have been mostly extended for the convenience of the reader.*]

Ffor the much honoured WILLIAM LENTHALL, Esquire, Speaker of the Common's House.

Sr.

Wee gaue you an account in our last Letter of all our proceedings in the west and returne to Bazin stoke where we met with his Exies and the Lord Manchester's forces, which happy vnion the Lord hath blessed. The King being at Newberry, vpon ffriday last we marched to Thatsham, and quartering beyond the Towne, that euening we disputed some hills for our securitie, which we gained. The next morning (being Satturday) wee drew vp our Armie within vew of Newbury, and obserued the King's Armie to stand betweene two Riuers and the Passage betweene vs and Newbury strongly guarded and fortified, the difficulty of entering there was easily perceiued. We then (considering the King expected present supplies from Prince Rupert, and that two brigades of his horse were gone to Banbury) thought it not fit to delay, and vpon aduise resolued to diuide our Armie, and to fall on two wayes. That night his Exies. and the Citty ffoot, with all our horse (but two thousand that were lef with the Earle of Manchester) marched on the right hand about 4 miles. The next morning (being the Lord's day) we aduanced early and by two in the afternoone we were within a mile and a halfe of the Towne vpon a large heath, then we fell into the Lands and hedges, and marched not aboue one quarter of a mile before we came in sight of the enemie, who had blocked vp our way with a strong brestworke, and in it fiue peeces of Cannon, and for theire better advantage they were vnder the ffauour of Dennington Castle, theire best peeces being there. Vpon our approach theire cannon plaid hard vpon vs, the place being a narrow heath gaue not leaue to bring vp our body. The hedges hindred our horse very much. Theire Cannon made our ground very hott. There was no way left but to fall on with horse and ffoote, and that without delay; which put in execucon (the sunne not being aboue an hower high), his Excies. ffoote (both officers and souldiers) went on vndauntedly, and fought neuer men better. Your horse aduaunced with the ffoote, the enemies horse sallied out and fell vpon vs, wee beat them backe, tooke the Earl of Cleueland and his Liut. Colonell and two of theire standards. Your horse and ffoote fell in with the Enemie into theire workes, which put theire whole Armie into an extreame confusion; many of theire men ranne through Newbury; your's tooke theire fiue peeces of Cannon and 4 besides, in all nine. The enemy had then beene totally routed, but for theire reserues of hedges and Brestworkes w$^{ch}$ held your's for long in dispute, that night preuented our ffull prosecucon. Your's were come euen to the open ground where the last of the enemy stood. But it not being possible to distinguish ffreinds from enemies in the night, we gave off shooting, wayting for the morning; hoping to have found the enemy on that ground. In the night they drew all off to the Castle with carriages and cannon; wee then expected to have found the ffoote and horse vpon the Castle hill in the morning, but wee quickly vnderstood that the Baggage was secured with the cannon at the Castle, and that the souldiers both horse and ffoote were shifting for themselues; some informed us they went Wantage way to Oxford, others Wallingford, others Hungerford, others Winchester way, we found some went confusedly all these wayes. The greatest parte went to Wallingford, and thither wee followed with as much speed as our horse and dragoones could march, soe fast that wee lost many horse. The less able ffoot marched very hard, the horsemen carrying theire Armes, and gained Wallingford early in the morning. The King rode away from the battell about halfe an hower after sunn sett. He entered Oxford [The writers were misinformed; the King retreated to Bath.] early next morning, some say about one hundred and fifty of his best horse attended him. Had the sun but stood still two howers, he had found more seruants, but what God doth is best. The Earle of Manchester fell on for the gaining of his passage, but it proued (answerable to our thoughts) very difficult, we heare great comendations of the gallantrie of his ffoote. The enemies workes were well fortified, and Master Dolman's house was to them insteed of a Castle, they went on w$^{th}$ that resolucon and made theire approaches soe neare that the enemy kild some ffew braue officers and souldiers. The Citty Regim$^{ts}$ did well, of those killed dead on both sides, the number is vncertaine, some of yours officers and souldiers are wounded, but not very many. They tooke some of yours prisoners, amongst the rest Maior Vrry, but left all behind them. This morning in Towne and ffeild were taken about 1000 musketts, how many since we cannot tell. Wee heare that at the least 1000 prisoners were taken, wee tooke many straglers, some within a mile of Wallingford, we cannot for the present pursue them further that way, that passage being theires. Wee desire to give God the glory, He was our God at Cherrington in the spring, and now at Newbury in the ffall, we hope this is a great step to the Conclusion of the Kingdomes misery, we intreat that as God hath heard our and your prayers, soe wee may all returne him thanks. We are now at Newberry and will improue this mercy to our vtmost, the season of the yeare vnfitts vs for constant abiding in the ffeild, the pacience and suffering of our souldiers are beyond our expressions, wee presume your thoughts are vpon them. Lett vs but receiue your comaunds and we will obay as becomes

S$^r$.

Yo$^r$ ffaithfull seruants,

Newberry,
28 of Octob, 1644.

WILLIAM WALLER.
ART. HESILRIGE.

Nouemb. 12th, Tewsday, 1644.

That which ensueth was transcribed out of a coppy of a Letter sent from Sert. Maior. Gen. Skippon to the Earle of Essex, Lo. Gen., which coppy onely was read in the House of Commons, for the Earle of Essex sent not the originall, and the superscription of this Letter was not transcribed in the said Coppy.

May it please Yor. Excy.

What though our too late Intelligence and other interveening accidents the King's Army yesterday releiued Dunnington Catle and drew out his carriages thence, ere our fforces could be gotten together to the place viewed by some of vs the day before as fittest to interpose betweene the Castle and theire coming. In the afternoone he drew downe his horse, ffoot, and cannon vpon vs who conceived it most convenient to stand vpon our owne defence with all our ffoot and cannon within those sorry works which we had cast vp, but the same day the rather because our horse all held theire Rendevouz vpon Newberry Wash on the other side of the Towne, and having to march through the Towne before they came on that side where our ffoot were engaged, the enemy after he had placed 2 great and 2 small peeces of cannon charged vs with great resolucions both with horse and ffoot, and were, (blessed bee the Lord whom alone is our constant strength, refuge, and helper), most boldly resisted and repulsed soe that but once and at one place they came on where and when (being soundly pelted especially by the Musquetiers of Yor. Excies. Regiment) they soone recoyled, and being set further of by a forlorne hope of musquetiers commaunded by Capt. Horsey, presently drew of theire cannon and betooke them to an orderly retreat which could not bee interrupted as was wished, because ere night came too farre on, the horse were hardly enough come ouer to vs. All the ffoot stood theire ground very orderly and resoluedly expecting the enemies charging them on all sides, as they threatened by theire drawing vp. This day the King's Army marched leasurely and souldier like from the further side of the Castle (whither they retreated last night) Wantage way; it is said to haue drawne vs out of our strength, and that he might the rather thereby haue had advantage (we being necessitated to march somewhat about to come at him because of the Castle), soe to haue got into Newberry behind vs, and soe to haue had the freeway to Basing, or to have forced vs to fight with him vpon great disadvantage, he hauing the Libertie to choose his owne ground, where vppon it was resolued wee should march backe to Newberry, where all our ffoot forces lie miserably pestered. And truly my most noble Lord, if there be not some speedy course taken for setling them in some fresh Quarters, where they may bee encouraged, recollected, and recruited, I very much feare that all the Armies will be very much weakened, and preiudiced, especially that vnder Yor. Excies. immediate commaund. This I humbly presume in duty to acquaint yor. Excy. with and that (if it may stand with the publike seruice), Yor. Excy. would please, (who I know is most sensible of our condicon), to vse the best meanes Yor. Excy. shall thinke most meet that we might seasonably haue a good winter quarter at Reading, if it might bee, being the most likely place to get them together againe in. I humbly begg pardon for my great boldnes, and beseech the Lord to watch ouer Yor. Excy. for good, I euer remaine,

Yor. Excyes. most humble and faithfull servant,

Newberry, 10 of November, 1644.                      Ph. Skippon.

Nouember, 13th Wensday, 1644.

The Letter of which the coppie ensueth was read in the House of Comons on Wensday, the 13th of Nouember, 1644.

Ffor the Comittee of both Kingdomes sitting at Derby House.

My Lords and Gentlemen,

According to Your Commaunds we hold it fit to giue you a constant accompt of the enemies' motions. Yesterday they marched to Lamburne and Wantage, they carryed with them but two peeces of ordnance out of the Castle, and have left ten there for want of drafts to carry them so suddainely away. We heare this day that they are marched from Lambourne to Malborough. Some of our intelligence is, that a part of theire Army is gone by Wantage. As we heare more certainty of the enemies motions, we shall giue Your Lordships an account of it and expect your orders and directions, which we shall obey as

Yo<sup>r</sup>. Lopp<sup>s</sup>. most humble seruants,

E. MANCHESTER.   WILLIAM WALLER.
W. BALFORE.      ART. HESILRIGE.

Newbury, 11th Nouember, 1644.


*From a MS. belonging to the Earl de la Warr. ("Fourth Report of the Historical MSS. Commission," p. 297.)*

"Oct. 30, 1644.  CHAS. MURRY to SIR JOHN BERKELEY.

"About three in the afternoon Waller and Essex came with a resolution to carry all clear before them, which they had not much failed of, if they had known how ill our horse and some of Prince Maurice's foot behaved  The truth is, they had beaten our foot from the pase [pass], and routed most of our horse before ever they ...... them; but Lord Barrard [Bernard Stuart] that knows not how to retreat, charged so handsomely that he beat them back before they could see the disaster we were in; it was dark, they could not pursue. Amongst us was nothing known but utter ruin and loss of all, so that the King was advised, with his son and some lords and three troops (having but one way to pass to go away) which my Lord Bar. commands, to get away and join Prince Rupert; so the King got to Dennington Castle by 9 at night, and thence took guides that brought him safe next day by night to Bath. It seems that after the King had gone, the army rallied and marched that night to Wallingford, and found that we lost not above 200 or 300 men, and six cannons lost at the Hill toward Hungerford: for at the other pass and at a house which Geo. Lile maintained we beat them sufficiently at the same instant that the rebels were so successful at the other end. No man could have done action of more courage or resolutiou than he did that day; he killed above 500 and took two cannons." (2½pp.)

## V.—NEWBURY CHURCH AS A PRISON AND HOSPITAL.

At the time of the War, Newbury Church was used both as a prison and a hospital. There is a most interesting petition among the State Papers, in the Public Record Office, from John Bonwak, a distinguished sufferer in the Royal cause, and prisoner at Newbury. Shortly after the Restoration he sued for some compensation. The signatures attached to his petition are by men of note and name. He alleges that he had been Clerk of Reigate, and at the time of his petition was Rector of Newdigate, near Dorking, Surrey. He asks for letters mandatory to the University of Cambridge for his D.D. degree. He had left Christ's College, Cambridge (as many other University men did) in 1643, and entered the army to fight for the King. After the Second Battle, he says, he was stripped, imprisoned, and almost starved to death in Newbury Church. Thence he marched barefoot to London House, and was there again imprisoned. He escaped, and ventured his life for the Restoration. Attached to his petition, as testimony, is the *clarum et venerabile nomen* of Jeremy Taylor, also that of Lord Mordaunt and eight others, who testify that, rather than comply with the ruling powers, he had refused several good livings, and, with his wife and six children, had remained on one of £20 per annum.

In 1646, when the town of Newbury was in the hands of the Parliament, part of the garrison were quartered in the Church, which was subjected to all sorts of sacrilegious profanation and plunder. The lead was either stripped off the roof or demanded by the soldiery, and with other Church property was only preserved by the Churchwardens paying what was considered an equivalent value. Shortly after the death of Cromwell, at which time some little attention appears to have been bestowed on the Church, there are several entries in the Churchwardens' books of charges for clearing out the rubbish from the interior; and for making good the injuries which the building had sustained during the preceding stormy and eventful era.

---

## VI.—BOXFORD.

There is no parochial record at Boxford of any local incidents connected with the military operations which took place in the immediate neighbourhood during the years 1643-4-5; but in the Register for the succeeding year, there is the following entry—"Thomas Adams, souldier of Cap. Pym's troope was buryed April ye 5, 1646." In one of the later Parish Books the following curious memorandum is made:—

"Thomas Dore declar'd in ye presence of us whose names are hereunto subscribed, that he remember'd in the Oliverian rump times, when subjects rebell'd and did wh<sup>t</sup> seem'd right in their own eyes, that William and Ralph Coxhead pull'd down and carry'd away ye very well turn'd decent rails fixed and placed across the rising upper part of the Chancel to separate the Communion Table, and that they were carry'd by the above-named persons to one Edwd. Pokes

APPENDIX. 225

[? Pocock], (Schoolmaster), who then lived on Westbrooke side, who with his scholars triumph'd and rejoiced with those Puritans over this sacrilegious spoil and broke in pieces and burnt the same. Attested and declar'd in the presence of Anthony Tassell, rector, and Lucy Tassell, April 11, 1721."*

There is a tradition preserved in the village that the Parliamentary soldiers, on more than one occasion, stabled their horses in the church.

In this Church there is a monument, of neat design, to the Rev. Jas. Anderton, rector of the parish, who died in 1672. It has the appearance of marble, but it is made of clunch or hard chalk. The inscription describes Mr. Anderton as "a determined defender of the orthodox faith, even among the Rebels." This clergyman figures conspicuously in the 'Life of Oliver Sansom,' the Berkshire Quaker, with whom he had a long religious controversy.

## VII.—BUCKLEBURY.

The Registers of this Parish (remarkably perfect from the first year in which such records were appointed to be kept, 1538) contain the following interesting entries.

"1644, April 20. Wm. Basset being slaine by a souldier was buried.
" ,, April 29. Richd. Buxie a soldier of the Kinge was slaine by a Parliament souldier at Chappell Row and buried.
"1645, Oct. 29. Mr. Richard Warde a Lieutenant for the Parliament was slaine and buried.
" Dec. 9. Henry Hall being slaine was buried."

Guy Carleton was Vicar of this parish during the troublesome times of the Civil War. Walker gives the following account of him:—" He was of a good and ancient family in Cumberland, and educated at Queen's College in Oxford, where he became successively *Poor Child, Taberder, Fellow,* and *Proctor.* Upon the breaking out of the Rebellion he faithfully adhered to his Majesty's interest, and did him considerable service. He was first driven from his rich living in the North; afterwards, coming into Berkshire, he was patronized by Mr. Gravets

---

* However much such excesses as were practised at this period are to be lamented, it must be borne in mind that the destroyers were acting in many instances against their will, and in strict accordance with an Ordinance which had passed the Houses of Lords and Commons, and which enacted that all altars and tables of stone, with candlesticks, basons, &c., should be taken away and demolished; and also that all communion tables should be removed from the east end to the body of all churches and chapels; all rails before any altar or communion-table, likewise, to be taken away, and the chancel levelled; all crucifixes, crosses, images in and upon all and every church or churchyard to be destroyed; and none of the like "superstitious ornaments" to be allowed in any church, chapel, or other place throughout the land  The execution of this order was delegated to the Churchwardens of each parish, with severe penalties in case of default. Exception only was made to the monument of any King, Prince, or nobleman, "which hath not been commonly reputed to be taken for a saint." Complaints having been made to the Parliament of laxity in performing this Order of the House, a second Ordinance was issued to the Committee of each County, peremptorily enforcing the execution of the decree. See 'Journals of House of Commons, Aug. 27, 1643, and Aug. 19, 1645.'

2 F

of Hartley Court, who presented him to the living of Bucklebury, in the right of his Guard Sir Henry Winchcombe, from whence also he was driven by the Tryers. After which he was likewise seized and imprisoned in Lambeth House, whither his wife secretly conveyed him a cord, by the help of which he let himself down through a window towards the Thames; but, the cord not reaching to the ground, he was forced to drop from it, and in the fall dislocated one of his bones, but a boat being provided for him, he was soon carried off, and lay concealed during the cure, to pay for which his poor wife was forced to sell her very bed. After his recovery he fled beyond the seas to his Majesty; in the meantime one of his daughters was maintained by Mrs. Gravets; and his wife and two other daughters were supported in London, partly by some charities, and partly by their own labour. Mr. Carleton returned with his Majesty from beyond the seas, became one of his Chaplains, D.D., Dean of Carlisle, Prebendary of Durham, and in 1671 was advanced to the Bishopric of Bristol, and in 1678 translated from thence to Chichester. He died in the year 1685." 'Sufferings of the Clergy,' pt. ii. p. 214.

The old Vicarage in which Guy Carleton resided while at Bucklebury, a picturesque old house, is still standing, unaltered, at the western side of the churchyard.

## VIII.—THE LICENSE OF WAR.

The following letter, from one of their own officers, will convey some idea of the excesses committed by the Parliamentary soldiers in this neighbourhood, and of the grievous evils attendant on a state of civil warfare, such indeed as were also attributed with perhaps equal truth by the Parliamentary party to the Royalist soldiers.

From Col. Wm. Ball to Speaker Lenthall; dated from Reading, March 1, 1645.

"Sir, I have been 10 days at Reading upon the command of the House for the ordering of the recruits for the army, and find the employment very troublesome; yet the service succeeding indifferently well answereth my paines and expectations; but that which exceedingly affects me is the continual clamour of the soldiers at Newberry and country people thereabout, the soldiers having almost starved the people where they quarter, and are half-starved themselves for want of pay, and are become very desperate, raging about the country, breaking and robbing houses and passengers, and driving away sheep and other cattell before the owners' faces. Every day bringeth more instances of these outrages. I shall mention only two amongst others the country people are now relating unto me. Some of the soldiers were driving away the sheep of Andrew Pottinger, of Wolhampton, a freeholder of £60 per annum, a very considerable man for the Parliament, having a wife and 6 young children, who endeavouring to secure his sheep, the soldiers struck him on the head so that he became presently speechless, and dead within four hours, to the great grief and sorrow of the neighbourhood. Another party of nyne soldiers, armed with muskets, came yesterday to the house of Mr. Illsley, of Beenham, and broke open his door, to the great affright of his wife, he being absent, and hearing of it, got together his neighbours and so beat the soldiers that they were all wounded and not able to return to their quarters. I will give many more instances were it necessary, but this I thought fitt to discover unto you, that the soldiers and country people are all grown desperate, and continue one against the other that we are like to have little other than killing and robbery, if there be not a speedy supply of money for the soldiers. I beseech you to take the opportunity to acquaint the House with the condition of these parts, which under the most terrible time of the enemy was nothing so badd. I am sorry, I have such a badd subject, and shall therefore conclude, craving leave to subscribe myself, Sir, your humble servant, WILL. BALL."* (Tanner MSS., Bodl. Libr., vol. 60-2, No. 491).

Another case of outrage and pillage, in this instance countenanced by the Parliamentary officers, occurred at the house of the unfortunate Sir Humphrey Forster at Aldermaston:—"While Sir Humphrey, Sir Richard Kingsmill, his lady, and some other friends, consisting of Mr. Francis Smith, Mr. John Wright, Mr. Thos. Grove, Mr. James Weare, Mr. John Awberry, and Mr. John Young, were quietly sitting at dinner, a party of 60 or 80 Parliamentary troopers, headed by three officers, with swords drawn and pistols cocked, burst into the room, to the great terror of the company, having previously dangerously wounded the butler at the door, and demanded that all the apartments in the house should be showed them. This was readily granted by the affrighted Sir Humphrey, who was in terror of his life, one of the troopers telling him that the wounds his man had received ought to have been in his (Sir Humphrey's) heart. After examining the house, and taking every valuable article they thought worth their attention, these servants of the Parliament broke open the stable doors, while others searched the Park, and succeeded in carrying off eight valuable horses, which they fully equipped with saddles, bridles, &c. To prevent any alarm being given, four of the troopers were quartered in the house for the night. Capt. Waldron, Lieut. Seymour, and the other officer were all old offenders, having been previously bound over for robbery and other barbarities committed in the County of Wilts." (Tanner MSS., Bodl. Libr. vol. $\frac{57}{1}$, No. 199.)

The 'Mercurius Aulicus,' the chief Oxford paper, of Thursday, Nov. 14, 1644, referring to the inhumanity of the Parliamentarians, recites the following instances of "the bloudy disposition of the Rebells, as well to their own creatures as His Majesty's good subjects." But such tales as these must be taken *cum grano salis*, no story being too foul or too false to be refused a place in the Journals and pamphlets issued almost daily by both parties. "We have it most certainly advertised that the day after the last Newbury fight when His Majesty's army was drawn off, the good Earle of Manchester went into Mr. Doleman's house at Shaw (near Newbury), where he found some wounded souldiers. Colonell George Lisle (who so gallantly commanded those Guards the day before) left a note in the house, wherein he certified that certaine hurt men (some whereof were His Majesty's souldiers, the rest were prisoners, whom the Colonell tooke in the last fight), which could not at present be removed from that place, without hazzard of the poor men's lives. Therefore desired all

---

* This was not the Capt. Ball, a famous Royalist freebooter, stationed at Reading in 1644, whom Sir Jacob Astley complains of in a letter given in Warburton's Prince Rupert,' vol. ii, p. 358-9.

gentlemen, officers, and souldiers, whom it might concerne, to afford them protection and assistance, as he had done, for as muche as the poore men were unable to help themselves. But the Lord Kimbolton [Manchester] and his Rebells, no sooner entered the house, but most barbarously they knockt these poore wretches' braines out, not merely his Majesty's souldiers, but their owne men also (for the bloody fit was now upon them), lifting up boards, breaking down wainscot, and pulling out the very barres of the windowes, pretending that His Majesty was concealed in that house, else (said they) the Popish Malignants would never have fought so desperately to maintaine it. Therefore they vowed to find him (the poore men's blood not dry upon their hands), else they would put the Maister of the House to death. In conclusion (having left that house) they did all mischief imaginable to the owner of it (Mr Doleman), leaving him not so much as cloaths to put on, nor anything else either in or about his house.

"Nor was their behaviour much better to their well-wishers thereabouts, for when that Faction, out of their zeal, brought them divers carriages loaden with provisions, these grateful Rebells took from them both their horses and carts in requital of the curtesie. And to make their accompt just, they took a farewell survey of their deare Society at Newbury, and for a Farewell plundered the town most equally, leaving them to contemplate the Reward of Rebellion, which is to be used worse by those for whose sake they have been most seditious."

The following day, 'Mercurius Aulicus' has another little incident to relate;—A royalist soldier (a Welchman *), having been taken prisoner, and finding no way of escape, promised to take up arms for the Parliament. On perceiving the Parliamentary army preparing to leave Newbury, and being at that time sentinel outside the prison, where some 30 royalist soldiers were confined, he gave the prisoners his lighted match and a horn of gunpowder, for them to put into the lock, and blow open the door. This was so well done that the Welchman and the 30 other soldiers all came safe to His Majesty's army. "Had the Rebells thus escaped," adds 'Aulicus,' "they would surely have said it was a miracle."

The Anti-Royalist Journal, 'Mercurius Britannicus,' repudiates the "slander" against the Earl of Manchester "about the Shaw-house business;" and as to the breaking down of the wainscot, &c. in search for the King, satirically asks, "Has his ill-success in the late battle made a great king so little as to escape into a mouse-hole?"

The following anecdotes will show to what peril property was exposed, which had to pass the Western road:—In January, 1645, a large company of Wiltshire carriers and clothiers having started from London, and entered into a composition with Sir John Boys, the governor of Donnington Castle that they should be unmolested in their route by the Royalists, on payment of £3 for each waggon, were proceeding on their way near Marlborough, when they were met and captured by a body of cavalry, who were marching from Basing House to Bristol. Col. Massey, the governor of Gloucester, having heard of the circumstance, and ascertaining that the captors as well as their booty were still at Marlborough, instantly drew out 200 horse, and came so unexpectedly upon them, that though they made a show of resistance at the entrance of the town, he drove them in again, took thirty prisoners and fifty horses, and restored the wains to the carriers.

---

* There was a strong contingent of Welchmen in the King's service engaged at Newbury.

Among the prisoners were Sir Anthony St. Leger, their commander, and Sergeant-Major Hyde. In the following month of May, a party of West-country clothiers obtained from the Royalist Governor of Devizes a pass for London, and entered into a bond to pay him more than £400 excise on the cloth they were to convey to London. As they approached Newbury, Sir John Boys sallied out on them and demanded the full amount in the King's name. No expostulations could save the poor clothiers, they were forced to raise the money in Newbury, and after some days started on their expedition. They had not gone far before some Royalist troopers from Wallingford Castle pounced upon them, seized their teams, baggage and all, and took them into the castle, where the governor, Col. Blagge, not only forcibly detained their goods, but suffered his troopers to search their pockets. The end of it all was that, after much vexation and delay, the carriers obtained their final discharge by consenting to pay an additional £10 on every pack of cloth, or leaving an equivalent in value. (Waylen's 'Hist. Marlborough,' pp. 220—2.)

Notwithstanding what has been above stated with regard to the lawlessness of both the Royalist and the opposing forces, there is favourable evidence in another direction, in the following letter from a gentleman named Anthony Vaux, dated "Newburie, Nov. 4, 1642," to a friend in London. Giving an account of the proceedings of his Majesty's troops in Berks, the letter shows that, at least in the early days of the war, there was little demoralization among the soldiers of the Royalist army.

"Rt. Worthy Sir. Cannot but be obliged unto you for your continuall favours unto me and my son Robert at Lincoln's Inn. I have understood by your letter the forwardnesse of the City of London, and the strength of men, ordnance, and other implements of engines in all places for the resisting of His Majesty's forces. I confess possession is IX points of the Law, so their managing the City with strength is a sure ground of resistance, but I believe to little purpose? for on Tuesday, I rid to Oxford and through the roads of His Majesty's army, which exceeds the number of your relation; and having spent the day in the city, I came late to my house at Newburie, and there was no injury offered me by the way, or had forcibly taken from me the value of a point, though it hath been related that neither horsemen or footmen, waggon or carrier can travell about but the soldiers make them their prey. I assure you they are kept in good order without doing pillage as is related."

The writer further adds that while at Oxford he saw at least 50 burials, and "in an hour's respite" as many more, which he concludes were some of those slain at the late fight (Edgehill). At his Inn, "the Catherine Wheel," he chanced upon Secretary Nicholas, with whom he drank part of a pint of wine, and learnt the King's intentions, which he relates. He mentions that Reading has been pillaged of at least 5000 yards of cloth; and that divers troops of horse and foot are billeted at Thatcham, besides great store at Newbury. Reference is also made to the issuing of the King's warrant for plate and money, for food and sustenance for the troops, which is being brought to His Majesty in abundance, the treasure being conveyed upon wheels, and the money coined while travelling. It is a most excellent invention, he says, of Leniell, his Majesty's engraver, who, it was thought, was cut off at the last fight at Kineton (Edgehill).

On the other hand, the following letter from Sir John Boys,

## THE SECOND BATTLE OF NEWBURY.

governor of Donnington Castle, to Prince Rupert, instances the insubordination in one of the King's regiments quartered in Newbury in 1644, and shows the difficulties experienced in maintaining military discipline and obedience at such a period of anarchy and disorder:—

"S$^r$. when I wrott to yo$^r$ Highness last, I was in hope I shoold have had no cause to complaynd of the Regimt. of Coll. Nevills ; quartered in Newberry, but since I cannot prevayle w$^{th}$ the officers from keeping their souldiers from high mutenyes, I beseech yo$^r$ Highnes to give som order herin, that farther Inconvenyencies may be avoyded. I shall only aquaint yo$^r$ Highnes w$^{th}$ one or two particulars; wherby yo$^v$ may Judge of their Caryadge in Generall ; three nighte since, the Capt. of the watch going the Round, hearing a great noyse (it being very late) went in desireing those troopers to be quiete in their quarters w$^{ch}$ they wear so far from, that they very much abused the Capt. of the watch, who comitted one of them to his Gaurd, and in the morning whilst he was gon to the Lieut. Coll. to aquaint him of his souldr$^s$. misdemenor, and so to leave him to him selfe, an officer of the Regmt. w$^{th}$ divers w$^{th}$ him, came and forst the Gaurd and tooke the prisoner from thence w$^{th}$ an addition, of mvch unbeseeming language, since w$^{ch}$ tyme I being desired by divers to take notice of an Extreme leaude yonge fellow living in Newberry whoe entytelled himselfe Capt., whoe w$^{th}$ his Companyons have comitted many outradges in the Cuntry by Robbing, and doinge all Villaynes, hering he was in his Howse in the Towne, sent to apprehend him, but ther being a man of Lieut. Coll. Standishes in the howse w$^{th}$ stood the officer and kept the door ag$^{st}$ him, for w$^{ch}$ I sent for him to know why hee did soe, whoe was so Uncivill to mee in his langwage that I caused the Marshall to sett him on the horse, ‖ for w$^{ch}$ both the officers and souldiers have vowed a revenge, and this day (for no cause) a Trooper came to a foot souldr. and cutt his Head to ye Brayns soe y$^t$ the Chirurgeon assures me he cannot live, and presently after ther being many officers and souldiers together come to the Gaurd, and cryd draw all, for weell have the foote out of the towne and though their Lieut. Coll. was by, wold not Chek any of them for this mutenye, as this gent. Capt. Taylor can fully satisfie yo$^r$ Highnes. S$^r$. I shall only accquaint yo$^u$ w$^{th}$ one thinge more and so leave it to yo$^r$. Highnes, since my coming heyther I have often desired Lieut. Coll. Standish to keep out Gaurds and patrolls going, w$^{ch}$ he absolutly refuses, and doth not keepe so much as a Sentinel at the Towns end, and whether it being Contempt or having little use for it they have only once, or twice received the word from mee. S$^r$. I have spent divers years as a souldr. abroad, and am Confident I doe Competantly understand the Comaund his mat$^{ie}$ has heer pleased to instruct me w$^{th}$, and that I aught not to suffre any thing that shoold detrackt from the Comaund given me, it being an vndervalueing to his mat$^e$ whoe gives it, but S$^r$. my Respecte and obedience to yo$^r$. Highnes leades me this way, beseeching yo$^u$ ther may be some speedy course taken by yo$^r$. Highnes letter to them for the avoiding farther mutenys, and that they may asist us in watching, w$^{th}$ out w$^{ch}$ those foote w$^{ch}$ quarter in Newberry cannot be safe, and I beseech yo$^r$. Highnes believe I shall never be wanting in my reddy obedience being, Yo$^r$. Highnes,

Dennington Castle,             Humblest servant,
Jan. 30th, (? 1643-4).             Jo. BOYSE."

(Add. MS., 18981. Rupert Correspondence, 1644, vol, 2, f. 15.)

---

‖ A wooden machine used as a military punishment. A wooden horse.

APPENDIX. 231

IX.—THE CAPTURE OF LADY FORTH, COUNTESS
OF BRENTFORD.

*Extracted from " Memoirs of some Actions in which Collonel John Birch
was engaged, written by [Roe] his Secretary."* *

[The text where printed in italic type denotes corrections made in
the MS. by Col. Birch. The original reading is given in the lettered
foot-notes.]

\* \* \* \* \* \* \* \*

"And the next day neere the evening, the Lord gave a great
victory [the action at Newbury on the 27th Oct.], though the evill
prosecution of it vexed you more then the other cheered you. However, with a few other gentlemen that were there with you, *and suche
as you could gather up,* the pursuite was followed by you.*a* And after
noone you being well wearied in the twoe nights and dayes (before)
you dismissed your partie, and yourselfe wayted on by Maior Ashley,
your regiment quartermaster, at that time, my selfe, returned late at
night towards Newberry, where the head quarters were. And rideing
easily 2 miles short of Newberry in the way from Hungerford, my
selfe being before you, I heard a noise of horse and coaches comeing
down the way towards vs.*b* Wherevpon I giveing you notice, you
stood a little, and presently affirmed it was the enimy; for we had
neither horse nor coaches at the head quarters. And they comeing on
ffast, you had noe more time, but only to vtter these words, "What
ever you see me doe, lett the like bee don by you." This was about
*eightc* of the clocke at night, the 30th day of October, 1644, the moone
shineing pretty light: and instantly therevpon you turnd your horse
in a broad cart way into the feilds on your right hand *out of the comon
road to Hungerford.* And instantly after vs about three pikes length
they come into the feild the same way ; and comeing on fast some of
them were got vp even with us; but your face being towards the
west, and the moone being in the east-south-east, your face was soe
shadowed thereby that they could not easily discover you ; but as, as I
suppose, takeing you to bee of their owne company, passed on with
their whole partie, consisting of 96 mounted men, three coaches and a
coach-wagon, with 30 led horse, as you presently tould your quartermaster, saying you had counted them, which I was at that time in too
great a feare to doe. And soe soone as the last of this company was
done, you turned backe your horse and wee likewise: and haveing
gon backe about 40 paces, you mett on(e) of their company, to whome
clapping your pistoll you bid him hold his peace, and turne backe
with you, else hee was a dead man; which he did; and carrieing him
backe into the lane hee confessed hee was one belonged to the King's
Lord Generall, the Earle of Forth, whoe then past by ; and those with

---

\* 'Military Memoir of Col. John Birch,' edited by the Rev. T. W. Webb, M.A.,
F.R.A.S. Printed for the Camden Society, 1873.

*a* "vnto Hungerford and 4 or 5 miles beyond " cancelled.

*b* "the comeing downe" cancelled. The 'Mercurius Aulicus' of 4 Nov. 1644,
states that Lord Forth escape† from the Castle during a dense fog, which had
prevailed for some time. The route he took would appear to have been from the
Castle to the village of Bagnor, where two fords were crossed, and the Lamborne
Road reached ; thence to Stockcross and int⁾ the Bath Road by Gravel Hill. Here,
probable it was, that the horses and coaches were heard " coming down.' Distances
given in those days, when there was a want of accurate information generally, are
not to be relied on.

*c* "eight" altered to "10."

him are his guard ; and in the coaches his ladie and some other ladies, and the coach wagon was full of his bagadge, hee being come out of Donington Castle into which hee was forced to fly the night before in the battaile. Vpon this relation you instantly turned for vs and said, 'I knowe not in what way God will bring it about; but I am very confident that all these coaches, horses and men will bee mine: nay they *are* mine. Come, therefore; letts vse the meanes.' And vpon that rid sharply with your prisoner towards Newberry; and comeing there gave this account to the Lord Manchester of what you had seen, and what danger you had escaped, desireing of him a partie of horse, and you would give him a good account of that company. But hee haveing long watched was so extreame heavy with sleepe, you could not have one ready word from him. Wherevpon you thought of another course, and that was, to goe to the houses where souldiers lay, and see if you could gett vp a partie by your perswasion, and for hopes of prize, which you failed not to promise them, as was afterwards well performed. By this meanes you gott vp 47 resolved horse, *whereof foure weare trumpeters;* and away you marched; and vpon the way Lieftennant Caltroop asked you how many you judged the enimy to be: to which you replyed, 'They are 30'; and then turned to your quartermaster and said 'If my heart faile mee not, noe bodies else shall for the number;' and soe went on, your selfe being still a distance before to discover any noyse, and likewise to finde the way they were gone; which you did at every turneing with your bare hands, feelling in the darke which way the coach wheeles turned; it being now about 2 of the clocke and somewhat darke. Thus wee went on about 16 miles; yourselfe still before; and being at a turneing and feeling which way the wheeles had gon, one standing neere by you, at a gate, as you after informed vs, vsed these words 'What rouge is that there?' for then it was neere breake of the day and very darke. You doubting, as indeed it was, that the wyly generall might have left a reareguard, and hee might bee a centry, and you had better goe to him: possibly you might make good the gate till wee came vp (whoe weare eleven score yards behind) rather then lett him and his ffellowes come out vpon you; which assuredly they would doe, if they were souldiers. Thereupon you takeing out your rapier and holding the point of it downeward vnder your rocket, went to the gate to him with your horse as hee was then in your hand ; your pretence being to aske him the way: but another *coming out to*[d] him clapt his face over the gate close to you, and though darke yet discovered you, and pulling out his sword, with *an oathe,*[e] not to be named, as you after informed vs, said you were a Roundhead: but you being more readye then he believed, made such a hole in his skinn as brought a groane from him. The other starting, but not seeing the danger, you said with soe loud a voice, that wee heard, whoe were then *a good way*[f] short, 'What's the matter, gentlemen, doe you mean to abuse a man travelling on his way?' and with that more of them coming to the gate and endeavouring to fforce it, you made it good with your rapier, vntill instantly the trumpet (whoe had charge what to doe some hours before) comeing up, and finding you engaged, sounded a charge. Wherevpon the partie rushing upon that rearegaurd, being twelve, were quickly dispatched; and from some of them that were then alive, you did learne that the Earle of Forth was then refreshing himselfe in that village: which soe sone as you herd, you

---

[d] standing by.     [e] another (!)     [f] 40 paces.

guest, as indeed it was, that the enimy would take the alarum and drawe into a body, and then the business might be hazarded. And therevpon, instantly, the lane being pretty broad, and day appearing at the very instant, God was soe good as to direct the timeing of that business, you *ordered the former devision being neare*[g] thirty prime men and horse to *go on with you*[h] the rest of the partie being almost tired were to march on 3 score paces after, and one trumpeter with them sounding a march; and soe to continue till they had ffurther order from you. In this posture marching a good trott, the first partie, where your selfe was, entering into a little *comon*[i] in the midle of the village, there, close by you, was the Lord Ruthven draweing his men together, and at that very instant the trumpets that were behinde sounded a march and you cried aloud, "Gentlemen, letts not stay for the body of horse but fall on them instantly;" which at a high trott was done and they presently routed, haveing not draune 40 together. This was noe sooner done, but, musket shot distance, as many more, whoe had then taken the alarum, were then gott together. Some of your partie seeing them said, 'Looke, Sir, backe yonder is a partie more.' You replied, 'The same are rallied againe, down with them:' and imediatly vpon a full gallop you charged them. During theis 2 charges all the coaches and wagon were runne away.[j] This busines being pretty well over, and all that were in those twoe parties fallen or taken, with the generall's armes in his trumpet;[k] none escaped but the Earl himselfe, Collonel Fielding, and three more, who by reason of the goodness of their horse, after they had mett with some blowes, leapt of the comon into the closes, you being between them and the lanes end, by which meanes they escaped. Your selfe presently, and about *twelue*[l] more whoe were able, pursued after the coaches, and haveing gon at a great speed four *or five* miles you were close at them in a village, where God was wonderfully seen for you. For a *considerable part* of the Queen's regiment of horse quartered then there, who could time enough to the flight: which you discovering *by seeing souldiers stir hastily about*, presently cried to the people as you were vpon a hard speed after the coaches, 'Gentlemen, lay out quarters in this towne presently for my Lord Manchester's regiment of horse:' and further called loud to your quartermaster, whoe then was most gallantly as hee had been all the morneing at your backe, sayeing, 'Quartermaster, in the next village let Sir William Waller's regiment quarter.' Vpon this and heareing the trumpets, whoe were then farre behinde, *sound*, all the *souldiers* there, three times the number of your partie, runn away; and before our faces, some ridd out back wayes: most footed it into the woods; and you had an opertunity to ffall on the partie with the coaches, whoe never offered to strike, but cried for mercy; not one man of them escaped; coaches and coach wagon and all the ladies taken, with 57 men brought prisoners; and of their whole partie but the 5 aforesaid escaped. Of horses of theirs, and those tooke from the Queen's regiment flieing as aforesaid you brought away 107, besides twenty one horse that were on the coaches and wagon. And now being 20 miles from Newbury, and in the enemies country, yet it pleased God soe to bless you that you brought safe away that day all the prisoners to your quarters neere Nuberry; although your partie was soe small that you were forced some times to

---

[g] drew out.    [h] for a forlorne; and.    [i] towne.
[j] "and a partie with them," cancelled.
[k] i.e. the flag attached to the trumpet.    [l] 20.

put one man to guard 3 prisoners. This mercy of God, though I doubt not but you have it in perfect memory, yet his hand being soe plainely discovered in it, I could not omitt it, and hope the time you spend in reading of it will not seem long."

NOTE.—It is impossible to speak with certainty as to the place where the carriages were captured; but from the distance stated, Marlborough would seem to be the town referred to; for it is about 20 miles from Newbury, and at that time was occupied by a body of the King's troops. It is also related in one of the Diurnals, that no sooner had the King passed through Marlborough in his flight from Donnington Castle, than a small company of the enemy came dashing through the town, enquiring which route the King had taken.

Now although this adventure has been thus minutely recited, and Birch, by revision and correction, assented to every item, and claimed to himself the credit of the whole, yet it is curious to find a competitor starting up with an opposite claim, and appropriating to himself the origin and management of the exploit. A Lieutenant-Colonel Thorp, vindicating his character from some aspersions in the 'Mercurius Aulicus,' brought out in the ensuing spring a very different version; and his account introduces us to the obscure names of some others of the party. His case is thus stated:—"At the last fight at Newbury he was commanded upon the guard betwixt Newbeury and Dennington Castle after the fight; he then receiving intelligence from Col. Birch, drew some fourty men and horse from the guard; so he desired Col. Burch to go along with him; there were under his command, officers as followeth: Cap. Draper, Cap.-Lieutenant Evans, Cornet Mathews, Cap. Draper's Cornet; the intelligence was, that my Lord Ruthin, the King's Generall, his Lady, and divers more with him [had escaped]. So they pursued them some eight miles, where they tooke the General's lady, and some prisoners of quality with her, three coaches, and about fifty horse and men, a wagon with much goods in it; so Lieutenant-Col. Thorpe sent the lady and the prisoners towards Newbury, with Col. Birch and some of the troopers; the said Lieutenant-Col. pursued the Generall some nine miles further, and rid in view of him the most of that way, but he having but some two men with him, and his horse being weary, he returned back to Newbury, where he and the rest of the party divided the spoile. This was done without the losse of a man. This is the true relation of this piece of service." 'Kingdom's Weekly Intelligencer.' April 8, 1645. Note by the late Rev. John Webb, M.A., F.S.A. to the 'Military Memoir of Colonel John Birch,' p. 187.

## X.—DONNINGTON CASTLE.

"CAPT. KNIGHT'S RELATION OF THE SIEGE OF DENINGTON."\*

"Wee are Come to December 1645, and Dulbere w$^{th}$ Cromwell hauinge Surprissed that same housse and garrisson of Bassinge, the s$^d$ Dulbere w$^{th}$ too Reagiments of horsse and thre of foote marches into Newbery, of whose S$^r$. Jo. Boys beinge advertised fires Dening-

\* 'Clarendon State Papers,' No. 2062; Bodleian Library.

# APPENDIX. 235

ton towne and other Ajatiente villages,* as was comanded by the Lds. and Counsell at Oxford. hope is of A noble facultie. his matie and the Lds. at Oxford conceaued good hopes as expectinge A brave Resistaunce to be made by these men who in A former seege hade done soe gallantly, and of the noble gouerner Sr. Jo. Boys, A psone Examplarye for vallore and fidillitie. Dulbere being thuse prevented of his quarters of Denington towne, wch was within halfe A mile of the Castell, and also of other Ajatiente Villages and howses, loges his partie of foote in Newbery, and quarters his horsse in the Ajatiente villages, soe yt Denington Castell may bee sd to bee now bloked, but not beseged, for yt Dayllie the Castillians made sallyes, broughte in contribution and such prisoners as Reffused to paye, and the Cuntrye peoplle, as to a marte, dayely brought in all sorts of provissions, soe faire A corrispondancy the Gouerner Sr. Jo. Boys keepte wth the peoplle of the Cuntrye yt hee was of them generally beloued, and treuley he Allwayes gave them A better price for thire Comodities then they could haue fownde att any of the Ajatiente marketts, and treully soe good A Justiser was Sr. John yt England had not A beter Regullated guarrisson, nor better beloued of the Countrye then was this of Denington. Sr. Jo. and his, not to Seame Remisse or necligente, are studiouse to make all necessary pvissions [provisions] to preserve the place, and Consideringe Colonell Browne hade in the former seage made his battery one the northe side of the Castell and yt from a place called the Queen's oake † the Castell might bee easilly stormed, beinge A leuell [level] and the Castell on all other pte standinge vppon A hill, hee thirefore made A mounte vppon the sd leuell some (200) paces of the Castell, trenche And pallasads it, the walls beinge heigh, Canone pffe [proof], and the tope made of greatte thicknes and stronge, as couered over wth brickes and Earth proped wth greate beames and layed over with packes of woll [wool] to prevente the execution of morter Granadas.

"The winter beinge very Rude and viollente Dulbere Could not laye

---

* 'The Commons' Journal,' 9th April, 1646, has the following entry:—"The humble petition of the poor inhabitants of Dennington in the county of Berks; shewing that their houses, stables, barns, and divers other buildings, together with their goods and household stuff, were burnt and consumed by command of Sir John Boys, governor of Dennington Castle, amounting to the sum of Five thousand, two hundred and eighty-three pounds and eighteen shillings, to the utter undoing of the petitioners, their wives, and many children; they consisting of two-and-thirty families, was this day read.

"The Articles upon which Dennington Castle was surrendered was likewise read.

"The House called upon a report, in the hands of Mr. Lisle. And

"It is ordered that the debate concerning Sir John Bois, and the articles for rendition of Dennington Castle, be taken into consideration next after the said report."

More momentous affairs than the question of the poor sufferers at Donnington having subsequently occupied the attention of the House, this seems to have been the only notice taken of the matter. An ancestor of the writer resided in the parish at the time; and as owner of property destroyed, he signed the petition The baptism of his daughter Alice is the second entry in the parish-register of 1646; the earlier records are supposed to have been lost during the war. Capt. Money, who was connected with this family, commanded a company in the regiment of Col. Montagu, better known as the Earl of Sandwich, who raised a regiment for the Parliament in 1642. At the battles of Marston Moor, Newbury (1644), and Naseby, this regiment particularly distinguished itself, and also played a prominent part in the Siege of Bristol and Basing House.

† The memorable oaks mentioned by Evelyn, in his 'Discourse on Forest Trees,, as growing in Dennington Park, near Newbury, appear to have stood between the Castle and the little homestead on the north side, belonging to the Castle Farm, precisely in the spot mentioned by Capt. Knight. There are still two or three very fine oaks in this field.

A Closse seage to the Castell, nor well bloke it vppe now that the Ajatiente villages and howsses were burned, and that Castell Cittuate vpon A Hill and the Cuntrye About it very blitte [?bleak], hee thire fore keeps hime selfe w<sup>th</sup>in the towne of Newberye. No guarrisson of his Mat<sup>ies</sup> was better maned then this of Denington, for besides the ordinary guaruisson Souldery, thire are Come to S<sup>r.</sup> Jo. 140 men that marche of [off] from Winchester to Wodstocke, and are now com to Dennington. Dulbere Acts littill, only att times to Ayere his souldery, drawes of of his hool<sup>le</sup> [whole] to face the Castell. Nor is S<sup>r.</sup> Jo. Boys Idlle [idle] but Consults for the holding out the seage, and consideringe y<sup>e</sup> scarcittie of horsmeate sendes Away All the superfluitie of his horsse for Wallingford, only keepinge a sellecte number of 40, and such gallants they were y<sup>t</sup> y<sup>e</sup> Enimie neuer faced the Castell w<sup>th</sup> theire horsse wthout some losse. Maior Stuard [Major Stuart] who then commanded the Rebells horsse iu chiffe, A man of Action and of A turbillente spirite and greate Creuillte [to] All Royalliste, vsed more then Emullitarye [emulatory = emulative] offitiousnes to prejudice the guaruison, in fine soe Ressollute A man hee was y<sup>t</sup> hee is Reported to pistoll such of his troopers as turned taylle. An excellente discipline, for its most pbable A valliante leadere makes daring and bowld soulders, where on the Contrary no good Service is to be Expected from a Cowardly Comander, and sertainty stuard Comand As stoute A Regiment as was in y<sup>e</sup> Rebells service, besids hee was A justice and well Advised soulder, hee toke vpp his quarter at Kings Clere, thireby keepte his Regiamente in view, and too secure his quarters made turne pikes att the streets and bloked all the Avenues,—the Kentish Reagimente beinge the other y<sup>t</sup> wayted vppon Dulbere ware not soe surcomspecte but toke vppe A more larger quarter—loging att Burclere and other Ajatiente Villages. S<sup>r.</sup> Jo. Boys y<sup>t</sup> may in soe mannare be s<sup>d</sup> to bee A man that tackes Reste in Action, getts information of the quarteringe of the Enemies horsse and findinge An Impossibillitie to deall w<sup>th</sup> Stuarte Resoulves to attempte some dissigne vppon his Cuntreymen the Kentish Reagiamente [Sir Jo. Boys was a Kentish-man] and knowinge y<sup>t</sup> hee hade not horsse Suffitiente to beate vpp theire quarterres sends out a partie of 100 foote whoe passinge hegge and diche in the deade of the nighte felle vppon ptie [party] of the Kentish men's quarters, and besides prisoners brought Awaye About 80 horsse Armes and good pillage, nor doese Sir Jo. lette Dallebere to snorte w<sup>th</sup> out feere in his hotte beed at Newbery, but gives hime alsoe soe stronge An Allarme that the greatist pte of his men Rane out of the towne, and hime selfe w<sup>th</sup> the Rest, drew out of the towne, standinge all the Reste of the night in Armes. Maior Stuard stormes att this disgrace of the Kentish Regiamente, and for a braueada the next daye faces the Castell, and to puocke [provoke] S<sup>r.</sup> Jo. to Sallye sends out a Comanded ptie from the Reste of his maine bodie, S<sup>r.</sup> Jo. sends out a partie of his Castillians, who seinge they might well charge the Enemie being A good distance from their maine bodie and w<sup>th</sup> all secured by A good partie of muscitteres layd in Ambuscada to secure thire Retreate, falles vppon this partie of the Enemie and Routts them, killes many and taikes sume prissoners. Stuarte Advanced to the Rescue, but by the orderly Retreate of the Castillians and o<sup>r</sup> partie of foote, Stuarte was frustrate of his intention, soe hauevinge tacken soe poore A Reuenge Returned to his quarters w<sup>th</sup> shame, the Kentish Regimente Attributs the blame of their losses to their landlords as fauores of the Caualleres [Cavaliers], Remoues thire quarters to Wodhaye [Woodhay], and for securitie Croudes them selues vppe in some fewe howsses. S<sup>r</sup>. Jo. is Advertised where they are and howe loged, drawes out A partie of 120 ffoote whoe puided [provided] w<sup>th</sup> sleeges [hammers] and hachatts for the breaking vpp of doores and hauinge hande granades to through [throw] in att windoes Amongste them, passed heage and diche and in the deade of the night, falles vppon the Rebelles in foure howsses, Repartinge them selve, as S<sup>r.</sup> Jo. Commanded, in to 4 parties, 30 in A Companyne, in fine o<sup>r</sup> [our] partie breake vpp thire doors vppon them, tooke 26 officers and souldery, and mitte haue taken many more if they would, but vaulloinge [valuing] their horses more than the men they brought of betwixte 80 and 90 horses, Armes, and plunder. S<sup>r.</sup> Jo. neaded not at this time to haue Alaremed dulbere in Newberye for the Rest of the Kentish Reagimente in a greate Confusion Rane to the heade quarters and soe Allaramed Dulbere y<sup>t</sup> hee drew out of the towne and stoode all nighte in armes, in fine, Aftere this Dulbere changed his Course, for now hee sleepte all daye and wachte all night. The Kentish Reagemente hauinge now loste (200) or more of thire horsse were acquesed by Dulbere of slothe and Negligence, and hime selfe Reeeaued A like checke from the p'liamente, soe y<sup>t</sup> to preuent the like disgrace hee keeps A stronge gaurd of horsse daye and nighte betwixte Denington and Newberv. It wore tediouse to Recounte all the passages and scirmishes passed betwixte the Castillians and Rebels, the wholle seage beinge spente in suche like actions and beatinge vpp of quartteres.* The Kentish Reagiamente drawes them selues in to Bolsome howsse, A place duble motted [moated], but S<sup>r.</sup> Jo. Boys would not leauve them soe, and to that purpose, Communycates his Rossollution w<sup>th</sup> Colonell Blakke [Blagge] of Wallingforde, who joynes with S<sup>r.</sup> Jo. sends A partie of 150 horsse w<sup>th</sup> whome Sir John Joynes his, and besides 120 foote with firelokes and other materialles fitte for beatinge vppe of quarteres, thease togeather sette out of Denington Castell, and Comes to balsome howsse, the Enimies quarter.† A place

---

* In the month of August, 1645, Sir John Boys "beat up" the quarters of a party of Parliamentary troops under Dalbier, engaged in the siege of Basing, and brought off a Colour, with two officers, and seven other prisoners to Donnington Castle.

† Whitelocke, the Parliamentary Historian, gives a somewhat different version of this affair, but it is not to be wondered at considering the strength of party feeling at the time. He says :—"A party from Wallingford and Dennington fell upon the Parliaments quarters at Kintbury, near Newbury, took Mr. Web, but killed none, the Parliamentary party killed a knight and two more of theirs and they being allighted to plunder the town [the village of Kintbury] a Cornet with a part of a troop of the Parliaments, took twenty of the King's Horse, and two men." A family of the name of Webb were residing at or near Inglewood, which is not far from Balsdon, at this period. The "Mercurius Britannicus," a Parliamentary organ, for the week ending March 30, 1646, which commences—" Here's Victory upon Victory, Heaven smiles upon us, scarce a cloud to be seen ahead : The Cavaliers Sun is set in the West, but ours is in the Meridian!" has a satirical fanfaronade upon a letter from "Academicus," a Royalist journal, referring to the garrison at Balsdon. It states that the Cavaliers hearing the Kentish regiment quartered near Kintbury, had resolved to burn the Book of Common Prayer, sent a party of Horse "to see the manner of the Ceremony, and 35 of their men were tooke, there not being above ten left of seven score of them." This also requires to be taken "cum grano salis." The old manor-house of Balsdon, Balston, or Balsome is situated in a picturesque and secluded spot of no great elevation, about a mile and a half from the village of Kintbury, and is surrounded by a double moat as described by Capt. Knight. The ancient house having been allowed to fall into a ruinous condition was pulled down about fifty years since, and nothing now remains upon its site but portions of the foundations, and a Well on the N side, which was originally within the interior area of the house. The inner moat which encompassed the principal building is oval, and from 9 to 12 yards wide, inclosing a space of about ¾ of an acre, having a N and S. diameter of 34 yards, and an E. and W. diameter of 48 yards. This inner ditch or fosse is of considerable depth, always well filled with water, and well stocked with

## THE SECOND BATTLE OF NEWBURY.

Able to haue w$^{th}$ stoode any parttie y$^t$ had uot brought Canone w$^{th}$ them, but whether these presuminge one the strengthe of the place thought S$^r$. Jo. woulde not have attempted to beate them vpp in a place of y$^t$ strength, or how: Securitie distroyed them, for as they Coke shure slepte w$^{th}$ out keepinge guard or sentenells the Royallists come vnexpectedly vppon them, broke vpp thire gatts, and surprissed them. This laste action totally brake the Kentish Rigemente who were once 4 or 500 horsse. in sume maior Stuarte has preserued his Regiments w$^{th}$ littell losse to his no little glorye, who in his owne psone [person] vpon a scirmish vnfortunatley shotte that braue gent. liustenante Colonell Smith,* liustenante Colonell to S$^r$. humphery Benette, where of he shorttley deyed.

"S$^r$. Jo. Boys to Revenge Smythe's deathe inquires out Stuart's Rendesuves, And hauinge intelligence y$^t$ hee [was at] Knights howsse of Greenhame† to a greatte Supper, to whose dafter [daughter] he

---

fish. The position of the Drawbridge is marked by the spot on the W side where the moat has been filled up to form a passage to the garden; but both the remains of the ancient passage itself, and of the old house were existing within the memory of the present occupier (in 1883) of the adjacent cottage. The outer moat has been partly obliterated but is traceable on the N.E. side (24 yards long), E side (64 yards), S side (84 yards), and W side (44 yards). Upon the banks of the inner moat on the S.E. side, and within the outer fosse numerous flowers not indigenous to the place spring up during the summer, and several venerable fruit-bearing and other trees are still growing on this spot. Outside this again on the W. is an open space partially surrounded by a ditch, which may well have contained the outbuildings of the old manorial residence. The Manor of Balsdon was arciently in the family of Polhampton; at a later period in that of the Darells. The Loders were of Balsdon Park in 1667; and it was most probably in their hands at the time of Sir John Boys' exploit. The Park comprised about 124 acres. An account of Balsdon Manor is given in the 1st Vol. of the Newbury Field Club Transactions. pp. 132-4.

* This Lt.-Col. Smith was buried in the chancel of Newbury Church, as appears by the following entry from the Churchwardens' Accounts, given at the Vestry on 20 Sept. 1645,—

"Received of Dr. Barker, for Burying Colonel Smith in the Chancel 0 13 4."

Dr. Hugh Barker, who was an eminent physician residing at Newbury in the 17th cent., was probably the Colonel's medical attendant. He is described as "the first physician in the country," in a petition to Mr. Secretary Williamson from a Mr. Dobson, of Newbury, dated 1666, requesting the Secretary's influence with the newly restored King, in order that a daughter of a neighbour of his. "a gentlewoman of good stock, whose husband was loyal to the late King" might be privately touched for the King's evil. Dr. Barker was great nephew to Sir Christopher Barker, Garter-King-of-Arms, who, by virtue of his office, made the grant of Arms to John Winchcombe, eldest son of Jack of Newbury, which is given *in extenso* in the 'Hist. of Newbury,' pp 149, 150.

† Greenham Manor-house, the scene of this tragic occurrence, formerly stood close to the old chapel which has been recently taken down. Part of this site of the house is now occupied by the modern church. John Knight, of Newbury, by his will, bearing date 1550, leaves to Elizabeth his wife the parsonage of Greenham and Crokeham and the free chapel of Crokeham, which was attached to the old mansion at Chamberhouse. In 1643, Roger Knight, of Greenham, was one of the Sequestrators of Delinquents' estates for the county of Berks; and in Thatcham Church there was formerly a memorial for Roger Knight, Esq , of Greenham who died in 1653, aged 69. Among the Ashmolean MSS. in the Bodleian Library there is a very curious letter from Mr. Roger Knight, junior, of Greenham, probably a son of the above mentioned, to the Astrologer Lilly, affording a remarkable instance of credulity and impostnre. Mr. Roger, finding himself involved iu a troublesome "affaire du cœur," desired Lilly's judgment in the matter. He thus minutely describes his birth, personal appearance, and temperament, for the Astrologer's guidance:—"I was borne 3 weeks before my time, on the 16 Aug., 1619, neare Newbury. but what hour I cannot tell. I am very tall of stature but stoop a little at the shoulders. I am leane, have a thin flaxen hair, of a longish vissage, and a pale complexion. gray eyed, haveing some impediment in my upper lippe which hath a small mole on the right side thereof, also on the right side of my forehead another little mole. I am of melancholly disposition, having been all the time of my life in an unsettled condition." He here mentions that his father had propounded a match for him, and

was a servante [suitor], the sᵈ Sʳ. John sendes out a partie of (60) ffoote, who came vpon them soe sudently betwexte 7 and 8 of the cloke [clock] in the yeavininge [evening] in marche, that they fowned the doores oppen and Stuarte att super setting by the side of his mʳˢ· [mistress], the man would take no quarter [and] was shotte deade in the place, many prissoners were taken wᶜʰ not worthe the nomingnatinge I lette passe, in sume, this was the last beatinge vppe of quarters.*

"Wee are now come to the moneth of Aprill,† and Dulbier takes the field, faces the Castell, and the same night falles a digeinge vnder the maye poolle‡ wᵗʰin 15 score [?paces] of the Castell, Sʳ· John could

---

describes his ladye love's horoscope and astrological characteristics, and asks Lilly whether he had better make any attempt to again bring about the business, his first essay having failed ; if so, what time of year would be best suited to renew his court; and he naively wishes to know if he may rely on the Astrologer's promise that he shall "be settled" by November. In conclusion, Roger, to be prepared for the worst, requests to be informed, "in case none of the things prophesied should come to pass," whether there is no probability for him to travel "beyond sea," which he much desires. An answer was to be sent by the Bristol post, addressed Mr. Roger Knight, junior, Greenhame, neare Newberry, to be left with the postmaster at Speenhamland. Mr. Roger adds, that he shall be glad to know if questions can be solved by letter, as there were divers persons of his acquaintance in the neighbourhood of Newbury, "who have had experience," and desire to employ the Astrologer's skill, but cannot make the journey to London. He encloses an 11s. piece for Mr. Lilly's "present paines." This letter is dated "Sept. 8, at halfe an hour after 4 in the afternoon." but the year is not given. As reference is made to previous visits to the Seer in 1647 and 48, it was probably written Sept., 1646, at which time Roger would have been 30 years old. (Ashmolean MS. 423, 130. Bibl. Bodl.) Mr. Roger Knight, junior, appears to have overcome his "unsettled condition," as in 1673 he is described, in Blome's 'Britannia,' as residing at his paternal estate at Greenham ; but the sequel to his love story is not recorded.

Lilly,§ in relating his astrological career, mentions that he was well acquainted with the "Speculator" John à Windsor, a scrivener, sometime living in Newbury. This Windsor, he says, was club-fisted, wrote with a pen betwixt both his hands, and was much given to debauchery, so that at some times the Dæmons would not appear to the "Speculator"; he would then suffumigate; sometimes, to vex the spirits, he would curse them, and fumigate with contraries. Upon Windsor's examination before Sir Henry Wallop, knt. he said that he once visited Dr. Dee, in Mortlake, and out of a book, which lay in the window he copied out that call which he used when he invoked.—It was that which near the beginning of it hath these words.

"*Per virtutem illorum qui invocant nomen tuum,
Hermeli, mitte nobis tres Angelos*," &c.

Windsor, Lilly adds, "had many good parts, but was a very lewd person. My master, Wright, know him well, and having dealings in those parts (Newbury) made use of him as a scrivener."

* The following incident in connection with the siege of the Castle, is related in ' Perfect Occurrences of Both Houses of Parliament and Martial Affairs,' for the week ending 11th March 1645-6. "A partee of Dolbier's men, surprised 9 of Donnington men [of the Castle garrison] in Bagnoll [Bagnor] drinking, amongst whom some Officers, Colonel Boise the Governour hearing of it, sent out a partee, who set fire on four or five houses in Bagnoll [Bagnor] to be revenged for the losse of his men."

† This relation was probably written from memory and the events occurring in March. 1645-6, are, from some fault in the recollection, said to have taken place the following month.

‡ *The maye poolle.* There is no traditional spot where a Maypole stood in the village of Donnington, but we know that the Maypole had its place in almost every village equally with the parish church and the parish stocks, and there is no reason why there should not have been a spot appropriated for this homely May-day pageant in one of the fields adjacent to the Castle. From Capt. Knight's description, it would appear that the *maye poole* was standing during the siege in 1646, but this does not seem very probable as Parliament had, on the 6th April, 1644, ordained that "all and singular Maypoles that are or shall be erected shall be taken down," and had enforced their decree by penalties. Now as the "May-pole hill" is likewise referred to in Major Ryves' letter, printed on a subsequent page, the probabilities are

§ 'Hist. of his Life and Times,' p. 145.

not degeste such Ruffe pceedings of the Enemie, Commands a sallie w$^{th}$ horsse and foote at heighe nowne, the Enemie leyinge carelesly in thire trenches, not suspectinge a sallye, for y$^t$ they sawe the gatte shute and the brige drawne * but in this they were very much deceaved for S$^r$. John had A privatte Sallye portte made w$^{th}$in the bulworke trenche and pallissathes filed vpp w$^{th}$ earthe, w$^{ch}$ now hee clered and through it passed his horsse and foote vndiscovered, this partie was Comanded by Capt. Donne who soe sodenley ffell vppon the Enemy that they beate them out of thire works, killed' Aboue 80 personse vpon the place, brought Awaye Above (60) prissoners (4) Collores and many hundred Armes. Dulbere stricked [? stricken] w$^{th}$ this losse marches w$^{th}$ all his forces, horsse and foote to Regaine his trenches w$^{ch}$ he deed w$^{th}$out disputte, and the nexte daye plants A morter pece, and the same daye shootte 17 vppon the Castell, An oold weake Rotten howse y$^t$ w$^{th}$ this one dayes worke was well ney all shattered to peces, however Dulbere knew he hade to deall with A braue Enemie and hime selfe hauinge Received soe many Rubes from the Castillians was in disgrace with the Pliamt Assayes to gaine S$^r$. Jo. and the garrison by treatey, and to that purpose writts S$^r$. John that the L. Hopton hade giuen vpp his Armey in the weste to Generall Fairefex, the L. Astley was latly Routed att Stowe of the owlde weste [Stow-on-the-Wold], Chester surrendered, and y$^t$ hee could expecte no Reeliffe, thire fore hee Advised hime to yealde betimes, whilles hee may be able to give hime Conditions, and y$^t$ this Advice pceded from hime of mere loue as to him selfe and soe many gallant men w$^{th}$ him, to whome hee bore much honor and love, finally that this was done ag$^t$ most of the wills of his officers. S$^r$. Jo. called A Councell of Warre, Comunycatts Dulbere's l're [letter] w$^{th}$ his officers, in sume the Resoulte of this Councell was not to belcve Dulbere vppon his beare worde, but if it were soe y$^t$ the s$^d$ Dulbere should be moued to grante passes to too gent. of the Castell to gooe to Oxforde to the Kinge, to Acquainte hime w$^{th}$ the Condition of the Castell. and to knowe his mat$^{ies}$ Reassollution, in fine, this Dulbere Curtiously granted, and Capt. Osborne and Capt. Done, † too noble gent. were sente to his mat$^{ie}$ to Oxford, who sente to S$^r$. Jo. Boys that hee should gette the beste Conditions hee could for him selfe and his, and y$^t$ if possiblely hee could, he should marche of to Oxford and bringe of All the Artillery of the Castell w$^{th}$ hime. Vppon the Returne of those gent. a ply [parley] was helde with Dulbere where in the Conclusion was to surrender the Castell.

---

certainly in favour of a May-pole having stood near Dalbier's intrenchments, which are easily approachable by a sunken road from the village of Donnington. It has been suggested that an old Maple tree standing just within the park gates and near the place indicated by Capt. Knight, at the angle of Dalbier's intrenchments may have been the object which the Parliamentary soldiers fell "a digeinge vnder." But this conjecture is now scarcely tenable when we find a second authority explicitly mentioning the "May-pole hill," and further Stubbs, a contemporary writer in describing May-day customs uses the term May-pole in almost identical form as Capt. Knight. He says, "Their cheefest jewel they bring from thence (the woods) is their *Maie poole*."

* The gate here referred to appears to have been the palisaded gate closing the passage through the earthworks; and the bridge was likely to have been opposite to the existing entrance because that was most sheltered from the enemy's artillery, and the bridge was probably construced to cross the ditch of the field-work that surrounded the battered building

† In addition to these two gallant officers, the name of another of Sir John Boys' associates in defence of the Castle is preserved to us.—Mr. Robert Stradling, of the ancient family of the Stradlings of St. Donats, Glamorganshire. A biographical notice of this officer is given on a subsequent page.

## APPENDIX. 241

"The Castellians were to marche Awaye to Wallingeforde w$^{th}$ bagge and baggage, musketts chargd and primed, mache in Coke, bullate in mouthe, drumes beatinge, and Collurers ffleyinge. Every man taken w$^{th}$ hime as much amunishion as hee could Carye. As honourable Conditions as Could be given. In fine, thus was Denington Castell surrendered."

---

XI.—THE FOLLOWING LETTER IS OF CONSIDERABLE INTEREST AS A FURTHER EXPLANATION OF AN EPISODE IN THE SIEGE OF DONNINGTON CASTLE, OF WHICH WE HAVE ALREADY HAD A ROYALIST'S VERSION IN THE PRECEDING RELATION OF THE SIEGE BY CAPT. KNIGHT.

It is entitled—"Newes from Dennington Castle or A true Copy of Major Willlam Rives his Letter, in Vindication of himselfe and others. Wherin is related the Condition of the Leaguer before it, and the manner of the late Sallie from the Castle, with what losse was on both sides. Licensed and Printed according to Order. Printed for Henry Twyford, at the signe of the three Daggers in Fleet Street, neare the Temple. Aprill, the first, 1646." *

"Newes from Dennington Castle,
or a Copy of Major Rives
his Letter, &c.

Sir,
It was my fortune yesterday to bee very much ingaged, but it pleased God to give me deliverance. On Tuesday last wee drew forth of this Towne [Donnington], and faced the Castle on the Hill next *Shaw*, where we sent them a Summons, which was not totally refused, but they desired three dayes time to send to his Majesty. This was taken as dilatory, and that night to begin the siege, I had orders with three Companies of mine, which were my owne, Captaine Doves and Captaine Knowles, and with Major Blagrave's four Companies to begin the works, and to raise a redoubt on the side of the May-pole hill,† which was performed that night without the losse of one man. The next morning we began to heighten our Worke, but about seven of the clock the enemy observing our Horse-guard drawne off, fell out on us most desperately with all their Horse, and neere all their Foote, and beat in our by-guard, which was to discover cleere to the Castle. Our guard was scarcely in to give us allarme, but their Horse were in with them, and ere we could have any notice fired their Pistolls on our men in the pitt where they were, which I had stickadoed round; to prevent the falling in of their Horse. At the same instant their Foot fell on to the other side of us, and beat in our Pyoniers, who, retreating in some disorder to their Armes,

---
* The author is indebted to the courtesy of Messrs. Pickering & Co, 66 Haymarket, London, for a copy of this tract.
† See Note on "The May-poolle," p. 239 *ante*.

2 H

caused some distraction amongst our men. But of my owne Company of Gray-coates being next hand, I rallyed some suddenly, thinking to have manned our imperfect redoubt, but ere I could doe it, their Horse were in it; out of which I drawing my selfe some musketteers to the corner of it, beate them out, aud killed one of their Horses. As soon as my Ensigne saw that, hee fell on the man with his sword, and either killed or wounded him; But their Horse and Foot comming on, he was forced to retreat to his Colours. And the Enemies Foote possessing the trench of our Redoubt next the Castle under shelter of our Worke, fired on us in the pitt, where their Horse could not breake in. These did I by about twenty Musketteires of my own Company beat back, but they being well seconded, came on againe, and fell in from the hill side of the pitt, whiles their Horse fired on the other side which was open. This put our men in such a maze, being so suddenly, that they in the reere runne away in confusion, which occasioned my men being diserted to run also. My owne Company which were formerly of the King's party fought very wel, knocking it out at Musket stocke, till they broke many of their Muskets. And one of my Corporals beat a Trooper from his Horse with his Musket, and tooke his Sword, but the man was rescued ere he could kill him; we got two Carbines, and some Pistolls of such as were killed, or wounded by us. And since I understand by some of my wounded Soldiers prisoners (came off since) wee killed and wounded as many of theirs, as they of ours, only the losse of our Colours, which might well have beene saved, had there beene any Horse-guard, or that Major Blagraves' men (though I cannot impeach him in his person) had seconded me as they might, but run first. At the crosse Lane neere Dennington towne I forced some men to stand and fire, which forced the enemie to retreat in hast. And as soone as my men got more Ammunition, having spent their owne on service, I advanced againe to my post, and almost finished the Redoubt ere night. This night Colonel Martin finished it, and drew a line from Dennington Lanes to shelter our approach, and this night or tomorrow we plant our Cannon and great Mortar. And although we have a desperate Enemie, who the first night shot, and [in] one sally fought like divels, yet I hope we shall be able suddenly to give a good account of the place. And had all done like the gray-coates (however some say they run away to the Castle) they never durst attempt us. And truly my Ensigne with them fought gallantly; And of six only of them taken, there are foure wounded, and yet prisoners in expectation of exchange. Ere long I presume you will heare that wee shall repaire our honour, which is greater than our losse.     I am,

Your humble servant,

From the Leaguer before Dennington,   WILLIAM RYVES.*
  the 26 of March, 1646.

FINIS.

---

The redoubt and temporary work thrown up by the besiegers shortly before the surrender of the Castle, so fully described by Major Ryves

---

† The name of this officer, by a typographical error, is spelt "Rynes" in the pamphlet from which a copy of the Articles for surrendering the Castle was transcribed, and hence is so printed at p. 209. It should read "Major Ryves," not "Rynes."

APPENDIX. 243

in the preceding letter; and memorable as the scene of the last sortie made by Sir John Boys, in which his men,—to use the words of his admiring adversary "fought like divels," are remarkably perfect at the present day.

There are traces of a line of parapet and ditch very close to the park gates, and from this there was a clear range to the south side of the Castle gateway. The direction of the shot-holes clearly indicates that this point was the position whence the projectiles were discharged. From this work on which "our Cannon and great Mortar" was probably planted, owing to its proximity to the only well metalled road of approach—a point of importance in the transit of such heavy ordnance—the edge of the hill breaks abruptly into a small escarpment, and then opens out into a wide pit corresponding exactly to that Major Ryves describes. It is situated about 70 yards from the angle of the intrenchment before referred to; and is about 30 yards wide, and 10 feet deep on the West, or "hill side of the pitt"; and "open" on the east side as represented by Major Ryves. The flanks (sides) of the pit gradually decline to the natural level of the lower ground; but a complete shelter and defence was afforded by this excavation from an attack on all, save the open side, had the Parliament men "stood to their guns." This escarpment continues in a northerly direction towards "Dalbier's Mead," where the formal surrender of the Castle took place, and it affords excellent cover for the "covering party" which remained under arms while the working party and pioneers continued the redoubt. But it is quite possible that the edge was improved for defence, and according to the Major's own statement the pit itself was stockaded to prevent the sudden rush of the Royal horse, of which his men seem to have had a wholesome dread. Towards the northern end of the escarpment is a deep and rather wide trench running at right angles to it, and this may have been one of the roads of approach from the Donnington lanes to which the Major refers. Just to the right-front of the pit is distinctly marked the ditch line of the square redoubt referred to, the entrance to which was from the angle nearest the pit. It measures 72 feet along its front face, and 66 feet on either of its side faces, but the ditch on the rear side is only 41 feet long, leaving a space of natural ground between it and the open face. This space is close to the pit referred to by Major Ryves, and it can be easily seen that this is the point where the Major placed his men to check the enemy's foot who had gained the ditch of the redoubt nearest the Castle.

## XII.—THE DISMANTLING OF THE CASTLE.

It appears that, after the surrender of the Castle, and withdrawal of the garrison, the forces of the Parliament, in whose custody it was placed, dismantled the fortress, and carried away a quantity of lead. timber, and other goods and materials belonging to Mr. Packer; and that he obtained an Order from the House of Lords to search in Newbury and other places for the property unjustly disposed of. The execution of this Order gave rise to serious affrays in Newbury and

Basingstoke between Mr. Philip Packer, son of Mr. John Packer, the owner, and a certain Ensign Robins, who had appropriated some of the lead. An account thereof is set forth at large in the Lords' Journals. The following deposition, made by Mr. Philip Packer, introduces the name of our old friend, Mr. Gabriel Coxe; and as the incidents narrated are illustrative of the period, their insertion in full may be excused.

"Philip Packer, of the Middle Temple, gentleman, maketh oath that while he was in Newbury, in county of Berks, to seize upon such lead as he could there discover to have been brought from Donnington Castle, and having seized divers parcels in Newbury by virtue of an Order of the Hon. House of Peers, one Robins, an ensign in the Farnham regiment (and under Capt. Bruer as this deponent is informed), came to Mr. Coxe's (where this deponent lodged in Newbury) on Saturday night, 25 April, with one Lieutenant Brooks of the same regiment, and finding this deponent sitting at the table after supper, about 9 at night, said to this deponent, 'Sir, you have taken away my lead.' This Deponent replied, Sir, 'tis more than I know.' The ensign, with his sword undrawn in one hand and a pistol in the other, presented the pistol to this deponent's breast, and swore by God he would have his blood or his lead, and bad him, 'if he was a gentleman to give him presently satisfaction with his hand, or else he would post him upon the gallows as a slave and a base fellow.' This deponent bad him be advised what he did, for it was in disobedience of an Order of Parliament, and before them he would give him satisfaction, but conceived it was not to be demanded by the sword (or to that effect). He swore he would not depart the House till he had satisfaction, and that he would have his life or his lead. Mr. Coxe desired him to depart his house and to express satisfaction in another place, which he would not do, but still demanded satisfaction for the lead, and would have drawn this deponent out of the house to have given satisfaction, and swore he would break open the place where this deponent had laid the lead. But would not depart the house till Mrs. Coxe, the gentlewoman of the house, was in so great fright with his rude and insolent carriage that it was justly feared she would suffer much in her health, thereupon, with great threatenings, he left the house. And further this deponent saith that on Monday in the afternoon, April 27, the said Ensign met this Deponent in Basingstoke, and told him he was not now in Newbury, and that he had a sword on, and so followed him into the Bell Yard,† where this deponent went, and laying hands on his horse and bridle,

---

† The Bell Inn at Basingstoke, which still survives, was a notable hostelrie in the 17th century; and it was here, according to local history, that the Marquis of Winchester, Sir Robert Peake, and some other royalists made prisoners at the taking of Basing House, were lodged before being sent up to the Parliament in London.

In a work written by John Taylor, usually styled the Water Poet, printed in London in 1636, he enumerates the various Inns and Taverns that he visited; and mentions three Taverns at Newbury, as being kept respectively by John Greenaway, Thomas Howes, and Anthony Linch. At the same time there were two taverns at Speenhamland under Richard Cox, and James Garroway. The following Inns in the neighbourhood are alluded to in this very scarce work :—At Wantage, a Tavern kept by Edward Gallant, at the sign of the Elephant. At Enborne, one by Anne Plantin. At Theale, one by John Bowyer. At Thatcham, one by Robert Humphrey. At Lambourne, one kept by — Daintree, at the sign of the Two neck'd Swan. At Hungerford, one by Thomas Smith. At Reading, Taverns were kept by John Domelaw, Elizabeth Foster, John Bayley, Richard Alexander, John Skot, and George [sic] Dnell, [? Daniel, or Dunell], at the George. "A Catalogue of taverns in ten shires about London." Lond:, 1636, 12b, Brit. Mus. C. 306, 37.

APPENDIX. 245

bad this deponent come down and give him satisfaction for the lead he stole, and drew his sword and struck the Deponent upon his arm, whereupon the Deponent drew his sword for his defence, and presently there came in two troopers under Capt. Terry, of Surry, whom the Ensign, as this Deponent believeth, called thither, being of his intimate acquaintance, who did abet him and would not suffer this Deponent to go or send for any of the magistrates. This Deponent shewed them the Order of the Lords, which they said was not sufficient being subscribed only by John Browne, and no Lord's hands to it. He told them that he had done what he did by that Order, and what they did was in disobedience to it, so till this Deponent had given satisfaction under his Hand they would not give him liberty to go out of the place. All which or words to the same effect this Deponent affirmeth to be true.

"Jur. 20 Maai, 1646. PHILIP PACKER."
"Thomas Heath."

Gabriel Coxe, of Newbury, gentleman, made oath and corroborated Packer's statement. Philip Packer further made oath and said that Barnard Reives, of Basingstoke, grocer, confessed to the Deponent that he had in his possession three tons of lead which belonged to Donnington Castle, but refused to deliver the same without a sum of money to be paid him at the delivery.

---

XIII.—DEPOSITIONS OF WITNESSES AT THE TRIAL OF KING CHARLES I., AS TO THE PRESENCE OF THE KING AT THE TWO BATTLES OF NEWBURY.*

*Gyles Gryce*, of *Wellington*. in *Shropshire*, Gent., sworn and examined, deposeth, That he saw the King in the Head of the Army at the second Fight near Newbury.

*John Vinson*, of *Damorham*, in the County of *Wilts*, Gent., sworn and examined, saith, That he did see the King at the first Newbury Fight, about the month of September, 1643, in the Head of his Army, where this Deponent did see many slain on both Sides. This Deponent also saith, That he did see the King at the second battle at Newbury, about the month of November, 1644, where the King was at the Head of his Army in complete armour, with his sword drawn ; and this Deponent did then see the King lead up Col. Thomas Howard's Regiment of Horse, and did hear him make a Speech to the Soldiers, in the Head of that Regiment, to that effect — that is to say, *That the said Regiment should stand to him that Day, for that his Crown lay upon the Point of the Sword; and if he lost that Day, he lost his Honour and his Crown for ever;*—And that this Deponent did see many slain on both sides at that Battle.

*George Seeley*, of *London*, Cordwainer, sworn and examined, saith, That he did see the King at the head of a Brigade of Horse, at the Siege of Gloucester, and did also see the King at the first Fight at

* 'The Journal of the Trial of K. Charles I.' State Trials, vol. i, pp. 1031, 32.

*Newbury*, about the month of September, 1643, where the King was at the head of a Regiment of Horse; and that there were many slain at that Fight on both sides. This Deponent also saith, That he did see the King at the second Fight at *Newbury*, which was about November, 1644, where the King was in the middle of his Army.

*John Moore*, of the City of *Cork* in *Ireland*, Gent., sworn and examined, saith, That at the last Fight at *Newbury*, about the month of November, 1644, he this Deponent did see the King in the middle of the Horse, with his sword drawn; and that he did see abundance of Men at that Fight slain upon the ground, on both sides.

*Thomas Ives*, of *Boyset*, in the County of *Northampton*, Husbandman, sworn and examined, saith, That he did see the King in his Army at the first Fight in *Newbury*, in Berkshire, in the month of September, 1643, and that he did see many slain at that Fight; he, this Deponent, and others, with a Party of Horse, being commanded to face the Parliament's Forces, whilst the Foot did fetch off the dead.

*James Crosby*, of *Dublin* in *Ireland*, Barber, sworn and examined, saith, That at the first fight at *Newbury*, about the time of Barley-Harvest, 1643, he'this Deponent, did see the King riding from *Newbury Town*, accompanied with divers Lords and Gentlemen, towards the Place where his Forces were then fighting with the Parliament's Army.

*Samuel Burden*, of *Lyneham*, in the county of *Wilts*, Gent., sworn and examined, saith, That in or about the month of November, 1644, he did see the King at the last Fight at *Newbury*, riding up and down the Field from Regiment to Regiment, whilst his Army was there fighting with the Parliament's forces; and that this Deponent did see many men slain at that Battle on both sides.

*Michael Potts*, of *Sharpereton*, in the county of *Northumberland*, Vintner, sworn and examined, deposeth, That he, this Deponent, saw the King in the Head of the Army in the Fields about a mile and a half from *Newbury-Town*, upon the Heath, the Day before the Fight was, it being about Harvest-tide in the year 1643. And he further saith, That he saw the King on the day after, when the Fight was, standing near a great Piece of Ordnance in the Fields. And he further saith, That he saw the King in the second *Newbury* Fight in the Head of his Army, being after or about Michaelmas 1644. And he further saith, That he saw a great many men slain at both the said Battles.

---

## XIV.—A LETTER FROM THE EARL OF MANCHESTER TO THE HOUSE OF LORDS, GIVING AN OPINION ON THE CONDUCT OF OLIVER CROMWELL.

[Tanner MSS., vol. lxi, fol. 205.]

My Lords,
                                                          Dec<sup>r.</sup> 1644.
    In obedience to your commands I shall give your Lopp<sup>s.</sup> an account of that which with much trouble I have of late laboured under: the discontents that have bin in that army w<sup>ch</sup> I have the honor to comaund. My Lords, when I found these differences in my

army to grow to some height, and considered the inconveniences thatt might thence ensue, I brought to London twoe persons of my army that were most concerned in these differences, and did represent to the Committee of both kingdoms the danger and prejudice that might thereby arise to the publique service, if some speedie course should not be taken for removeall thereof. But the Comittee of both kingdoms, holding it unfitt at that time to take them into their consideracion, when there was a necessitie of putting the armies to present action against the common enemie, directed mee to endeavour that they should be composed, or at least laid aside till further leisure, in the time of our winter quarters. This advice I willingly embraced, and did apply myselfe w$^{th}$ my full endeavours to quiett those distraccions for the present; but this hath not satisfied the armies of some who I heare (upon what grounds I cannot imagine) doe fixe upon mee the character of being a discountenancer of honest and godly men, I cannot but wonder at soe high a slander, and if this relate to those of my owne army, wherein I hope there are many honest men, though differing in judgment to what I professe, yett I shall appeall to them whether I have at any time been failing in my respects unto them; and I can say that upon some of them I have looked w$^{th}$ that value und esteeme, as that the choice and approbacion of most of the comaunders in the army have bin in their power. Lieftennant Generall Cromwell shall be my compurgator in this particular. Hee knowes that I alwaies placed him in cheefest esteeme and creditt with mee. But it is true that of late I had not given soe free and full a power unto him as formerly I did, because I heard that he used his power soe as in honor I could not avowe him in it, and indeed I grew jealous that his designes were not as he made his professions to mee; for his expressions were sometimes against the nobilitie; that he hoped to live to see never a Nobleman in England, and he loved such better than others because they did not love lords. He hath further expressed himselfe w$^{th}$ contempt of the Assembly of Divines, to whom I pay a reverence, as to the most learned and Godly convention that hath bin these many ages, yett these he termed persecutors; and that they persecuted honester men than themselves. His animositie against the Scottish nation, whome I affect as joyned w$^{rh}$ us in solemne league and covenant, and honor as joyntly instrumentall w$^{th}$ us in the common cause, yett against these his animositie was such as he told me that in the way they now carried themselves, pressing for their discipline, he could as soone draw his sword against them as against any in the King's army; and he grew soe pressing for his designes as he told mee that he would not deny but that he desired to have none in my army but such as were of the Independent judgement, giving mee this reason :—

That in case their should be propositions for peace or any conclusion of a peace such as might not stand with those ends that honest men should aime at, this army might prevent such a mischeefe.

I must confess these speeches, some of them spoken publiquely, others privately, yet soe soone as I saw they had a publique influence on the army, made me jealous of his intencions; and therefore I did not communicate my councells to him w$^{th}$ that freedome that formerly I had done, and I hope this shall not make such an impression upon the hearts of others that are godly, even of such as are of his judgement soe as to derogate from my esteeme in soe high a measure as to thinke mee fitt to be stiled an enemie to Godly men. My conscience bears mee witnes that my affections are still sett upon such as love Christ in sincerity with the highest value, nay, I can in the cleerenes of my heart profess that to those who have sought thus to traduce mee my prayers shal be that God of mercy would pardon of their uncharitable and unchristian carriage, and my endeavours shalbe as far as it may stand with the vindication of my owne integritie to returne good for evill.

Indorsed: Concerning Leiutenaunt Generall Cromwell, referred Xber 4o, 1644.


## XV.—BIOGRAPHICAL NOTICES OF SOME OF THE OFFICERS AND OTHERS,

MENTIONED IN CONNECTION WITH THE SECOND BATTLE OF NEWBURY.


### § 1.—ROYALIST OFFICERS.

PRINCE MAURICE. Third son of the King of Bohemia, entered into the service of Charles I. about the same time with his brother. He was not of so active and fierce a nature as Rupert; but knew better how to pursue any advantages gained over the enemy. It is said that he wanted a deal of his brother's fire, and Rupert a great deal of Maurice's phlegm. He laid siege to several places in the West, and took Exeter and Dartmouth. His most signal exploit was the victory at Lansdown. The Prince perished in a hurricane off the West Indies in 1654.

DUKE OF RICHMOND. James Stuart, eldest son of Esme, third Duke of Lennox, and Catherine, daughter and heir of Sir Gervase Clifton, was born in Blackfriars, London, April 6th, 1612. After the death of his father he was placed by his mother under the especial care and protection of Charles I., to whom he was nearly related. He was appointed Lord Steward, Warden of the Cinque Ports, and Privy Councillor; and created Duke of Richmond in 1641. He married Mary, only daughter of George Villiers, first Duke of Buckingham, who had been previously contracted in childhood to Charles, eldest son of Philip, Earl of Pembroke. He was sent to travel in France, Italy, and Spain, for the benefit of his education, and from the time of his return to England, at about twenty-one years of age, he never was absent from the King's person, but shared in all his councils, and attended him in every change of fortune till the secret flight from Oxford, when the King left behind him all the members of his household and of his Privy Council. The Duke resumed his post after this event whenever he was permitted to do so by those into whose hands the King had fallen, and he even accompanied him finally a short distance from Newport on the road to Hurst Castle; then, forced to take leave, he was never again allowed to see the King alive. He obtained permission, with three others, to attend his funeral; and was one of the four who are said to have offered their own lives to save that of their master. He died 30th March, and was buried in Westminster Abbey 18th April 1655. He was

# APPENDIX.

succeeded by his only son Esme, who died in his minority in Paris. His only daughter married Richard Butler, Earl of Arran, second son of the Duke of Ormonde.

LORD BERNARD STUART. The youngest of five sons of Esme, Duke of Lennox, all of whom served in the royal army, and brother to James, first Duke of Richmond. He was slain at Rowton Heath, about two miles from Chester, Sept. 26th, 1645. His brothers, Lord D'Aubigny and the Lord John Stuart, both fell in the King's service. It is stated by Lord Clarendon and others, that Lord Bernard Stuart was created Baron Stuart of Newbury and Earl of Lichfield, in consideration of his gallant behaviour near the latter city. It was intended that these titles should have been conferred on Lord Bernard, but he died before the Patent passed the Great Seal; hence he never was Earl of Lichfield or Baron Stuart of Newbury, because it was the Great Seal only that would have entitled him to bear those titles. He died simply Lord Bernard Stuart. Charles Stuart, only son of George, Lord D'Aubigny (who was slain at the battle of Edgehill), and nephew of Lord Bernard Stuart, was created (10 Dec., 1645) Baron Stuart of Newbury, Berks, and Earl of Lichfield, and succeeded his cousin Esme, 10 Aug., 1660, as third Duke of Richmond, and sixth of Lennox. He died at Elsinore, while ambassador to Denmark, 12 Dec., 1672, without surviving issue; and his titles became extinct. There is no doubt, that the titles of Earl of Lichfield and Baron Stuart of Newbury, were conferred on Lord Charles Stuart, in consideration of the services of his uncles, and especially to perpetuate the titles which were intended to have been conferred on his uncle Bernard.

EARL OF NEWPORT. Mountjoy Blount was a natural son of Charles Blount, Earl of Devonshire, by Penelope, daughter of Walter Devereux, first Earl of Essex, and divorced wife of Robert, Lord Rich. He was created Lord Mountjoy of Mountjoy Fort by James I., and Baron Mountjoy of Thurveston, co. Derby, and Earl of Newport by Charles I. He was Master of the Ordnance, and one of the Council for War in the royal army. He died at Oxford and was buried in Christ Church Cathedral 15 Feb. 1665-6. The title became extinct in 1681, on the death of his youngest son Henry, third Earl.

EARL OF BERKSHIRE. Sir Thomas Howard, second son of Thomas, first Earl of Suffolk, by his second wife, Catherine, eldest daughter and co-heir of Sir Henry Knevet of Charlton, Wilts, Kt., and widow of Richard Rich, Esq. He was created, 22 Jan., 1621-2, Baron Howard of Charlton, and Viscount Andover, installed K.G., 13 Dec., 1625, and advanced to the Earldom of Berkshire, 7 Feb. 1625-6. He died 16 July, 1669, aged about ninety. His grand-daughter Frances, daughter of Thomas, third Earl of Berkshire, married Sir Henry Winchcombe, Bart., of Bucklebury, ancestor of the late Winchcombe-Henry-Howard Hartley, Esq., of Bucklebury, Berks, and Lyegrove, Little Sodbury, Gloucestershire.

EARL RIVERS. John Savage, eldest son of Thomas, first Viscount Savage, by Lady Elizabeth D'Arcy, daughter and co-heir of Thomas, first Earl Rivers, succeeded his maternal grandfather as second Earl Rivers in 1639. He died 10 Oct. 1654. The title became extinct on the death, in 1728, of John fifth Earl, who was a Roman-Catholic priest.

LORD CAPEL. Arthur Capel, born A.D. 1603, son of Sir Henry Capel and Theodosia Montagu, sister to Lord Montagu of Boughton. Sir Henry died in the lifetime of his father, and Arthur Capell succeeded to his grandfather Sir Arthur Capel's estates. In November, 1626, he married Elizabeth Morrison. In April, 1640, he was chosen Member of Parliament for the County of Hertford, and again for the ensuing Parliament in November, 1640. On the 7th August, 1641, he was created Lord Capel of Hadham. At the breaking-out of the Civil War he raised a troop of horse in defence of the King. He was appointed one of the Prince of Wales's Council during the campaign in the West, and accompanied him to Jersey. In March, 1646-7, he returned to England, and again took up arms for the King; and, together with Lord Norwich, Sir Charles Lucas, and Sir George Lisle, defended Colchester against the attacks of Lord Fairfax. After more than eleven weeks' siege they were obliged to surrender. Lord Capel was subsequently tried by a high court of justice, erected for the purpose of trying Lord Norwich, and others. He was sentenced to death, and with exemplary firmness died on the scaffold, March 9th, 1648-9. "He was a man," says Lord Clarendon, "that, whoever shall, after him, deserve best of the English nation, he can never think himself under-valued, when he shall hear, that his courage, virtue, and fidelity, is laid in the balance with, and compared to, that of the Lord Capell."

LORD HOPTON. Ralph Hopton, son of Robert Hopton, of Witham, Somerset, was created Baron Hopton, of Stratton, co. Cornwall, 4 Sept., 1643, with remainder, failing his issue male, to Arthur Hopton, his uncle and his issue male. After exerting himself in the House of Commons, for the King's cause, he joined the army, and obtained a well-earned peerage for the signal victory he obtained in conjunction with Sir Beville Granville, and his Cornish army, over the Parliament's forces, under the command of the Earl of Stamford, at Stamford Hill, near Stratton, in Cornwall, May 16th, 1643. Lord Hopton is described as "a worthy man and excellent officer, who sought no favours from Oxford, severely repressed pillage, everywhere protected the people, and while fulfilling what he considered the duty of a faithful subject, did it with all the humanity of a good citizen." A character which a study of his history fully verifies. Towards the close of the first war,—in January, 1645-6, Hopton accepted the command of the remnant of the King's forces in the West; and on the 16th of February following, met with a disastrous defeat from Fairfax at Torrington—the death-blow of the King's affairs in the West. Being driven down to the very extremity of Cornwall, Hopton vainly endeavoured to recruit the small force which still remained faithful to him. With honourable consideration for his position, Fairfax offered the most generous terms if he would surrender, but he declined to treat. He however gave his officers of horse leave to conclude articles, which was accordingly done, and the army disbanded. Hopton retiring to Scilly, where he joined the Prince of Wales. He died at Bruges in September, 1652, s.p., when the title (his uncle Arthur having died s.p.) became extinct.

LORD COLEPEPER. John, Lord Colepeper, was descended from a branch of the very ancient Kentish family of Colepeper settled at Bay Hall, near Pepenbury. He was the son of a knight of the same name, living at Wigsell in Sussex; and he spent some years in foreign parts, doing good service as a soldier, and was reported to be of great courage, but of a rough nature; his hot temper leading him too frequently into quarrels and duels When he married he settled in the County of his ancestors, where he soon became popular amongst his neighbours; and, in consequence of the knowledge of business which he exhibited, and the ability with which he conducted it, he was frequently deputed by them to the council-board, and at length was

APPENDIX. 251

knighted, and elected Member for Kent in the Long Parliament. The King, sensible of his value, admitted him to his privy council, and in January 6, 1642, made him Chancellor of the Exchequer. During that eventful year, with the assistance of Lord Falkland and Edward Hyde, though sometimes disconcerted by the King's hasty measures, he did what he could to serve his Majesty. He acquired great influence, but his counsels were not always very wise or temperate. To his advice is attributed the King's consent to pass the Bill for removing the Bishops from the House of Peers, the transference of the court from Windsor to York, and the attempt to obtain possession of Hull. On January 28, 1643, he was promoted to the Mastership of the Rolls, an office for which his previous education had in no degree prepared him. He took it as adding to his dignity and profit, without regard to its duties. As a counsellor, he was used on the most private occasions, and was added to the junto which, as a cabinet-council, managed the King's affairs; as a soldier, he was ever by the King's side, and took part in all his battles with the most distinguished bravery. In reward for these services, the King, on October 21, 1644, created him a peer, by the title of Lord Colepeper, of Thoresway in Lincolnshire, and named him one of the Council of the Duke of York. He died July 11, 1660, and was buried in the church of Hollingbourn in Kent, in which and the neighbouring parish the family property, including Leeds Castle, was situate. By his first wife, Philippa, daughter of Sir George Snelling, knt., he had one son, who died young. His second wife, who was his cousin, Judith, daughter of Sir Thomas Colepeper, of Hollingbourn, knight, brought him four sons, the three elder of whom enjoyed the title in succession, which then, for want of male issue, became extinct in 1725.

LORD GORING. George, Lord Goring, was the son of George Goring, Earl of Norwich, and Lady Mary Nevile. In consequence of the numerous debts he had contracted at home he went abroad in 1633, entered foreign service, and distinguished himself in the Low Countries, receiving a wound at the siege of Breda, which lamed him for life. In 1641, he was made governor of Portsmouth, and betrayed to the Parliament the intentions of the King to bring the army to London; and he continued greatly in favour with the popular party until 1642, when he declared for the King. In 1644 he superseded Lord Wilmot in the command of the Horse, and served in the West, where the want of discipline in his troops, and the licentiousness of his own conduct, materially injured the cause he had espoused. He suddenly quitted the country in 1645, and never returned. His habits of intoxication continued to the end of his life, and he died at Madrid, in 1662, having embraced the Roman-Catholic faith, and, it has been stated by some writers, having entered the Order of Dominican Friars. He married Lettice, daughter of Richard, Earl of Cork, but had no children. The Earl of Norwich survived his son George, and died January 1662-3, when he was succeeded by his son Charles, at whose death without issue, in 1672, the title became extinct.

SIR JOHN BOYS. The exploits of this gallant royalist have been fully narrated in their proper place. Rather encouraged than daunted with past dangers he zealously adhered to the royal cause in every fortune, and when not in prison he was actively concerned in most of the daring enterprises to overthrow the authority of Cromwell and his parliament. In August, 1648, he was engaged in an unsuccessful attempt to raise the siege of Deal Castle, and was one of the seven royalists who having been in arms against the Parliament since the first of January, 1647-8, it was proposed by the Commons should be banished the kingdom. However, on the question being put to the House that Sir John Boys be one of the number it passed with the negative. In 1659 he appears to have been a prisoner in Dover Castle "for tendering an Address or Declaration for a Free Parliament," but was released by order of the House of Commons, 23 Feb. 1659-60. He lived to see the Restoration; and then petitioned Charles II. for the appointment of Receiver of Customs at Dover. The original petition, which describes Sir John Boys, as "one of yor Maties gent. of yor Privy Chamber in Ordinary," is preserved among the State Papers in the Public Record Office, and is endorsed "Done." Sir John died at his house at Bonnington in Kent, in 1664. The following inscription, is on a black marble slab over his grave, in the aisle of a chapel in the north chancel of the parish church of Goodnestone-next-Wingham, Kent, "Underneath rests Sr. John Boys, late of Bonnington, Kt., whose military praises will flourish in our Annales as laurells and palmes to overspread his grave. Dun[gan]non in Ireland may remaine a solemne mourner of his funerall; and Dunington Castle in England a noble monument of his fame, the former for the losse of its expert governer the latter for the honour of its g[alla]nt defender. To crown such eminent loyalty and [va]lour ye King royally added to his antient scutchon a crown. Leaving no other heires male than man[l]y deeds to keepe up his name his inheritance decended to his three daughters Jane, Lucy, Anne. In his [5]8th yeare, being discharged from this militant state below he was entertained as we hope in that triumphant state above, Octob. 8th, 1664." Above the inscription are the arms of Sir John Boys (or, a griffin segreant sable, on a canton azure, a crown imperial or). Stephen Tucker, Esq., Somerset Herald, has not been able to find any record at the Heralds' College as to the Royal augmentation. The crown was not an uncommon augmentation to the arms of Royalists in those days; and the omission of any enrolment may be due to the troubled state of the times. The pedigree of Sir John Boys at the Heralds' College is signed by his father (Edward Boys) in 1619 ; there being eight antecedent generations to the gallant Royalist. "John" (son of Edward) is there said to have been aged 14 years and upwards In Dring's Catalogue of Lords, Knights, and Gentlemen who compounded for their estates, Sir John Boys, of Bonnington, Kent, is set down as having paid £0312 10. 0. He is returned as having been in arms against the Parliament in both the first and second war, and as entitled to the Manor of Bonnington, Kent, on the death of Edward Boys, Esq. Royalist Comp. Papers, Ser. 2, vol. 36, fo. 491. There was also a John Boys, of Old Sock, co. Somerset, gent, a captain in his Majesty's army, who yielded up himself upon the surrender of Bridgewater to the Parliaments' forces. Royalist Comp. Papers, Ser. 2, vol. 30, fo. 710. Sir Edward Boys, M.P. for Dover in the Long Parliament was Governor of Dover Castle for the Parliament. Major John Boys being Lieutenant-Governor of the same fortress.

SIR BERNARD ASTLEY. Son of Sir Jacob Astley. An eminent commander in his Majesty's army. After admirable service in six fights and eight sieges, he died of wounds received in a brave sally out of Bristol, Sept. 4th. 1645. He especially signalized himself at the Second Battle of Newbury.

SIR JOHN CANSFIELD. Frequently written "Campsfield"—Of Cansfield, a township in the parish of Tunstall, Lancashire. Commander of the Queen's regiment, raised in Lancashire, in the second battle of

APPENDIX. 253

Newbury, where he is said to have saved the life of Charles I. and the Prince of Wales by a decisive charge. Capt. Symonds says that Colonel Cansfield was knighted near Newport Pagnell 'for the Oney [Olney] buisnes.'

SIR WILLIAM BROUNCKER, frequently written BRONKARD. Sir Wm. Brouncker, kt., born 1585, was eldest son of Sir Henry Brouncker, Lord President of Munster. He became a Gentleman of the Privy Chamber to K. Chas. I., and was Vice-Chamberlain to K. Chas. II., when Prince of Wales. He was created Viscount Brouncker in the Irish Peerage 12 Sep. 1645, and dying shortly after, was buried in Christ Church Cathedral, Oxford 20 November in that year. The title became extinct in 1687-8, on the death of his youngest son Henry, third Viscount.

SIR WILLIAM ST. LEGER. He was knighted in his father's lifetime; served in the Parliament of 1639 for Kilmallock; commanded a regiment in the war with the Irish; and, after it ceased, went, in November 1643, to Bristol, to assist the King in England. With Col. Myn, he took over 1000 foot and some horse; and did great service in harassing the garrison of Gloucester. He fell in the Second Action at Newbury, 27 October, 1644; and not having been married, his brother succeeded to his estate. His descendant, Arthur St. Leger, was created by patent, 23 June 1703, Baron Kilmadow and Viscount Doneraile. Sir Anthony St. Leger, commanded Prince Rupert's Life Guard at the Second Battle of Newbury.

SIR JOHN OWEN. Of Klinenney, co. Caernarvon. He was wounded at the taking of Bristol in 1643. Tried by the High Court of Justice, with the Duke of Hamilton and Lord Capel, he was sentenced to death, but subsequently pardoned. He is said to have served in 7 battles, 9 sieges, and 32 minor actions.

SIR THOMAS HOOPER. Lieutenant-Colonel of Dragoons. Knighted for taking General Wemys (General of Sir William Waller's Artillery) at Cropredy Bridge. Symonds's 'Diary,' p. 2.

SIR RICHARD PAGE. Of Kingsthorp, co. Northampton. Knighted at Leicester, 2 June 1645, after it was taken by storm. He had been "first on the escalade" at this memorable siege, which was one of the best fought and defended actions of the war.

SIR RICHARD LANE. Sir Richard Lane was a lawyer, "the Prince's solicitor and attorney." See Lloyd's *Memoires*, 594.

SIR THOMAS BASSET, OR BASSETT. General of the Ordnance to Prince Maurice. He was, with his brother Francis (a Cornishman, governor of St. Michael's Mount), knighted at Crediton, co. Devon, about 30 July, 1644. He was second son of James Basset, of Tehidy, co. Cornwall, by Jane, daughter of Sir Francis Godolphin, kt., but none of the pedigrees of the family give any further particulars about him.

SIR HUMPHREY BENETT. Of the Benetts of Pythouse, Wilts. Col. Thomas Benett was Prince Rupert's Secretary, and the family were staunch adherents to the royal cause.

SIR JOHN GRANVILLE. Son and heir of Sir Bevil Granville, who fell at the Battle of Lansdown, July, 1643. Created Baron of Kilkhampton and Bideford, Viscount Granville of Lansdown, and Earl of Bath, April 20th, 1661. He died August 22nd, 1701.

SIR JOSEPH WAGSTAFFE. Wounded at Lichfield, 1643. Engaged in the western rising, 1655, and was with difficulty persuaded by his companions from hanging the Parliamentary Judges and the High Sheriff of the County, who had fallen into their hands at Salisbury. After the failure of the enterprise he escaped abroad.

## THE SECOND BATTLE OF NEWBURY.

SIR CHARLES LLOYD. Governor of Devizes. Knighted 8th of December, 1644.

SIR EDWARD WALKER. Author of the 'Historical Discourses,' &c., was successively, Rouge-Croix Pursuivant, Chester Herald, Norroy, and Garter-King-Of-Arms, in which last Office he was succeeded by Sir William Dugdale. See more of him in "Athenæ Oxonienses." He died 19 Feby. 1676, being then one of the Clerks of the Privy Council to Charles II.

COLONEL WILLIAM ASHBURNHAM. There is no record of this gentleman having been knighted, although he is spoken of in a contemporary MS. referring to these transactions, as "*Sir* William Ashburnham," He was the second son of Sir John Ashburnham, of Ashburnham, Sussex, M.P. in 1640, who, with other loyal members, was expelled the House for his fidelity to the crown. He subsequently took an active and distinguished part during the civil war, was maj.-gen. in the royal army, and col.-gen. (1644) of co. Dorset. After the Restoration, he was appointed Cofferer to the King. He married Jane, third daughter of John, first Lord Butler of Bramfield, and widow of James Ley, first Earl of Marlborough, but died without issue in 1679.

COLONEL LEKE. Who fell at the Second Battle of Newbury, was the son of Sir Francis Leke, knt., of Sutton, co. Derby, elevated to the peerage, 26 Oct., 1624, as Baron D'Eyncourt, whose two sons both laid down their lives in the King's service. Lord D'Eyncourt, who himself took an active part in the war, became so mortified (it is said) by the execution of Charles I. that he clothed himself in sackcloth, and, causing his grave to be dug some years before his death, laid himself therein every Friday, exercising himself frequently in divine meditation and prayer. The Barony of D'Eyncourt and Earldom of Scarsdale became extinct on the death of the 4th Earl, who died unmarried in 1736. Burke's 'Dormant and Extinct Peerages,' p. 319.

COLONEL ANTHONY THELWALL. "A branch of the Worshipful family of the Thelwalls of Plasyward, near Ruthin, in Denbighshire; known for his brave Actions at Cropredy (where his majesty trusted him with a thousand of the choicest men he had, to maintain, as he did bravely, the two advantageous villages, Burley and Nelthorp), and at the Second Newberry fight, where he did wonders with the reserve of Sir George Lisle's Tertia; and had done more, had he not been slain for not accepting of Quarter." Lloyd's 'Memoires,' p. 661.

COLONEL GILES STRANGWAYS. "Of Melbury Sampford, in Dorsetshire. This worthy gentleman, who was descended from one of the most ancient and respectable families in Dorsetshire, was representative in Parliament for that County, and one of the Privy-Council to Charles II. In the time of the Civil War, he had the command of a regiment in that part of the royal army which acted under Prince Maurice in the West. In 1645 he was imprisoned in the Tower for his active loyalty, where he continued in patient confinement for more than two years and six months. There is a fine medallion of him, struck upon this occasion: on the reverse is represented that part of the Tower called Cæsar's, with the inscription—*Decusque adversa dederunt*. When Charles fled into the West, in disguise, after the battle of Worcester, Col. Strangways sent him three hundred broad pieces; which was, perhaps, the most seasonable present the royal fugitive ever received. This, however, was but a small part of the sum which is to be placed to the account of his loyalty; for the house of Strangways paid no less than £35,000 for its attachment to the Crown. He died 1675.

COLONEL HOGHTON. Slain at the second battle of Newbury. Son of

# APPENDIX. 255

Sir Richard Hoghton, Bart., of Hoghton Tower, Lancashire, by Catherine, daughter of Sir Gilbert Gerard, of Gerard's Bromley, co. Stafford, knt., Master of the Rolls. Hoghton Tower between Preston and Blackburn, was fortified for the King during the Civil Wars by its gallant owner, Sir Gilbert Hoghton; and is described by Dr. Whitaker, in his *History of Whalley*, as the only specimen in his neighbourhood of a true baronial residence, with two courts, crowning the summit of an elevated ridge, and appearing at a distance like a fortified town.

CAPTAIN CATELYN. A member of a Norfolk family, one of whom, Sir Robert Catelyn, was Lord Chief Justice in the reign of Queen Elizabeth. Capt. Catelyn, commanded a troop of horse in Sir Edward Waldegrave's regiment, and fell in the Second Action at Newbury, while engaged with the royalist force on the Speen side. He was buried at Speen, as the parish-register thus records:—"1644, Oct. 31, Thomas Catelyn a gentleman of Norfolke."

ROBERT STRADLING. This gentleman was a member of the ancient family of Stradling of St. Donat's. In a petition addressed to the Bishop of London, by Robert Stradling, shortly after the Restoration, desiring the Bishop's influence with Secretary Nicholas to obtain the petitioner the place of Messenger to the Queen, he encloses certificates in his favour from Sir John Boys, Sir John Robinson, Sir Edward Savage, and Sir Philip Musgrove, testifying to his services at Donnington Castle, in Ireland, Scotland, the Isle of Man, and Shetland. In a subsequent petition, the former not having received attention, the petitioner mentions that he went with the Countess of Derby to join his Majesty on his arrival in Scotland, but fell ill in 1651, and has suffered much by imprisonment,* loss of estate, &c. He annexes the previous certificates, with another by Richard Egerton, to the effect that "Robert Stradling was Cornet of Horse in Sir George Booth's rising, and always ready for design in the King's service." The certificate of Sir John Boys is as follows:— "I doe Certify that this gent. Robert Stradlyn was under my command in the garrison of Denningtton Castle, and did venture his life for his late Mats service, and that he was faithfull in his Trust. Jo. Boys. July xviij$^{th}$." State Papers, Domestic Series, Charles II, vol. 55, No. 3. i.

CAPTAIN SYMONDS. The author of the "Diary of the Royal Marches," frequently referred to in this volume. He was, as he tells us in the family pedigree, which he entered in his Essex collections, a native of the parish of Black Notley, co. Essex; and at the commencement of the Civil War joined the royal standard. He was committed prisoner as a delinquent 25 March, 1643, but escaped 21 October, the same year, and attached himself to the King's service. He served in the King's troop under Lord Bernard Stuart, in the battle of Cropredy Bridge, Lostwithiel, Newbury second battle, the relief of Donnington Castle, Naseby, and the relief of Chester, where Lord Bernard Stuart was slain. He subsequently served with Sir William Vaughan at Denbigh and other places. The date of his death is unknown.

---

* The name of Robert Stradling and his coat of arms, cut by him on the stones of the chamber in the Round Tower of Windsor, in which he was imprisoned, with the date, 1648, is still to be seen, with those of other royalist prisoners.

## § 2.—PARLIAMENTARIAN OFFICERS.

EARL OF MANCHESTER. Edward Montagu, son and heir of Henry Montagu (first Earl of Manchester), M.P. for Huntingdon in the first Parliament of Charles I., was raised to the Upper House in 1626, with the title of Baron Montagu of Kimbolton, and was associated in the charge of high treason with Pym, Hampden, Strode, Holles, Hesilrige, whose arrest Charles attempted in his famous and fatal *coup d' état*. He defeated the Earl of Newcastle at Horncastle in June, 1643, and distinguished himself by his victory over Prince Rupert at Marston Moor, in which engagement Cromwell acted as his Lieut.- General, but in reality guided him. He refused to sanction the execution of the King, and retired from Parliament (where he held the office of Speaker) until 1660, when he assisted at the meeting of peers who voted for the restoration of Charles II. He was deputed by the Lords as their Speaker to congratulate the King on his return to the Capital, and shortly after the Restoration, was appointed Chamberlain of the Household, and held other posts of dignity strangely out of keeping with his antecedents. The Earl died at Whitehall, May 5th, 1671, at the age of 68 years. He had been five times married. The present ducal house of Manchester is descended from his second marriage.

SIR WILLIAM WALLER, son of Sir Thomas Waller, Constable of Dover Castle, and Margaret, daughter of Sampson Lennard, Lord Dacre, served in the Netherlands, in the same camp with Sir Ralph Hopton; and was in the army of the confederate princes against the Emperor. He was one of the most able and active of the Parliamentary Generals; and, being for a considerable time victorious, was therefore called, William the Conqueror. He was defeated at the battle of Lansdown, near Bath; and afterwards wholly routed at Roundway Down, near Devizes. The "Conqueror's" fame sunk considerably from this time; but he afterwards had the credit of defeating his former fellow-soldier, Lord Hopton, at Alresford. A few months later, he was beaten by the royalists at Cropredy, in Oxfordshire; and repeated reverses led to his being deprived of his command in 1645. He was imprisoned by the Independent Parliament, and confined until the King's Restoration. He died at Osterley Park, near Hounslow in 1668. The Wallers of Newbury were descended from the youngest son of this eminent commander.

SIR ARTHUR HESILRIGE. Eldest son of Sir Thomas Hesilrige, of Nosely, co. Leicester. Sir Arthur Hesilrige brought forward in the House of Commons the suit for the attainder of the Earl of Strafford. The soldiers of Sir Arthur's troops were so completely armed that they were called by the other side "Hesilrige's Lobsters," because of their bright shells with which they were covered, being perfectly cuirassed. They were the first that made any impression on the King's cavalry. Hesilrige was one of the King's judges, but did not sign the death-warrant. He died in the Tower shortly after the Restoration.

Thomas, brother of Sir Arthur Hesilrige, married (at St. Luke's, Chelsea, Middlesex, 6th Sept. 1632) Rebecca, daughter of Thomas Sheafe, D.D., Dean of Windsor, and rector of Welford, near Newbury. Heath's 'Chronicle' mentions Sir Arthur's brother, Thomas, as suborning witnesses to vilify the King; and hs evidently served the Parliament so faithfully as to secure honourable burial within West-

APPENDIX. 257

minster Abbey, and thus rendered his memory so obnoxious that his remains were included amongst those disinterred after the Restoration, and thrown into a common pit in the Churchyard. Dr. Sheafe, Rector of Welford, who died in 1639, at the age of 80, a short time before his death published a work entitled 'A Plea for Old Age.'

MAJOR-GENERAL CRAWFORD. Laurence Crawford, of the family of Crawfords, of Jordan Hill, Renfrewshire. The name of Crawford is rendered in some degree memorable from the circumstance of his being the original authority for imputing cowardice to Cromwell. The accusation is given at large in Holles's Memoirs. He was killed at the siege of Hereford, Aug. 17, 1645, when in his 34th year; and was buried on the N side of the Lady Chapel of Gloucester Cathedral, where a monument with half-length figure in white marble was erected, but destroyed by the authorities after the Restoration.

LIEUTENANT-GENERAL MIDDLETON. Fought in the First Battle of Newbury. Of Donnington Castle fame. "A person," says Clarendon, "who liv'd to wipe out the memory of his youth, for he was but eighteen years of age when he was first led into Rebellion." Lt.-Gen. Middleton had at the Battle of Edgehill with his own hands taken the royal standard. This was recovered by Capt. John Smith, brother to Lord Carrington, and an officer in Lord Grandison's Regiment of Horse, who was knighted the same evening by the King for the deed. Capt. Smith fell at Cheriton-fight, 29th March, 1644. He quitted the service of the Parliament when they cashiered the Earl of Essex, and made their New Model Army. He was taken prisoner after the Worcester fight; and, when he was sufficiently recovered of his wounds, he was removed to the Tower, where his friend and comrade Massey, the defender of Gloucester, who had likewise joined the royalist party, and fought at Worcester, was daily expecting the vengeance of the Commonwealth. When the time of their trial approached, Middleton found means to make his escape and got safe to France; and within a few days after, Massey had the like good fortune, "to the grief and vexation of Cromwell," who, Clarendon states, "thirsted for the blood of those two persons."

LIEUTENANT-GENERAL LUDLOW. Edmund Ludlow was a native of Wiltshire, having been born at Hill-Deverill, or in its neighbourhood, where his father, Sir Henry Ludlow, resided. He was M.P. for the County of Wilts in the Parliament which began Nov. 3rd, 1640, one of the Council of State,—Lieutenant-general of the horse,—and Commander-in-chief of the forces in Ireland. He entered with zeal into all the measures of the Republican party; and tells us himself, in his 'Memoires,' that he "had the honour of being one of the late King's judges." About the time of the Restoration he retired into Switzerland, where he remained in obscurity until the Revolution in 1688, when he repaired with other deputies, to London, to offer to raise men for King William's service. His further progress, however, in this measure, was quickly arrested by Sir Edward Seymour, who moved a resolution in the House of Commons, that they should address his Majesty to bring Ludlow to trial as a regicide, which he no sooner heard of than he returned to Switzerland. He died at Vevay, in the year 1693; and his remains were interred in the church of that town, under a monument erected to his memory by his widow. His memoirs, which are curious and apparently accurate, were printed after his death.

COLONEL RICHARD NORTON. Of Southwick, near Portsmouth, and Old Alresford, Hants. He was Governor of Basingstoke, and Cromwell's favourite "Dick Norton." He witnessed the Second Fight at

2 K

Newbury only as an amateur, but got so far in assisting Ludlow, who was in danger, that he was wounded. Richard Norton, the grandson of "Dick," was the last heir male of that family, and by his will bequeathed Southwick Park, Hants, and all his other estates, to the amount of £6000 a year, together with personal property of the value of £60,000, to the Parliament of Great Britain, in trust for the use of "the poor, hungry, thirsty, naked strangers, sick, wounded, and prisoners, to the end of the world." The will was, however, set aside; and the estates eventually devolved to the Thistlethwaytes, maternally descended from the Nortons. Charles I. was at Southwick when the Duke of Buckingham was assassinated by Felton at Portsmouth.

LIEUTENANT-COLONEL WHITE. On the 20th Nov., 1651, it was ordered by the House of Commons that the petition of the widow of Lt.-Col. White, "who was slain at the last Newbury fight." be referred to the Committee of the Army: and on the 26th August, 1652, it was resolved that lands of the value of £200 per annum be settled "upon Elizabeth White, late wife of Lieutenant-Colonel Walter White," and her children in full of all demands. Col. White was a member of the Wiltshire family of this name at Grittleton. A Lt.-Col. Walter White, Governor of Bristol Castle, died 3 June, 1643.

COLONEL SIR RICHARD INGOLDSBY. Second son of Sir Richard Ingoldsby, of Lethenborough or Lenborough, Bucks, by Elizabeth, daughter of Sir Oliver Cromwell, of Hinchinbrooke. Col. Ingoldsby was one of the Commissioners of the High Court of Justice for the trial of his Sovereign, and signed the warrant for his execution. He was one of the chief confidants of the Protector; Governor of Oxford Castle, and one of the Lords of the Upper House. When he found the cause of his relative Richard Cromwell desperate, he strenuously exerted himself in promoting the restoration of the exiled King Charles II.; and so effectually recommended himself to his favour, that he not only procured his pardon (being the only one of the regicides who received a free pardon), but was made a Knight of the Bath. He married Anne, daughter of Sir George Cooke, one of the Judges of the Court of King's Bench, and widow of Thomas Lee, Esq., of Hartwell, near Aylesbury. He died in 1685, and was buried at Hartwell.

COLONEL JOHN BIRCH. "In the sphere in which he moved, he was among the remarkable personages of the time; by no means inferior to those whose names are better known, though not more deserving of being recorded. He attained to considerable distinction in the field and in the senate; and, after a long share of personal exertion and sufferings, survived the troubles and dangers of a stormy and eventful struggle, and ended his days in retirement and peace." Preface to the 'Military Memoirs of Col. John Birch,' edited by the Rev. T. W. Webb, M.A., F.R.A.S. See more of him in that work.

CAPT. MASON. In Webb's 'Civil War in Herefordshire,' (1879, vol. ii, p. 106), the following curious particulars are given of the dress of this officer:—"Capt. Mason, who afterwards acted as a sequestrator in Herefordshire, appeared at the Second Battle of Newbury habited in the following officer's uniform—"with a sword about his neck and a black scarfe about his middle, in a black velvett doubleet, and a scarlett paire of breeches laced with two silver laces at the knees, being a Captain." He was supposed to have been there on the side of the King, which he afterwards denied, when it was necessary that he should vindicate his conduct against Parliamentary enquiry.

APPENDIX. 259

CAPT. RICHARD WOLFALL. Of Wolfall, in the parish of Hayton, co. Lancashire. One of the slain in the second battle of Newbury.
CAPT. THOMAS WHITTINGHAM. Of Claughton, co. Lancashire. Also slain at the second battle of Newbury.

## XVI.—HISTORICAL NOTICES OF THE MANOR & CASTLE OF DONNINGTON.

So little is known of the early history of the Manor of Donnington, that it is hoped the following notices may prove an interesting addition to the later annals of its memorable Castle.

1086. *Domesday* shows that William Lovet held, in Berks, Aneborne and Mortune, also Deritone,* in the hundred of Taceham. The third place is that now called Donnington. These places were afterwards held of the Honour of Skipton-in-Craven, Yorkshire.

1166-7.—The next earliest document in which the name of Donnington appears is the Pipe-Roll of the Exchequer, 13 Henry II. (about 1166-7), when, among the names of vills amerced, occurs that of Dunintona, held by Gervas de Sanervilla. which is amerced at half-a-mark. In the account of the aid levied in the following year for marrying the daughter of Henry II., which is found in the Black-Book of the Exchequer,† it is stated that Wm. de Sandrevill holds four knights' fees of the said Honour of Skipton, and Gervas de Sandrevill has a fifth fee, ‡ of which the lord of Skipton could not have the service. From the previous extract, it is clear that this fee is Dunintona; and that even as early as this period the service for it had been alienated from the Honour of Skipton. It is to be remembered that the returns in the Black-Book of the Exchequer do not show the knights holding in different Counties, but those holding of different Honours. Many Honours had fees in several Counties, but the return for the whole is entered under the County in which was the *caput honoris*. There is a Manor still called Sandrevill in the parish of South Moreton, near Wallingford, which Lysons states to have belonged to a family of that name in the reign of Edward I.§

1213. Donnington was in the hands of Gilbert Fitz-Reinfrid in the fifteenth year of King John (1213); and for some unexplained reason, on the 16th Nov. of that year‖ the Sheriff of Berks was directed to transfer it to the custody of Peter Fitz-Herbert, to whom

---

* 'Domesday Book:' Facsimile of the part relating to Berkshire, 1862, p. 11.
† 'Ebor,' p. 22.
‡ For every grant of a certain quantity of land, called a knight's feud, fief, or fee, the grantee was bound to do personal service in the army of the granter or feudal lord, forty days in every year, if called upon. "But," says Blackstone, "this personal attendance growing troublesome in many respects, the tenants found means for compounding for it, by (first) sending others in their stead, and in process of time by making pecuniary satisfaction to the owner in lieu of it. This pecuniary satisfaction came to be levied by assessment, at so much for every knight's fee, under the name of 'scutages.'" It was first levied in 5 Hen. II., 1158, but was abolished by Statute, 12 Car. II. cap. 24. This was the origin of the modern land-tax.
§ 'Magna Britannia; Berkshire,' vol. i. p. 316.  ‖ 'Close Roll,' vol. i. p. 273.

also Philip de Columbar's neighbouring land of Sac (Shaw) was committed.

1216. Gilbert Fitz-Reinfrid returned to his obedience in this year; and his charter, submitting himself to the King, is entered on the Charter-Roll.* One, amongst the things which he had to do, was that he should give the daughter of Richard de Copland as a hostage.

1232. In the sixteenth year of Henry III. there was a final concord between Philip de Sandrevill, Plaintiff, and Richard de Copland and Johanna, his wife, Defendants, for one knight's fee in Donnington, which was allowed by the Plaintiff to be the right of the Defendants and the heirs of Johanna, for which the Defendants gave the Plaintiff 66 marks.

1237. Accordingly, in the 'Testa de Nevill,'† the collectors for the aid for marrying the King's sister account for 1 mark for one knight's fee, which Richard de Cocland held in Donington of the Honour of Wallingford; "Cocland" being either a mistake or misspelling for Copland.

The Honour of Skipton, or a great part of it, passed in the reign of Henry II. to the Earle of Albemarle;‡ and the 'Testa de Nevill'§ shows that Philip de Sandrevill held land of the Earl of Albemarle in South Moreton and Enborne.

These were two of the places held, at the taking of *Domesday*, by William Lovet (see above); but nothing is said of the third (Deritone), the Lordship of which had now passed from the Honour of Skipton. This, combined with the extracts from the 'Pipe-Roll' and the 'Black-Book' of the Exchequer, proves that by "Deritone" the modern *Donnington* is meant.

1243. In the third volume of the 'Monasticon,'‖ Robert, Bishop of Salisbury, is shewn to have confirmed to the Priory of Wallingford the tithes of the demesne of Richard de Coupland, in the vill of Davinton, and also of the mill there. By this, no doubt, Donnington is meant; and for this reason: Shaw, which adjoins Donnington, is not mentioned in the Charter, yet the 'Taxation of Pope Nicholas'¶ shows that the Priory had a pension of 13s. 4d. from Shaw. It is, however, only a confirmation of the grant, which might have been, and probably was, made a hundred years earlier.

It is far from improbable that the Berkshire Coplands were a branch of the Cumberland family of the same name, and of whom there is an Inquisition, 26 Edward I. (1298),** when one Alan was found to be son and heir of a Richard Copland, and 21 years old.

1279. In an "Inquisitio post mortem"†† of this date mention is made of another Richard de Copland; and, by reference to the 'Calendarium Genealogicum,'‡‡ it will be seen that Joanna de Hertrugge, wife of Richard de Copland, was "soror" and "coüterina" of Philip de Hertrugge, that is to say, she was sister by the same mother. Joanna is said to be 40 years of age; she clearly therefore could not be the Joanna mentioned in the fine of A.D. 1232; but that age makes it probable that Richard, her husband was the son of Richard, Defendant in the fine. The next document which will be quoted shows Richard to have held Donnington, and that he died before 1284.

---

\* Ibid, 221, b. † 'Testa de Nevill.' p. 119.
‡ Dugdale's 'Baronage,' vol. i. p. 626.
§ Page 124. ‖ Dugdale's 'Monasticon,' vol. iii. p. 12. (Ed. 1673),
¶ Page 187 b. \*\* 'Calend. Inq. post mortem,' 25 Edw. I., No. 6.
†† 'Cal. Inq. post mort.,' 7 Edw. I., No 28, ‡‡ Page 283.

# APPENDIX. 261

1284. On the 'Assize Roll,' 12th Edward 1.* is a suit in which Alan de Copland seeks from Nigel de Sandrevill, the manor of Donyngton by Shaw, as that in which the Defendant had ingress by intrusion on the death of Richard de Copland, to whom Plaintiff had demised it for life. The Defendant did not defend the suit on its merits, but demurred, pleading he did not hold the whole manor, two other persons holding small portions of it. The Plaintiff could not deny this, and was consequently nonsuited.

1288. It is evident that Alan had eventually got possession of the Manor, for, by a fine, 18 Edward I., between Master Thomas de Badburber, Plaintiff, and Alan de Copland, Defendant, for the Manor of Duninton, Defendant allowed it to be the right of the Plaintiff.

This Plaintiff's name was derived from Adderbury in Oxfordshire, and is spelt, as was that of the place, in many different ways.

1291. Thomas de Abberbury had a grant of free-warren over Donnington and Bradley in the twentieth year of King Edward I. The following is a translation from the original charter:—

"For Master Thomas de Abberbury. The King to his Archbishops, etc. greeting. Know that we have granted and by this our Charter have confirmed to our beloved Master Thomas de Abberbury, that he and his heirs for ever may have free-warren in all his demesne lands of Doninton and Bradelee, Berks, provided however that those lands are not within the bounds of our Forest. So that no one shall enter those lands to hunt in them, or to take in them anything which pertains to the warren, without the license and will of Thomas himself or his heirs, under forfeiture to us of £10. Witnesses—the Venerable Father Robert, Bishop of Bath and Wells; John de Vescy; Guy Ferre; etc. Dated at Wigton, the eleventh of September, 1221." †

1299. In an "Inquisitio post mortem" ‡ concerning the lands of Edmund, Earl of Cornwall, of this date, mention is made of Donington among the rents and fees appertaining to the Honour of Wallingford, which confirms the opinion already expressed.

1306-7. The Inquisition upon Thomas de Abberbury furnishes us with a description of the Manor at this time. It is as follows:—§

Possessions of Master Thomas de Abbresbury, Dynynton, Berks. "Extent," dated 23 May, 35 Edward I.:—

Manor held in chief of the King of the Honour of Wallingford by service of half a knight's fee. A capital messuage with garden worth 6s. 8d. a year; 120 acres of arable land, 30s.; 50 acres of worse land, 4s. 2d.; 2½ acres of meadow, 3s. 9d.; 3 acres of pasture, 3s. 6d.; sheep pasture, 12d.; wood, 2s.; two water-mills, 40s. At Miggham 3 acres meadow, held of the Prior of Sandelford, 3s. Water-mill there, held of the Prior, 30s. 2 acres of meadow in la Wydmede, held of the Abbot of Reading, 2s.

| | | | |
|---|---|---|---|
| Two free tenants | | | 11d. |
| Villani | Total of their rente | 27s. | 3¼d. |
| | ,, their work | 27s. | 10¾d. |
| | Tallage | 18s. | 10¼d. |
| Cotarii | Rents | 12s. | 10½d. |
| | Work | 2s. | 6d. |

Profits of Court 12d.

---

* Berks, m. 6.  † 'Charter Roll,' 20 Edw. I., No. 8.
‡ 'Cal. Inq. post mort.,' 20 Edw. I., No. 44 (26 and 52).
§ 'Cal. Inq. post mort.,' 35 Edw. I., No. 44, translated.

Walter de Abbresbury, brother of Thomas, is next heir; 30 years of age and more.
22s. to be paid to the Prior of Sandleford by Miggham Mill.

Held also lands in Steple-Aston Manor } Oxon.
Sulthorne Manor

,, Migham } Berks.
Eneburne

1323. Of Walter, brother of Sir Thomas Abberbury, we are enabled to obtain little information; but in this year (1323), in conjunction with his son Richard, he granted certain lands in the parish of Abberbury to the Cathedral Church of Winchester.*

It is stated by Grose, in his 'Antiquities af Berks' (p. 5), that Walter Abberbury gave the King (Edward II,) 100s. for the Castle.† It was thought by the late Mr. Henry Godwin, F.S.A., that the license to build, given by the succeeding King (see further on), indicated that the new structure was a re-edification of a former building; and this doubtless was the case, since we see by the Inquisition of 1306-7, that "a capital messuage" was then attached to the Manor.

1385-86. At this time (9th Richard II.) the Manor was in the hands of Sir Richard de Abberbury, who had been guardian to the King in his minority, and had obtained the license to build anew and crenellate his castle at Donnington. The license is expressed in these terms:—

"The King to all his bailiffs and faithful subjects, to whom, etc. greeting. Know that of our special grace we have granted and given license for ourselves and our heirs, as much as in us lies, to our beloved and faithful Richard Abberbury the elder, that he may build anew and fortify with stone and lime, and crenellate a certain Castle on his own land at Donyngton, Berks; and may hold that castle so built, fortified, and crenellated, to him and his heirs for ever, without disturbance or hindrance by us or our heirs, justices, escheators, sheriffs, or other bailiffs or officers of ours whatever. In testimony of which, etc." This instrument was acknowledged by the King himself at his Manor of Henley, 11th June, 1385.‡

1397. It cannot be determined with certainty in what year' Sir Richard de Abberbury the elder died, as the Inquisition taken after his death is not to be found at the Record Office. It may, however, be inferred that he was living in 1397, for he had a son of the same name, to whom, by the description of Mons. Ric. Abberbury le fils, § John of Gaunt, by his will, dated 3rd February, 1397, bequeathed a legacy of 50 marks.

There is some difficulty, owing to the similarity of christian names, in identifying the various members of this family; but we have evidence of the existence of a Richard de Abberbury, the younger, as late as the twelfth year of Henry VI., 1433, when the name occurs in the list of Berkshire Gentry returned by the King's Commissioners.

---

* 'Patent,' 17 Edw. II., p. 1, m, 23.
† Grose took his authority for this from Urry's 'Life of Chaucer,' published about 1726. In 1731 the fire took place at Ashburnham House where the Cotton MSS. were kept, and it is very probable that the original document from which Urry derived his information was destroyed at that time.
‡ 'Rot. Pat.' 9 Ric. II., pt. 2, m. 7.
§ 'Donnington Castle,' by H. Godwin, Esq., F.S.A. 'Archæologia,' vol. xliv; and 'Trans. Newbury D. Field Club,' vol. ii.

He represented this County in the Parliaments of 17 and 20 Richard II. Alice, the wife of this Sir Richard de Abberbury, junior, was the only daughter and heiress of John Cleet, Knight of the Shire for Berks in the Parliament of 36 Edward III. Her first husband was Edmund Danvers.

1400. It has been asserted that the Castle and Estate of Donnington belonged to Geoffrey Chaucer, the poet, whose death is recorded to have taken place on Oct. 25th in this year; but there is no evidence to show that it was alienated by Sir Richard Abberbury during the poet's life-time. A deed-poll of Thomas Danvers, son of Alice, Lady Abberbury, by her first husband, Edmund Danvers, is dated at Donyngton, 1414, 2 Hen. V., which seems to imply that it still continued to be their residence.*

Our researches are assisted at this point by several important documents, some of which are printed *in extenso* in the late Mr. Godwin's paper on Donnington Castle in the 'Archæologia,' and in the second volume of 'Transactions of the Newbury District Field Club.'

1414-15. From a Fine dated the second year of Henry V., between Thomas Chaucer, Edward Hampden, John Golofre,† and William Beck (Plaintiffs), and Richard Abberbury, knight, and Alice his wife (Deforciants), of the Manor and Castle of Donnington, we ascertain that the said Richard Abberbury and Alice his wife conveyed to Thomas Chaucer and his Trustees the Manor and Castle of Donnington for 1000 marks of silver.‡

By a Fine of a shortly subsequent date, Edward Hampden, John Golofre, and William Beck granted to John Phelip and Alice his wife, for the like consideration (1000 marks of silver), the said Manor and Castle of Donnington, to them and their heirs for ever. In the event of Phelip and Alice dying without heirs, remainder to Thomas Chaucer and his heirs.§

At an "Inquisitio post mortem," taken at Wallingford, 21st October, 1415, on the Monday after the feast of St. Luke, as to the estates of which Sir John Phelip died seized, the Jury say that Edward Hampden, John Golofre, and William Beck (now deceased) were seized of the Manor and Castle of Donnington, and of one croft, one carucate, called Meredene, &c., and that they had given and granted the same to Sir John Phelip and Alice his wife and their heirs.‖

It appears from a Fine, dated Hilary term in the third year of Henry V., made between Thomas, Earl of Dorset, Hugh Mortemer, Will. Hankeford, knt., Thomas de Stonore, Henr. Somer, Rich. Wyot, Henr. Aston, John Warefeld, and Geoffry Prentys, clerk (Plaintiffs), and Thomas Chaucer (Deforciant), of the Manor and Castle of Donnington, that Alice Chaucer, the wife of John Phelip, knt., held the same for the term of her life, and that it ought to revert to Thomas Chaucer on the death of his daughter Alice. The effect of

---

\* Clarke's 'Hundred of Wanting,' p. 88.
† There were two John Golofres living at the same time. One, a Knight who married Philippa Mohun in 1389, and died before 2 Hen. V. (1414-15), when his relict married Edward, Duke of York. Another John Golofre died, seized of the manor of Fyfield, in 1433. In the late Mr. Godwin's article on Donnington Castle, these two persons appear to have been confounded. It is there said that John de la Pole, Earl of Lincoln, married the daughter of Sir John Golofre. No authority is given; but, as Lysons says the same, the statement was probably taken from him. The Inquisition on John Golofre shows this, however, to be erroneous.
‡ 'Pedes Finium,' 2 Hen. V., No. 3, co. Berks.
§ 'Pedes Finium,' 3 Hen. V., No. 2, co. Berks.
‖ 'Cal. Inq. post Mort,' 3 Hen. V., No. 42.

this document would evidently be a conveyance in trust. The remainder is conveyed to the Earl of Dorset and others for ever.*

Alice, the only child and heiress of Thomas Chaucer and Matilda his wife, daughter of Sir John de Burghersh, was born in 1404; and, according to the frequent practice then prevalent, was married in her childhood to Sir John Phelip, Knight; the object of these early marriages being to secure the property of the heiress as soon as possible, and to provide against escheats.

Sir John Phelip and Sir William Phelip, Knight of the Garter, who in right of his wife was Lord Bardolph, were brothers. Their mother was Juliana, daughter of Sir Robert Erpingham, of Erpingham, in the County of Norfolk. It is shown by the Inquisition taken shortly after his death, that Sir John Phelip died on the 9th October, 1415; and that he had attained the age of thirty-one years. His brother, Sir William Phelip, took a distinguished part in the French wars of Henry V, participated in the triumph of Agincourt, and was subsequently present at the storming of the Castle of Caen, and at the protracted siege of Rouen.

The exact degree of relationship between Thomas Chaucer and the Poet has yet to be discovered, and, as no fresh evidence has been advanced on the subject, it is not necessary to enter at length into this long-disputed controversy.

The following chronological notes, however, resulting from some recent researches, may be submitted to the consideration of those pursuing the enquiry.

Sir Payn Roet, knt., *alias* Guyn King-of-Arms, a knight of Hainault, had two daughters—

1.—Philippa, married to Geoffrey Chaucer.†
2.—Katherine, wife of Hugh Swinford, knt., and mistress, (afterwards wife) of John, Duke of Lancaster. She died 10 May, 1403, and was buried at Lincoln (of which See her son Henry was Bishop).

The children of Katherine by the Duke were (besides others)—

1 —John de Beaufort, a knight in 15 Rich. II., (1391-2), and created Earl of Somerset 20 Rich. II., (1396-7): died 1409, leaving his son Henry 9 years old.
2.—Henry, made Bishop of Lincoln in 1397, and of Winchester in 1405: died 11 April, 1447, aged 80. It is needless to mention others.

If this be correct Henry was born in 1367, and John, therefore at least in 1366.

Geoffrey Chaucer is said to have died in 1399 or 1400, that is, three or four years earlier than his wife's sister.

In the fasimile of National MSS., Part 1. ('Athenæum,' 13 Jany. 1866), is a letter to Henry IV., from Henry, Prince of Wales, dated 1402 (and which cannot be before that year, as it speaks of the marriage of Henry IV. and Joanna of Navarre), wherein he says:— "As I trust to God your humble leige-man, my cousin Chaucer, hath plainly informed your Highness at this time."

If there be no good evidence to prove that Geoffrey Chaucer died

---

* 'Pedes Finium,' 3 Hen. V., No. 1, co. Berks.

† The evidence on the 'Issue Rolls' tends to prove that Chaucer married a namesake or cousin. The earliest payments of Philippa's pension (presumably *before* her marriage) were received by her as Philippa *Chaucer*, but the later payments were received by Geoffrey for her, who is *then* described as her husband.

APPENDIX. 265

before 1402, this letter shows that he must have left male issue by the sister of Katherine Roet, since no other Chaucer but such issue would have been of kin to the Prince.

Thomas Chaucer died 13 Henry VI., on the Thursday after St. Edmund (20 Nov.), 1434, leaving Alice, daughter and heiress, aged 30. We may suppose that Thomas Chaucer had married about 1400; and he could not have been married more than two or three years earlier than that. If this be so, and if he were son of Geoffrey, and about the age of his first-cousin John Beaufort, he was 34 years old when he married. Instead of this, may not Thomas have been the grandson of Geoffrey? and, if so, who was his father?

Alice (daughter and heir of Sir Thomas and Lady Chaucer) soon after the death of Sir John Phelip married Thomas de Montacute, Earl of Salisbury, who was soon afterwards killed in the memorable siege of Orleans. The Earl was succeeded in the command of the English troops before that city by William de la Pole, Earl of Suffolk, who was forced by Joan of Arc to raise the siege, and was taken prisoner. He contrived, however, to escape to England, and married Alice (Chaucer), the widow of his comrade in arms, "The brave Earl of Salisbury." After enjoying great favour at Court, he was charged with treason, and beheaded at sea in 1450. The story of his death is a mournful episode in English history, and has been often told.

Alice (Chaucer) survived her last husband many years; and, dying in 1475, was buried near her parents in Ewelme Church. The altar-tomb bearing her effigy "is hardly surpassed in beauty," says Skelton, "and certainly not in the extreme excellence of its preservation, by any monument in England." It is one of the three known examples of female effigies decorated with the Order of the Garter. It is figured in Gough's 'Sepulchral Monuments.'

John de la Pole, son of Alice (Chaucer) and William, Duke of Suffolk, was confirmed in his father's estates and honours in 1463, and held the Manor and Castle of Donnington. He married Elizabeth Plantagenet, sister of Edward IV.; and died in 1491. John de la Pole and Elizabeth lie buried in Wingfield Church, in Suffolk, where, in the chancel, there is a large altar-tomb with effigies of herself and husband. Their arms are in a window of the south aisle of Iffley Church.*

John, Earl of Lincoln, eldest son of John de la Pole, by his wife Elizabeth Plantagenet, and consequently nephew to Edward IV., being engaged in the conspiracy to raise the impostor Lambert Simnel to the crown, fell at the battle of Stoke, in 1487, in the life-time of his father. In the first year of Richard III., 1485, he had obtained a grant of the manor of Woodhay, and of the Lordships of Basingstoke and Andover; but he being attained, his next brother Edmund succeeded to his father's titles and estates.

Edmund de la Pole, the last in lawful succession to the dukedom of Suffolk, was deprived of his title by attainder, and his honours were forfeited to the Crown. He was beheaded on the Eve of the Ascension in 1513, and left no male issue. His other brother Richard de la Pole, called the "White Rose," was afterwards slain, fighting in the French army, at the battle of Pavia in 1528.

In February of 1514, Charles Brandon, Viscount L'Isle, the friend of Henry VIII. from youth, was created Duke of Suffolk, in tail-male, and received from the King a grant of the Castle, Park, and Manor

---

* E. Marshall's 'Account of Iffley,' pp. 102, 3, Oxf. 1870.

2 L

of Donnington, Berks, being part of the possessions of Edmund de la Pole, late Duke of Suffolk, attainted.*

Charles Brandon, Duke of Suffolk, was Henry's chief favourite, and had married secretly, Mary, the King's sister, and widow of Louis XII. In contracting this union without the permission of Henry VIII., both parties exposed themselves to the risk of his serious displeasure, which, to Suffolk, as his own subject, might have proved fatal. But the French dowager-queen and her English husband crossed the Channel and took up their abode in their Manor in Suffolk, without venturing near the Court. A reconciliation was in a short time effected; the accomplishment of which was greatly owing to the good offices of Cardinal Wolsey, who appears to have been a staunch friend to the young couple.

In a letter from the Queen-dowager of France, to Henry VIII,, dated Letheryngham, Suffolk, 9th September, 1515, she thanks him for permitting 'my lord,' her husband, to repair to him on his coming to Donyngton, which had greatly comforted him. Had the time been convenient, she would gladly have accompanied her husband in this journey, but hopes they will both see his grace, as he wrote in his last letters, 'which is the thing that I desire more to obtain than all the honour of the world.' Desires to be remembered to her sister the Queen, and the Queen of Scots, and hopes to hear of the prosperous estate of her niece the Princess.†

Frances Brandon, Duchess of Suffolk, the eldest of the two surviving daughters of Charles Brandon by this marriage, on whose issue the Crown was settled by the will of Henry VIII., ended in prison a life, which for variety of wretchedness has had few parallels. She had seen her daughter, Lady Jane Grey, beheaded: her own and her daughter's husband had shared the same fate: her daughter Catherine, after having been repudiated by the Earl of Pembroke, was imprisoned in the Tower: and her youngest daughter Mary was most unequally matched to an inferior officer of the household.

The Duke of Suffolk, it appears from several letters addressed to Wolsey, from Donnington, and preserved among the State Papers, frequently resided at the Castle. Symonds, in his 'Diary,' mentions that the following quarterings were to be seen in many of the windows of the Castle in 1644:

Quarterly, 1 and 4, Barry of ten argent and gules, over all a lion rampant or, crowned per pale gules and argent [Brandon]; 2 and 3, Quarterly; 1 and 4, Azure, a cross moline or [Bruin]; 2 and 3, Lozengy, gules and ermine [Rokesley], The whole within the garter, and surmounted by a coronet or [Brandon, Duke of Suffolk].

As also this impaling;

France; impaling, quarterly France and England; the whole surmounted by a crown [Louis XII. and Mary Tudor].

Divors lyons heads also, and this motto very often: LOIAVLTE OUBLIGE. [Crest and Motto of Brandon.]‡

1535. By an Act, 37th Henry VIII. cap. 38, an exchange of lands was confirmed between the King and Charles, Duke of Suffolk; and by an Indenture bearing date 19 July of the same year, made

---

* 'Pat.' 5 Hen. VIII, pt ii m. 28.
† 'Cal. State Papers,' Hen VIII. vol, ii., pt. 1, No, 2347.
‡ Symonds 'Diary of the Marches of the Royal Army;' ed. by C. E. Long, M.A., p. 145.

between the Right Honourable Thomas Audeley, knight, Chancellor of England, Thomas Cromwell, Esquire, Chief Secretary to the King and Master of the Rolls, Sir Bryan Tuke, knight, Treasurer of the Chamber, Christopher Hales, Attorney-General, and Richard Ryche, Solicitor-General to the King, on the one part, and the Right Noble Charles, Duke of Suffolk, on the other part, the same Duke bargained and sold, &c., the Manors, Castles, and Lordships of Ewelme, Donyngton, Langley, West Bradley, West Compton, and Buckland, in the County of Berks, together with other Manors in the County of Oxford, the Manor-house and place of Southwerke, commonly called the Duke of Suffolk's Place, in the County of Surrey, with all Houses, &c., and the Park there, and also the offices of the High-Stewardship and Constableship of the Castle of Walyngford, Berks, in exchange for the reversion of the fee-simple of the Manors of Philberdes (otherwise called Phelbartes), Long Wittenham, Fiffed, Eton, Frydysham (otherwise called Freleford), and Gartford, in the Counties of Berks and Oxon, the reversion belonging to and the Manors of Southwolde, Dysenage, and others in the County of Suffolk.

Donnington Castle was thus again acquired by the Crown; and Thomas Cromwell, writing to Sir Richard Rich, Solicitor-General to the King, from Tewkesbury Monastery, July 29th, 1535, states that he is ordered by the King to reply to Rich's letter respecting this transaction with the Duke of Suffolk, as follows:—As to the leases, which, it was supposed, were made by the Duke of Suffolk, the King says he does not know that the Duke or his officers had made any lease since the conclusion between them of this bargain. As he is informed that the Duke or his officers have offered to make leases since that time, he considers this to be unkindness and ingratitude in the Duke, if it can be proved. Touching the decay of Ewelme and Donnington, the King answered that, whatever the Duke has spent upon them, it will appear in what decay they stand; whoever views them will easily perceive that good sums of money will not easily repair them. The King himself hath viewed Ewelme when lately there, and for Donnington the house is not only in decay, but also the keeper of the same, Mr. Fettyplace, hath both consumed and destroyed the deer and game there, and also wasted the woods in such wise as it is thought he hath not only forfeited his patent, but also right ill-deserved to have either fee or thanks for any good service he hath done there.*

1547. Charles Brandon, Duke of Suffolk, died in 1545. Upon the death of Henry VIII., in 1547, the Castle passed to his son Edward VI., who in the fourth year of his reign (1550), in fulfilment of the will of his father, the late king, and with the advice of his Council, granted by Letters Patent to his sister, Lady Elizabeth, various lands in several Counties, including the lordship and manor of Donyngton, with all the deer and beasts in the park, and the liberty of park within the said park, the Castle of Donyngton, Berks, with all rights and appurtenances, the whole town of Newbury, with all appurtenances, formerly parcel of the lands and possessions of the jointure of Lady Johanna, Queen of England [Lady Jane Seymour], the Manor of Hamstead-Marshall, etc., the whole being of the yearly value of £3106 13s. 1½d. To be held by a yearly rent of £106 0 1½, to be paid to the Court of Augmentations, or until the Councillors named in King Henry's Will shall arrange a marriage for her, in accordance with the said will.†

---

* 'Miscellaneous Letters,' Series III, vol ii., No. 96. Public Record Office.
† 'Pat.' 4 Edw. VI., pt. 3, m. 25.

1551. The above-mentioned Letters Patent were surrendered on 23rd April of the following year (1551) by the Lady Elizabeth personally appearing before the King in his Court of Chancery; and the enrolment was accordingly cancelled. On this surrender, another grant was made to the Princess in substitution of the former grant, including, with other lands mentioned in the previous grant the Lordship and Manor of Donnington, the Castle of Donnington, and the Manor of Newbury—the annual value of the whole being estimated at £3064 17 8½. To be held at a rent of £109 13 7, for life, or until marriage, as before.*

1600. On the 15th of May, in the forty-second year of Queen Elizabeth, a grant of the Castle and Manor of Donnington was nominally made to Nicholas Zouche, and Thomas Hare, Esquires, and their heirs, nominees of Charles, Earl of Nottingham, Baron Howard of Effingham, to protect it against escheat. In the following year, the said Nicholas Zouche, Esq., and Elizabeth his wife obtained license to alienate to the said Charles, Earl of Nottingham, and Catherine his wife, and the heirs of the said Earl, the Castle and Manor of Donnington, Winterborne-Davers (alias Winterborne-Danvers), Winterborne-Mayne. Leckhampstede, the Park of Donnington, and 40 messuages, 40 gardens, 20 tofts,† 4 water-mills, 3 dovecotes, 40 orchards, 1000 acres of arable land, 100 acres of meadow, 500 acres of pasture, 300 acres of wood, 300 acres of gorse, 100s. of rent, free warren, view of frankpledge in the town aforesaid, Bussock Courte, Speene mores, Uplamborne (alias Lamborne), Northcroft, Horspoole-Furlonge,‡ Newbury, Shaw, Thatcham, Henwyke, Spynamlande, Shawborne, and other places, together with the presentation and free disposal of the Hospital of Donnington, and all tithes and oblations in Donnington, Newbery, Speene, Winterborne-Davers, and Winterborne-Mayne, and the Advowson of the Church of Newbury, co. Berks, the Borough of New Lymington, and the Manor of Old Lymington and New Lymington, with other lands in the Counties of Southampton and Surrey. All these were to be holden by the grantees as follows:—With the exception of the lands in Southampton, to the use of the said Earl and Catherine his wife for their lives; with remainder to William Howard, son and heir apparent of said Earl, and his heirs male; remainder to Charles Howard, Esq., son and heir of William Howard, knt., brother of said Earl deceased, and heirs male; with remainder to Francis Howard Esq., second son of the said Sir William Howard, knt., deceased, and heirs male; with remainder to the right heirs of said Earl for ever. Worth £40. Fine on alienation £13 6 8. *Note in the Margin:*—"The cause of this small rate was for yt my Lo. purchased these lands in other men's names upon trust, and, all these dyinge but one, was forced to take ye same back from ye Survivor and his wiffe, as well for barringe of dower of ye wiffe of him that had yt in trust, as also for my Lo. his further securyty." §

1603. Sir Thomas Edmonds, in a letter to the Earl of Shrewsbury, dated Woodstock, Sept. 11, 1603, ‖ says, "I suppose your Lordship is

---

* 'Pat.' 5, Edw. VI., pt. 4, m. 11.
† Toft: a messuage or house, or rather a place where a messuage once stood, that is fallen or pulled down.—*Bailey.*
‡ A meadow belonging to Donnington Priory is still known by this name. The word "furlong" occurs often in the names of fields in Beds and Bucks.
§ Alienation Office: 'Entries of Licenses and Pardons,' v. 7, p. 313 d.
‖ 'Memoirs of the Peers of England during the reign of James I.,' by Sir Egerton Brydges; p. 171.

no less entertained with the pleasures of your hunting than we are here; so as you do not expect to hear any novelties from us during this time. Since the time that your Lordship left us, we have wholly spent our time in that exercise; but the Queen [Anne, of Denmark] remained at Basing till the King's coming hither, and she hath as well entertained herself with good dancing, which hath brought forth the effects of a marriage between my Lord Admiral [The Earl of Nottingham] and the Lady Mary Stuart. His Lordship, in his passage hither by the way of Newbury, hath recovered the possession of Donnington Castle from the Lady Russell,* she being absent in Wales with her daughter the Lady Herbert."†

This letter is also printed in Nichols' "Progresses of James I." In what way Lady Russell became interested in Donnington Castle is at present unknown; and, as Mr. Nichols remarks, we are not likely to gain further information as to the dispute than this letter gives us.

1615. In this year another dispute arose as to the ownership of the Castle and Manor, which at this time were in the hands of Lady Anne, widow of William, Lord Howard of Effingham. Being summoned to show by what title she entered upon and held the said Castle, &c., she stated that William, Lord Howard, was seized of the Castle and Manor of Donnington, &c., in demesne as of fee, &c.; and, being so seized, by Indenture, dated 10 October, 13 James I., between William, Lord Howard, of the one part, and Peter Vanlore, of the other part, he (William), bargained and sold to Peter Vanlore the said lands, &c., by which means Peter Vanlore became possessed of the same, but without having first obtained the King's license. (King James, however, by Letters Patent, dated 13 May, 14 James I., pardoned this alienation.)

She said further, that Peter Vanlore, senior, being thus seized, the King by Letters Patent, dated 1 April, 14 James I., gave license to Peter Vanlore, senior, to alienate the Castle and Manor of Donnington, &c., to Anne, Lady Howard, widow, late the wife of William, Lord Howard, of Effingham, for life; with remainder to Elizabeth, daughter and heir of William, and to the heirs of Elizabeth, and in default of such heirs to the right heirs of Anne.

Whereupon a fine was levied at Westminster in Trinity Term, 14 James I., between Anne, Lady Howard, Plaintiff, and Peter Vanlore, senior, Deforciant, of the Castle and Manor of Donnington, &c., which Peter Vanlore conveyed to Anne, as appears by an Indenture, dated 30 March, 14 James I., made between Peter Vanlore, senior, of London, Esq., of the one part, and Anne, Lady Howard of Effingham, late wife and sole-executrix of William, Lord Howard of Effingham, of the other part. By virtue whereof, Anne had entered upon and hitherto was seized in demesne as of free tenement for life. Judgment was therefore given in favour of Anne.

This Roll‡ contains a long list of places besides Donnington. It includes the Park of Donnington, also a meadow called Lorde's Meade, *alias* Horsemead, in Donnington, also two water-mills at Donnington, also a messuage near the bridge of Newbury between the tenement of Ralph Gunter, on the north part, and the Church Lane, leading to the Mill, on the south part, and extending in length from the High Street on the east part to the "Almes" on the west

---
* Elizabeth, daughter of Sir Anthony Cooke, and widow of John, Lord Russell, second son of Francis, Earl of Bedford.
† Wife of Henry, Lord Herbert, son of the Earl of Worcester.
‡ 'Memoranda Roll' (Lord-Treasurer's Remembrancer), Hilary, 14 James I., Roll, 205.

part, then or lately in the tenure or occupation of Catherine Lichpole and John Lichpole, otherwise Chaundeler, or their assigns, or the assigns of one of them. All the places mentioned passed under the conveyance here set out.

The two water-mills at Donnington are contiguous; and until recently they have been held by two different owners; one mill belonging to the Castle estate, the other to Mrs. Parry, whose family at one time were the proprietors of the adjacent Priory.

The messuage in Newbury comprised the premises well known in later years as the "Globe Inn," which before the dissolution of the Monasteries formed part of the possessions of the Priory of Wherwell, Hants.

William, Lord Howard of Effingham, who was summoned by writ to several Parliaments during his father's life, married Anne, daughter and sole heir of Lord St.-John, of Bletsoe. He died before his father, in 1615, and was buried at Chelsea, leaving Elizabeth, his only daughter and sole heir, who became the wife of John, Lord Mordaunt, afterwards Earl of Peterborough. Charles Howard, Earl of Effingham, the Lord High Admiral (which office, Fuller says, he resigned to the Duke of Buckingham, in the reign of James I), died at Haling House, Surrey, December 14, 1624; and was buried in the family vault in the chancel of Reigate Church.* He was succeeded in the title by Charles, his son by his first wife, Katherine Cary.

Lady Anne Howard died in June, 1638; and was buried in Westminster Abbey. In the letters of administration granted to her only child, Elizabeth, Countess of Peterborough, 20th of June, 1683, she is described as of Hawnes, Co. Beds; but she died in the parish of St. Bartholomew the Great in London.

Sir Peter Vanlore, above-mentioned, was a rich merchant, born at Utretch. He died in 1627; and in Tylehurst Church, near Reading, there is an elaborate and curious Jacobian monument to Sir Peter and his lady, with a long eulogistic inscription, commencing with the following lines:—

"When thou hast read the name, here lies Vanlore,
Thou need'st no story to inform thee more."

Further on, however, we learn, that Sir Peter was an industrious merchant, beloved by three English Monarchs; and that he died very rich, having lived four-score years—

"The greatest part in one chaste wedlock spent;
Utrecht his cradle—Tylehurst loves his tomb."

Sir Peter is supposed to have had a temporary interest in the Manor of Tylehurst by alliance with the Kendricks.

1623-44. John Chamberlayne is described in the Rolls of the College of Arms for 1623, as of "Donnington Castle," Berks;† and Symonds, the writer of the 'Diary of the Marches of the Royal Army,' informs us that the Castle in 1644 was "the habitacion of Mr. Packer, who bought it of Mr. Chamberlayne." A diligent search at the Record Office has failed to find a license given to Anne Howard to alienate, or a transfer to Chamberlayne; but this is no reason for doubting Symonds's statement. There is a John Chamberlayne described as of Sherborne, Co. Oxon ('Close Roll,' 22 James I., p. 16, m. 5); and

---

* 'Worthies,' Surrey, pp. 83, 84.
† 'Transactions of the Newbury District Field Club,' vol, ii, p. 39.

# APPENDIX. 271

another John Chamberlayne, as of Beaulieu, Co. Southampton ('Close Roll,' 19 James I., p. 11, m. 7). The latter is most probably the person who was for a short time the owner of the Castle. *

At the commencement of the Civil War, the Castle was unquestionably the property of John Packer, Esq., and in his hands when it was garrisoned for the King. Mr. Packer was born at Twickenham, Middlesex, about 1572, and appears to have been in public employment (at one time in the Signet Office); and to have been of considerable social distinction. A letter, dated 17 January, 1610, addressed by him to Sir Thomas Edmonds, Ambassador at the Court of Brussels, will be found in the "Court and Times of James the First;" 1848, vol. i. p. 104: and Camden, in his 'Annals,' states that the Marquis of Buckingham, Baron Haye, and the Countess of Dorset were sponsors at the baptism of one of Mr. Packer's children, in Westminster Church, 24 June, 1618. He acted as Secretary to George Villiers, first Duke of Buckingham, and a collection of letters relating to State Affairs, collected by him, and known as the "Fortescue Papers" was published by the Camden Society in 1871. A number of other important State Letters and MSS. were discovered amongst the Packer papers at Bucklebury in 1881. He was buried at St. Margaret's, Westminster, 15 February, 1649.

His will, dated 20th July, 1645, with a codicil, dated 2nd May, 1648, was proved, 27 Nov., 1649, by his relict Philippa. He was residing in a house within the College of Westminster, but described himself as of Shellingford, Co. Berks, Esq.; and stated that his lands had been sequestered by the King's forces, excepting the Manor of Groombridge (in Speldhurst), Kent, where he had built a chapel, and which he bequeathed to one of his sons, who still held it in 1696. He had married Philippa Mills, of the city of Westminster, gentlewoman, daughter of Francis Mills, Esq., of Southampton.† In a letter dated 12th Dec., 1604, written by John Packer to Sir Ralph Winwood, he speaks of his "good friend" Sir Thomas Lake (Principal Secretary of State to James I.), who first procured him the reversion to the Privy Seal; and he mentions that he is "now at the Court." Sir Dudley Carleton, writing to Sir Ralph Winwood in 1610, refers to Mr. Packer as having been sent as Envoy to Denmark, and alludes to " John Chamberlaine," with whom Mr. Packer was, it seems, familiar.

In 1647, 23 Charles I., John Packer, of Donnington Castle, was one of the Committee appointed by an ordinance of the Parliament for the "Visitation and Reformation of the University of Oxford." His sons, Robert and Philip, were members of University College, and subscribers to the new works at that College about 1675 ; and in one of the windows of the Hall are inserted the arms of the Packers— Gules, a cross lozengy, between four roses argent. Their brother, William, was one of the "Tryers for Approbation of Public Preachers" in 1653. The residence of the Packers at Shellingford, about two miles to the north-east of Faringdon, was an ancient stone building, called '·Shellingford Castle." It remained unoccupied many years, and was at last taken down. A few outbuildings, a large walled garden and some aged yew-trees, surrounding a fish-pond, are now all that remain to indicate the dwelling-place of this once important family. Mr. Robert Packer, M.P. for Wallingford in the Long

* We may also mention that a John Chamberlayne had been Mayor of Newbury in 1601 ; and that this name frequently occurs in the town records about this period.
† See note to the baptism of Mr. Packer's daughter, in Chester's ' Westminster Abbey Registers,' p. 66.

Parliament, and who died in 1684, appears to have been among those members, some of whom were imprisoned or secluded, and others seized by the army on the 6th December, 1648, for having voted the day previously, "That the King's answers to the proposition of both Houses were a ground for peace."

After the Civil War was over, Mr. John Packer had some of the ruinous parts of the battered Castle taken down; and with part of the materials was erected the mansion now standing near it, and called "Donnington-Castle House."

## XVII.—DESCRIPTION OF DONNINGTON CASTLE.

At an altitude of 403 feet above the level of the sea, and overlooking the wooded vales of the Kennet and Lambourn, which meet below, amidst green meadows and cultivated fields a little east of the ancient town of Newbury, stand the historic ruins of Donnington Castle. On the southern verge of the Snelsmore plateau, which stretches away northward, the noble old gate-house, still perfect on its eastern front, is a prominent landmark, though partly hidden by venerable elms, which now shade the war-worn slopes, where trench and rampart once aided in the defence of this famous stronghold.

From the battlemented roof of the gatehouse can be seen a panorama of wide extent and picturesque beauty. Bounded by hills on several sides, the landscape embraces many ancient, and probably pre-historic, marks of human habitation, warfare, and sepulture. On the Chalk range to the South, the great earth-walled camps of Ladle Hill and Beacon Hill bear such evidences; and Walbury is another similar indication of efforts to preserve tribal, if not national existence. Borough Hill, Bussock, Oare-borough, and Grimsbury, on spurs and elevations north of the Castle, attest similar, and perhaps contemporary life among the invaded and the invaders. Near by, on lower ground, to the West, between the Kennet and the Lambourn, but at some distance above their confluence, the earthwork enclosing the site of Roman Spinæ is traceable; but the somewhat later Romano-British cemetery in the further suburb of Newbury is obscured by modern buildings. It is possible that Donnington Hill itself was the site of an earlier stronghold, of pre-historic date; and its mediæval castle the survival or representative of the *oldest* local fastness.

The scenes of many later doings of historic interest lie amongst the heaths and wooded valleys in the southern distance. Away on the Hampshire Hills to the South-east, and overlooking Kingsclere, in its peculiar retired valley picturesquely enclosed by an ellipse of low chalk hills, may be seen a weather-beaten clump of trees, marking the site of Freemantle Park, the favourite Hunting-lodge of the early Norman and Plantagenet Sovereigns, and especially of King John. This is known also as Cottington Hill, having belonged to Francis, Lord Cottington, Lord-Treasurer and Master of the Wards under King Charles I. During the Commonwealth it was granted to Bradshaw, "President of the High Court of Justice," but restored to the Cottingtons at the Restoration.

# APPENDIX.

To the right hand at the foot of the Downs, stands the old Manor-house of West Woodhay (incorporated in a modern building), erected by Rudyerd, the Cromwellian statesman, a thoroughly honourable and upright politician; and there he ended his days with that peace which he had vainly endeavoured to procure for his distracted country. Further, in the western distance is Chilton-Foliot, where Bulstrode Whitelock, the confidential Secretary of Cromwell, wearied with the toil of ambition, retired shortly before the Restoration, and contentedly occupied his leisure hours in compiling the "Memorials" of those "Affairs" in which he had himself so conspicuously figured.

Nearer to Newbury are the Commons of Greenham and the Wash, where Lord Essex and his determined soldiers fought their way successfully towards London, in spite of the gallant but misdirected energy of the too impetuous cavaliers.

Many a midnight march and bold assault woke the hillsides and country lanes, and blocked the streets of the old town, when Rupert's dare-devil squadrons broke in on the steady tramp of the "trained-bands" armed for Parliament. Numbers of the dead of both sides, slain in the "First Battle of Newbury," lie buried in heaps on the Wash, or here and there in quiet church-yards, at Newbury and the surrounding villages.

From right to left below Donnington Castle flows the Lambourn, through the village of Donnington, with its old mill, ancient *Maison Dieu*, and Priory. In the neighbouring parks are many pleasant houses; and chief of these is "Shaw House," close to the church which occupies the place of its picturesque predecessor, on the site of Saxon if not British occupation, as shown by relics of both these periods which have been discovered in the churchyard soil.

From the Castle top can easily be seen the elevated camping ground of the Parliamentary army on Clay Hill, and the slopes which those Puritan warriors descended "singing of Psalms," on that Sunday morning in October 1644, when they attacked the old mansion at Shaw without success. While further afield the eye can trace the route of Cromwell's famous flank-march through Chieveley and Boxford, and the spot where he fell on Prince Maurice and the unprepared Cavaliers on the heath at Speen.

The Castle itself, however, wrecked as it is at present, had its own stirring times. For, invested by the Parliamentary forces in 1645-6, but defended skilfully, bravely, and persistently by Colonel (Sir John) Boys, it long withstood "crashing shot and bursting shell," until battered and untenable it was left a ruin within the humble but unconquered earthworks of the faithful garrison.

To the ordinary observer the remains of the old castle present little to denote an unusual capacity as a fortress; but from its command of important roads, and its naturally strong position, it became in the hands of a skilled and determined soldier one of the most important military posts in this part of England.

In their present condition the ruins of the Castle are now limited to the Gate-house, looking east, consisting of its two towers, the intervening frontage, and a small portion of its north side-wall. This is continued along the old foundation-lines with a rough garden-wall and masses of fallen masonry, showing a square enclosure with subordinate towers at the four angles in addition to those of the Gate-house. The western wall, however, was bent outwards forming a very obtuse angle. The interior area was of very limited extent. The angle-towers, both in character and altitude, were probably similar to those of the Gate-house.

2 M

The latter consists of a rectangular building, 26 feet by 19 feet, containing two storeys. It projects from the eastern wall, so as to flank the adjacent towers of what was the main structure, and is completed by two towers, similar to those of the Castle itself. The entrance lies between these, and opens into a stone-groined and vaulted hall, 23ft. 6in. by 11ft 9in., in which are still visible, the grooves and aperture for a portcullis, worked from the floor above, to protect the inner doorway, 8ft. 7in. by 7ft. 10in.

The remaining walls are massively constructed of rubble-work of flint and chalk, and are nearly 5ft. thick on the ground-floor, and 3ft. 9in. in the upper storey. Each storey is lighted by loopholes and windows; and these, from the nature of the mouldings, belong to the Early Perpendicular period of Architecture. The two upper stringcourses on the towers are enriched with some boldly carved gargoyles.

The aspect of Donnington Castle at various periods may be observed in the following views which have been published:—

1.—A sketch, as frontispiece in Ashmole's "Antiquities of Berkshire."
2.—"North-east view of Donnington Castle in the County of Berks," by S. and N. Buck, 1732. In Buck and Sayer's "Views of Castles," &c.
3.—A view from the West; in "The Antiquities of England and Wales," by Francis Grose, Esq., F.S.A., vol. i., 1773. Groups of posts stand before the gateway.
4. Vignette sketch from the North, on the title-page of "The Beauties of England and Wales," by E. W. Brayley and John Britton, 8vo, vol. i., 1801.
5.—Donnington Castle, a view of what remains of; in Woolnoth's "Castles of England."
6.—Vignette sketch of the "King's Camp before Donnington Castle," on Title-page of Cattermole's "Illustrated History of. the Civil War," drawn by George Cattermole, engraved by Brain, 8vo, 1844.
7.—Donnington Castle, taken from a field adjoining the road to East Ilsley from Newbury, drawn by W. Turner, R.A., engraved by W. and L. Byrne. In Lysons' "Magna Britannia, Berks."

The Gate-house is surmounted by a flat roof, enclosed by a parapet or breastwork, 6ft. 9½in. high, above which the towers still rise to a further height of 9ft. 4in. Both these and the walls themselves are crenellated. The embrasures are 2ft. wide, and 3ft. 6in. below the top of the coping-stone; the thickness of the wall is 14in. The actual height of the towers from the ground to the coping is 64ft., making the total altitude of the Castle above mean level of the sea 466ft. 9in. The entire length of the building, from the Gate-house entrance to the outside of the west wall, is a little more than 140ft.; and the mean width, between the inner walls, about 80ft.

At the outside of the eastern wall of the Gate-house, and protecting the entrance, are the remains of a wall on each side, about 15ft. high, by 10ft. in length, and 2ft. 8in. in thickness. This, possibly a Porch or Barbican, may have been added after the erection of the Castle.

The towers are entered from the Entrance Hall by arched doorways 6ft. 9in. high by 2ft. 2in. wide; and the southernmost of the two has a winding stone staircase (a portion of which, destroyed during the siege, has since been replaced by wooden steps), giving admission to the different floors.

There is no trace of a staircase in the North Tower; but it is furnished with a doorway on the ground floor, and another on the roof, similar to those of the South Tower. Communication with this tower is obtained on each storey.

In the north face of the wall of the main building, rather below the present surface of the ground, is a small Sallyport or Postern, 3ft. high by 1ft. 6in. wide, with an arched roof and a stone floor. This, however, has not been traced throughout; and the approach from the interior was probably made by a doorway and flight of steps in the thickness of the wall.

The existing enclosure nearly follows the ancient trace. It is built up from the débris of the building evidently on or near the old foundation; but does not represent the true thickness of the former walls.

There are numerous traces of shot-marks on the south and north sides of the Gate-house; and its south tower, having lost a considerable portion of its wall at the upper storey, has been repaired with brick-work. There are but few shot-marks on its front. It is indeed evident that the shots must have been fired, in one case, from the fields on the south side of the road leading from Donnington to Speen (the Grove-road), which brought down "three towers and a part of the wall;" in another from Snelsmore Common, reducing the northern side; and, thirdly, from the rising ground just within the Park-gate. In all these positions remains of field-works have been discovered and identified, from their agreement with contemporary descriptions, as the site of siege-batteries.

There can be no doubt, therefore, that a considerable part of the main building of the Castle, with its corner towers, was battered down by the fire directed from these points, to which, owing to its elevated position, the Castle was exposed; while the work of destruction was completed by the shells fired from "the cannon and great mortar piece" mounted on the battery raised by Major Ryves near the Park-gate, the position of which is shown on the Plan at p. 242. The construction of field-entrenchments, by which the defence could be more firmly maintained, and the enemy's approaches checked, must have been soon found to be indispensable. These, we learn from the Diary of Capt. Symonds, were constructed from the money raised by a weekly contribution levied on the Hundreds of Kintbury-Eagle, Compton, and Faircross, including the town of Newbury. Faircross Hundred paid about £60 a week; and the cost of the works is stated by Symonds to have been £1000, equal perhaps to £3000 at the present value of money. In considering these fortifications, it must be borne in mind that they are situated on the hill not overlooked by any neighbouring heights easily accessible for cannon or within what would have been an effective gun-shot range at the time. Snelsmore Common, on the north-east, is no exception to this statement, as it is level with the hill on which the Castle stands, and of which, indeed, it is but the continuation. On this side, therefore, defenders and assailants, the besieged and the besiegers, met on equal terms, as far as position was concerned. The neck of land between Snelsmore Common and the Castle Hill is narrow, a kind of *col*, the ground on either side sloping rapidly,—on the western side to the marshy swamps of Bagnor, and on the east to an open valley, which was commanded by the Royalists' works.

The outline of the fortifications surrounding the Castle is irregular, and may be thus described:—Two bastions, of limited extent, are traced—one opposite the north-western tower, and one outside the centre of the southern face of the main building. In the latter case, the work is very salient, being traced on the slope of the hill itself on account of the narrowness of the plateau. These are united on the western side by a line of parapet, broken outward into a sharp salient angle of nearly 90°, to the edge of the hill. A short curtain (the part of a rampart between two bastions) unites this southern bastion with a demi-bastion or bastion (it is difficult to determine which), situated opposite the southern tower of the Gate-house, the road to the Castle passing through the curtain. This demi-bastion is connected with the north-western bastion, first mentioned, by a parapet, broken outward to form a salient (with an angle of about 90°), similar to that on the west face ; and this completes the circuit.

Apparently, the ditches or trenches of the works were triangular, and somewhat shallow. But this is not remarkable, seeing in several cases that they are carried along the edge of the hill; while the parapets were of considerable height outside, as their exterior slopes were continued by scarping the hill-side to the bottom of the ditches. Their thickness does not seem to have exceeded 8 feet, which is about the dimensions of parapets in light modern works.

The trees which are now numerous on the slopes and summit of the hill could not have existed at the time of the siege ; for they would have afforded considerable cover; as did also the outbuildings of the Castle, which were held as an outpost.

To the elevation of its position and the excellent protection afforded by the Castle itself against the short-ranged artillery of the period (the projectiles of which moreover had but little penetrating force), and to the skill and gallantry of Sir John Boys and his garrison, must the lengthy defence of Donnington be chiefly attributed. But there is little doubt that the Castle itself must have speedily become untenable, and that the real defence at last, was practically confined to the excellent earthworks; another illustration of their value as compared with fortresses of stone.

The stabling, barn, stores, and other adjuncts to the Castle occupied the site of the present "Castle farm," at the foot of the hill. Considerable remains of the barn (see p. 135), and the walls of other buildings, still exist on the north, east, and south sides of the farm-yard ; but, as the premises have been rebuilt and altered from time to time, the direction of the walls cannot be determined with accuracy. They appear to have enclosed three sides of a quadrangular court, and to have been constructed of the same material as the Castle, that is of flint and chalk rubble, strongly cemented together, and very massive throughout.

Having in the foregoing Chapters of this Book told our story of Donnington Castle and the two Battles of Newbury, we must leave these pleasant, familiar scenes, and the ivied wreck of the old fortress—a melancholy spectacle of fallen sovereignty, but still a standing monument of valorous defence, unbending loyalty, and imperishable fame. Many a place within eyeshot, once disfigured with violence and bloodshed, has been decked afresh by nature's aid, and has been thus removed from human sight, and almost from memory, did not the dumb but speaking Ruin at Donnington indicate the whereabouts of camp and gunner, of horse and foot ; and here and there, a cluster of farm-buildings and the remains of old manor-houses, unnoticed and nearly forgotten, survive to recall to memory the scene of many a daring assault and brave defence.

These things are now made plain to us by old letters and age-stained records left by friends and foes, by narrow partisans and men of greater minds. Amidst the chequered landscape flow on the

Kennet and its sister Lambourn, bright and fair; winding, but ever steadfast to their goal, and serving everything along their course with such benefits as they alone can give. So runs a stream of honour, bravery, and virtue among historic deeds, checked here and diverted there, but good and bright with the heroism of the self-devoted, and the patient weary watching of the faithful. These have never ceased to bring forth their good results; they have revivified spent and wasted minds with hope and energy, making dark times bright again, and renovating the country with the better features of order, security, and peace.

# INDEX.

Abberbury, Thomas de, at Donnington, 261
Abingdon unsuccessfully attacked by Prince Rupert, 198
Agreement between Charles I. and the County of Berks, 125
Aldbourn Chase, the fight on, 15
Aldermaston, Essex's march by, 66, 81
Alice Chaucer, 264, 265
Altars, images, &c. to be destroyed, Ordinance for, 225
Armour, old, at Shaw House, 172
Articles of the Surrender of Donnington Castle, 208
Artillery at Donnington Castle, 147, 188
,, of the Royalists near Salisbury, 140
,, Parliamentarian, near Enborne, 49, 51, 75
,, the Royalist, on Wash Common, 39, 46, 75
Aston, Sir Arthur, at Oxford, 139
Ashburnham, Col. William, 254
Ashe, Simeon, at Shaw, 166, 175
Assault on Newbury by Sir John Boys from Donnington, 195
Astley, Lord, at Stow-on-the Wold, 210
Astley, Sir Bernard, at Shaw House, 153; notice of, 252
,, Sir Jacob, at Edgehill, 38; (Lord Astley) at Shaw, 152; notice of, 101
Aston, Sir Thomas, 101
Attack on Essex's rear after the First Battle of Newbury, 80
Auxiliaries (London), list of the Regiments at Newbury, 77
Bagehot, Col. Thomas, 105
Bagnor, surprise of Dalbier's men at, 239
Baker, Sir Richard, on the Battle at Newbury, 70
Balfour, Sir William, 108; at Speen, 166, 168

Ball's (Col. William) letter to Speaker Lenthall, 226
Balsdon (Balsome), attack on, 237
Banbury, relief of, by Lord Northampton, 146
Barker, Dr. Hugh, 238
Basset, Sir Thomas, 253
Basing, relief of, 139, 195
Batteries at Donnington, 275
Battery at Speen, South of Donnington Castle, 146; on Snelsmore Heath, north of Donnnigton Castle, 148
Bear Inn, the, at Hungerford, 194
,, the old, at Newbury, 94
Beaurepaire, house at, 68
Bedford, Earl of, 97
Belasyse, Lord John, 97
Bell Inn at Basingstoke, the, 244
Benett, Sir Humphrey, notice of, 253
Benett's (Sir Humphrey) brigade of horse at Shaw, 154; at Speen 169
Berks, agreement respecting the Contribution from, 125
,, Commissioners for raising money and prices in, 118
,, list of the sequestrators for, 116
,, list of those who made the Protestation in, 113
,, public feeling of, in 1643, 123
,, sums set on the towns in, for Ship-money, 121
Berkshire, the Earl of, 249
Bertie, Hon. Henry, 99
Biggs' Cottage at Enborne, 33
,, Hill at Enborne, 57
Birch, Col., captures Lady Brentford, 183; notice of, 258; his account of the capture of Lady Forth, 231
Biographical Notices, 88, 106, 248, 256, &c.
Birkenhead, J., editor of the Mercurius Aulicus, 72

# INDEX. 279

Blagrave, Daniel, 120
Blue Regiment of the Trained-bands, 78
Boxford, incidents at, 224
,, on the line of the flank march, 162
Boys, Col. John, knighted on Red Heath, 145, 214; Sir John, at Donnington Castle, 31, 134; biographical account of, 251
Boys' (Sir John), defence of Donnington Castle; letter to Prince Rupert. 230
Brandon, Charles, 265, 267
,, Frances, 266
Brentford, Countess, the capture of the, 183, 231
,, Earl of, at Donnington Castle, 183
Bridge at Newbury, 168
Bristol, taken by Prince Rupert, 8
Brocas, Bernard, 68, 102
Brooke, Mr. Thomas, of Whitchurch, 213
,, Sir William, 107
Brouncker, Sir William, 253
Browne, Mr.,'of Shefford, 196
Browne, Richard, 120
Brown, Sir John, at Shaw, 152, 171
Bucklebury Heath, the Parliamentary army on, 157
,, parish registers at, 225
Bulstrode's (Sir Richard) Memoirs of the Reign of Charles I., extracts from, 219
Bumper's Hill, on Wash Common, 64
Burden, Samuel, 246
Byron, Lord, on the cause of the defeat of the Royalists at Newbury, 70
,, on the fight at Aldbourn Chase, 15, 22
,, Sir John (Lord Byron), notice of, 89
Byron's (Lord) account of the Battle on Wash Common and Enborne Heath, 42, 44, 51, 56
Camp, Parliamentary, on Clay Hill overlooking Shaw, 159
Cansfield, Sir John, at Speen, 168, 176; notice of, 252
Capel, Lord, 249
Carleton, Guy, of Bucklebury, 225
Carnarvon, Lord, killed on Enborne Heath, 56; notice of, 89

Carnarvon's (Lord), account of the Battle on Wash Common, 40
Castle farm at Donnington, 276
,, Inn, the, at Marlborough, 192
,, of Donnington, historical notices of, 259 et seq.
Catelyn, Captain, 255
Causes leading to the Civil War, 1
Cavalry, the royalist, on Wash Common, 48
Chamberlayne, John, 270
Chandos, Lord, 98
Charles the First, his character and conduct, 140, 212
,, on Wash Common. 47, 245
,, trial of, 212
Chaucer, Geoffrey and Thomas, 263, 264, 265
Chieveley on the line of the flank march, 163
Chilton House, 32
Chirurgeons, seal of the, found on Wash Common, 65
Churchmen combined with Puritans against Charles's measures, 1
Church, Newbury, as a prison and hospital, 224
Cirencester, surprise of Royalists at, 13, 14; taken by Prince Rupert, 8
Clare, Earl of, 97
Clarendon, Lord, on the results of the Battle at Newbury, 73
Clarendon's (Lord) notice of the flank march, 163
Clay Hill near Shaw, 153, 158
Cleveland, Earl of 96, 169
Clifton, Captain, 106          [29
Cloth-working trade at Newbury,
Codrington, Robert, 112
Codrington's (R.) account of the fight on Aldbourn Chase, 17 ; of the battle on Wash Common, 57
Colepepper, Lord, 250
Colours taken from the Royalists, 68
Commentaries on the battle on Wash Common, 59
Commissioners for raising money and forces in Berks, 118
Compton Downs, the Parliamentary army on, 181
Conditions of the surrender of Donnington Castle, 208
Constable, Sir William, 107
Contribution from Berks, agreement respecting, 125

## INDEX.

Cope (or Copped) Hall, near Enborne, the fight near, 44, 49, 51
Cornwall, state of affairs in, 133
Coxe, Gabriel, of Newbury, 42, 124, 245; petition of, 42
Crawford, Earl of, 97; General, 257
Crockham Heath, Lord Essex at, 36
Cromwell, colonel of regiment of horse, 6; General, at Shaw, 161 *et seq;* at Speen, 166, 170
,, General, in the Earl of Manchester's Army, 142; joins Fairfax before the battle of Naseby, 203
,, Oliver, the Earl of Manchester's letter about, 246
Cromwell's accusations against Lord Manchester, 199
,, cavalry in Speen fields, 168
,, horse stationed on the Wash Road, 185
Cropredy Bridge, Royalist success at, 132
Crosby, James, 246
Crosby, Lady Anne, petition of, 62
Dalbier, Col., at Theale, 82; siege of Donnington Castle by, 204 *et seq;* notice of, 110
Dalbier's (Col.) letter on the feeling at Newbury, 31
Dalbier's Mead at Donnington, 209
Dalton, Col. Thomas, 61
Daniel, petition of, 65
Dark Lane, near Wash Common, 51, 76
Deadman's Lane near Theale, 80, 82
Deane, General, 109
D'Ewes' (Sir Simonds) Diary, extracts from, 220
De Gomme (or de Gomez), Sir Bernard, engineer to Charles I., 187
De la Pole, Edmund, 265
,, John, 265
Depositions of the Witnesses at the Trial of Charles I., 245
Deputation to the King from Gloucester, 10
Derby-house Committee, the, 137
Description of Donnington Castle, 272
Descriptive accounts of the Second Battle of Newbury, 219
Digby, Lord George, notice of, 98
,, on the cause of the Royalists' defeat at Newbury, 70

Digby's (Lord G.) letter to Prince Rupert, 144
Discovery of Lord Essex's Vault and Coffin, 86
Disposition of the King's troops before Newbury, Nov. 9, 1644, 186
Dissensions in Manchester's Army, 143
Dolman, Sir Thomas, of Shaw, 216
Dolman's (Sir Thos.) house at Shaw, 152 *et seq.*
Donnington Castle summoned to surrender, 1644, 182
,, artillery at, 147, 188
,, blockaded by Col. Horton, 146
,, Capt. Knight's account of the siege of the, 234 *et seq.*
,, description of, 272 *et seq.*
,, earthwork defences of, 275
,, garrison of, 134, 147
,, Major Ryves on the siege of, 241
,, published views of, 274
,, the dismantling of, 243
,, the final siege of, in 1645, 203 *et seq.*
,, the military value of, 31
,, the regalia removed from, 188
,, the relief of, 144, 184
,, the siege of, in 1644, by Col. Horton, 146
,, the supplies for, 134
,, the surrender of, 208
Donnington, historical notices of the Castle and Manor of, 259 *et seq.*
,, petition of the poor of, 235
,, siege-batteries at, 275
,, village of, 273
Dragoons, the, 39
Dunce, Mr., of Newbury, 215
Dunch, Edmund, 119
Earthwork defences of Donnington Castle, 135, 275
Earthworks at Newbury Marsh, 185
,, on Snelsmore, 148
,, on the Maypole Hill at Donnington, 243
Edgehill, the battle of, 7
Elizabeth, Princess, 267

# INDEX.

Enborne Heath, 37; the fight on, 55
Enborne, Lord Essex at, 33
Entry into London, Lord Essex's, 68, 73
Essex, biographical notice of the Earl of, 106
Essex, Lord at Bradfield and Reading, 155, 157
,, in Cornwall, 133
,, relieves Gloucester, 12
,, the flag and motto of, 47
Essex's (Lord) escape from Cornwall, 136
,, vault discovered in Westminster Abbey, 86
Eure, Col. Thomas, 104
Eyston of Hendred, 124
Failure of the attack on Shaw House, 174
Fairfax, Sir Thomas, at Newbury, 202; commander-in-chief of the New Model Army, 200
Falkland Farm near the River En, 53; on Wash Common, 51, 53
Falkland, Lord, biographical notice of, 92; his character, 54, 63; on the Ship-money, 123; shot when charging through a hedge in Dark Lane, 51, 52, 76
Falkland Place in Newbury, 95
Falkland's (Lord) death, described by Lord Byron, 52; by Clarendon, 53
Faringdon, the Royalists at, 198; unsuccessfully attacked by the Parliamentarians, 198
Fast, solemn in London, 159
Fawley, Manor-house at, 197
Fight, the, on Aldbourn Chase, 15, 17, 20; on Speen Heath, 161
Fielding, Colonel, 43, 61
Flank march by Lord Essex past Newbury, 34, 41, 74
,, by Waller and Cromwell, from Shaw round to Speen, 161 et seq., 273
Fleetwood, Capt. Charles, 111; Dr. James, 149
Flight of the King from Oxford to Newark, 211; to Bath, 175
Fogge, Rev. Robert, 150
Forces, Parliamentary at Aldbourn Chase, 14
,, Royalist, at Aldbourn Chase, 16
Forster, Sir Humphrey, 156

Forth, Earl of, 88
Forth, Lady, the capture of, 231
Frechville, Sir John, 101
French noblemen at the fight on Aldbourn Chase, 19
Fuller on the Battle at Newbury, 69
Gage, Col., knighted at Oxford, 182
Gage's (Col.) relief of Basing, 139
Garrard, Mr., of Kingwood, 189
Garrison of Donnington Castle, 147
Gate-house of Donnington Castle, 273, 274
Gate of Gloucester, inscription on the South, 12
Gerard, Col. Charles, 104
Gloucester besieged by the King, 9
Gloucester, deputation from, to the King, 10
Golofre, John, 263
Goodman, Dr. Godfrey, 184
Goodwin, Col. Arthur, 109
Godwin's (Colonel) letter on the march to Newbury, 30
Grandison's (Lord) letter about the disaffection of Newbury, 29
Granville, Sir John, 253
Great Shefford, manor-house at, 196
Greenham Common, Lord Essex's march over, 66, 81
,, Manor-house, attack on, 238
Grey, of Groby, Lord, 107
Gryce, Gyles, 245
Guizot, M., quoted, 1
Gun public-house on Wash Common, 39
Guns, old, at Shaw House, 172
Guyer's Lane, near Wash Common, 50
Gwynne, Captain, 106
Hammond, Captain, 111; Col., at Shaw, 173
Hampden, colonel of a regiment of foot, 6
Hampden's opposition to the Ship-money Tax, 3
Hamstead, Lord Essex at, 37
Henrietta Maria, the influence of, 2; the Queen, not present at Newbury, 82
Henrietta-Maria's letters from Oxford, 83
Hesilrige, Sir Arthur, 256
Hesilrige's (General) letter to Speaker Lenthall, 220
Historical notices of the Manor and Castle of Donnington, 259 et seq.

2 N

# INDEX.

Hoby, Peregrine, 116
Hoghton, Colonel, 254
Holland, Cornelius, 121
Holland, Earl of, 96
Holland, munitions of war from, 6
Hooper, Sir Thomas, at Shaw, 152; notice of, 253
Hopton, Lord, 250
Horton's (Col. Jeremy) blockade of Donnington Castle, 146
Hospital at Enborne, the, 67
Hotham, Sir John, holds Hull, and is proclaimed a traitor, 6
Howard, Charles, 268
„ Lady Anne, 269
Hull, Charles I. at, 6
Hungerford Park, 33
Hungerford, the Parliamentary army at, 33; the Royalists at, 193
Hunt, Captain, 111
Hurry, Col., at Aldbourn Chase, 19, 20; in the attack on Essex's rear, 66; in the skirmish near Enborne, 44
Hurry, Sir John, at Donnington Castle. 183; biographical notice of, 101; turns traitor and joins Manchester's army, 146
Hursley, old seal at, 179
Impolicy of Charles the First's measures in Parliament, 4
Influence of Queen Henrietta-Maria, 2
Ingoldsby, Sir Richard, 258
Inns or taverns in Berkshire, 244
Inscription on the coffin-plate of Lord Essex, 87
„ on the gate at Gloucester, 12
Interment of the dead after the First Battle of Newbury, 63; after the Second Battle of Newbury, 179
Ives, Thomas, 246
Jacob's Mead near Skinner's Green, 49
James the First, his notions, 2
Jermyn, Lord, 98
Johnston, Sir Archibald, 142
Juxon, Capt. John, 79
Kineton Heath, battle of, 7
King, the, *passim*.
King's (the) answer to the deputation from Gloucester, 10
Kingsmill, Mr., of Sydmonton, 213
Kingwood near Lamborne, 189

Kirke, Sir Lewis, 100
Knight, John, of Newbury, 238
„ Roger, of Greenham, 238
„ Stephen, 176
Knight's (Capt.) account of the siege of Donnington Castle, 234 *et seq.*
Knight's feud, fief, or fee, a, 259
Knollys, Sir Francis, 116
Lambourn, passage of the, at Boxford, 154, 162; at Shaw, 152, 164, 165
Lane, Sir Richard, 253
Leather guns used at Shaw, 172
Legge, Col. William, 103
Leke, Colonel, 254
Lenthall, William, 118
Letter from Sir Thomas Edmonds to the Earl of Shrewsbury, 268
„ from the Earl of Manchester on the conduct of Oliver Cromwell, 246
„ from the King to Prince Rupert in 1644, 138
„ from Thomas Cromwell to Sir R. Rich, 267
Letter of Major William Rives relating to the siege of Donnington Castle, 241
Letters about outrage and pillage by both armies, 226 *et seq*.
Letters from the King to Prince Rupert, 24
Life-guards, troop of the King's, 26
Lilly, the astrologer, 238
Lindsey, Earl of, 95
Lincoln, John Earl of, 265
List of the Prisoners removed out of Ely House, 1643, 79
„ regiments of the Trained bands and Auxiliaries of the City of London that were at Newbury, 77
List of Royalists whose estates were sequestered by the Parliament, 123
List of Sequestrations in 1643, 116
Lisle, Sir George, at Shaw, 173; notice of, 100
L'Isle, Viscount, 265
License of War, 226
Lloyd, Sir Charles, 254
Long Lane at Shaw, 153, 171
Losses of the Parliamentarians at Speen and Shaw, 178
Losses of the Royalists at Speen and Shaw, 175

## INDEX.   283

Losses (the) in both armies by the First Battle of Newbury, 60 et seq.
Lucas, Sir Charles, 99
Ludlow, General, at Shaw, 160; notice of, 257
Luke, Sir Samuel, 108
Lushy Gully near Enborne, 71
Macclesfield, Earl of, 105
Manchester and Cromwell on Compton Downs, 181
Manchester, Earl of, at Shaw, 164 et seq.
  ,,  on Oliver Cromwell, 246
  ,,  notice of, 256
Manchester's (Earl of) Army, 142
  ,,  assault on Shaw-house, 170
  ,,  attack on Donnington Castle, 147
  ,,  hesitation and refusal to pursue the King, 180, 190
  ,,  reply to Cromwell's accusations, 199
Manor of Donnington, historical notices of the, 259 et seq.
Manor of Newbury, the dower of the queen, 28
Mansel, Sir Anthony, 101
March of Lord Essex from Aldbourn Chase to Newbury, 22; from Cirencester to Aldbourn Chase, 14; to Cirencester, 13; to Gloucester, 11; to London from Newbury, 65 et seq.; to Newbury, 32
March of the Royalists from Whitchurch to Newbury. 145; from Cornwall to Salisbury, 138; from Donnington to Marlborough, 189; from Aldbourn Chase to Newbury, 21; from Gloucester to Newbury, 24, 26
March, the King's, to Newbury from Salisbury, 213
Marlborough stormed, 8; the Royalists at, in 1644, 190, 192
Marquis de Vieuville, death of the, 18, 21; portrait of the, 19
Marsh, Newbury, earthworks in the, 185
Marston Moor, the battle on, 132
Marten, Henry, notice of, 116
Mason, Captain. 258
Massey, Governor of Gloucester, 9; his subsequent career, 12

Matchlock, the old, 58
Maurice, Prince, the King's nephew, 7; at Speen, 153; notice of, 248
Maypole at Donnington, 239, 241
Meldrum, Sir John, 110
Mercurius Aulicus, the, 72; Britannicus, the, 72
Meyrick, Sir John, 107
Middle Class, importance of the, 1
Middleton's (Colonel) attack on Donnington Castle, 135
  ,,  General, 257
Milton, Christopher, 124
Milton's (John) opinion of Charles I., 140
Molyneux, Lord, 99
Money, Capt., 235
Monkey (or Monks') Lane, near Greenham, 66
Moore, John, of Cork, 246
  ,,  Sir Francis, of Fawley, 197
Morgan, Colonel, 104
Mortar, monster, at Donnington, 148, 206
Mottoes on the colours taken from the Royalists at Newbury, 68
Murray's (Charles) letter to Sir John Berkeley, 223
Needham, M., editor of the "Mercurius Britannicus," 72
Newberry, County Cork, 28; title of Earl of, 105
Newbury, assault on, by Sir John Boys in 1644, 195
  ,,  Baron of, 105
  ,,  Charles I. in, 215
  ,,  Church as a prison and hospital, 224
  ,,  history of, 27
  ,,  in Saxon, mediæval, and later times, 28
  ,,  lists of those who made the Protestation in, 114
  ,,  Lord Saltoun's capture at, 128
  ,,  Marsh, fortified, 185
  ,,  occupied by Royalists 25, 34, 41, 152
  ,,  public feeling of, in 1642, &c., 29
  ,,  the bridge at, 168
  ,,  the First Battle of, 37 et seq.
  ,,  the Parliamentary army at, in 1644, 131

## INDEX.

Newbury, the Royalists at, in 1644, 130
,, the Second Battle of, 128 et seq.
,, title of Earl of, 105
Newman, Captain, 28
New Model Army, 200
,, Ordinance, the, 200
Newport, the Earl of, 249
Nonconformists at Newbury, 29
Northampton, Earl of, 95
North Heath on the line of the flank march, 163
Norton, Colonel, 257; his letter about the Second Battle of Newbury, 178
Nottingham, Earl of, 96, 268
Nottingham, the King at, 6
Oaks at Donnington, 235
Officers in the Royalist Army in Cornwall, 214; see Parliamentary; see Royalist.
O'Neill, Col. Daniel, 104
Owen, Sir John, 253
Oxford, the King escape from, 131
,, invested by Fairfax, 203, 211
,, the King's return to, 182
Packer, John, 271; Phillip, of Donnington, 244
Padworth, military chest found at, 67; Prince Rupert's attack on the Parliamentarians near, 66, 81
Page, Sir Richard, at Shaw House, 152, 172, 176
,, notice of, 253
Parliamentarians repulsed at Shaw House, 174
,, Successes of the, in 1643-4, 129; in 1645, 1646, 210
,, victorious at Newbury, 66
Parliamentary army at Newbury in 1644, 131
,, movements of the, in Berks, in 1644, 155
,, Commissioners, letters of the, to the Derby-house Committee, 154 et seq.
,, forces at Newbury in 1644, the state of, 192
,, and officers on Wash Common, 43
,, officers with the army at Speen and Shaw, 160
,, officers and troops engaged in the siege of Donnington Castle, 204

Parliamentary officers killed at the battle on Wash Common, 62
,, officers at the Second Battle of Newbury, 256
,, troops bivouacing on Wash Common after the Battle, 58
Parliament, King Charles's last, 4
Parliaments, Charles the First's disregard of, 2
Percy, Lord, 98
Perkins of Ufton Court, 124
Petition from Berks against the Ship-money, 122
,, of the poor people of Donnington, 235
Petitions, 42, 62, 156
Phelip, Sir John, of Donnington, 264
Pile, Sir Francis, 116
Pinchbeck, Colonel, 105
Platt, Col. Richard, 104
Pontefract Castle, the last to hold out for Charles I., 211
Porter, George, 106
Potts, Michael, 246
Powle, Henry, 117
Preston, skeletons found at, 23
Protestant feeling at Newbury. 29
Protestation, the, made in Berks, 1641, 113
Public feeling of Berks in 1643, 123; Newbury, in 1642, &c., 29
Pudsey, Major, and another deputed to answer the King, 10
Puritans at Boxford, 224; combined with Churchmen against Charles' measures, 4
Pursuit after the Royalists too late, 180
Pye, Sir Robert, of Faringdon, 118, 198
Pym, Capt. Charles, 111
Queen, influence of the, 2; not present at the Battle of Newbury, 82; returns with money from the Continent, 8; visit to Holland by the, 5
Ramsbury, silver coins found at, 23
Rawdon, Col. Thomas, 105
Reading taken by Lord Essex, 8
Recusants some of the, 124
Red Field, near Shaw, 159, 160
Red Heath (near the Wash), 217
Red Hill, 217; Field, 219
Red Regiment of the Auxiliaries, 79; of the Trained-bands, 77

INDEX. 285

Reformers, the English, 1, 29
Reform of the Army, 200
Regalia removed from Donnington Castle, 188
Relief of Banbury by Lord Northampton, 146; of Basing by Sir H. Gage, 196; of Donnington Castle, 144, 184
Results of the Battle at Newbury, 72
Retreat of Charles I. to Donnington Castle and Bath, 175; of the Royalists at Speen, 167; of the Royalists to Wallingford and Oxford, 174
Return of the King to Oxford, 182
Returns of those who made the Protestation in Berks, 1641, 113
Richard Colonel, 103
Richmond, the Duke of, 248
Rivers, Earl, 249
Robartes (or Roberts) Lord, 107
Royalist Army at Salisbury, the state of the, 138
,, drawn up before Newbury, Nov. 1644, 185, 187
,, in Cornwall, 214
,, forces at Speen and Newbury in 1644, 151
,, before Newbury in 1644, 222
,, Officers at the Second Battle of Newbury, 248
,, Officers killed at the battle on Wash Common, 60
,, with the army at Speen and Shaw, 159
,, troops. and commanders the, on Wash Common, 40, 42, 43
,, retreat of, from Wash Common into Newbury, 58, 74
,, reverses at Newbury, 66; at Speen, 167
Royalists disasters of the, in 1643-4, 129; in 1645, 1646, 210
,, license of the, 196
,, the, at Hungerford, 193
,, at Newbury in 1644, 130
Rudyerd, Sir Benjamin, notice of, 118
Rupert, Prince, biographical notice of, 89; on Wash Common, 46, 48, 55; the King's nephew, 7
Rupert's (Prince) attack on Essex's rear near Greenham, 66
Ruthven, Patrick, Earl of Forth, 88

Ryves' (Major W.) letter relating to the Siege of Donnington Castle, 241
Sackville, Hon. Edward, 43
St.-Barbe, Capt. Francis, 111
St.-John, Colonel, 103
St.-Leger, Sir William, 253
Sallies by Sir John Boys from Donnington Castle, 148, 195, 206, 207
Sally, final, from the Castle, 240, 241
Saltoun's (Lord) capture at Newbury, 128
Scutage and land-tax, 259
Seal, old, of the Commonwealth at Hursley, 179
Second Battle of Newbury, descriptive accounts of the, 219
Seeley, George, 245
Self-denying ordinance, the, 200
Sequestrators of Estates for Berks in 1643, 116
Seven members, seizure of the, in Parliament, 5
Seymour, Lord Francis, at Marlborough, 192
Shaw Church, 273; House, 152 et seq.. 273; Charles 1. at, 174, 215, 216; the attack on, 221
Shaw, passage of the Lambourn at, 152 165
Sheffield, Colonel, 110
Ship-money, history of the tax called, 3, 121
Shrewsbury, the royal army at, 7
Siege-batteries at Donnington, 275
Siege of Donnington Castle, 1644, 1645, 146. 203, et seq.
,, Capt. Knight's account of the siege of, 234 et seq.
,, Major Ryves' letter concerning the, 241
Skinner's Green near Enborne, 36, 49; fight at, 52, 53
Skippon, General, at Speen, 169; in Cornwall, 137; notice of, 108; on Enborne Heath, 45, 55
Skippon's, General Ph., letter to the Earl of Essex, 222
Skirmish between Oxford and Faringdon, 208
,, Slings (the), near Enborne, 36, 37
Snelsmore Heath, 174; battery on, 148, 275

Speenhamland, near Newbury, 94, 152, 218
Speen Heath (or Hill), 153; Waller and Cromwell on, 161, 166
Speen, action at, 166
,, Marsh (or moor), 153
,, Royalists at, 151, 153
,, the fight at, 219, 220, 223
Spencer, Henry (Lord Sunderland), 91
Springer (or Springett), Sir W., 43
Standard-bearer, Sir E. Verney, the, 6, 7
Standard, the raising of the King's, at Nottingham, 6
Stapleton, Sir Ph., at the Battle on Wash Common, 71; notice of, 107
Stapleton's cavalry on Enborne Heath, the decisive charge of, 55
Stow, encounter at, 13
Stradling, Robert, 255; Sir Edward, 101
Strafford, attainder of the Earl of, 5
Strangways, Col. Giles, 254
Stuart, Lord Bernard, 249
Suffolk, Duke and Duchess of, 266, 267
Summons, Col. Horton's, to Sir John Boys to surrender Donnington Castle, 147
,, General Middleton's to surrender Donnington Castle, 135
Sunderland, Lord, killed on Enborne Heath, 56; notice of, 91
Supplies raised at Marlborough, 193
Surprise of Royalists at Theale, 82
Surrender of Donnington Castle, 208
Symonds, Captain, 255
Symonds' (Capt.) account of the attack on Waller at Andover, 141
Tanfield, Sir Lawrence, the tomb of, 92
Taxes raised by King Charles, 3
Taylor, Dr. Jeremy, at Newbury, 38
Thanksgiving for the safety of the King, 67
,, in London after the Battle of Newbury, 69
Thatcham, skirmishes near, 157
Theale, Essex's march by, 67, 81
Thelwall, Col. Anthony, 254
Thorpe's (Col.) account of the capture of Lady Forth, 234
**Tilden, Mr. Hopestill, 79**

Towers, Mr., of Frobury, 213
Town-hall, the old, at Newbury, 67
Trained-bands of London at Speen, 166
,, in the Battle of Newbury, 70
,, list of the regiments of the, that were at Newbury, 77
,, on Wash Common, 46, 48
,, under Sir James Harrington, 140
Trial of Charles I., witnesses at the, 245
Trundle Hill near Enborne, 75
Tumuli of the dead on Wash Common, 64
Twisse, Dr. William, notice of, 29, 111
Vault, the, of Lord Essex discovered in Westminster Abbey, 86
Vachell, Tanfield, 117
Vanlore, Sir Peter, 269, 270
Vavasour, Sir William, 101
Venn, Colonel, 82
Vieuville, death of the Marquis of, 18, 21; portrait of, 19
Views of Donnington Castle, published, 274
Villiers, Col. Edward, 103
Vinson, John, 245
Vyne, the, 68
Wagstaffe, Sir Joseph, 253
Waldegrave, Sir Edward, 100
Walker, Sir Edward, 254; his account of the Royalists before Newbury, Nov. 9, 1644, 185
Waller, Sir William, at Andover, 140; at Shaftesbury, 141; at Shaw and Speen, 168 et seq., 179; defeated at Cropredy Bridge, 132; notice of, 256
Waller's (Sir William) letter to Speaker Lenthall, 220
Wansey, Major, in the rear at Shaw, 161
Warrant for raising Supplies at Marlborough, 193
Warwick's (Sir Philip) letter about the Siege of Gloucester, 9
Wash Common, Lord Essex at, 37; the battle on, 38 et seq.
Well, said to be poisoned, 183
Westminster Abbey, Lord Essex's vault and coffin in, 86
West Woodhay, manor-house at, 273

White, Colonel, 258
Whittingham, Capt. Thomas, 259
Wilmot, Lord, 89
Witch-murder at Newbury, 84
Witnesses at the Trial of Charles I. 245
Wodehouse, Sir Michael, 101

Wolfall, Capt. Richard, 259
Woodd, Capt. Basil, 105
Yellow Regiment of the Trained-bands, 78
Yew-tree Cottage on Wash Common, 53
York, Charles I. at, 5

www.ingramcontent.com/pod-product-compliance
Lightning Source LLC
Chambersburg PA
CBHW071812230426
43670CB00013B/2435